Jerry Baker's
Great Green
book of
Garden
Secrets

www.jerrybaker.com

Jerry Baker's
Great Green
book of
Garden
Secrets

Handy Hints, Timely Tonics, and Super Solutions to Turn Your Yard into a Green Garden Paradise!

by Jerry Baker,
America's Master Gardener®

American Master Products, Inc.

Published by American Master Products, Inc.

Executive Editor: Kim Adam Gasior
Project Editor: Cheryl Winters Tetreau
Interior Design and Layout: Sandy Freeman
Cover Design: Kitty Pierce Mace
Copy Editor: Erana Bumbardatore
Indexer: Nanette Bendyna

Jerry Baker
P.O. Box 1001
Wixom, MI 48393

http://www.jerrybaker.com

Printed in the United States of America

6 8 10 9 7 hardcover

To: All of you faithful "Garden Liners" who
have followed me and my tips, tricks, and
tonics all of these years. Your loyalty, support,
and belief in me and my methods have helped
us create a cleaner and greener America
for future generations to come. Thanks.

Contents

Introduction **VIII**

CHAPTER 1 **Gardening 101** 1

The Best-Laid Plans **2**
Be Choosy **20**
Starting from Seed **24**
Jerry Tells All About…Gardening Basics **35**

CHAPTER 2 **Time to Get Dirty** 47

Soil Secrets **48**
The Art of Composting **57**
Out and About **64**
Toolin' Around **83**
Jerry Tells All About…Soil Improvement **85**

CHAPTER 3 **Let's Water, Weed, and Feed** 95

Water, Water, Everywhere **96**
Chow Time **110**
Take My Weeds, *Please!* **123**
Jerry Tells All About…Garden Care **131**

CHAPTER 4 # Show Off Your Green Thumb   151

Plentiful Produce   **152**
Fabulous Fruits & Berries   **160**
Garden Beauties   **166**
Handsome Houseplants   **181**
Jerry Tells All About...Successful Growing   **195**

CHAPTER 5 # Land Hoe!   215

The Grass Is Always Greener...in *My* Yard!   **216**
Luxurious Landscapes   **233**
To Tree or Not to Tree   **244**
Jerry Tells All About...Landscaping   **261**

CHAPTER 6 # Gathering Up the Garden   271

Reap What You Sow   **272**
Putting the Garden to Bed   **284**
Lasting Mementos   **294**
Filling the Pantry   **299**
Jerry Tells All About...Harvesting   **311**

50 Fabulous Fixers, Mixers & Elixirs   **321**

Index   **332**

Introduction

You might say that I've been puttering around plants since I was knee-high to a midsummer cornstalk. I inherited my green thumbs from my wise Grandma Putt, who taught me how to treat plants as friends—with kindness, respect, and love. They always rewarded her with beauty and bounty, and now they're my rewards, too. She was my garden guide, leading me down the magical path to plentiful produce, fabulous fruits and berries, garden beauties, and handsome houseplants. Why, when I was a young lad, she appointed me her No. 1 apprentice—a position I gladly accepted!

Grandma Putt planted the seeds of garden wisdom inside of me and watched them flourish. No matter how many roses, radishes, or rhododendrons I plant, I still get excited as I watch them them grow. It's an excitement I never want to lose, and neither should you!

So now it's my turn to share my lifetime of gardening secrets with you. It's the best gift on earth–and for the earth—that I can give you. Tucked inside these pages are tons of down-home tips, tonics, and tales that are guaranteed to give you a healthy lawn and garden for many years to come. As you flip through these pages, you'll quickly see why this is the one and only book you'll need to turn your yard into a blooming success, and yourself into a gardening genius!

Right from the start, you get the inside scoop on dirt, the secrets behind sowing seeds, the behind-the-scenes benefits of composting, and the truth about tools of the terrain. You'll discover how easy it is to grow gorgeous geraniums, splendid strawberries, and radiant raspberries with only a minimum of effort, and without sacrificing your weekends.

You'll also find tips, tricks, and techniques for each season. Now, I can't control Mother Nature, but I do know a thing or two about how to handle her many moods! If you pay close attention to her seasonal signs, you'll know when it's just the right time to plant, water, and harvest. But if you try to fool Mother Nature, you usually end up being the fool! It's much better to have her on your side, and I'll show you how to do it.

You'll also learn how to use common household stuff, like brown grocery bags, baby shampoo, Murphy's Oil Soap, and even beer for fabulous results in your garden. Want proof? Check out "5 Fast Uses for Sugar" (at right). You'll find thousands more terrific tips like these inside, plus easy-to-read charts, step-by-step instructions, and oodles of recipes for both you and your plants.

Through the years, a lot of folks have asked me loads of questions. How should I plant this? When is the best time to harvest that? Or, how can I get the biggest bang for my gardening buck? Well, I've finally put together everything-you-always-wanted-to-know collections of answers called "Jerry Tells All About…" that are featured at the end of

MIXERS & ELIXIRS

5 Fast Uses for Sugar

1. Get rid of nematodes by tilling 3 pounds of sugar per acre of soil in early spring and late fall.

2. Make a fertilizer for strawberries and rhubarb by combining 5 pounds of dry garden food with ½ cup of sugar.

3. Trap insects in a gooey mess by sprinkling flour and powdered sugar on plants in the morning before the dew dries.

4. Feed hummingbirds with a mix of 1 part sugar and 4 parts hot water; replace the mix every three to five days.

5. Remove gasoline spots from lawn areas by sprinkling a mix of 6 cups of gypsum and 1 cup of sugar over the area and watering frequently.

Jerry's Secrets

Before you head to the shed for your wheelbarrow, rake, and hoe, heed my Three Green-Thumb Gardening Rules:

Rule 1: Plan before you plant.

Rule 2: Read before you reap.

Rule 3: When in doubt, see Rules 1 and 2.

each chapter. So the next time you're stumped, take a gander, and see if the answer to your gardening question is somewhere in there.

Now, I don't know about you, but the last thing I want to do is wade through a thicket of words, or spend precious daylight hours holed up in the house with my nose buried in a book. I'd much rather be outside with my hands buried in some soil, tackling my next garden project. That's why I made sure to cultivate the chapters so that you have lots of easy entrances and exits. You can go in, find the answer, get out, and put your new-found knowledge to good use where it belongs—in your yard! If you arm yourself with my time- and money-saving knowledge, use a little common sense, and follow my Three Green-Thumb Gardening Rules (at left), your yard will soon be the envy of the neighborhood.

So, are you rarin', roarin', and ready to hoe, sow, and grow? Well, if you are, read on, and I'll *guarantee* that you'll have the best dang garden you've ever seen!

Jerry Baker

"With a little common sense and preplanning, you can have the greenest grass, the prettiest flowers, and the tastiest fruits and vegetables on your side of the fence."

Gardening 101

The Best-Laid Plans

When it comes to planning your garden, one thing's for sure: *haste makes waste*. So take the time to sit down and really think about your lawn, garden, and landscape before you do anything. You're going to be spending your hard-earned money on trees, shrubs, seeds, and seedlings, so I can't emphasize this enough: Plan before you plant, and you won't be disappointed!

A PICTURE PAINTS 1,000 WORDS

No, you're not painting a masterpiece, but you will be drawing your dream landscape! So first thing, do what professional landscapers do—sit down with paper (preferably graph paper, but even an old grocery bag will do), pencil, and ruler, and draw your yard.

Make sure you include your house, walkways, driveway, outbuildings (such as a garage or tool shed), patio, pool, stone or concrete walls, and fences—in short, anything and everything that's nailed down to the ground.

Draw your yard to scale, using a scale of 1 inch on paper equals 1 foot in your yard. Use one sheet (or more) for the front yard, one for each side yard, and one (or more) for the backyard. Be sure to include the locations of trees, shrubs, flowerbeds, and other plants or planting areas.

Above all else, take your time, and don't leave anything out. Remember, this isn't a race! It will be well worth the hour or so you spend on your drawings because when you're done, you'll have a plan you can use forever, whether you're ordering your plants, tools, and gardening accessories from a reputable mail order catalog or you're stocking up at your garden center.

Jerry's Secrets

Be the (wo)man with the plan—use a different-color pencil to draw in your newly purchased plants on your master plan. That way, you can follow the progress of your yard and garden from season to season.

CLEAN UP YOUR ACT

Before you do any digging, tilling, or planting, you must clean up your yard and last year's garden (if you had one). It's the only way to ensure a happy, healthy yard and garden this year. Best of all, it's a simple, four-step process.

Step 1. Take a stroll around your yard with pencil and paper. Write down any problems you see or any chores that need to be done immediately. Then go back inside, sit down with a cup of hot coffee or tea, and go over your list, numbering the items in order of importance.

Step 2. Repair any tree limb, stem, or trunk damage. Wash the affected areas and seal with a mixture of 1 tablespoon of antiseptic mouthwash and 1 tablespoon of liquid Sevin per 8 ounces of latex paint.

Step 3. Gently rake out any winter debris from under your shrubs and off of your lawn. Shred the debris by running it over with your lawnmower until it's finely chopped up, and then add it to the compost pile or put it on the garden to be tilled under later.

Step 4. Bathe your yard, and I mean all of it—from the biggest trees to the littlest plants—with my "Rise-'n-Shine Clean-Up Tonic," below.

Rise-'n-Shine Clean-Up Tonic

MIXERS & ELIXIRS

1 cup of Murphy's Oil Soap
1 cup of chewing tobacco juice*
1 cup of antiseptic mouthwash
4 drops of Tabasco sauce

Mix all of the ingredients together in a 20 gallon hose-end sprayer jar, filling the balance of the jar with warm water. Apply this mixture liberally to everything in sight (except the kids and the dog).

*To make the juice, take three fingers' worth of chewing tobacco from the package, place it in the toe of a nylon stocking, and place the stocking in a gallon of boiling water. Let the tobacco steep until the water is dark brown.

PLAN FOR THE LONG HAUL

Perennials aren't once-and-done plants, so plan carefully for these yearly bloomers. Since a single group of perennials rarely provides continuous bloom, you'll need to select different varieties to ensure continuous color throughout the growing season. One other bit of advice—always give perennials plenty of room to roam.

DON'T FORGET THE WEATHER

All of your best-laid garden plans can be washed down the drain if you don't consider the weather. Don't attempt to till, seed, weed, or set out bulbs or plants without first seeing whether Mother Nature is going to cooperate. Believe you me, you don't want her to wash out, blow out, burn out, or freeze out all of your hard work!

Even though weather-watching and predicting has theoretically become scientific and sophisticated today, the simple truth of the matter is that Mother Nature can still give us the inside scoop on the coming weather. If you pay attention to Mother Nature, it won't be long until you can use her signs to help you plan your days. Here are just a few of Mother Nature's weather signs:

WINTER SIGNS

• Skinny rabbit tracks in the snow mean that a thaw is close at hand.

• Fat rabbit tracks in the snow mean that a thaw is a long way off.

• If the beaver adds more wood to the north side of his home, winter will continue.

• If the snowdrifts face north, spring will come early.

• If the trees split their bark, it will be a dry, warm spring.

• When the deer reappear, spring is near.

• When the pine needles sweat, spring is an early bet.

SPRING SIGNS

• When the leaves on the trees turn their backs to the west, a storm is just around the corner.

• Red sky at night, the next day is a delight.

• Red sky in the morning is a storm warning.

• When the bees leave the flower patch, the rains are a'coming.

• When the fireflies are heavy, the weather will be bright and sunny for the next three days.

Getting Edgy

A perennial border needs careful watching, especially if grass grows right up to its edge. In that instance, the front-row plants may flop over and make it hard to mow the lawn. So make your landscape chores a whole lot easier by arranging your perennial beds so that they border a brick, gravel, concrete, or flagstone walk. This will keep the edge nice and neat, which means less work for you!

SUMMER SIGNS

• When the anthills are small, it will be a dry, hot summer.

• When birds fly close to the ground, it will rain soon.

• If the hay field bends to the northeast, the weather will stay hot.

• If the earthworms leave their homes in the ground, a heavy rain is on the way.

• If the cows and horses huddle in a field, a storm is on the way.

• If a rooster crows at noon, the rains will come soon.

• If a cow bellows three times in a row, a storm is not far behind.

FALL SIGNS

• When the leaves drop early, the Indian summer will be short, and winter will be mild.

• When the sugar maple buds are fat in the fall, winter will be short and sweet.

• When the leaves fall late, winter will be hard.

• When the hornets' nests are fat and low, winter will be cold.

• When the hawks fly low, there will be much snow.

• When the squirrels gather green nuts and do not chatter, it will be a severe winter; chattering squirrels foretell a milder winter.

• If the crickets sing in the chimney, it will be a long winter.

• When the clouds in the sky look like horses' tails, frost is coming.

• If the crows do not frighten in the cornfield, it will be a hard winter.

• If the squirrels' tails are extra fluffy, it will be a cold winter.

• If the moss on the north side of the tree dries up in the fall, it will be a mild winter.

MIXERS & ELIXIRS

Flower Surge

50 lbs. of peat moss
25 lbs. of gypsum
10 lbs. of garden food
4 bushels of compost

Mix together and work well into the soil in all of your flowerbeds.

MIXERS & ELIXIRS

Perennial Punch

Jump-start your flowerbeds by overspraying them with this one-two, powerful punch.

1 can of beer
1 cup of liquid dish soap
1 cup of antiseptic
   mouthwash
½ cup of regular cola
   (not diet)
¼ tsp. of instant tea
   granules

Mix all of the ingredients together in a large bucket. Then pour into your 20 gallon hose-end sprayer, and apply to 100 square feet of planting area. Let the soil sit for two days, and then you can plant.

FOUR Ps TO GARDENING SUCCESS

While you're in the garden-planning stage, get out a big calendar, and print "Garden Chores" on the front cover with a bright, bold marker. Then open it up, and circle the most important dates in the coming year, such as your wedding anniversary, your spouse's and children's birthdays, vacation days, and so on. Next, I want you to prepare a list of your most important gardening chores by month, numbering them in order of importance, and mark those chores on your calendar.

Then, get yourself four index cards. On the first, write PRIDE. On the second, write PATIENCE. On the third, write PERSISTENCE. And on the fourth, write PRAYER. Tack up your calendar and index cards where you'll see them every day. That way, you'll stay focused on the matters at hand, and if your garden isn't a success, at least you'll gain some points with the big guy upstairs.

IT PAYS TO BE CHOOSY ABOUT PERENNIALS

Since you'll be living with perennials for many years to come, you'll never regret choosing them wisely from the start. Follow these guidelines for perennial pleasure!

❧ Match sunlight requirements of the perennials to your planting locations.

❧ Create beds of complementary colors like blues and oranges, reds and greens, or purples and yellows.

❧ Vary plant heights to add interest to your landscape.

❧ Coordinate bloom times—as the blooms on one variety die, the blooms on another should begin to flower.

Build a Border

A border of small trees or a hedge around your garden will give you what farmers have grown for years—hedgerows that attract birds and keep them from stealing seeds in the field. Good trees for birds are red cedar (Virginia juniper), birches, dogwood, flowering crabapple, hawthorn, and the taller mountain ash. All have berries or fruit that birds love.

FEED THE BIRDS

Sometimes, gardens are literally for the birds! You can plant your garden with individual flowers matched to specific types of birds, or you can let your garden grow wild, in which case you'll get all kinds of birds.

To have a garden full of fine feathered friends, supply these bird necessities:

Food: trees, berried shrubs, and plenty of feeding stations.

Water: a birdbath that you can keep full, a small bird pool (even a plastic one), ponds, and streams or other moving water.

Cover: shrubs, vines, and trees to protect your friends from marauders.

Safe nesting sites: good cover or trees.

Birds of a Feather

…will flock to your yard if you plant the trees they love. Here are some examples of their favorite cuisine.

PLANT THIS	TO ATTRACT
Hawthorn	Cedar waxwings (they love the berries)
Mountain ash	Robins
Any fruit tree (Japanese persimmons are particularly good, as birds linger in them for a long time into the fall)	Mockingbirds, cardinals, and sparrows
Pear trees	Baltimore orioles (they prefer to hang their nests in the haven of pear trees)
Shrubs and flowers with red hues, such as coral honeysuckle, red salvia, Turk's cap, cypress vine, and hibiscus	Ruby-throated hummingbirds

Jerry's Secrets

Contact your local Audubon Society or a local nursery to help you find the perfect plantings for the fine feathered friends that call your part of the country home. You can also contact the National Wildlife Federation for plenty of help with a back-yard wildlife or bird program. Their address is 8925 Leesburg Pike, Vienna, VA 22184. Call them at (703) 790-4000, or check out their Web site at www.nwf.org.

SEEDS THAT AIM TO PLEASE

If you're not going to plant a garden to attract birds, but instead you plan to set out feeders, use the list below as a guide to some of the more common birds and their seed preferences.

The best time to begin a feeding program is in early October, when birds start looking for a winter food supply.

One word of warning: If you don't intend to keep a regular feeding program going—that is, every day without fail—don't consider starting one. Birds come to rely on the food that is being put out, and when that supply is cut off, it causes needless hardship (and even death) for the birds that have been using your station as their only food supply. This is a less-serious problem in heavily populated areas where there is more than one feeding station, but it is extremely important in rural areas, especially during severe weather.

Jerry's Secrets

Serious bird watchers know that birds will visit a feeder more readily if you provide a cover of bushes or shrubs nearby. And try to keep the feeder in the sun and out of the wind. Remember—the early bird gets the seed, so watch for your feathered friends in early morning when they're most eager to feed.

American goldfinch: millet, sunflower, thistle

Blue jay: peanut, sunflower

Cardinal: millet, peanut, sunflower

Chickadee: peanut hearts, suet, sunflower, thistle, wild bird food mix

Cowbird: millet, proso

Evening grosbeak: sunflower

Finch: millet, suet, sunflower, thistle

Grackle: cracked corn, sunflower

House finch: millet, peanut hearts, suet, sunflower, thistle

House sparrow: cracked corn, millet, sunflower

Junco: cracked corn, hulled oats, millet, peanuts, suet, thistle

Mourning dove: cracked corn, millet, peanut hearts, sunflower

Purple finch: millet, sunflower, thistle, wild bird food mix

Red-bellied woodpecker: cracked corn, suet, sunflower

Song sparrow: millet, suet, sunflower, thistle

Towhee: millet

Tufted titmouse: peanut hearts, suet, sunflower, thistle

White-breasted nuthatch: suet, sunflower

White-crowned sparrow: cracked corn, millet, peanut hearts, sunflower, wild bird food mix

White-throated sparrow: cracked corn, millet, peanut hearts, sunflower, wild bird food mix

BECKON THE BUTTERFLIES

Who doesn't enjoy the sight of butter-flies fluttering about the yard and garden? Here's what you'll need to entice these beauties to your neck of the woods:

Sunlight. Locate your but-terfly garden in a sunny area. Butterflies are cold-blooded in-sects, so they need plenty of sunlight to warm their wing muscles enough to allow them to fly.

Shelter. It's easier for butter-flies to fly and feed in a calm area, so provide shelter from wind and rain.

Hang Around for Hummingbirds

To entice hummingbirds to your yard, hang long strands of orange polyester yarn on trees and shrubs near your hummingbird feeder. For more permanent attraction, plant trees and shrubs that have red or orange berries and flowers.

Water. Butterflies cannot drink from open water, so wet sand, earth, or mud are the best water sources. Sink a pail into the ground, fill it with mud, and place a few sticks on top for the butterflies to perch on.

Food plants. Young butter-flies need food, so include some plants that butterfly larvae eat. These include bloodflower, elm, fennel, milkweed, passion-flower, senna, and wild cherry.

Nectar plants. Butterflies find nectar flowers by their col-ors—the insects are attracted to "hot" colors like yellow, orange, red, and purple. The best nectar plants include azaleas, butterfly bushes, Mexican sunflowers, New England asters, verbena, and yellow cosmos. Some but-terfly species will accept rotting fruit, stale beer, and sugar or honey water.

Butterflies need flowers that provide a platform to perch on while they probe for nectar with their proboscis. It's easier for them to probe simple flowers, so it's best to avoid double flowers.

Butterflies are generally around from spring into fall in most parts of the country, so you should plant flowers for a succession of blooms through-out the growing season.

PEST PATROL

Bug-Be-Gone Spray

While you're attracting birds, butterflies, and other friends to your gar-den, keep bugs at bay with this potent spray.

1 cup of Murphy's Oil Soap
1 cup of antiseptic mouthwash
1 cup of chewing tobacco juice*

Mix all of the ingredients together in a 20 gallon hose-end sprayer, and soak your plants to the point of runoff.

*To make the juice, take three fingers' worth of chewing tobacco from the package, place it in the toe of a nylon stocking, and place the stocking in a gal-lon of boiling water. Let the tobacco steep until the wa-ter is dark brown.

WEEKEND WATER GARDEN

For a weekend's worth of work, you can have a beautiful water garden that will attract birds and small wildlife while creating a re-laxing retreat for you and your family. Water garden kits are avail-able at many garden centers and through mail-order catalogs. The key to a long-lasting and attractive water garden is planning.

1. Choose the location carefully. Place your water garden where it can be viewed and appreciated from the house. If you want to grow water lilies or lotuses, be sure to locate the pond or pool in a spot with full sun for at least five hours each day.

2. Be sure the soil at the site is well drained. Boggy, wet soil can distort the shape of an artificial pool and can eventually crack the liner. A pool placed in sandy or crumbly soil also has to be spe-cially prepared, to keep the sides from caving in.

3. Keep clear of trees. If the pool or pond is directly under trees, falling leaves will decay and muck up the water, harming fish and plant life and clogging the pumps and filters.

4. Locate the pond near water and electricity. The pool or pond will need to be filled with a hose and will occasionally need to have water added to replace what you lose through evaporation. Plus you'll need electricity to run the pump.

5. Make it deep. Shallow pools and ponds cloud up quickly with excess algae. Submerged plants, floating plants, and fish do better in water that's about 18 to 24 inches deep—or even deeper, in colder climates.

6. Do your homework. There are three ways to create a pool or pond. A flexible plastic liner is lightweight, inexpensive, and can be cut to any shape, but installation is time consuming.

Prefabricated fiberglass pools are more expensive but more durable than plastic liners. They also perform better on sloping ground and are easier to install.

A concrete pool lasts the longest, if it's in-stalled correctly. Inadequate mixing or reinforcement of the concrete can cause cracking, so it's best to hire a professional.

THINK SMALL

Do you have a small yard, but long for a vegetable garden? Don't despair—there are a number of dwarf and compact vegetable plants that will thrive in even a Lilliputian garden. Here's a look at just some of the many varieties available:

Cucumber: 'Bush Champion', 'Spacemaker', 'Bush Whopper', 'Pot Luck', 'Patio Pik', and 'Bush Crop' are all high-quality dwarf varieties.

Pumpkin: A vining-type pumpkin can easily overgrow a small garden, but 'Cinderella' has a desirable bush character and produces pumpkins that weigh 8 to 11 pounds. Since the bush pumpkin produces in about 90 days, don't plant it too early. For Halloween pumpkins, plant in June.

Tomato: Cherry tomatoes like 'Tiny Tim' and midsize tomatoes like 'Patio', 'City Best', and 'Stakeless' are good for container growing and home greenhouse growing.

Watermelon and cantaloupe: In general, these are temperamental and require the best conditions to grow. Because the dwarf character is so strong, seed quality is poor. The quality of the melons is usually less than desired, too. If you have the space to grow standard varieties, I recommend that you do so. If you attempt to grow watermelons, I suggest that you start them inside in containers, and then transplant them to the garden once it warms up.

Winter squash: Burpee's 'Butter Boy' has large fruit of the butternut type on smaller vines. Burpee's 'Butterbush' has much smaller fruit that produces in a smaller space. Burpee's 'Bush Table Queen' is an acorn-type squash that is a semibush. Their yields are high, but these vines do not tolerate heat or stress conditions. All produce acceptable quality squash.

Keep 'Em Close

Nearness makes the heart grow fonder—kind of. Keep your vegetable garden as close to your house as you can—it's more convenient to tend to and water your garden for a few minutes each day if it's just a hop, skip, and a jump from your back door.

PEST PATROL

Marigolds to the Rescue!

Marigolds are a mighty mosquito repeller, so plant them in and around your outdoor living areas and vegetable garden to help keep pesky mosquitoes away.

FALL FOR BARGAINS

Fall is the best time to plant for many reasons, including the low, off-season prices. After the long, cold winter, your local garden centers stock their shelves for spring, and while they're at it, they price their merchandise to make their seasonal profits, which is only fair. But come August, they drastically reduce their prices on leftover plants, tools, and fertilizers to clear out inventory and make room for the next spring's blooms. So fall is *the* time to buy.

Buy all of the garden supplies you need, as well as any tree, shrub, evergreen, perennial, rose, or any other potted, packaged, balled, or bareroot plant. Believe you me, given the choice, plants would prefer to spend the winter at your family homestead rather than in a cold, lonesome parking lot. Smart shoppers can also find bargains through their local parks and recreation departments, which sometimes sell extra trees at wholesale prices.

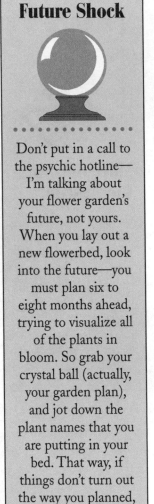

Future Shock

Don't put in a call to the psychic hotline—I'm talking about your flower garden's future, not yours. When you lay out a new flowerbed, look into the future—you must plan six to eight months ahead, trying to visualize all of the plants in bloom. So grab your crystal ball (actually, your garden plan), and jot down the plant names that you are putting in your bed. That way, if things don't turn out the way you planned, you'll know what varieties to avoid planting next year.

GET OFF TO A ROSY START

If you're including roses in your landscape (and you should), be sure to plant them where they'll feel right at home. They need well-drained soil that will not dry out near a handy watering facility. They also need at least a half-day of full sunlight, but keep in mind that the morning sun is not particularly advantageous.

A windbreak or shelter to the north and west is almost a necessity in severe climates. Fences, hedges, and buildings all make very effective protection for roses.

Naturally, rose-growing requirements vary enormously with local conditions, but genuine success with roses can seldom be achieved unless they have good drainage, some sunlight, and shelter from strong winds. And no matter when or where roses are to be planted, you'll need to prepare their beds well in advance of their arrival. Select the location, design the garden (if there is a design), and dig, fertilize, and let the bed settle before planting roses.

BUILD A BED A BIT AT A TIME

When you decide to put in a brand-new planting bed, you've got to be prepared to do a lot of digging and soil amending. But don't despair—you can work at it a little bit at a time, as I did one summer when I decided to put in a perennial bed that

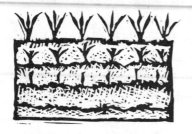

would run 100 feet down the entire fenceline on the west side of my backyard.

I began preparing the bed by digging and spading a little bit every time I got a chance. (That usually meant about twice a week, because that's how often I mow my lawn.) The grass clippings became part and parcel of the new bed.

In early fall, I added mower-shredded leaves until I had a 2 × 100-foot flowerbed that was ready for action. And the best part was that the whole bed was made with a minimum amount of aggravation and backaches!

LILY LOCALE

I just love lilies; they're the darlings of my flower garden. If you've never had the pleasure of tending to these beauties, you may not realize that their location has to be chosen very carefully to ensure good growth. Here's what they need to get off to a good start:

Perfect drainage. A gentle slope will do. If your site is level and your soil is heavy, you need to build and prepare raised beds for the bulbs.

Air circulation. A good breeze can keep many garden pests and diseases away.

Sunlight. At least until 2 P.M. Filtered sunlight or semishade brings out the more delicate colors, but makes weak stems and soft flowers. Don't plant lilies near walls, walks, or driveways that reflect sun or heat.

Jerry's Secrets

Take some advice from someone who knows—make your beds a manageable size, especially if you are a first-year gardener. That way, you can keep them looking good and still have the time to enjoy them.

Easy Peonies

Select a sunny, well-drained place for your peonies. They will tolerate some shade, but should only have sun for half of the day. Don't plant them too close to large trees or shrubs that will rob them of the food and moisture that they need to grow.

GO WILD WITH BULBS

Spring-flowering bulbs offer a wide variety of colors, heights, and flowering periods. Since bulbs are easy to grow, let your imagination run wild as you plan your garden. Colors, heights, and flowering times are the keys to colorful and creative plantings. Here are some tips for bulb success:

❧ Note the blooming period for each bulb variety. Plant shorter, early-blooming bulbs among tall, late-season flowers. The late bloomers will camouflage the withered foliage after the shorter flowers have faded.

❧ Plant low-growing bulbs at the front edges of garden beds, so shrubs and taller flowers won't hide them.

❧ Bright-colored flowering bulbs bring vibrant color to a neutral setting. Try them in the rock garden or alongside a brick wall.

❧ If your garden or window box is visible from indoors, try using colors that complement your curtains or porch decor.

❧ Plant scattered clusters of early-flowering bulbs, such as crocus, throughout your lawn to get that "natural" look.

Jerry's Secrets

Don't throw away old, broken umbrellas. Tear away the material and use the metal ribs for long-lasting flower supports. Paint them green, and no one will even notice them in your garden.

An Annual Event

Since most perennials are spring or fall bloomers, you won't have much summer color in your perennial beds unless you plan ahead and bring in some annual reinforcements. Plant annuals to fill in the gaps in your perennial beds, and you'll be rewarded with colorful blooms all summer long.

GONE WITH THE WIND

It isn't a pretty sight to see the tops of your flowers blowing away on the first gusty day that comes along. So to keep your flowers from losing their heads, plant tall, top-heavy plants near windbreaks—your house or garage, a wall, a hedge, or anything else that will provide much-needed protection from wind damage.

Know Your Annuals

Before you spend time, effort, and money on choosing and planting annuals, familiarize yourself with their habits to make the most of these bloomin' beauties. Here are my suggestions for the best use of annuals in your yard.

USES	BEST ANNUALS
For borders	Balsam, bells-of-Ireland, cosmos, flossflower, flowering tobacco, hound's-tongue, knapweed, larkspur, madwort, marigold, mealy-cup, petunia, scarlet salvia, snapdragon, spider plant, statice, zinnia
For color	Amaranth, basil, canna, dusty miller, flame nettle, perilla
For cutting	Aster, bells-of-Ireland, blanket flower, carnation, coneflower, cosmos, dahlia, daisy, gerbera, globe amaranth, knapweed, larkspur, marigold, nasturtium, painted-tongue, petunia, pincushion flower, sage, snapdragon, statice, verbena, zinnia
As edging	Begonia, calendula, candytuft, cupflower, dusty miller, dwarf bachelor buttons, flame nettle, flossflower, forget-me-not, gazania, globe amaranth, heliotrope, icicle plant, impatiens, lobelia, madwort, pansy, phlox, periwinkle, petunia, pinks, purslane, snapdragon, verbena, wishbone flower, woolflower (dwarf varieties), zinnia
For partial shade	Balsam, begonia, bush violet, calendula, flame nettle, flowering tobacco, forget-me-not, impatiens, lobelia, pansy, sage, wishbone flower
For rock gardens	Candytuft, dusty miller, gazania, icicle plant, madwort, pansy, verbena
For seashore areas	Dusty miller, hollyhock, lupine, madwort, petunia, statice
In window boxes	Cupflower, cascade petunia, flame nettle, lobelia, madwort, thunbergia, wax begonia
As groundcovers	Creeping zinnia, cupflower, forget-me-not, icicle plant, lobelia, Mexican ivy, morning glory, nasturtium, periwinkle, purslane, sweet alyssum, sweet pea, thunbergia, verbena

THE KINDEST CUT OF ALL

Every home garden should include an area that has been set aside especially for cut flowers. As enjoyable as flowers are in the garden, most of us also want some in the house, to use as centerpieces or just to brighten a room.

Locate your cutting garden in a fairly out-of-the-way place, but not too far from the house, or you'll never get out there.

Choose a sunny spot where there is good, well-drained soil; if there's any doubt, improve the soil with plenty of organic materials like compost, manure, and peat moss before you plant.

By planning and planting a cutting garden, you:

❧ won't have to detract from your display beds and borders by cutting from them;

❧ can grow flowers especially for cutting in orderly rows, just like vegetables;

❧ can weed, water, and perform other maintenance chores quickly and easily.

GIVE SHRUBS A FIRM FOUNDATION

If you're planning to plant shrubbery along the foundation of your home, keep in mind that the soil is usually very poor. The builder usually fills this in with whatever is available at the time, and more often than not it includes pieces of brick, concrete, drywall, and the like. So before you plant, I want you to dig a hole a minimum of 3 × 3 feet, remove all of the soil, and replace it with a good, rich mix of compost and manure.

SMART CONTAINER CHOICES

If you're planning a container garden on your patio or deck (or anywhere else, for that matter), I heartily recommend you use plastic containers. Now, don't turn up your nose at that suggestion—I'm not talking about the boring, cheap-looking white, dark green, or black plastic containers that many nurseries and garden centers supply. I'm talking about the really attractive ones that look just like clay or molded concrete, but which are far more practical. They won't break, they retain moisture longer on hot surfaces than clay pots do, they clean up easier, they store easily, and they are relatively inexpensive. Plus, moss and mold don't build up on them in the shade. What more could you ask for?

If you must, barrels, boxes, and stoneware containers can also be used, but just remember that when you need to move your plants, the weight of the containers will really get you down!

MUM'S THE WORD

These late bloomers are the bright lights of the fall garden—mums really put on a show just as the gardening season is winding down. To get the most out of your mums, plan carefully before you plant.

❧ Select a site that gets at least half a day of sun.

❧ Plant them in fertile, well-drained soil. Soil can be improved by adding compost, peat moss, or any other rich organic matter.

❧ Mums that are already flowering can be planted in any location that needs a splash of color, but keep in mind that they will grow best in an area that gets lots of sun.

❧ Plant them in spring, because spring-planted mums have a better chance of survival the first year than those planted in fall. The extra time in the ground gives their root systems a chance to get up and running before winter sets in.

Jerry's Secrets

Take it easy—cut pictures from gardening magazines, mail-order catalogs, or booklets that you've picked up at your local garden center to plan your dream garden on paper right in the comfort of your living room!

Perfect Potting Soil

Here's how to make the perfect blend of soil for all of your container-grown garden plants.

Mix in 3 equal parts:

Sharp sand
Clay loam
Organic matter or professional planter mix

Per cubic foot of soil mixture, add:

1½ cups of Epsom salts
¾ cup of coffee grounds (rinse them clean first)
12 eggshells (dried and crushed to powder)

Mix it all together, and use it to make your plant friends feel comfy and cozy, and right at home.

VEGETABLES ON THE VERANDA

When planning a container garden, don't limit yourself to a few cherry tomatoes or peppers. Many vegetables are easily adapted to container gardening. Plant early varieties and those that are developed especially for containers whenever possible to ensure green thumb success.

🌿 Many vegetable seeds can be sown directly into their final containers. These include kale, garlic, self-blanching celery, potatoes, beans, peas, carrots, and cucumbers. Radishes, spring onions, lettuce, and spinach are also easy to grow from seed. Sow several types, and plant the seed at weekly intervals. Then you'll be able to harvest continually throughout the season. Thin the seedlings when they are still small.

🌿 Runner beans, peas, and cucumbers can be grown in containers. Just keep in mind that they require staking.

🌿 Dwarf cucumbers, peas, and cherry tomatoes will thrive in well-drained hanging baskets.

🌿 Even carrots can be grown in containers, but choose deep containers and a carrot variety that is stump-rooted.

🌿 Potato transplants grown from seed or seed potato tubers can be grown in containers. Plant one transplant or tuber with a maximum of three eyes in a large pot. Don't place more than one plant in a pot, or your yield will be greatly reduced. Protect these plants from frost in spring and early fall.

🌿 Many herbs—such as chives, basil, bay, marjoram, thyme, mint, parsley, and sage—can be successfully grown in hanging baskets or containers. They can easily be brought indoors when the weather turns colder.

GO FOR A WINNING TEAM

If you think of your vegetables as team players and yourself as their manager, you'll realize how important it is to place each player on the field in the position where they'll perform the best. Here are some tips for managing your vegetable garden team all the way to the world championship!

❧ Plant perennial crops, such as asparagus, artichokes, and herbs, in a separate area so they won't get in the way when you're cultivating annual crops or plowing up the garden in spring or fall.

❧ Group plants together according to the time it takes them to reach maturity. On one side of the garden, place the fast growers: radishes, turnip greens, mustard, spinach, leaf and bibb lettuce, and green onions. On the other side of the garden, plant the slower-growing vegetables: peas, beets, carrots, Swiss chard, kale, head lettuce, collards, broccoli, cabbage, cauliflower, bulb onions, and early potatoes. This allows you to harvest the fast growers without disturbing their slower-maturing teammates.

TREE TERRITORY

Before you plant trees, check for proper drainage in the planting area. Dig several holes 3 feet deep or so, fill them with water, and then step back and watch what happens. Repeat several times if necessary. If water stays in the hole for one or more days, or if it drains away in less than three minutes, then drainage is poor and you should choose another location.

Pole Partners

If you're thinking of growing pole beans, plan to plant them right next to your corn. That way, the bean vines can grow up the corn stalks for support. In return, the beans supply much-needed nitrogen to the corn.

Be Choosy

There's nothing as sad as seeing folks make the mistake of buying and planting flowers, trees, and shrubs that are destined to fail for the simple reason that they're the wrong plants for the wrong location. You can avoid a whole lotta heartache simply by doing a bit of homework before you buy your plants.

Walk around your neighborhood to see what's thriving in your neighbors' gardens. Talk with your local nurseryman or county extension agent to find out which plants are best suited for your particular area. And know what to look for and what to look out for when purchasing seeds, bulbs, and plants. Being choosy about your plants is the smart way to start your garden.

On a Roll

If you can't find a suitable site for your flowers—put 'em on wheels! Make a movable bed out of an old toy wagon. Drill drainage holes, add a thin layer of gravel, top with soil, and plant. To put your flowers in a new location, simply move the wagon.

SET YOUR "SITES" ON EVERGREENS

Evergreens require perfect drainage, so select their sites with care. Always plant evergreens outside the drip line of your house—falling ice can very easily break branches and split stems to the ground.

Also, be sure to familiarize yourself with the growth and spreading habits of your evergreens, so you can plant accordingly to avoid overcrowding. That cute, little, 2-foot baby that you bring home can soon grow into a 12-foot monster!

You can plant evergreens anytime from March to November. If you're starting with a balled-and-burlapped tree or container stock, be sure to have the bed ready within a few days of your purchase. If you're digging your own tree or using bareroot transplants, it's best to plant in early spring, as soon as you can get a shovel into the ground.

KEEP 'EM IN THE DARK

What, other than mushrooms, would grow in dark, damp conditions? Well, believe it or not, there are quite a few flowering plants that don't mind being situated in shady, moist areas of your yard. Take your pick of these:

🌿 Try the wild hyacinth, which is available in blue, white, or cream. This easy-to-please plant will grow in shade or full sunlight wherever the ground is wet.

🌿 Sweet-smelling lily-of-the-valley thrives in moist soil and full to partial shade.

🌿 Crimson flag, native to South Africa, will grow nicely where it's warm and damp.

🌿 Elephant's ear, aptly named for its huge leaves, grows well in warm, moist areas, and will actually thrive in just a few inches of water in a shallow pool.

SHRUB-A-DUB-DUB

Choose your shrubs with care—you're going to be living with them for a long time to come. So take a tip from professional landscapers, and choose shrubs that look good throughout the seasons. Here's what to look for:

Blooms. There are many varieties that bloom at various times throughout the year. And some offer blossoms followed by berries in brilliant shades of red, orange, deep crimson, brown, or black. One, the sapphireberry, is turquoise blue.

Foliage. Look for shrubs that are attractive even when they're not in bloom. Do you like leaves that are large or small? Do you prefer bright, glossy, green leaves or those that are duller gray-green? And what about shape? Leaves can be round, oval, heart-shaped, serrated, or many-fingered.

Wood. Consider the color and shape of the trunk, branches, and twigs when they are bare. Handsome bark and twig color in winter are just as important as (in the colder climes, maybe more important than) blossoms in spring.

I PINE FOR VINES

A fast-growing annual vine can be a lifesaver—it will hide unsightly spots and add beauty to your landscape. One of your best bets is the popular morning glory. This vine is what we call a twiner, so give it something to wind around.

I love morning glories because they will thrive in poor soil and will grow just about anywhere as long as they have adequate sun. On cloudy days they will stay open, but on sunny days the flowers will close up by noon. So the moral of the story is to place the plants where they don't get direct sun in the early morning and thus will stay open longer.

Other good vining choices are cathedral bells, cypress, marble vine, and gourds.

Bulb Alert

Steer clear of bulbs with mushy gray spots on them. They're not worth carting home, because they won't recover. But don't worry if the bulb's papery skin is loose. This is completely normal. And don't be concerned about a few nicks—they won't affect the development of otherwise healthy bulbs.

BUYER BEWARE

Nurseries and garden centers offer many perennials for sale. Buying the plants (seedlings) instead of growing them from seed is a great way to get off to a fast start, but there are some things that you should look out for when purchasing perennials.

🍂 Avoid plants that have been in warm areas for too long. You'll know them by their pale yellow stems and leaves.

🍂 Choose plants that are short, compact, dark green, and that look healthy and strong.

🍂 Buy only named varieties. They are bred to have specific characteristics, so you can easily research their disease resistance, heat and cold tolerance, and plant habits if you so desire.

WANTED: ALIVE, <u>NOT</u> DEAD!

It's not easy to tell whether a flowering tree is alive when you buy it because in most instances, you're buying it when it is dormant. But some super sleuthing can help you solve the mystery.

First, look for signs of new growth, such as small bud breaks. Then, if none are visible, gently peel back a small piece of bark in two or three places up the trunk to see if it is moist and green underneath. Say goodbye to any tree that doesn't pass these two tests.

HAPPY HOUSEPLANTS

The surest way to have healthy, happy houseplants is to buy them already grown to the size and shape you want. If you only need to water and fertilize your plants enough to keep them healthy, you will greatly increase your chances of success. Use this shopping list to make sure you get the plants that are best suited for you:

Plants for any conditions: Aglaonema, aspidistra, cissus (Venezuela treebine), crassula (jade plants), dieffenbachia, ficus, philodendron, sansevieria, schefflera, scindapsus, syngonium

Plants for dry conditions: Bromelaids, cacti, peperomia, sansevieria, scindapsus, zebrina

Plants for large tubs: Dieffenbachia, dracaena, fatshedera, ficus, palms, pandanus, philodendron, schefflera

Plants for low temperatures (50° to 60°F at night): Bromeliads, cineraria, citrus, cyclamen, English ivy, German ivy, Jerusalem cherry, kalanchoe, primrose

Plants for moderate temperatures (60° to 65°F at night): Christmas cactus, chrysanthemum, gardenia, grape ivy, palms, peperomia, pilea, ti plant, tuberous begonia, wax begonia

Plants for high temperatures (65° to 70°F at night): African violet, aglaonema, cacti, caladium, croton, dracaena, ficus, gloxinia, philodendron, scindapsus, schefflera, succulents, sygonium

Plants for low light: Aglaonema, ferns

Plants for medium light: Begonia, dieffenbachia, dracaena, palms, peperomia, philodendron, schefflera, scindapsus, syngonium

Plants for high light: Cacti, croton, English ivy, sansevieria, any succulent

MAIL MALADIES

Plants that you buy through the mail, no matter how carefully they are wrapped, are most likely to have two strikes against them: Their package may have been crushed or traumatized by other, heavier packages en route; and in all likelihood, they have been stored in a close, warm room for too many hours in the postal facility.

So the survival of these plants depends on your quick action—get them into the ground without delay! This, of course, applies to any plants you buy, whether through the mail or from the local nursery—don't let them languish in the back seat or trunk of your car, and don't leave trees on the driveway, patio, or front porch for days on end.

Starting from Seed

Believe you me—nothing beats the satisfaction of planting tiny seeds and watching them blossom into big, beautiful flowers and mouth-watering vegetables. While starting from seed means a little extra effort and a longer wait for your plants to arrive, it doesn't take a lot of skill, the cost is minimal, and the satisfaction you get is immeasurable.

SEEDY CHOICES

Whether you buy seeds in seed packets or on seed tapes, be sure that they have a current-year date stamp. You can buy seed packets in any garden center, through the mail, or on the Web. The advantage of the latter two is variety—you'll find a lot more varieties available through seed catalogs or on the Web than you will in your local nursery or nearby garden center.

Most of the seed companies now sell seed tapes. These are long strips of laminated paper coated with water-soluble material, and the seeds are already spaced on them. You prepare the soil, place the seed tape on top, cover it lightly with soil, firm it down with your hand, and water. The seeds sprout, and the paper dissolves from the moisture in the soil.

While seed tapes are more expensive than seed packets, they are less expensive than flat-grown plants. Another advantage is that they are quick and handy. And if you have kids or grandkids who want to help you garden, seed tapes are the perfect solution to wayward seeds. The kids get a kick out of "planting," and you'll know that the seeds have been sown right where you want them, not scattered across the lawn!

Make Sure You Pass This Test

The smart gardener tests his or her vegetable seeds before planting. Simply fold them in a strip of blotting paper and stick the paper in a pan of moist sand. If the sand is kept moist and warm for several days, the best of the seeds will sprout. From a good batch of seeds, about 75 out of every 100 seeds will sprout.

Go Soak Your Pots

Soak clay pots in a mild soapy-water solution for a day or so before using them. If you start with dry pots, they'll wick all of the moisture out of your potting soil, and you might as well be planting in the Sahara Desert.

ROW, ROW, ROW YOUR SEEDS

To get picture-perfect plants all in a row, follow these six steps to success:

1. Start by setting a stake at the beginning and end of each row. Then stretch string between the stakes to keep your rows nice and straight.

2. Make a furrow with your hoe handle, adjusting the depth to the seed you're planting.

3. Sow seed thinly. Shake it from a cut corner of the packet or use an old salt shaker.

4. Use a corner of the hoe blade to draw soil over the seed. Don't allow stones or soil clods to cover it up.

5. If your soil is heavy, sprinkle weak tea water (see recipe at right) on it to help germination and make crusting less severe.

6. Thin young plants as necessary to provide growing space.

MIXERS & ELIXIRS

Weak Tea Water

1 twice-used tea bag
1 tsp. of liquid dish soap
1 gal. of water

Steep the tea bag in the soapy-water mixture until the water is slightly colored. Use as needed.

BAN THE BIRDS

Newly planted annual seeds, which are very near the soil surface, are tempting morsels for the birds to snatch. To keep birds at bay, try one of these tried-and-true techniques:

Netting. This is one of the best safeguards. It lets light in while keeping birds (and many insects) out.

Screening. A homemade portable screen will deter birds. Cut old window or door screens into 18-inch-wide strips, and nail them to old lath to make a framework. It doesn't look pretty, but it gets the job done.

Noisemakers. Use noise, motion, and light reflection to frighten birds (and small animals, too) away. Here are some quick, easy, and inexpensive ways to do this:

🐦 String the tops and bottoms of metal cans to make chimes that clang in the breeze and reflect sunlight.

🐦 Crumple aluminum foil into balls and suspend them throughout the flowerbed to reflect sunlight.

🐦 Hang strips of cloth so they'll gently sway in the breeze.

🐦 Hang small mirrors here and there to reflect sunlight.

Natural Bug Juice

½ cup of marigolds
½ cup of geraniums
½ cup of garlic
10 gallons of warm
    water

Chop the marigolds, geraniums, and garlic very finely, and mash them until they are liquid. Mix with the water, and sprinkle over and around your vegetable garden.

SPEEDY SEEDS

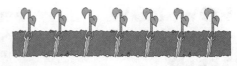

You can speed up the sprouting time of seeds by soaking them in a mix of 1 teaspoon of dish soap, 1 teaspoon of ammonia, and 1 teaspoon of instant tea in 1 quart of warm water for 24 hours. Then place the seeds in a piece of old nylon stocking tied up with a twist tie. Let the seeds dry out, remove them from the stocking, and plant them.

SUMMER STARTERS

Before planting perennial seeds in summer, select a good location—one that is at least a little protected from the weather and which does not dry out. A cold frame or an unheated hotbed is much better than the open ground at this time of year because the cover can be closed to prevent drying out as well as to prevent the seed from being washed out by heavy rains.

The seed itself may be sown in shallow rows, a few inches apart, or it can be broadcast evenly over the entire area. Then, instead of disturbing the soil to cover the seed, try sifting a little fine vermiculite (⅛ inch deep) over it and pressing down lightly. Water with a fine mist. Afterwards, water whenever it becomes necessary.

If you planted in an open bed, cover the seeds with newspaper or burlap until germination takes place.

Scatter Far and Wide

Small-seeded greens such as spinach can be sown over a wide area rather than sown in rows. Simply scatter the seeds evenly from your hand as you walk. Avoid sowing in thick patches or strips. To ensure good rooting, walk over the sown area to press the seeds into the soil.

COSMOS AGAIN AND AGAIN

For many, many years I have considered cosmos to be indispensable in my garden. So in order to get a lot of early blooms, I have always started my plants indoors or in a cold frame, making sure I had the very earliest-blooming varieties. It never occurred to me that cosmos would easily sow itself.

A few years ago, some of my plants ripened seed, which scattered on the ground in the fall. Much to my surprise, the following spring a number of baby plants appeared and bloomed weeks earlier than those from spring-sown seed.

Since then, I have deliberately allowed a few of the largest and earliest blossoms to go to seed. The resulting young plants are far stronger than those started indoors or in a frame. I keep them well pinched-back to induce bushy growth and early flowering. And because the self-sown plants grow closer together than plants set out by hand, they support one another and rarely need staking. Talk about a time saver!

Slow and Steady

Start the seeds of slow-sprouters, such as onions, parsley, and beets, under a strip of burlap. This creates a nice warm environment that lets moisture in and encourages sprouting. Once the seeds have sprouted, remove the burlap to avoid growing leggy seedlings.

OVER HILL AND DALE

Plant seeds for large vegetables—such as squash, corn, and melons—in hills or mounds of soil. Plant three or four seeds in a cluster a foot or more in diameter. Then make a furrow around the perimeter of each hill for watering. Hill planting enables the roots to grow out from a central point and gives them more room to grow than they would have in a row.

Jerry's Secrets

Summer is a good time to start perennials from seed for blooms the next spring. The ground is warm, so the seeds start readily and still have time to produce good growth before activity ceases with the coming of the cold winter weather.

WINDOWSILL SALAD

For salad fixings in no time, plant radish, lettuce, and tomato seeds in containers and set them out on your windowsill.

Plant radish seeds ¼ inch deep and 1 inch apart in a 9 × 12-inch cake pan. Scatter lettuce seeds on the surface of the soil in another cake pan, and cover with ⅛ inch of soil. Set the pans in a sunny windowsill, and keep the soil damp. The plants will be ready for your salad bowl in 8 to 10 weeks.

Grow 'Tiny Tim' tomatoes in clay pots on the windowsill, and they'll be ready in 12 to 14 weeks.

MIXERS & ELIXIRS

Super Seed Starter Solution

¼ cup of barnyard tea*
¼ cup of soapy water
¼ cup of brewed tea
2 gallons of water

Mix all of the ingredients together, and spray on newly planted seedbeds and seedlings.

*To make barnyard tea, mix equal parts of manure, peat moss, and gypsum with a handful of garden food. Put it in cheesecloth, and soak it in warm water until the water is dark brown.

PLANT A-PEEL

Orange, lemon, and grapefruit rinds don't have to be banished to the compost pile! Instead, use them as neat indoor plant starters.

1. Cut the fruit in half, and clean out each half-rind.

2. Poke several holes in the bottoms and sides of the rinds to provide drainage.

3. Fill the rinds with soil, then plant them with their own, or any other kinds of seed.

4. After the seeds sprout, bury the rinds in the garden when you set out the plants.

What's in a Name?

After you've sown your seeds, it will be awhile before plants stick their heads up through the soil. By the time they do, you may be scratching your head, wondering what the heck you planted there in the first place! To avoid this confusion, label your planting beds. Record the plant name and date of sowing, and leave room on the label to record the transplanting date, as well.

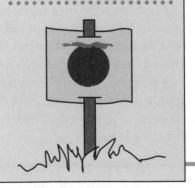

REFRIGERATE THE LEFTOVERS

If you find yourself with left-over seeds after the spring planting season, don't throw them out! You can store them for use next year. Seal them in their original packets, put the packets in small, airtight jars (like baby-food jars) with lids, and then tuck them away in your refrigerator.

Be sure the temperature stays between 36° and 45°F. (Check with a thermometer and adjust the fridge setting as needed.)

SOW YOUR ROSES

If you don't mind waiting a few years to see the blooms, you can grow roses from seed. (The plants may produce a few flowers the second summer after planting, but they generally don't blossom until the third year.) Just follow these simple steps, and sit back and be patient!

1. Let rose hips mature on the plant until they begin to crack open. Snip them off, and remove the seeds.

2. Plant the seeds in a prepared seedbed, and cover them lightly with sifted peat or sand. Water them and cover with clear plastic.

3. When the seeds sprout, cover the young plants with jars, and mulch heavily around their bases to protect them during the winter.

4. Remove the jars in spring after all danger of frost has come and gone.

Give 'Em a Pat

Here's a trick growers use in commercial greenhouses: To get seedlings to grow hardier and sturdier, lightly brush your hand across them several times a day.

Curb Your Dog

There is nothing worse than having neighborhood pets tramping through your flowerbeds. Keep dogs and cats away from your precious blooms by dusting crushed, dried red peppers or red pepper (cayenne) powder in and around the beds.

Bulb Basics

Bulbs are flowers-in-waiting—prewrapped packages of leaves and flowers ready to burst into bloom. The good news is that bulbs are practically foolproof. However, even the most experienced green thumbers can use a helping hand now and again to get the most from these beautiful bloomers.

MIXERS & ELIXIRS

Bulb Breakfast

10 lbs. of compost
5 lbs. of bonemeal
2 lbs. of bloodmeal
1 lb. of Epsom salts

Mix all of the ingredients together in a wheelbarrow. Before setting out bulbs, work this hearty breakfast into every 100 square feet of soil in your bulb planting areas.

MAY THE FORCE BE WITH YOU

When autumn leaves are falling, you can get a head start on bulbs that don't usually bloom until spring—such as crocus, galanthus, hyacinth, narcissus, scilla, and tulip. Here's how to get them growing for winter blooms:

1. In October or early November, plant the bulbs in pots, keeping them at 40°F for two to three months. You can keep the potted bulbs outdoors or in a cold room indoors. If you keep them indoors, the room must be dark and the temperature must be kept at 40°F. Water the bulbs every day so that the soil doesn't dry out.

2. As an alternative, you can refrigerate crocus, hyacinth, narcissus, and tulip bulbs at 40°F for two months instead of planting them in pots. At the end of two months, plant the bulbs in bowls.

3. In mid-January, when the shoots are well out of the necks of the bulbs, bring the pots or bowls into a cool, bright room that can be kept at 55°F. Expect blooms in about a month.

Note: Once bulbs have been forced, don't try to store them for replanting in your garden, as you would with outdoor-flowering bulbs. Unfortunately, the results are usually disappointing, so keep them indoors.

HANDLE WITH CARE

Lily bulbs are never completely dormant. They must be revived as soon as possible after digging. If the bulbs you buy are slightly limp on their arrival, place them in wet peat moss for a few days. They'll soon freshen up, and you should then plant them immediately.

Never plant new lily bulbs where other lilies have failed to grow and never plant them in heavy, soggy soil. Lilies cannot be treated like tulip or daffodil bulbs, which can be dried out and go completely dormant. Above all else, drainage is paramount!

You Can Fool Mother Nature

If you want to see your bulbs bloom a bit earlier than nature intended, plant your spring-flowering bulbs in a warm, sunny spot, such as against a wall. The result? Beautiful blooms a week or two earlier than usual.

If, on the other hand, you want to delay the bloom time, plant your bulbs in a cooler spot, such as on a northern hillside.

KEEP 'EM HIGH AND DRY

For a glorious spring display, plant spring-flowering Dutch bulbs in the fall. They will thrive in full or partial sun, but will actually do just fine in almost any location, as long as they have good drainage.

Bulbs will rot in standing water, so avoid areas of your yard that are prone to flooding, like at the bottom of a hill. If you have moist areas that just won't go away, don't despair. Crocuses, clivias, irises, caladiums, cannas, and white fawn lilies are all moisture-loving bulbs that can turn your eyesore into a beautiful spot.

PEST PATROL

Give Your Bulbs a Bath

To keep your bulbs bug-free, treat them to a nice, warm bath before putting them into their planting bed. Here's what you'll need:

2 tsp. of baby shampoo
1 tsp. of antiseptic mouthwash
$\frac{1}{4}$ tsp. of instant tea
2 gal. of warm water

1. Mix all of the ingredients in a bucket. *Carefully* place the bulbs into this mixture.

2. Stir gently, then remove the bulbs one at a time, and plant them.

3. When you're done with the bath, don't throw out the bath water with the babies. Instead, give it to your trees and shrubs as a special treat—it'll make them rise and shine, too!

TOOLS FOR TUBERS (AND BULBS AND CORMS)

If the promise of a colorful spring garden finds you out-of-doors on a crisp November day, don't be daunted by the bushels of daffodil bulbs, boxes of tulip bulbs, and bags and bags of teeny-weeny crocus corms all around you. With the right tools, tucking away those bulbs for the winter will be a snap. Here's the lowdown:

Garden trowel. This makes a very quick and handy bulb planter. To use it like professional Dutch gardeners do, grab the handle so the inner curve of the spoon faces you, then stab straight down into the soil like you're using an ice pick. (The depth of the blade when plunged to the hilt should sink to about 8 inches, the perfect depth for planting larger bulbs.) Just pull back on the trowel to open a pocket in the soil, tuck the bulb in with the pointed end up, remove the trowel, and smooth the soil down. This technique allows you to get a good rhythm going.

Bulb planter. Sold in garden centers and in specialty catalogs, it comes in two versions: a hand tool bulb planter and a stand-up model with a long handle that gets you off your knees. Both make it easy to dig neat, circular holes of the proper depth for bulbs. Their cone shape pulls out a plug of soil as you withdraw the tool. You just plop the bulb into the hole and replace the soil. Some gardeners swear by these, while others think they're too much fuss.

Planter bit. This is my favorite. It fits any $3/8$" or larger electric drill. This bit makes a 3" round hole so quick, you won't believe it. Planter bits are available from garden catalogs, or visit us at www.jerrybaker.com.

Spade. One great planting technique is to naturalize crocuses or other small bulbs in your lawn. One way to do this is to simply cut a slice into the turf with a spade, push forward on the handle to open a pocket (like the trowel technique), and slip in a few bulbs.

Another spade technique calls for making a spade cut in the turf on three sides. Then you peel back the grass "carpet," place the bulbs in the trench, and roll the sod back in place.

Of course, the spade is also the tool to use for planting a large quantity of bulbs in a bed or border. Simply dig a trench to the

---

Jerry's Secrets

Handle your bulbs with care. Inside each dead-looking bulb is a small-but-perfect plant waiting to bloom—but not if you treat it too roughly. Never carelessly drop a bulb into the bottom of a shopping bag or box; you'll bruise more than their egos, and chances are they won't recover.

proper depth. (Hint: If you place the soil on a sheet of plastic until you're ready to replace it in the trench, you'll make a neater job of it.) Then place the bulbs in neat, evenly spaced patterns, and replace the soil.

Kneeling cushion. This is one item many gardeners deem a must. A good, soft kneeling cushion not only adds to your comfort and keeps you warm and dry, but also keeps you from sinking into your well-prepared soil. Inexpensive and washable versions are available at most garden centers.

Best Bulb Depths

Use these planting depth guidelines to ensure bulb success.

BULB	PLANTING DEPTH	BULB	PLANTING DEPTH
Allium		Lily	3 times the diameter of the bulb
Giant onion	7–8"		
Drumsticks	4–5"	Narcissus	
Crocus	3–4"	Large cup	6"
		Poeticus	6"
Daylily	6–8"	Trumpet	5–8"
Fritillaria		Snowdrop	3–4"
Checkered lily	4–6"		
Crown imperial	4–6"	Siberian squill	3"
Glory of the snow	3–4"	Striped squill	3"
Grape hyacinth	3–4"	Summer snowflake	4–5"
Grecian windflower	3–4"	Tulip	6–8"
Hyacinth	4–6"	Wood hyacinth	3"
Iris	4–6"	Winter aconite	3–4"

DARLING DAYLILIES

These bulbs make great additions to your landscape. With over 500 daylily varieties to choose from, you're sure to find just the right colors and shapes you're looking for.

Daylilies bloom from early spring until late fall, and they'll grow in almost any soil. A big plus is that they are seldom bothered by bugs or diseases.

Plant daylilies from April through November, mulching around fall-planted bulbs to prevent winter frost heaving.

Daylilies prefer sun, but they will do reasonably well in partial shade. Avoid low, wet spots where water collects and high spots over ledges where the soil is thin.

Spacing varies based on the look you're after. Use these guidelines for dramatic daylily effects:

Mixed perennial flower border: Allow a 16- to 18-inch circle for each daylily if you're going to divide and replant it in a few years. Allow a 24- to 30-inch circle if you plan on leaving the clump intact.

Landscape setting: Space the plants in a triangular pattern with each plant 24 inches from its neighbor. For a distant effect of grand clumps, space five to seven plants 12 to 18 inches apart in a cluster. Leave several feet between each cluster or group of daylilies.

Edging along a walk: Space the plants 12 to 18 inches apart in a single row.

Knee Pleasers

Save money and make your own kneeling cushion. Fill an old water bottle partway with water for a cushiony pad, or make a variation of the old Scout "sit-upon" by folding newspapers into a thick pad and enclosing them in a piece of old shower curtain, a grocery bag, or an old pillowcase.

Jerry Tells All About...
Gardening Basics

Q. I've tried planting packets of wildflower seeds without much success. How and when do I plant them?

A. I put my wildflower seeds, mixed with a little soil and just a sprinkle of tea water, to sleep in the refrigerator for a week prior to sowing them as early in the spring as possible.

Q. What type of evergreen can I plant in a wet area to make a nice-looking hedge?

A. I've found Canadian hemlock to be the ticket—it makes a great hedge, looks rich, and it's thick. The American arborvitae is a good second choice, if the area isn't too wet.

Q. When is the best time to plant evergreens?

A. Take a map of the United States, and draw a line from the coast of Massachusetts to the top corner of the Kansas-Missouri border. Continue the line south to the middle of Texas and west to the middle of Arizona. Next, follow it right up the middle of California, Oregon, and Washington. You can plant evergreens south and west of this line all winter long, and north of this line in early spring and fall. But no matter what part of the country you live in, when you plant evergreens, do so when the days are warm and the nights are cool.

Q. What flowers should I plant to attract hummingbirds?

A. Just about any flower that's bright red will do it. I've had a lot of luck with impatiens, petunias, and begonias.

MIXERS & ELIXIRS

Black Spot Remover

When black spot attacks your roses, fight back with a weapon you can gather from your garden:

15 tomato leaves
2 small onions
¼ cup of rubbing alcohol

Chop the tomato leaves and onions into very, very fine pieces, and steep them in the alcohol overnight. Apply to your rose bushes with a small, sponge-type paintbrush, hitting the tops and bottoms of all the leaves.

Q. I've had problems growing flowers on the north side of my house. I would like to know what kinds of flowers are best for that location. I've tried petunias, but they just bloom once, and the next bloom is very small. What can I do?

A. First of all, prepare your flowerbeds by overspraying them with this mixture: 1 can of beer, 1 can of regular cola (not diet), 1 cup of baby shampoo, 1 cup of antiseptic mouthwash, and ¼ teaspoon of instant tea granules, mixed together in a large bucket, then applied with your 20 gallon hose-end sprayer. Then plant any shade-loving flowers, like begonia, impatiens, or coleus. That should do the trick!

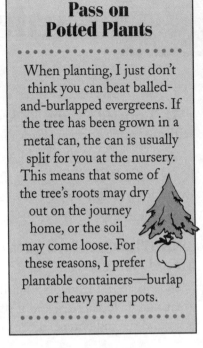

Pass on Potted Plants

When planting, I just don't think you can beat balled-and-burlapped evergreens. If the tree has been grown in a metal can, the can is usually split for you at the nursery. This means that some of the tree's roots may dry out on the journey home, or the soil may come loose. For these reasons, I prefer plantable containers—burlap or heavy paper pots.

Q. I love rhododendrons, but I don't have a northern location where I can plant them. Am I out of luck?

A. Not really. Rhododendrons like shade, but will tolerate some sun. Any exposure will do if you can shade the plants with, let's say, a large tree. Azaleas, mountain laurels, and lily-of-the-valley are all great friends of the rhododendron, and they like the same acid soil in a moist and shady spot.

Q. What flowering shrub should I plant for long-lasting fragrance and white flowers?

A. Double mock orange blooms almost all summer long, and it smells great. They grow to 5 or 6 feet tall, so plan accordingly.

PEST PATROL

Caterpillar Killer Tonic

To keep caterpillars in check and away from your plants, mix up a batch of my killer tonic.

½ lb. of wormwood leaves
2 tbsp. of Murphy's Oil Soap
1 gal. of water

Simmer the wormwood leaves in 2 cups of water for 30 minutes or so. Strain, then add the liquid and the Murphy's Oil Soap to 2 more cups of warm water. Apply with a 6 gallon hose-end sprayer to the point of runoff. Repeat as necessary until the caterpillars are history!

Q. What kind of shrub can I plant in wet soil?

A. Two of my favorites are the red twig dogwood and the speckled alder. Both just love the moisture.

Q. I have packaged vegetable seeds that are over a year old. Can I still use them?

A. You can try—just keep them tucked away in the refrigerator until you're ready to plant them.

Q. After dusting my dahlia bulbs with medicated baby powder and wrapping them in newspaper in fall, I put them in the refrigerator. When I checked on them, I discovered that they were rotten. What went wrong?

A. Dahlias are bulbs that should be dry stored, not refrigerated. So this year, when you dig up your bulbs, store them in a cool, dry place.

Bulbs Need Drainage

Planting hardy bulbs in poorly drained soil will shorten their lives—new bulbs will be poorly developed, flowers will be smaller, and the bulbs will rot.

Q. Last year, I dug up my tulip bulbs, but I never got a chance to replant them. Are they still good?

A. They may be, but you'll never know until you plant them! When you do, make sure you pack this organic lunch for them: 10 pounds of dry manure or compost, 5 pounds of bonemeal, and 2 pounds of Epsom salts mixed together and worked into every 100 square feet of soil.

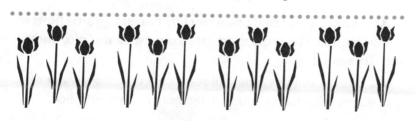

MIXERS & ELIXIRS

Bulb Booster

Bulbs need a complete, balanced diet to grow their very best. So to boost your bulbs to new heights, sprinkle this mixture on top of the growing beds in early spring, just as the foliage starts to break out of the ground.

2 lbs. of bonemeal
2 lbs. of wood ashes
1 lb. of Epsom salts

Q. I have an amaryllis bulb. The first year, I had flowers, but last winter I only had leaves. I let it grow all summer, then took it out of the soil to let it rest. When I planted it again, it grew leaves, but no flowers. Help!

A. I plant my amaryllis in pots, and then sink them into the ground for the summer. Come fall, I cut the foliage back to 3 inches; set the plants in a cool, dry area; and keep them damp, not wet. Try this method with your plant—it should do the trick.

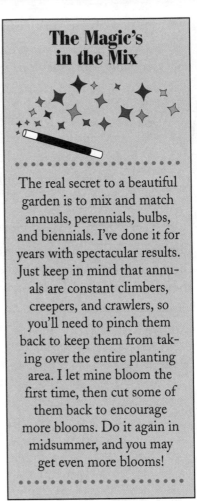

The Magic's in the Mix

The real secret to a beautiful garden is to mix and match annuals, perennials, bulbs, and biennials. I've done it for years with spectacular results. Just keep in mind that annuals are constant climbers, creepers, and crawlers, so you'll need to pinch them back to keep them from taking over the entire planting area. I let mine bloom the first time, then cut some of them back to encourage more blooms. Do it again in midsummer, and you may get even more blooms!

Jerry's Secrets

Bulbs need low temperatures to develop good roots and buds. So don't mulch them too early, or you'll cause premature leaf growth, which will weaken them. New plantings of tulips and daffodils benefit the most from mulching; older beds in milder climates really don't need it.

Q. How much sun is necessary for lots and lots of blooms?

A. I've found that five to six hours of morning sun is best, although the afternoon sun won't hurt.

Q. I've been told that when you buy nursery-grown flowers for the garden, you want short green ones with no color showing. True or false?

A. True! If you buy long, tall plants, they soon grow out of proportion. Short, fat plants can be more easily controlled.

Be Sweet to Your Annuals

Don't try to grow annuals (except marigolds, nicotania, and verbena) in soil with a pH below 6.5 because they can't tolerate the acidity. To sweeten the soil, add lime at the rate of 15 to 25 pounds per 500 square feet.

Q. What annual flower variety is the most popular?

A. Petunias are by far the number one favorite among both amateur and professional growers. They're followed closely by marigolds.

Q. I would like to plant my garden in an area that is now covered with Bermuda grass. How should I begin to prepare the area for my garden?

A. First, overspray the area with a warm soapy-water solution (1 tablespoon of liquid dish soap per gallon of water), and then follow with an application of KleenUp or another systemic grass and weed control. Finally, cover it with black plastic for a month or so.

Q. I have a small garden that I put potash on several years ago, and I still can't grow anything. Tomato plants stay the same size, flowers don't do anything, grass comes up but turns brownish red, and radishes poke up but don't grow. I have plowed deep and put lime on, but nothing seems to help. What can I do?

A. Build a better bed. With a rake, I want you to scratch the soil both north to south and east to west. Then apply

PEST PATROL

The Ants Go Marching

To keep local ant armies in check, try one or both of these mixtures.

Ant Control #1

4 to 5 tbsp. of cornmeal
3 tbsp. of bacon grease
3 tbsp. of baking powder
3 packages of yeast

Mix the cornmeal and bacon grease into a paste, then add the baking powder and yeast. Dab the gooey mix on the insides of jar lids, and set them near the anthills.

Ant Control #2

1 cup of sugar
1 tbsp. of boric acid powder
3 cups of water

Add the sugar to 3 cups of water, and bring to a boil. Then add the boric acid. Place the mix in small jar lids, and set the lids in the middle of ant trails or near anthills. Store any unused portion in a secure container, and keep everything out of reach of children and pets.

PEST PATROL

Keep Bugs from Bugging You-Know-Who

To keep bugs at bay when you're out working in your yard and garden, follow this advice:

• Avoid using heavily scented cologne, hair spray, hand lotion, or shaving lotion.

• Don't wave your arms to ward off an insect. Simply stand still until the pest flies away.

• Use a repellent that contains DEET, which is effective and safe if used according to directions.

• Pennyroyal, peppermint, eucalyptus, and citronella are all natural pest repellents that you may want to try.

• Cover yourself with tightly knit clothing. Wear a long-sleeved shirt with tight cuffs, and tuck your pant cuffs into your boots or socks. Avoid floral patterns at all costs!

gypsum at the rate of 10 pounds per 50 square feet, mixed with 1 pound of sugar. Cover the soil with a weed-block fabric, then surround your garden area with untreated 2 × 10s to create a raised bed. Fill to the brim with organic material—leaves, grass clippings, compost, and garden soil. That should do the trick.

Q. Could you please give me some advice on how to keep my neighbors' cats out of my flowers?

A. Try crushing moth crystals into a powder, and adding 2 tablespoons of cayenne pepper and 2 tablespoons of black pepper to the powder. Then spread the mix on the ground wherever you don't want the cats to go.

Q. Help! I'm being eaten alive every time I go outside! Do you have a formula that will control mosquitoes?

A. I sure do! Use your 20 gallon hose-end sprayer to spray the area with a mixture of 1 cup each of lemon-scented ammonia and lemon-scented dish soap. Spray three times a week early in the morning or late in the evening. This will keep the little buggers away.

Q. I've heard that marigolds will keep mosquitoes away, but I tried and had no luck. Why?

A. You probably planted one of the newer varieties. Try the giant, old-fashioned marigolds instead. Plant them in pots, and

Color Block Bulbs

The biggest mistake people make when planting bulbs in fall is to plant one bulb here and one bulb there, not realizing how sparse they're going to look come spring. *You must mass bulbs together!* Whether you're planting 20 or 200, you'll get the biggest bang by planting bulbs close together in groups or what I call "color blocks."

place them on the patio at night. That'll do the trick—even I can't stand the smell! The newer varieties don't work as well because they have no odor.

Clay is A-OK

I'm always hearing complaints from gardeners about their clay soil. The truth of the matter is that clay is the richest soil in the world—if you can break it up. Begin by gathering sand, grass, leaves, and gypsum. Till and spade all this into the clay. Keep working organic materials into your clay soil throughout the year, and you should be able to start planting the following year.

Q. Which annuals will do well in damp soil?

A. Begonia, impatiens, nicotania, and coleus will all tolerate dampness.

Q. What flowers would you use in a hot, dry location in the southwest?

A. You should try portulacas, asters, and zinnias.

Q. You always hear about people who have a brown thumb when it comes to houseplants. Well, I've got a brown thumb when it comes to outdoor gardening! Help!

A. First of all, I firmly believe that no one has a brown thumb when it comes to plants. You just need to know how to go about it properly. To grow your green thumb, just keep these four things in mind: (1) Pick good, fresh seed of a plant variety that's recommended for your soil and your

MIXERS
& ELIXIRS

Fungus Fighter

Molasses is great for fighting fungus and disease in your garden. So at the first sign of trouble, mix up a batch of this brew.

½ cup of molasses
½ cup of powdered milk
1 tsp. of baking soda
1 gal. of warm water

Mix the molasses, powdered milk, and baking soda into a paste. Place the mixture into the toe of an old nylon stocking, and let it steep in a gallon of warm water for several hours. Then strain, and use the liquid as a spray for your garden every two weeks throughout the growing season. I guarantee you'll have no more fungus troubles!

MIXERS & ELIXIRS

Garden Cure-All Tonic

At the first sign of insects or disease, mix up a batch of my Cure-All Tonic to set things right.

4 cloves of garlic
1 small onion
1 small jalapeño pepper
1 tsp. of Murphy's Oil Soap
1 tsp. of vegetable oil
Warm water

Pulverize the garlic, onion, and pepper in a blender, and let them steep in a quart of warm water for 2 hours. Strain the mixture and further dilute the liquid with three parts of warm water. Add the Murphy's Oil Soap and vegetable oil. Mist-spray your plants with this elixir several times a week.

part of the country; (2) make sure your soil drains well, and is rich with organic matter like leaves, grass, and compost; (3) feed your plants regularly with proper food; and (4) make sure you understand when, where, and how to water. That's really all there is to it!

Keep it Under Control

I've seen many folks lose lots of time, money, and effort trying to maintain enormous gardens that they just can't handle. So keep it under control.

I suggest you plant no more than a maximum of 25-foot-long rows if you're an experienced gardener, and 10-foot-long rows if you're a beginner. This will keep things manageable—and more enjoyable for you.

Q. I live near the ocean. What can I plant that will withstand the salty sea breeze?

A. Try alyssum, petunias, lupine, and dusty miller.

Q. Which flowering annuals like shade?

A. Try coleus, impatiens, lobelia, myosotis, calendula, browallia, nicotania, pansy, salvia, balsam, and begonia.

Q. What can I do to bulb roots so they don't rot or dry out when they are stored away for the winter?

A. When the foliage is yellow, dig up the root and remove the soil. Then wash the bulbs in a weak soapy-water solution, and let them dry for four to five weeks. Put them in a paper bag with a fungicide like Thiram, and shake well. Then place them in a box of dry peat moss, and store them at 50°F.

Q. Is it a good idea to use plastic as a mulch in flowerbeds?

A. I only use plastic in my perennial beds because I seldom move them. I don't like to use plastic in my annual and bulb areas because it is a pain to be constantly digging in. I use grass clippings instead.

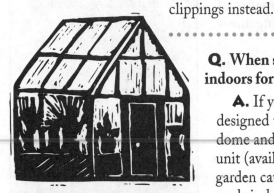

Bordering on the Sublime

I think every vegetable garden should have a border. It makes the garden look neat, and as though it were designed to fit into the yard, instead of just a dirt patch that's out of place. My favorite border plants are bushy herbs that can be picked for use and trimmed to be fat and low, like parsley. I use herb borders for my evergreens and flowerbeds, too. Whatever you do, experiment with different herbs in different areas of the garden to provide a variety of textures and scents.

Q. When should I start seed indoors for annual flowers?

A. If you have a specially designed tray with a plastic dome and soil-heating cable unit (available through most garden catalogs), you can start seeds indoors in March. Otherwise, start them in February, and transplant the seedlings three times during their growing phase to ensure stronger, healthier plants. Feed the seedlings monthly with any good plant food.

Q. I've tried two different varieties of forsythia, and I can't get either of them to bloom. Do you have any suggestions?

A. Forsythia will do well in any soil except unusually dry soil. So the next time you plant forsythia, make sure you add a lot of peat moss, shredded leaves, and sandy loam to the soil. Then mulch well around the plants with shredded bark.

Jerry's Secrets

A "wild" garden is pretty, but every bloom is better seen and enjoyed if the flowers are carefully stepped back according to height, with dwarf varieties in front and tall growers in back.

Q. I moved to a beautiful piece of property that has lots of hickory nut trees. I've had no luck planting vegetables or flowers. Is there anything I can do, short of cutting down the trees?

A. The hickory is related to the walnut, and it causes plants the same discomfort. Vegetables won't have a chance growing near hickorys, but you can try planting perennials that like shade and acid soil. I've had great luck with daylilies in this kind of situation.

Plant Irises in the Sun

I often see large groups of iris foliage without flowers in shady areas. While it's true that irises will grow and even multiply in the shade, their blooming is seriously impaired. So plant irises in a location that has a minimum of four hours of full sunlight each day.

Jerry's Secrets

If the annual seedlings you started indoors begin to look weak and gangly before it's time to set them out, try making a cold frame or window greenhouse to give them sunshine and fresh air.

Q. I'm starting from scratch, landscaping a hill that's a mixture of clay soil, red shale, and sandstone. What advice can you give me on what to plant to hold the hill up? Everything I now plant gets washed down the hill when it rains. I would eventually like to plant a vegetable garden here—is this possible?

A. Yes, you can plant vegetables or any other plants on your hill. But first you must terrace the hill with large stones, railroad ties, 2 × 6s, or some other materials that will help hold the hill in place. Then plant your garden horizontally across the face of the hill, in the terraced rows.

Q. Please tell me how to get seed to germinate by keeping it in a dark room.

A. Soak your seed in tea water and store it in your refrigerator for 24 hours or so. Dry it off, and plant in the evening. That's dark enough!

Q. I have three wisteria bushes that have never bloomed. How can I encourage them to flower? They are planted in soil that has a lot of red clay in it. They receive lots of sun, and their foliage appears to be healthy. Any ideas?

A. I want you to prune them very hard in midsummer, and cut out all new growth, leaving just four buds per vine. Then come fall, cut off all the long tendrils, root prune, and sprinkle ½ cup of Epsom salts underneath each bush.

Q. I have a new puppy, and would like a weed control that doesn't contain chemicals. What should I do?

A. Spot-shoot weeds with a mixture of 2 tablespoons of vinegar, 2 tablespoons of baby shampoo, 2 tablespoons of gin, and a quart of warm water.

Q. What's good to plant in partially filled wetlands?
A. Willows, birches, and cedars will all do well.

Some Bulbs Won't Wait

Don't keep tulips, daffodils, or hyacinths past the fall season to plant in spring because they won't flower. They need a long period of dormancy before they will bloom, so they must be planted in the fall in order to develop blooms for the following spring.

Q. How can I discourage rabbits from eating my garden plants, especially cabbage? No matter what I do, they keep coming back for more.

A. Mix 1 tablespoon of baby shampoo and 1 tablespoon of ammonia in a quart of water, and spray every third evening until the cabbage heads start forming.

Seedling Strengthener

To get your seedlings off to a healthy, disease-free start, mist-spray your plants every few days with this elixir:

2 cups of manure
½ cup of instant tea granules
Water

Put the manure and tea in an old nylon stocking, and let it steep in 5 gallons of water for several days. Dilute the resulting "tea" with 4 parts of warm water before using.

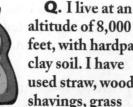

Q. I live at an altitude of 8,000 feet, with hardpan clay soil. I have used straw, wood shavings, grass clippings, chicken and rabbit manure, and builders' sand in the soil with no luck. What can do so that I can grow a garden and fruit trees?

A. More of the same every year. The secret is the constant use of baby shampoo once a month in-season, using 1 cup of shampoo per 20 gallons of water. Use it on both the lawn and garden areas.

Q. I got carried away putting fireplace ashes in my small garden. I've had no luck raising vegetables. I neutralized the soil, and used gypsum and basic fertilizer, all without results. Any suggestions?

A. I want you to overspray the soil with a mix of 1 cup of corn syrup, 1 can of beer, and ½ cup of liquid dish soap in your 20 gallon hose-end sprayer every three weeks this season.

Q. Can I grow rhododendrons in the shade, or do they need to be in full sun?

A. While it's true that rhododendrons will live and grow in heavy shade, they bloom much better when they're given a fair amount of light. Dappled shade suits them well, or better yet, plant them on the north side of a building, where they can get good sunlight, but not the direct hot rays of the midday sun.

Let's Get Edgy

Many folks discover that it's very hard to keep grass from creeping into their well-manicured shrubbery and flowerbeds.

The best control is to edge the bed with metal or plastic edging, wood strips, concrete, or bricks. Whatever edging you choose, remember to put it deep enough into the ground to keep grass roots from spreading under and into the bed.

PEST PATROL

Super Slug Spray

For slugs that are too small to hand-pick or be lured into traps, try this super spray:

1½ cups of ammonia
1 tbsp. of Murphy's Oil Soap
1½ cups of water

Mix all of the ingredients in a handheld mist sprayer bottle, and over-spray any areas where you see slug activity.

CHAPTER 2

"Your goal is to make bad dirt good, good dirt better,
and all dirt more appetizing for the flowers and vegetables
you are about to start growing."

Time to Get Dirty

Soil Secrets

No matter how good your plants look when you buy them, or how fresh your seeds may be, their (and your) success depends upon how well you prepare the soil in the beds you're making for them. As all good gardening professionals know, the best soil you can give your plants is one that will hold moisture while letting extra water run off. To accomplish this, you'll need to do some work clearing out the bedding area and fortifying the soil. The little bit of extra effort will be well worth it when you see your plants thriving.

BE PREPARED

There's one rule of thumb to remember when starting out—soil preparation will make or break your garden. Follow these simple steps, and you'll have the best garden in town!

1. When staking out your garden area, make sure that it is not in a pocket that will hold water, and not under or near large trees that will keep it in shade for most of the day.

2. Condition the soil by spreading 50 pounds of gypsum, 35 pounds of lime, and 25 pounds of dried cow, cattle, or sheep manure per 100 square feet of intended garden area.

3. Pile decaying leaves, grass, sawdust, and fireplace ashes on top of the soil-conditioning materials mentioned above.

4. As soon as the soil is dry enough to spade or plow, turn it over as deep as you can. Then let it set for three days. Rotary till the soil as fine as possible before you begin planting. Don't plant anything in your garden until the soil will crumble in your hand after being firmly squeezed.

Spring into Spading

Always spade or rotary till your garden in the spring, even if you did so when you added compost and other organic materials the previous fall. You need this second tilling because soil becomes compacted from snow and rain. If you just scuff it up with a rake, you won't give the seeds and seedlings a fair start in this brave new world.

Jerry's Secrets

The two best times to work organic material (what I call "garden fodder") into your garden are in the spring, before spading, and in the fall, after harvesting.

ASHES TO ASHES

Wood ashes are valuable soil builders in your garden. The best part is they're free—you can obtain them at no cost from your own (or a neighbor's) fireplace. Good-quality, unleached wood ashes contain 5 to 7 percent potash and 1.5 to 2 percent phosphoric acid; leached ashes contain about 1 percent potash and 1 to 1.5 percent phosphoric acid. Both have 25 to 30 percent calcium compounds, which help build good, strong, sturdy root systems.

Hardwood ashes contain more potassium than those from softwood lumber, but be forewarned—both kinds will lose much of their soil-enriching value if they are exposed to the weather, which causes the soluble chemicals to leach out. So the moral of the story is to keep the ashes covered until you're ready to use them.

Wood ashes should be applied to the soil some time in advance of planting. Don't mix them with manure or other high-

nitrogen materials, except what's already in the soil. Because of their low plant-food value, they can generally be used in any quantity in your yard without harm to your plants. An average application would be 5 to 10 pounds per 100 square feet, scattered on the freshly dug surface and then raked into the soil. As a final reminder, note that wood ashes should not be used on lawns around any acid-loving plants.

Way back when, folks burned coal to keep warm and, consequently, they had a lot of **coal ashes** available to them. They put the ashes to good use by mixing them with heavy clay soil to improve its texture. But don't use them as a fertilizer— the amount of potassium and phosphorus that the ashes contain is insignificant.

Nowadays, screened coal ashes are used on greenhouse benches under potted plants to ensure good drainage. Use them at the bottoms of borders or beds to protect roses or other moisture-sensitive plants from "wet feet" in poorly drained soil.

Squirrel Beater Tonic

To keep those pesky squirrels from chewing up everything in sight, douse your prized plantings with this spicy, sure-fire tonic:

2 tbsp. of cayenne pepper
2 tbsp. of Tabasco sauce
2 tbsp. of chili powder
1 tbsp. of Murphy's Oil Soap
1 qt. of warm water

Mix all of the ingredients together. Pour into a handheld sprayer, and liberally spray all of your plants.

PUT YOUR VEGETABLES TO BED

If you have real problem soil—heavy clay, poor drainage, lots of rocks—you can still grow a great vegetable garden by planting in raised beds. Use wood, bricks, rocks, or even cement blocks to frame in the area where you want your garden to be. If you use wood, buy rot-resistant wood such as cedar, cypress, or locust, or else you'll be replacing the wood in a few years. Make the bed no more than 3 to 5 feet across for easy access, and make it any length you desire. Or you can build several smaller beds that are easy to manage.

After you've set out the boundaries of your new bed or beds, fill them with a mixture of good sandy loam, homemade or store-bought compost, well-rotted manure, peat moss, dried leaves, and any other organic material you can get your hands on. Then, when the soil is good and crumbly, you're ready to grow!

Jerry's Secrets

If you have more money than time and energy, you can buy your mulching materials instead of gathering them from your yard or begging, borrowing, or stealing them from your neighbors. Manure, peat moss, straw, pine straw, and wood chips are all readily available at most garden centers.

WHY MULCH MATTERS

The short answer is…because. Besides keeping the weeds under control, a good mulch conserves moisture, cools the soil, and helps keep low-growing vegetables like squash, beans, and melons from getting dirty and water-spotted.

Mulching works wonders around America's favorite fruit. It prevents blossom-end rot on tomato plants by regulating the supply of moisture, and often results in a longer bearing season with greater yields.

Okra, eggplant, peppers, and all other long-season vegetables grow best when they're surrounded by a mulch that keeps their roots cool and moist during the long, hot, dry, mid-summer months.

So the long and short of it is…mulch matters!

Timing Is Everything

The best time to mulch is after a heavy rain before the weather gets too hot. Never apply a mulch when the ground is dry. If you do, the mulch will absorb any rain-water that happens to come along and allow it to evaporate before it can soak into the soil, where it will do the most good.

LEAVES, PLEASE

One of the few modern yard luxuries I allow myself is a leaf shredder. I tell you, I really enjoy shredding up leaves to make a nice mulch for my flowerbeds. I would heartily recommend one to any of you who can afford it. If you can't, then you can always spread the leaves out on your lawn and mow over them a couple of times with your lawnmower. Same result, at half the cost. If the trees in your yard don't generate enough fallen leaves, don't be shy about asking your neighbors to dump their leaves into your yard. You'll be glad you did. Then shred them up into mulch. And when you've got your flowerbeds and garden covered, add any leftover leaves to your compost pile.

CEDAR CONQUERS BUGS

I'm gonna let you in on a little professional landscaping secret—it really doesn't matter what type of wood chips, bark chunks, sawdust, or shavings you use in your planting beds, as long as you put shredded cedar underneath it. Think of this as creating a cedar closet especially for your plants.

For some reason, cedar chips seem to discourage insects from setting up shop when the chips are either laid on top of the soil or worked into it. To decide which method is best, simply survey your yard, determine which method is easiest for you to apply, and then, as the commercial says, just do it!

I also recommend using cedar chips underneath stone mulches to absorb heat. This prevents the soil beneath your plants from drying out, which in turn will save the roots from drying out. Remember, roots under any kind of mulch tend to stay near the surface.

After mulching your beds with a wood byproduct, spray with "Root-Rousing Tonic" (at right) to feed the roots below.

MIXERS & ELIXIRS

Root-Rousing Tonic

1 can of beer
1 can of regular cola (not diet)
1 cup of liquid dish soap
1 cup of antiseptic mouthwash
¼ tsp. of instant tea granules

Mix all of the ingredients in a large bucket, then pour into a 20 gallon hose-end sprayer and spray liberally over your planting beds.

THE POWER OF PLASTIC

Black plastic sheeting also makes an excellent mulch. It provides failsafe weed control, holds moisture in the soil, and—because dark colors absorb heat—keeps the soil beneath it 5 to 10 degrees warmer than it would be otherwise. (This is especially a plus in the colder parts of the country.) In addition, the warmer environment encourages plants to grow faster and mature earlier.

You can buy rolls of 1.5-mm black plastic sheeting just about anywhere. Once you've got yours, follow these simple steps to sheeting success:

1. Prepare and fertilize the soil when there is adequate moisture in the soil.

2. Center a roll of plastic over the row you're going to plant. Dig 3-inch-deep trenches parallel to the row along both sides, and 3 inches closer to the row than the edges of the plastic. Dig 3-inch-deep trenches at both ends of the row, as well.

3. Unroll the plastic over the row, smoothing out the wrinkles as you go. Place the long edges of the plastic in the trenches and cover with 3 inches of soil or stones. Anchor the ends of the plastic in the trenches in the same way.

4. Cut T-shape slits in the plastic through which you'll insert your large seeds or transplants. The slits will allow water to seep down into the soil underneath the plastic.

5. In very hot weather, spread a light layer of straw, leaves, or grass clippings over the plastic to prevent the soil under the plastic from becoming too warm. (Do this only if the plants are not growing close enough to provide the soil with adequate shade.)

Jerry's Secrets

One secret I've learned over the years is that a 3- to 4-inch layer of grass clippings will save you a heck of a lot of work and water in your planting beds. But before you mulch with clippings, put down a layer of either newspaper or weed-blocking fabric—they act as weed barriers and help retain water.

Read All About It!

Yesterday's news makes an excellent garden mulch. Put down three alternating layers of single newspaper sheets, then lay up to 3 inches of grass clippings over the top. The zinc in the ink will help prevent weeds.

MUCH ADO ABOUT MULCH

You can usually tell when a yard has been professionally landscaped—there's mulch just about everywhere! Give your yard that look by using mulch in flower and vegetable gardens, around trees and shrubs, and for walkways. Here's how to make the most of mulch:

Grass clippings: Spread them regularly in thin layers over vegetable beds and flowerbeds, or mix with leaves and spread in a thicker layer.

But be careful—don't spread grass clippings more than 4 inches thick, or they'll mat and stop water from penetrating down into the soil.

Leaves: Deciduous leaves can be used as mulch in the fall. Evergreen leaves can also be used, but they take longer to turn brown and decay.

Chipped or shredded woody waste: Spread 3 to 6 inches deep for a good-looking, long-lasting mulch or path material.

Cardboard: Layer it under paths to make them last longer; top it off with woody waste.

Pine needles: They're great as a mulch around acid-loving plants like rhododendrons, azaleas, and blueberries.

SQUEEZE ME TIGHT

Any gardener worth his salt knows that if you work soil when it's too wet or too dry, you can destroy its structure and make your gardening a real chore. So before you set out to work in the garden, give your soil a good old-fashioned squeeze test. Simply pick up a handful of garden soil and squeeze it. If it crumbles apart when you open your hand, it's too dry. If it clumps into a solid shape, it's too wet. But if it holds together without packing, it's just right, and you can get on with your digging.

Brew Some Barnyard Tea

Here's a Valentine's gift especially for your vegetable garden. In February, spread 50 pounds of manure, 50 pounds of peat moss, 25 pounds of garden food, and 25 pounds of gypsum over each 100 square feet of garden. Then just let it sit. This makes a great big batch of natural "barnyard tea," which seeps down into the subsoil, enriching it for your early spring plantings.

PREPARING POTTING SOIL

A plentiful supply of potting soil is really convenient for indoor gardeners, especially if you have a lot of houseplants. But if you have only a few plants, you may prefer to buy a commercially prepared potting soil called "professional mix."

On the other hand, if you have a lot of plants, it pays to make up a large quantity of potting soil in advance to keep on hand for use as you need it. You can store the prepared soil in plastic bags, small trash containers, or cans. And when you need it, it will only require moistening to make it ready for use.

Good soil is one of the most important factors in growing houseplants successfully. Straight, out-of-the-ground garden soil is seldom satisfactory because no matter what it is, from heavy clay to light sand, it becomes hard and caked in a pot. Your plants will live in such soil, but they will grow far better in a loose, friable soil. Both clay and sandy soils can be modified, chiefly by the addition of humus, into an excellent planting mix for houseplants.

Humus is added because it absorbs moisture quickly and releases it slowly, thus helping to retain even moisture in the soil. Humus may also acidify the soil slightly (particularly if the humus is peat moss), may supply some nutrients, and improves the texture of the soil.

Humus comes in many forms: peat moss bought at your local garden center, compost from your compost pile, or leaf mold. (Leaf mold is made by gathering leaves in the fall and putting them in an old pail or garbage bag where they are kept moist until they decompose.) If it's available, well-rotted manure can also be used as a source of humus.

When you're making your potting soil mix, drainage materials must also be added to the soil to ensure that excess water will drain away and keep the soil loose. Clean, coarse sand is an excellent drainage material. Vermiculite or perlite are good substitutes, and they are available at garden centers.

Use the chart on the opposite page to make the best potting soil for your needs.

MIXERS & ELIXIRS

Potted-Plant Potion

1 tea bag
1 tbsp. of whiskey
½ tsp. of baby shampoo
½ tsp. of ammonia
10% of recommended
   rate of any plant food
1 gallon of water

Mix all of the ingredients together, and use as a food and water source for your houseplants and outdoor container plants.

Make Your Own Potting Soil

GARDEN SOIL TYPE	POTTING SOIL RECIPE
Heavy	Mix one-third loamy soil dug from the garden, one-third humus, and one-third coarse sand or vermiculite.
Light, with a good amount of humus	Mix two parts soil, one part humus, and one part good drainage material.
Very sandy	Mix two parts soil with one part humus, and omit any type of drainage material.

Note: These basic potting soils can be easily modified to meet special needs. For example, add an extra handful of peat moss when you prepare soil for azaleas. For cacti, add a little more sand.

THE SEAWEED SECRET

Seaweed has been used down on the farm and in the garden for centuries. When liquid seaweed is applied to a plant, it increases the plant's ability to fight stress periods like drought, severe weather changes, and other garden challenges. The best news is that you don't need to live near the ocean to reap the benefits of seaweed. Both liquid and dry versions are available in garden centers. Here's what else seaweed can do:

🌿 speed up the germination of flower, vegetable, and grass seed;

🌿 activate enzymes in the soil;

🌿 supply energy to growing plants;

🌿 help the soil release nutrients so that plants can use them;

🌿 increase the size, quality, and yield of foliage, fruit, and berries.

Rung-by-Rung Herbs

An old wooden stepladder makes a quick-and-easy herb garden. Simply lay the ladder down on a flat area, fill in between the rungs with potting soil, and plant a different herb in each section.

MIXERS & ELIXIRS

Veggie Tonic

2 tbsp. of Epsom salts
1 tsp. of baby shampoo
1 gal. of water

Mix all of the ingredients together and use "Veggie Tonic" liberally to soak the soil around tomato and pepper plants as they flower, to stimulate their growth.

MANURE, FOR SURE!

While the "sweet" smell of manure will never compete with the fragrance of a rose, without manure, the rose would not have any fragrance at all! Manure is the great garden equalizer, returning organic matter back to the garden's soil, which is vital for growing happy, healthy plants.

Without fail, **animal manures** are available in every garden center in the country. The most common types are cow, sheep, poultry, and horse manure. You can buy manure fresh, dry (dehydrated), or in liquid form. But a word of warning—your neighbors will not appreciate it very much if you decide to add fresh manure to your garden in the spring or fall, even if you till it in!

Dry manures are less powerful in plant food value than fresh manures are, but dry manures are great soil builders because of the bedding straw and barnyard soil that is mixed into them. These processed manures also have less of an objectionable odor and can be used straight out of the bag at planting time.

Liquid manure, also referred to as "barnyard tea," is a rich, powerful source of plant food. But remember—a little bit of this fertilizer goes a long way! Apply it to your yard and garden with a sprinkling can, well diluted with water, and never allow it to touch the foliage of tender flowers. Liquid manure is also great to add to your hose-end sprayer when you're spraying the lawn, especially in the early summer. But take note: It really stinks!

Down the Drain

Here's a quick and easy test to determine how the drainage is in your garden area. First, dig a hole in the lowest part of your garden, about 1 foot wide by 1 foot deep. Then fill it full of water. If the hole drains quickly, then the soil is too light. If the water is still there the next day, then your soil is too heavy. The perfect soil should drain in about 30 minutes or so.

The Art of Composting

No matter what you might hear, composting does not take much time or effort, and there's no complicated formula to memorize. Composting is the process of turning clippings, leaves, and other yard and garden materials into a rich soil additive for use in gardens or around plants and shrubs. Just pile up lawn trimmings, vegetable parings, and other organic refuse, and wait for it to decompose. Compost piles work by generating heat and biological activity to decay organic materials.

Simple, right? Right, but there are times when the composting process doesn't work or your compost doesn't quite turn out the way you thought it would. The composting tips in this section will get you on track to making that perfect batch of "black gold."

BE NEIGHBORLY

Unless you live on acres and acres out in the country, far away from your nearest neighbors, you'll need to contain your compost in some way to hide the unsightly materials as they decompose. Here are several of the most popular compost container alternatives.

Bag: Something as simple as those large black plastic garbage bags will keep compost moist and speed up the heating process. They are ideal for small-scale composting. You can keep them anywhere—in the garage or basement, the side yard, or on a back porch.

Bin: You can make your own compost bin from logs, boards, bricks, concrete blocks, chicken wire, other fencing, or just about anything that can be made into an enclosure. As an alternative, you can purchase a plastic bin with a lid in most gardening and home centers.

Can: Remove the bottom of a metal garbage can, and you're ready to go! If this makes the can a little wobbly, support it between two stakes driven into the ground.

Fireplace: Put an unused outdoor fireplace or barbecue pit to good use by using it as your compost bin.

Jerry's Secrets

Your compost pile is not a toilet, so don't put dog and cat droppings in it. Dog and cat waste can carry diseases that can spread to humans, so never dispose of them in your compost pile or garden.

COMPOST CAMOUFLAGE

If you (or your neighbors) get tired of the view of the compost bin, you don't have to jump ship and abandon your efforts. Simply use the old noggin and camouflage your bin. Place a trellis or plant an evergreen hedge around it, or plant ornamental vines (such as gourds, morning glories, or sweet peas) alongside your bin; then train them to grow up the sides.

BIN BASICS

If you build a compost bin or wire-fence enclosure, I don't want you to make it taller than 5 feet, and be sure to leave one side open (or make it removable) for easy access to the compost.

Use removable slats on one side of a wood structure. On a fenced structure, tie or wire shut the fourth side to the corner post rather than nail it. Then you can roll back that section for access.

Also, make sure your bin has no bottom, so the compost will be accessible to the hardworking bacteria in the soil.

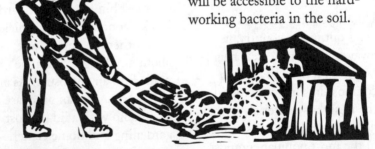

Jerry's Secrets

Don't place your compost pile too near trees, or you'll have uninvited guests (the trees) over for dinner — their roots will grow into your compost! And always try to set the pile on flat ground to prevent nutrients from leaching away.

KEEP COMPOST CLOSE AT HAND

You'll save a lot of time and effort by placing your compost bin close to your garden. Adding garden refuse to the pile and then using the resulting compost in the garden will be a heck of a lot easier and less time consuming if you don't have to trudge halfway across your yard just to get to the bin. Remember, you want this to be fast, fun, and easy!

Also, be sure to place your bin within easy reach of your garden hose, because you'll need to water your compost pile regularly. This'll help keep it going.

KEEP IT HEALTHY

Most folks don't follow the basic rules needed to have "healthy" compost piles. Then they wonder why it's not working. Remember, without healthy compost, you can't have a healthy garden. So here's how to keep your compost pile vigorous:

Cover the pile. Sunlight kills the bacteria that's needed to decompose the matter, so it's important to keep sunlight out of the compost pile. Use thick, black plastic to cover compost piles and chicken wire bins. (Black plastic absorbs heat and keeps sunlight out.) Use a lid to cover other types of bins.

Provide proper ventilation. A compost bin needs adequate venting through its sides and bottom to allow air to penetrate the pile. Inadequate ventilation slows down the heating process ("cooking") of the compost pile and causes bad odors. Don't over-ventilate, however, or your compost pile won't retain the necessary heat needed for proper decomposition.

Be picky about ingredients. Never compost grass clippings that have been treated with pesticides or herbicides. And don't put meats or cooking fats in the compost. This attracts varmints and creates bad odors. (Then you've really got problems!) Compost only those products that are high in carbon (like leaves and sawdust) or nitrogen (like grass clippings and vegetable peelings).

Keep things small. Smaller pieces compost better. Use an electric blower/shredder/vac that has a shredding ratio of at least 10 to 1 and an air velocity of at least 180 mph (check with your garden center). Shredding speeds up the breakdown of the pile.

Turn, turn, turn. Turn your pile twice a week to accelerate the process and ensure decomposition. If your compost is clumped and gooey, turn it more often and add high-carbon materials.

Water correctly. If a compost pile is too dry, it won't heat up and decompose. If it's too wet, the pile will smell from anaerobic decomposition. So what do you do? My general rule is to keep your compost pile as wet as a damp sponge.

Know when it's ready. Your compost is ready to use in the garden when it's dark brown or black and crumbly. When it's done cooking, make sure you use it.

Quick Cleanup

For quick and easy cleanup after you're done with your yard and garden work, place a bar of soap in the toe of an old nylon stocking or panty hose leg, and hang it near an outdoor faucet. Instead of making a mess inside the house, you can scrub up outside without even having to take the soap out of the stocking. Believe you me, this simple secret has saved many a gardener's marriage!

THE COLORS OF COMPOST

When you're building your compost pile, think "green" and "brown." Green materials are those that are wet and high in nitrogen. Brown materials are dry and high in carbon. Here's a quick rundown so you can keep track:

Greens: Coffee grounds, cover crops, eggshells, fruit wastes, grains, grass clippings, hair, leaves, manure, seaweed, vegetable scraps, and weeds.

Browns: Corncobs, cornstalks, hay, nutshells, paper, pine needles, sawdust, straw, vegetable stalks, and seeds.

Jerry's Secrets

To ensure proper ventilation of your compost pile, take a large PVC tube and drill holes along its length. Then place the tube upright in the center of the pile to encourage air flow through the pile.

ON THE VERGE OF A BREAKDOWN

Here are three surefire ways to encourage decomposition in your compost pile:

Call in the worms. Put earthworms in your compost pile. They aerate the soil with their tunneling, which will dramatically speed up the process—plus, you'll have a ready supply of bait for fishing.

Pour a drink. Dump a can of regular cola (not diet) on your compost pile. The sugar content and carbonation will help speed up decomposition.

Mix up a starter tonic. My favorite compost starter is an oldie but a goodie: Mix 1/4 bottle of beer, 1/4 cup of ammonia, and a gallon of warm water. Spray this on your compost pile to really get it cookin'!

Shred First

While most composters know to shred their household scraps before depositing them in the compost pile, many people still dump in leaves as they find them—usually whole. Be sure to shred leaves, too, to speed up the composting process. Remember, small is better.

REFUSE TO THE RESCUE

Your compost pile can contain many different kinds or organic refuse. Here's a list of the most common "ingredients" available to home composters. If your household doesn't generate enough organic waste to maintain your compost pile, ask neighbors for help. You can also try to obtain some of these materials from local farmers and lawn and tree service companies:

- Old produce
- Sawdust
- Spoiled hay
- Manures
- Chopped corncobs
- Chopped tobacco stalks
- Ground tree bark
- Cannery or winery wastes

USABLE COMPOST IN 14 DAYS

Everyone has their own favorite recipe for compost, and after you've done some experimenting, you will, too. Here's one of my favorite quick compost recipes to get you started:

Day 1: Shred your materials (leaves, spoiled hay, grass clippings, etc.) with a shredder or rotary lawn mower. You're going to make a 4-foot-tall pile in an area that's approximately 8 × 4 feet. Start with a layer of shredded materials, then add a nitrogenous material like manure, dried blood, or cottonseed meal. Mix the materials together. Continue building layers until you've got a 4-foot-high pile.

Day 2: The pile should begin to heat up. If not, it's time to add more nitrogen. Keep the pile moist, but not soggy.

Day 4: Turn the pile, be sure it's heating up (if it's not, add more nitrogen), and keep the pile moist.

Day 7: Turn the pile again, check to be sure it's still hot, and keep the pile moist. The interior temperature of the pile should have reached 180°F by now. You can check the temperature with a compost thermometer, which is available at garden centers and through mail-order garden catalogs.

Day 10: Turn the pile again. It should begin cooling about now.

Day 14: The compost is ready to use. It will not be fine humus, but at this stage, it is perfectly good for use in your garden.

Jerry's Secrets

Go vegetarian! Never, and I mean *never,* use meat, fish scraps, or cooking fats in your compost pile. Believe you me, they will attract varmints and insects, cause odors, and slow down decomposition of the pile.

USE IT OR LOSE IT

Once a compost pile has been broken down, you can (and should) use your new compost material in the following ways:

What's in the Pile?

Here's a look at some common compost materials and the nutrients they contain.

COMPOST MATERIAL	% NITROGEN	% POTASH	% PHOSPHORUS
Cattail reeds	2.00	.81	3.43
Coffee grounds	2.08	.32	.28
Corncob ashes	—	—	50.00
Corn stalks and leaves	.30	.13	.33
Crabgrass, green	.66	.19	.71
Oak leaves	.80	.35	.15
Pine needles	.46	12	.03
Ragweed	.76	.26	—
Tea grounds	4.15	.62	.40
Wood ashes	—	1.00	4.00-10.00

To improve garden soil: Apply a 3-inch layer of compost on top of the soil, and dig it in to a depth of 6 inches with a spading fork or rotary tiller. Side-dress around the roots of transplants (vegetables, bushes, trees, or shrubs).

As a mulch: Lightly hoe in compost as a mulch over bulb beds.

As a potting soil amendment: Use a 1:3 ratio of compost to water and mix with potting soil to supercharge your houseplants and indoor seedlings.

To seed a new lawn: That's right—compost is great for lawns, too! When putting in a new lawn, blend compost into the soil prior to seeding or sodding. As a general rule, apply 250 pounds of compost per 1,000 square feet of sandy soil; 400 to 600 pounds of compost per 1,000 square feet of loamy soil; and 1,200 pounds of compost per 1,000 square feet of clay soil.

As a winter seed starter: Mix compost with equal parts of sand and loam, and use it to start seeds indoors or in a cold frame.

COMPOST COCKTAIL

If you don't have the time, space, or energy to make your own compost, here's a quick compost cocktail that can still work wonders on your plants and in your garden.

Save your table scraps each day—peels, shredded vegetables, eggshells, tea bags, and so on (but no fat or meat). If you have a small household, a crock or large ceramic bowl will work nicely for scrap saving, or you can simply toss everything into a plastic bag.

Every few days, place the scraps in a food processor or blender and cover them with water. Add a tablespoon of Epsom salts to the mix, and liquefy.

Pour this cocktail onto the soil in your garden, lightly hoe it in, and you'll be as good as ("black") gold!

KEEP COMPOST DISEASE-FREE

Many folks add all kinds of discarded vegetation and yard waste to their compost piles, in the hope of increasing their future supply of humus. They figure quantity is better than quality. Don't fall into this trap, because although at first glance this seems like a good idea, looks can be deceiving.

What these folks may be unknowingly adding to their compost piles are numerous insects and a whole host of diseases that carry through from year to year in the form of eggs, grubs, inactive spores, or what have you. Oftentimes, these carriers are on, in, or under some kind of plant growth, so adding infected plant material to the compost pile now spells big trouble when you use the compost in your garden next year.

How can you tell what's good to compost and what needs to be destroyed? You can't always be sure, unless you're a darned good scientist. But you'll be on the right track if you make it a point to burn any plants and plant parts that you know to have been attacked by diseases or insects that bore or tunnel. Do not compost them. Remember: When in doubt, throw it out!

MIXERS & ELIXIRS

Compost Booster

To get your compost off to a roaring start, mix the following in a large bucket or container:

1 can of beer
1 can of regular cola (not diet)
1 cup of ammonia
½ cup of weak tea water*
2 tbsp. of baby shampoo

Pour this mixture into your 20 gallon hose-end sprayer, and saturate your compost pile every time you add a new foot of material to it.

*Soak a used tea bag in a gallon of warm water and 1 teaspoon of liquid dish soap until the mix is light brown.

Out and About

Well, all the garden planning is done. You've made your choices about the seeds, seedlings, and bulbs you're going to plant. You've composted, tilled, and prepared the planting beds. Now you're itching to get out in the dirt and turn those garden plans into reality. I don't blame you.

But before you do, read on, and you'll be rewarded with the most spectacular flowers, fruits, and vegetables you've ever seen. So grab your gloves, tools, and garden hose, and let's get growing!

MADE IN THE SHADE

You wouldn't like being set out in the hot sun with no clothes on, and neither do your plants! So remember, it's best to transplant in the evening or on a cloudy day. That's because the warmth of the sun evaporates water from the plant's leaves, making it more difficult for the plant to get established.

Shade your new transplants and protect them from drying winds with a newspaper tent or an inverted flowerpot for the first few days in their new location. Also, you can use any one of the anti-transpirant products available, like my WeatherProof, to lock the elements out and lock moisture in. This'll give your transplants a leg up in the world.

Jerry's Secrets

It's a fact of life — plants grown in rich, humusy soil are less likely to be attacked by insects and disease. And for added protection, be sure to purchase only plants that are labeled "disease resistant."

TOUGH LOVE

You gotta do it—plants grown from seeds started indoors need to be hardened off (toughened up) before they are planted outdoors. Hardening off refers to the gradual adjustment the plants must go through to face the rigors of the cold, cruel world. To harden them off, withhold water, lower the temperature in the room, and increase the ventilation. You can also place the plants in a cold frame or directly outside on sunny days (be sure to bring them back in at night). Gradually increase the exposure for a few weeks, and your plants will be able to "stand tall" when you transplant them to the garden.

FRIENDS 'TIL THE END

There's an old saying—make new friends, but keep the old; one is silver and the other's gold. Nowhere is that more true than when it comes to your garden. You should try new varieties, but certain plants (old friends) just seem to grow better.

By planting certain flowers, herbs, and vegetables together, you create the conditions each needs to grow and thrive. Companion plants help each other out by supplying nutrients the others need, or by warding off insects. Plant the following "friends" side by side in your garden and watch the results:

Companion Plants

VEGETABLE	COMPANIONS	VEGETABLE	COMPANIONS
Asparagus	Tomatoes	Kohlrabi	Beets, onions
Beans	Beets, cabbages, carrots, cauliflower, cucumbers, potatoes	Leeks	Carrots, lettuce, radishes, strawberries
Beets	Beans, kohlrabi, onions	Lettuce	Carrots, radishes, strawberries
Cabbage	Chamomile, dill, mints, potatoes, rosemary, sage	Onions	Beets
Carrots	Chives, leeks, lettuce	Peas	Beans, carrots, corn, cucumbers, radishes, turnips
Cauliflower	Celery		
Celery	Cauliflower, leeks, tomatoes	Potatoes	Beans, cabbages, corn
		Pumpkins	Corn
Corn	Beans, cucumbers, melons, peas, potatoes, pumpkins, squash	Radishes	Chervil, cucumbers, lettuce, peas
		Spinach	Strawberries
Cucumbers	Cabbages, potatoes, radishes	Tomatoes	Asparagus, celery, marigolds, parsley
Eggplant	Green beans		

LET 'EM GROW

Here's a little secret that professional growers use to ensure growing success—never transplant a seedling until it has at least four leaves. The second set of leaves, called the "true leaves," is needed to help the plant withstand the shock of being transplanted.

Don't Harvest Seeds

Many a gardener has sadly discovered that it's not a good idea to save any plant seeds from one year's harvest to plant the next season. These seeds may carry diseases and will produce not-true-to-type plants if cross-pollination has occurred.

USE UP THE LEFTOVERS

If you have vegetable seeds left over from last year's planting, you can use them if they were stored in a cool, dry place during the off-season. But here's a little professional secret—sow leftover seed thicker than you would new seed to ensure a good crop.

One Life to Live

Some vegetable seeds live longer than others. Here's a look at the longevity of some popular fruit and vegetable seeds.

SHORT-LIVED (usually not good after 1–2 years)	MODERATELY LONG-LIVED (good 3–5 years under good conditions)	LONG-LIVED (good more than 5 years under good conditions)
Leek, onion, parsley, parsnip, salsify, sweet corn	Asparagus, bean, brussels sprout, cabbage, carrot, cauliflower, celery, chicory, cress, endive, kale, kohlrabi, lettuce, okra, peas, pepper, radish, spinach, turnip, watermelon	Beet, cucumber, muskmelon, mustard, tomato

TRANSPLANTING: AS EASY AS 1, 2, 3

All right, your plants are hardened off, you've got a nice cloudy day, and you're all set to move them to their permanent home in the garden. Follow these simple steps to transplanting success:

1. Water the plants thoroughly 24 hours before transplanting them.

2. Dip the roots of the plants in soft mud, or soak them in a solution of my SGH-15+, then water with "Transplant Tonic" (at right).

3. Dig a small hole, set the plant in, and gently firm the soil around the roots. Water thoroughly, then cover the moist soil with dry soil.

RULES FOR RHIZOMES

Rhizome-rooted plants, such as irises, must feel the kiss of the warm sun as often as they can or they will not bloom well. So you should plant them with their roots below the surface of the ground and their rhizomes just on the surface.

The best way to do this is to dig a hole wide enough to accommodate the long rhizome, and then build up a small mound of dirt in the center of the hole. Set the rhizome on the mound so it will be almost even with the surface of the surrounding bed. Let the roots hang down, and cover them with soil, packing it carefully.

PROPER PERENNIAL PLANTING

Have you ever bought perennials by mail? If you have, then you were probably quite surprised when all you received was a mass of roots topped by a small bit of foliage. What's the deal?

Well, it doesn't matter how much foliage perennials have, it's the roots that count. So give them plenty of room to roam.

First, dig a hole large enough to accommodate the roots. Then spread the roots outward and downward in the hole. Press the soil firmly around the roots to remove any air pockets, and water well.

MIXERS & ELIXIRS

Transplant Tonic

½ can of beer
1 tbsp. of ammonia
1 tbsp. of instant tea
1 tbsp. of baby shampoo
1 gallon of water

Mix all of the ingredients together. Use 1 cup of the tonic for each plant you are transplanting.

TWO FOR THE PRICE OF ONE

I love perennials because you always get more than you bargained for—where else can you get all that beauty and grace, and plants for free, too? Nowhere else that I know of!

Perennials should be divided every few years to generate new growth and to keep your garden from becoming overgrown and crowded. Think of it as giving them a haircut. This gives you an opportunity to transfer a dazzling array of color to another area of your garden at no extra cost. Talk about a bargain!

Jerry's Secrets

I know it's here somewhere, but where did it go? If that sounds like you, then be sure to mark each planting site with the name of your plant. Some plants start later than others, and if you don't know what you planted where, you may accidentally dig up something that hasn't started to grow yet.

OUT OF MY DEPTH

Proper planting depth is key to growing powerful, perky perennials. But you don't have to memorize complicated depth charts. Just follow these simple guidelines for beautiful blooms year after year in your garden.

Planting Perennials	
PERENNIALS	**PLANTING GUIDELINES**
Carnation, creeping phlox, painted daisy	These plants have a fibrous root system, so their crowns (where their leaves and roots meet) must be planted above the soil surface.
Bleeding heart, peony	Plant deep enough so that the tips of the new eyes are just below ground level (about 2 inches).
Baby's breath, hollyhock, sweet pea	These plants have long tap roots, so they should be planted with their crowns just below soil level.

DIVIDE AND CONQUER

The best time to divide or move perennials is in the spring in cold climates and in the fall in warmer regions. Start with a razor-sharp spade; in this case, the sharper, the better. Cut right through the middle of each perennial clump that you want to transplant. If you're doing this in the fall, pull the spade out, lightly cover the plants with straw for the winter, and wait for spring. In the spring, dig up only the half of the plant you are going to move. This way, the plant will experience far less shock, and you won't have to give up a season of blooms.

An Egg-cellent Idea!

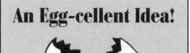

Dry eggshells in the microwave or oven and crush them underfoot on your garage floor. Then add them to any planting mix for a quick calcium fix. You can also soak them in water, and use it for the same results.

A MATCH MADE IN HEAVEN

Here's a little secret that professional pepper growers have known for years: Peppers love slightly acidic soil, so bury a book of matches under each plant when you set them out. The sulphur in the matches increases the soil's acidity, which will take your plants to new heights!

DARLING DAHLIAS

After the last threat of frost has passed, plant these tubers in any good garden soil, 4 to 5 inches deep, with an eye or sprout upright. For best results, plant in full sun, except in the warmest areas of the country, where afternoon shade is advisable. Do not allow the soil to dry out after planting, because dahlias require lots of moisture from the time growth begins until they're done blooming.

To get the most out of your dahlias, here's a little secret I use—pinch the tops off of the plants when they are about 1 foot high to make them stronger and more bushy.

PEST PATROL

Red-Hot Repellent

To keep insects or worms off of flower bushes or cabbage plants, lightly dust the plants with cayenne (red) pepper in the morning, while the plants are still wet with dew.

RAPID RHUBARB

If your mouth waters at the thought
of rhubarb pie (as mine does), then you'll
be happy to know that you can have your
fill of this tasty fruit practically all year long.
That's right; it's easy if you follow these simple steps.

In November, before the ground freezes solid, beg, borrow, or
buy (I betcha' thought I was gonna say steal) a clump of rhubarb
from a friend or local nursery. Make sure it is big, in good shape,
and has plenty of roots. Take it home, lay it in your garden, and
protect it with a layer of soil, straw, or mulch until mid-January.

In mid-January, bring the clump into your basement and place it
in a bushel basket. Fill the basket with soil mix. Water well, keeping it damp, but not soggy. Feed with "Compost Cocktail" (see
page 63). Use a grow light for six hours a day, and you will have
rhubarb indoors from February through March.

Come spring, simply plant the rhubarb in your garden, and
continue to enjoy your harvest for the rest of the year.

Jerry's Secrets

**Never try to repro-
duce hybrid plants
like roses and lilies
from seed — they'll
always revert to a
different and of-
ten undesirable
variety.**

ROSES ON THE MOVE

The best time to move
roses is when the bushes
are dormant, that is, when
the leaves have dropped
and scales have formed
over the growth buds for next
year. Many professional rose
growers prefer to move roses in
early spring, before any of the
new growth starts.

Bushes can be pruned at the
same time you move them to
compensate for root loss and to
remove any wood that has been
winter-killed. Then the bushes
should be remounded with soil
to prevent the stems from
drying out until the roots take
hold again.

Always try to move rose
bushes with as much soil
around the roots as possible.
Also, have your planting holes
ready so there's no delay when
transplanting your roses.

Garlic Gets 'Em!

Here's an old-time gardening
secret: Put one or two garlic
cloves among
your roses to keep
aphids and other
pests away.

LOVE YOUR LILIES

To get the most from your lilies, you need to treat them well right from the start. Give them a little tender loving care, and you'll be rewarded with lovely blooms.

Start at the right depth. Most bulbs don't need more than 4 inches of soil over them.

The exceptions are 'Cascade Strain' and 'White Elf', which should be planted with not more than 1 inch of settled soil over the tops of the bulbs.

Feed 'em well. Lilies have big appetites and they root deeply. They need porous, well-aerated soil that is rich in humus. Supplement the soil with a well-balanced plant food.

Mulch generously. Lilies love a good mulch of well-rotted cow manure, rich compost, or decaying leaf mold. Keep it nice and thick by applying it several times during the growing season. The mulch keeps the soil cool, discourages weeds, and eliminates the need for surface cultivation, which might hurt the stem roots of your growing lilies.

Keep out the competition. Lilies love being the center of attention and hate competition. Don't expect your lilies to compete with strong-growing perennials or shrubs. Instead, plant a shallow-rooted groundcover near your lilies to keep the ground shaded.

Don't Delay with Strawberries

Haste makes waste, but not when it comes to planting strawberries. It's best to set out your strawberries as soon as they arrive. If you must hold them for a day or two, keep them wrapped in the same plastic in which they arrived and put them in your refrigerator. If that's not possible, keep them in as cool a place as you can find, like a root cellar or in the basement.

CREATIVE CROCUSES

If you want to get a bit creative with your landscape and not have everything all tidily arranged in beds and gardens, try planting crocuses right in your lawn. That's right, *in* your lawn. They provide lots of early spring color, and when they're done blooming, you simply mow the tops off. They'll return the following year almost without fail. Now that's what I call low-maintenance landscaping!

MIXERS & ELIXIRS

Start-Up Meal

1 tbsp. of liquid dish
   soap
1 tbsp. of hydrogen
   peroxide
1 tsp. of whiskey
1 tsp. of Vitamin B_1
½ gal. warm tea water*

Mix all of the ingredients
together, and use to wa-
ter newly planted roses
to get them growing.

*Soak a used tea bag in a
gallon of warm water and 1
teaspoon of liquid dish soap
until the mix is light brown.

10 STEPS TO ROSE SUCCESS

If you follow these steps when planting your roses, then you'll
have blooms that you'll be as button poppin' proud of as you are of
your own children. (True rose growers will tell you that their roses
are their children.)

1. Purchase only the best unwaxed nursery stock. When it
comes to roses, you get what you pay for!

2. Carefully select planting sites with adequate drainage and
average garden soil. Be sure to give your roses good sun exposure
for at least half a day and, if at all possible, some shelter from
the wind.

3. Fill a bucket full of water and add 1 tablespoon of shampoo,
1 tablespoon of Epsom salts, and 1 tablespoon of instant tea granules. Let the plants soak for an hour or so before planting.

4. Dig a large hole (20 inches wide by 18 inches deep should
do it) to accommodate the roots of the plant without crowding
them—and save the topsoil.

5. Fill the hole one-third of the way with a small handful of
superphosphate, a mix of good-quality peat moss, and the topsoil you saved. Build a mound in the bottom
of the hole with this mixture.

6. Place the rose roots on the
mound so that the bud or graft
union is at or slightly below
normal ground level.

7. Fill the hole two-thirds full with
more of the soil/peat moss mixture,
then water slowly to settle the soil around
the roots and to eliminate any air pockets.

8. Wash down the rose canes with a mild soapy water solution
just before you cover them.

9. Add more soil, repeat watering, then feed with "Start-Up
Meal," at left.

10. Cover the entire plant with a mound of soil for protection
from severe weather. In areas where you get heavy freezes, cover
your roses with rose cones or a soil-and-leaf mixture.

DAYLILIES, THE BEST OF THE BUNCH!

Why do I say that? Because daylilies bloom from early spring until late fall, grow in almost any soil, and are seldom bothered by insects or diseases. Plus they pay for themselves many times over by spreading out with great big families. Here's the lowdown on how to get the biggest bang for your buck:

When: You can plant daylilies any time you can dig them up, from April through November. Fall-planted daylilies should be mulched to prevent them from heaving in the winter.

Where: Daylilies are sun-loving flowers, but they also bloom rather well in partial shade. If possible, plant them where they can get six or more hours of direct sunshine a day.

How: Spread the roots in a generous hole and cover the crown where the leaves and roots meet with only 1/2 to 1 inch of firmed soil. Water well, and that's all there is to it!

FLOWERS TO THE RESCUE!

Believe it or not, flowers can be a tree's best friends. How? Well, if you plant flowers around trees, they'll protect the tree trunks from lawn mower injury. And when you water the flowers, if you water deeply enough, this will help to keep the trees healthy during any dry periods.

The best flowers for this so-called "guard duty" are the shade-loving annuals such as impatiens, begonias, and coleus.

STRAWBERRY SECRETS

Before planting strawberries, soak the roots in my special mix of 1 tablespoon of baby shampoo, 1 tablespoon of Epsom salts, 1 tablespoon of instant tea granules, and 1 gallon of water. Then set the plants in the ground deep enough so that the roots are entirely covered with soil. Do not cover the crowns, though, or the plants will not form proper runners.

Press the soil firmly around each plant. If rainfall isn't adequate, water the plants frequently, especially during the first six weeks, or you'll lose them.

LASAGNA, ANYONE?

You can have a succession of flowering plants from the same bed by planting your bulbs in layers, with late bloomers at the bottom and early bloomers on top. It's the same way that my Grandma Putt used to make lasagna. Here's how:

1. Dig up your bed about 8 inches deep, and set the soil aside for use in another part of your yard.

2. Prepare a new soil mix by using 2 pounds of bonemeal, 5 pounds of gypsum, and 12½ pounds of peat moss per bushel of soil.

3. Set in the first layer of late-blooming bulbs (usually the larger ones like tulips). Cover with a layer of the soil mixture, being careful not to plant the bulbs too shallowly.

4. Continue planting bulb layers and covering them with the soil mix. Be sure to offset the bulbs so that one bulb does not sit directly over another, obstructing its growth. As you set each layer down, note where you've placed the bulbs.

5. To keep varmints away, lay some chicken wire on top and finish by mulching with leaves, light bark, or wood chips. Scatter moth crystals over the top.

DON'T GET TOPSY-TURVY

Have you ever held a bulb in your hand, turning it this way and that, trying to figure out which is the top and which is the bottom? Just about every one of us at one time or another will plant a bulb topsy-turvy.

While setting a bulb upside down won't kill it, it does put the new shoot at a disadvantage because it has to reverse course to grow up and out.

With some bulbs and tubers, it's anyone's guess as to which is the top and which is the bottom, but for most, there's an obvious difference. The top of a bulb comes to a point (either blunt or sharp), while at the base there is usually some sign of roots or a basal plate from which the roots originate. Remember—look for the nose, not the toes, and plant your bulbs "heads up"!

BE QUICK ABOUT IT

It's best, although not imperative, to plant bulbs as soon as possible after bringing them home. If you can't get to them right away and you find yourself with unplanted bulbs after cold weather has arrived, plant them anyway, because they won't keep indoors until next year. I've often found that if you put them in the ground, they'll generally surprise you by flowering in the spring.

THE STAKES ARE HIGH

Most folks don't think about supporting their perennials until it's too late. That, my friends, is a mis-stake! (Sorry—I just couldn't help myself!) You should always stake top-heavy perennials when you first set them out. Don't worry—as the plants grow, they will cover the stakes so that eventually the stakes will barely be noticeable.

You can use stakes made from wood, dowels, bamboo, plastic, metal, or wire. If they're made of wire, loop the top so that no one is injured when working in the garden. Metal stakes attract electricity, which supercharges the atmosphere surrounding your plants and stimulates their growth. (This is called electroculture, and it was all the rage way back when.)

The stakes should be 6 to 12 inches shorter than the height of the mature plant. Place the stakes behind the plants, sinking them far enough into the ground to firmly anchor them. They must be able to withstand the wind and the rain.

Tie the plants loosely with nylon panty hose strips. The nylon holds static—another electrifying bonus for your plants!

If you're using wire to tie the plants, make a double loop in the wire and place one loop around the plant and the other loop around the stake. Never loop the wire around both stake and plant—the plant will hang to one side, and the wire may girdle the stem.

LEAN ON ME

Don't know what to do with that ugly bare wall or fence? Plant a perennial border, and then use the wall or fence to support your top-heavy plants.

Tightly stretched wires set a few feet apart on brackets make the perfect support system. Allow them to extend several inches out from the wall or fence. If you don't want to permanently mount brackets, you can use a wooden trellis placed in front of the wall or fence to support the flowers.

Jerry's Secrets

Here's a neat idea—to support your tall plants, use a small, extension-type curtain rod. Then, as the plants grow, the rod can be adjusted so that is it always at the right height.

SPRING CLEANUP

A little early-spring "elbow grease" will get your perennials off to a great start. Follow these steps and I guarantee you, your perennials will absolutely thrive.

1. As soon as you can (even if there's a little snow left on the ground) remove all of last year's dead foliage.

2. Before new growth begins, sprinkle a mix of 5 pounds of natural organic flower food and 1 pound of Epsom salts per 100 square feet of garden soil.

3. Feed plants with "All-Season Green-Up Tonic" (see the opposite page) or my Fish Fertilizer+. Repeat every three weeks throughout the growing season.

4. One week later, use "All-Season Clean-Up Tonic" (see the opposite page) or my Total Pest Control. Repeat every two weeks for the rest of the growing season.

5. Keep the soil damp, but not soggy. If your garden is in full sun, you will need to water it more often.

6. Don't be afraid to thin, trim, and pinch back your plants. If you don't, they may soon take over the whole garden!

Hands Off

Here's a simple secret that'll save you a lot of heartache—don't handle, spray, prune, or pick vegetables from plants that are under stress from drought, extreme temperatures, or excessive humidity. So if your garden is very dry, water it, let the water soak in and evaporate from the leaves, and then go to work. Don't start a minute sooner!

BETTER LATE THAN NEVER

One of the best ways to keep the veggies coming throughout the season is to late plant some of the same vegetables you planted early in the spring.

Now mind you, some tender vegetables won't withstand frost, so they must be planted with plenty of time to mature before the first frost. These vegetables include bush lima beans, Irish potatoes, cucumbers, pole snapbeans, dry shell beans, winter squash, summer squash, and tomatoes.

To figure out when is the right time to plant these late crops, check your garden diary for the average date of the first fall frost in your area. Now count back the number of days it takes for the vegetables to mature. Plant them no later than this date.

The vegetables that are listed below can withstand frost, but not hard freezes:

Beets
Broccoli
Brussels sprouts
Cabbage
Carrots
Cauliflower
Chinese cabbage
Endive
Kohlrabi
Lettuce
Mustard
Onions
Peas
Radishes
Swiss chard
Turnip greens
Turnips

Green-Up and Clean-Up

MIXERS
&
ELIXIRS

Here's a pair of garden tonics that I use faithfully every year. You should, too, and you'll be *amazed* at the results.

All-Season Green-Up Tonic

1 can of beer
1 cup of ammonia
½ cup of liquid dish soap
½ cup of liquid lawn food
½ cup of molasses or corn syrup

Mix all of the ingredients together in a large bucket, then pour into a 20 gallon hose-end sprayer and apply to your plants.

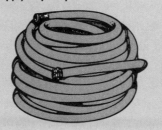

All-Season Clean-Up Tonic

1 cup of liquid dish soap
1 cup of chewing tobacco juice*
1 cup of antiseptic mouthwash
Warm water

Mix all of the ingredients together in a 20 gallon hose-end sprayer, filling the balance of the jar with warm water. Apply to your plants liberally to discourage insects and prevent disease during the growing season.

* Place three fingers of chewing tobacco in an old nylon stocking and soak it in a gallon of hot water until the mixture is dark brown in color.

Root Revival Tonic

Before planting any bare-root plants in spring, soak them in this mix:

1 tbsp. of liquid dish
    soap
¼ cup of brewed tea
1 tbsp. of Epsom salts
1 gal. of water

Let plants sit in this tonic for up to 24 hours. This will revive the plants, and get them ready to grow.

THINK THIN

Thinning and removing surplus plants should take place as soon as the best-growing plants become apparent. You'll know 'em when you see 'em. Why? Because crowded plants, whether vegetables or flowers, never develop to their fullest potential.

Thinning doesn't mean pulling plants out by their roots. If the plants are thick, pulling them out haphazardly may disturb the roots of those you want to keep. A far better method is to snip the stems off close to the ground when the plants are about 4 to 6 inches tall.

The remaining plants will grow vigorously, and their foliage will soon fill in the gaps left by thinning.

KEEP DISEASES AT BAY

When it comes to plant diseases, an ounce of prevention is worth a pound of fungicide. Here are some secrets on how to keep your plants healthy and strong.

❧ Don't plant in any wet, shady areas.

❧ Don't crowd plants together. Leave plenty of room for air circulation.

❧ Water plants early in the day so leaves can dry before nightfall. Fungal diseases thrive on wet leaves.

❧ Stake plants that need it, and keep all branches up off of the ground.

❧ Remove and burn diseased leaves, stems, and flowers. (Never put any of these in your compost pile.)

Butts Out

I'm often asked about cigarette smoking, and how it can affect your plants. Well, pipe, cigar, and cigarette smoke can ruin your tomato crop. So if you're a smoker, before working in the garden, wash your hands well to avoid transmitting tobacco mosaic—a disease that attacks tomatoes and potatoes—to your plants.

8 STEPS TO CUTTING SUCCESS

One of my favorite ways of propagating new plants from my favorite perennials is by taking stem cuttings. The best time to take cuttings is in spring or early summer. Here's how to do it:

1. Take a sharp knife or pruning shears out with you to the garden. Choose the plants you want to propagate, and cut a 2- to 6-inch segment from the top of a mature stem. The cut should be made 1/4 inch below a node, which is the joint at which a leaf joins the stem.

2. If there is a bud or flower at the top of the cutting, pinch it off to encourage the cutting to devote all its energy to root production. Pinch off the lower leaves as well, so that the bottom inch of the cutting is bare.

3. Don't try to root cuttings in the garden, or you are doomed to fail. You have to pamper cuttings if you want them to grow. Make your cutting nursery in flowerpots, wood or plastic flats, peat pots, or other containers at least 4 inches deep. Be sure your containers have good drainage.

4. Fill the containers with sterile rooting medium, such as perlite, vermiculite, shredded sphagnum moss, or sand. Wet the rooting medium thoroughly before inserting the cuttings. If you're using sand, tamp it after wetting, then wet it again.

5. Dip the bottom of each cutting into water, then into a powdered rooting stimulant like Rootone (available at garden centers). Shake off any excess powder.

6. Poke a 1-inch-deep hole into the rooting medium for each cutting. Insert the cuttings, firm them in, and water thoroughly.

7. Cover the container with clear plastic, and set it in a bright place. Keep the cuttings out of direct sun, though, or they'll cook.

8. Watch the cuttings closely. When new leaves appear, open the plastic so the young plants can get accustomed to fresh air. A few days later, carefully remove one of the cuttings from the rooting medium and examine the roots. If they are 1/2 inch long or longer, the plants are ready to be moved into the garden.

MIXERS
&
ELIXIRS

Flower Power

4 cups of bonemeal
2 cups of gypsum
2 cups of Epsom salts
1 cup of wood ashes
1 cup of lime
4 tsp. of baby powder
1 tsp. of baking powder
1 bucketful of dry
    peat moss

Mix the first seven ingredients into the bucketful of dry peat moss. Put a trowel's worth of this mixture in the soil when planting flowers to get them off to a great start.

MIDWINTER CHORES

February is a good time to take a leisurely stroll around your yard to see what needs to be done in order to see your plants safely through to spring. Here's a region-by-region rundown.

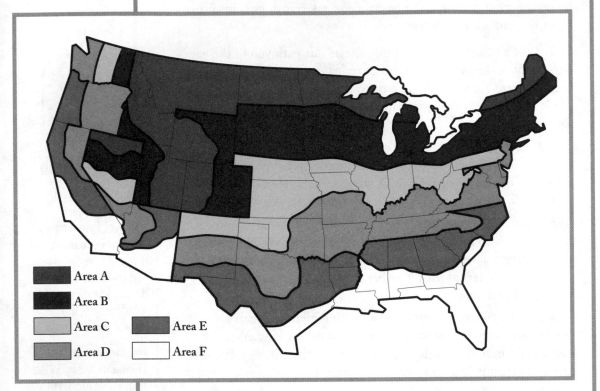

Area A
Area B
Area C
Area D
Area E
Area F

AREAS A & B

• Look for bent over, weighted down trees, shrubs, and evergreens, and listen for the drip, drip, drip sound of melting ice and snow. Although this water can drip during the day, it freezes up at night and breaks branches. So clear off any excess snow and break off any ice.

• Check your bulbs and perennials to see if any have been pushed (heaved) out of the ground by the cold. If so, gently press them back down and cover them up with a mulch.

• Prune sleeping trees, shrubs, and vines. Be sure to seal the cuts with a dab of interior latex paint mixed with a splash of antiseptic mouthwash.

• Check trees for bark

damage caused by mice, rabbits, and deer. Wrap trunks with aluminum foil, chicken wire, or hardware cloth as necessary.

• If the snow melts and you see bald spots in your lawn, sow a little grass seed now to give it a head start on germination in the spring.

AREAS C & D

• Spread a generous layer of organic lawn or garden food, or manure (at least two years old) onto your vegetable garden.

• Do any dormant pruning that needs to be done.

• If the weather cooperates, you can't beat a real early season dormant spray. The bugs will never know what hit 'em.

• Cut any dead wood on your rose bushes, and be sure to seal all cuts.

• Now's the time to get your early seeds started indoors.

• Order your summer-flowering bulbs and perennials now.

AREA E

• Clean out your lawn, shrubs, flowerbeds, and every other nook and cranny in the yard. Cleanliness is next to godliness in the garden, and I want yours to be a shrine!

• Shred all of the cleaned out material and use it on your garden beds as mulch or add it to your compost pile.

• Feed your lawn with a natural organic lawn food and 4 pounds of Epsom salts added for each 2,500 square feet of lawn area. Apply this mixture at half the recommended rate, two weeks apart.

AREA F

• Do all of the chores listed for Area E.

• Mix 3 pounds of gypsum and 4 pounds of Epsom salts into a 25-pound bag of lawn food, and apply it to your lawn.

• Plant to your heart's content (the rest of the country is green with envy!).

• Apply any organic lawn food in all flowerbeds and vegetable beds.

PEST PATROL

Scare-'Em-All Tonic

20 garlic cloves, peeled
1 medium onion, finely chopped
Cheesecloth
1 tbsp. of liquid dish soap
3 tsp. of glycerin
1 qt. plus 1 gal. of water
A blender

1. Place garlic cloves, onion, and 1 quart of water in a blender. Blend at high speed for 1 minute. Strain the mixture through the cheesecloth.

2. Mix the garlic-onion pulp with one gallon of water. Add the liquid soap and glycerin.

3. Spray on plants as needed to keep the bugs at bay.

MIXERS & ELIXIRS

Happy Herb Tonic

¼ cup of brewed tea
½ tbsp. of bourbon
½ tbsp. of ammonia
½ tbsp. of hydrogen
    peroxide
½ tsp. of liquid dish soap
1 gal. of warm water

Mix all of the ingredients
together, and feed to
your herbs during the
growing season.

HOW TO NURTURE HERBS

Once established, most herbs are fairly drought tolerant. Water them deeply only when necessary because most herbs don't do well in wet or poorly drained soils. Avoid heavy or frequent applications of fertilizer during the growing season, because over-fertilization can cause low oil production or leggy, stretched growth.

Established herb plants should be fed every six weeks during the growing season. Use "Happy Herb Tonic" (at left).

A PINCH TO GROW AN INCH

To maintain plant size and encourage branching, pinch off the growing tips of herbs periodically during the growing season. Begin pinching when the plants are 6 inches tall and continue to pinch after every 4 to 6 inches of new growth. This will help the plants remain compact and bushy, and will result in more abundant harvests.

KEEP BEDS CLEAN

After many years of experience, I can tell you that keeping planting beds clean will reduce insect and disease troubles. So throughout the growing season, remove old flowers as they fade and old leaves as they brown. Put all nondiseased foliage on your compost pile.

If your beds become too crowded, divide clumps of plants or dig up the extras to be transplanted or disposed of. Check with your friends and neighbors; I'm sure they'll take any extras.

In the fall, remove all top-growth of delphiniums, peonies, and irises, and discard.

Summer Snip Secret

As the gardening season begins to wind down in late summer, take a few minutes to stroll through your yard and gardens. Carry a pair of pruning shears with you, and cut off any small dead branches and foliage from any type of plant. This way, you'll be encouraging re-growth in the fall.

Toolin' Around

Trust me—you can't be a successful gardener without a good supply of garden tools. For too many years I tried to make do with inferior goods, but I found I was spending a fortune on cheap tools. So now I buy the best tools I can afford and treat them well. A little maintenance will keep tools in tiptop shape and ready for hard work year after year.

HANG 'EM HIGH

For a temporary garden tool rack, cut both ends from large fruit drink cans and nail the cans to a garden fence. Then slip each tool into a can, heads up and handles down, so they'll be at hand throughout the season. You may want to run a strip of duct or electrical tape around the rims of the cans to cover the sharp edges.

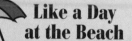

Like a Day at the Beach

During gardening season, store your hand tools in a pail of clean, dry sand. The sand will keep them rust-free when they're not in use.

GIVE TOOLS THEIR WINTER COATS

Before you put your garden tools away for the winter, clean them off and cover them with a light coat of WD-40. Then they'll be rust-free and primed for use next spring.

A SHARP IDEA

To keep pruning saws sharp, clean, and safely out of harm's way, use a length of old garden hose. Slit the hose lengthwise on one side and slip it over the blade as a cover.

CANNY COILS

Tripped up by that mess of kinky garden hose? Keep your hose from knotting and twisting by loosely coiling it around the bottom of an old garbage can or other large container.

Rust Buster

OK, so you forgot to clean and oil your tools last fall, and now they're rusty. Don't fret. You can get your rusty tools clean again simply by rubbing them with a soap-filled steel wool pad dipped in kerosene or turpentine. (Be sure to do this in a well-ventilated area and wear gloves.) Finish the job by briskly rubbing the tools with wadded-up aluminum foil to make them shine like new!

DON'T GO FROM GREEN THUMB TO ALL THUMBS

While gardening is the nation's #1 hobby and one of the most pleasurable pastimes, danger lurks, especially when you're using tools. It's always better to be safe than sorry, so keep these safety tips in mind:

❧ Keep a well-stocked first-aid kit in the tool shed and garage, as well as in the house, so you can always get to one quickly.

❧ Fatigue causes just as many accidents as carelessness does—in fact, fatigue *makes* you careless, too. So if you are feeling tired from your hard work, stop and rest. It'll still be there when you come back.

❧ Read and follow all instructions to the letter for your tools and other equipment.

❧ "A place for everything, and everything in its place." Put away all tools after you use them. Don't leave them around where they can be tripped over, especially if they have sharp edges.

Jerry's Secrets

Instead of throwing away that rusty old garden rake, use it as a tool holder. Hang it head-down in a convenient place, then hang your small hand tools heads-up between the rake tines.

MOWER MAINTENANCE

If you are mechanically inclined, springtime is the right time to perform lawn mower maintenance. Get a new plug, drain the old oil out (if you forgot to drain it last fall), and replace it with new oil. To get the gunk out, just add a cup of kerosene to the old oil before you drain it, and push the mower back and forth to mix it all up.

Have all of your mower blades sharpened and balanced. (Keep a spare on hand at all times.) Wash grass catchers in the laundry tub with a heavy-duty laundry detergent, and then hang them out to dry.

With these chores done, you're ready to get mowing!

Fork it Over!

An old kitchen fork makes a handy cultivation tool, especially in those hard-to-reach areas around delicate plants like herbs and when you're working with houseplants or other container plants.

Jerry Tells All About...
Soil Improvement

Q. This may seem like a funny question, but what's the difference between soil and dirt, and which kind do I need to grow a good garden?

A. Soil is a productive mix of decayed materials like leaves, grass clippings, sawdust, weeds, and shredded bark, while dirt is a collection of filth. For a good garden, any well-drained soil will do. Water should not puddle in pockets on top, but then again, the soil shouldn't be almost pure sand, or it won't hold any moisture at all.

Q. How can I put wood ashes to good use in my yard?

A. You should apply them to your garden at the rate of one bushel per 50 square feet. They can also be worked into a compost pile.

Q. I live in a landfill area where the soil is 90 percent sand, 9 percent clay, and 1 percent organic, with seashells mixed in. The soil pH is 7.7, and is high in sodium and calcium. What will lower the calcium level?

A. Calcium, as a rule, doesn't affect the pH. Time and regular applications of lime will do the job.

Use an Annual Rotation

Rotate your annuals just like you do your vegetables for variety in your yard. You'll also be able to cultivate better without using large quantities of fertilizer and soil conditioners.

MIXERS & ELIXIRS

Seedling Starter Tonic

Give your transplants a break on moving day by serving them a sip of my "Seedling Starter Tonic." This will help them recover more quickly from the transplanting shock.

1 tbsp. of Fish Fertilizer+
1 tbsp. of ammonia
1 tbsp. of Murphy's Oil Soap
1 tsp. of instant tea granules
1 qt. of warm water

Mix all of the ingredients together in the warm water. Pour into a handheld mist sprayer bottle, and mist the seedlings several times a day until they're back on their feet.

Q. Is it helpful to mix coffee grounds in the soil that my carrots and radishes grow in? Also, I use a lot of mushroom compost when I till my garden. I know it's good for humus, but are there any side effects?

A. The coffee grounds are great, and mushroom compost is good as long as it's not too fresh (right from the farm) because it can kill trees.

Q. If I put grass clippings, leaves, and other organic stuff in a pile, will they compost by themselves, or do I have to do anything to help it along?

A. You do have to pitch in to get things going. First, I want you to sprinkle fine soil ¼ inch deep on each 9-inch layer of compostable materials. Then overspray with a can of warm Coca-Cola that has been lightly shaken up. The soil contains the decaying bacteria and the Coke feeds the bacteria, which helps speed up decomposition of the pile.

Q. I've built a good porous base on my clay property, but the water backs up from beneath. What's the solution?

A. Get a tree auger that can be used on an electric drill, and drill holes 2 to 3 feet deep all over your garden, then fill them with gravel. These "French wells" will carry off excess water.

Jerry's Secrets

A good mulch will do more than cut down on weeds. Any of the rough mulches (grass, straw, hulls, or shells) can be spaded into the soil in fall to improve the structure and natural organic quality of the soil.

Keep It Light for Wildflowers

Almost all wildflowers require light, humusy soil. When preparing their new home, mix a sufficient amount of leaf mold or peat moss thoroughly into the soil to approximate the texture of the soil in their native habitat. And remember to be a good conservationist when you're harvesting wildflowers. Take them only if they are growing abundantly in the wild, and only if you can recreate the natural conditions in which they will thrive.

Q. The soil on the north side of my house develops moss. I would like to plant lily-of-the-valley there. How can I get rid of the moss?

A. You don't need to. The lily-of-the-valley is a good friend of moss, since they both like damp, shady spots.

Q. I'm confused—what's the difference between peat moss, sphagnum moss, perlite, and vermiculite, and what are they used for?

A. Peat moss is a fine, muck-based, decomposed plant material. Sphagnum moss is a coarser, fibrous moss that almost looks like dried seaweed. Perlite is an expanded rock material, and vermiculite is a layered insulation material. They all are excellent soil conditioners and rooting mediums.

HEAD FOR THE HILLS

If, despite your best efforts, your soil just isn't getting any better, don't give up on landscaping altogether! Take a tip from the pros, and mound plant. All you do is place hills of good soil in strategic locations around your yard, and then plant in the mounds. You can create some pretty original and spectacular designs and effects. Mound planting can be done with all kinds of plants; just remember to be aware of your permanent grade, and leave paths for water to run off and away.

Q. What's the best all-around type of soil for planting trees?

A. Most trees do well in sandy loam or a good clay loam. As a general rule, they don't do well in heavy clay.

Q. The soil in my yard is extremely sandy. What can I do to improve it?

A. The answer is to add gypsum at the rate of 50 pounds per 1,000 square feet, plus work in all of the leaves and grass clippings you can get your hands on.

Q. When should I add compost to my garden?

A. Fall is best—let it sit on top of the soil until spring, and then work it in very well.

Q. If I spade my garden in the fall, do I have to do it again in spring?

A. I only spade or rotary till in the fall if I need the exercise, and I do that before I add my compost or other material. I always spade again in the spring; that's a must. Soil gets compacted, or pushed down, from snow and rain. So if you just scuff it up with a rake, you won't give the new seeds a fair start.

Q. How do I prepare the soil for a new garden?

A. Start in the fall by removing the sod, and throwing it on your compost pile. Next, put a 6-inch-deep layer of leaves, grass clippings, ashes, wood chips, builder's sand, and

Jerry's Secrets

Bonemeal is useful to plants only when it's worked into the soil. It penetrates very slowly, so most of it is wasted if you simply sprinkle it on top of the soil.

The Lazy Landscaper's Checklist

Here's how to keep your flower gardening chores to an absolute minimum:

☑ Use bedding plants instead of seeds. Let the grower fuss over seedlings; bedding plants give you a running head start.

☑ Choose plants that don't need more fertilizer than what's added at planting. These include nasturtium, cleome, portulaca, amaranthus, and cosmos.

☑ Use prespaced flats to reduce effort. They have openings for roots, and are preplanted with bedding plants. Set the flat, plastic and all, into the soil, and hide the plastic with mulch.

☑ Choose low-maintenance plants with flowers that fall cleanly from the plant, like begonias, impatiens, coleus, alyssum, ageratum, lobelia, vinca, and salvia.

peat moss on the cleared area, and wait until spring to spade it in. Don't cultivate a new garden until the soil will crumble in your hand after being squeezed firmly.

Q. I've heard you suggest using human hair in the vegetable or flower garden. What does it do, and what is it used for?

A. Hair contains protein, nitrogen, and dozens of other super things. It really helps thicken plant roots and also deepens the color of the foliage.

Q. For the past three years, I've been unable to grow annuals. The roots don't grow beyond the size they were when I put them in. I've tried regular fertilizer, but have been unsuccessful. Any suggestions?

A. For each 100 square feet of flowerbed, I want you to spread this mix over the soil, then spade it in well: 6 bags of shredded leaves, 2 bags of grass clippings, 1 cup of Epsom salts, and ¼ cup of sugar. That should give your annuals something to grow on.

A Measure of Success

Here's a neat way to kill two birds with one stone—turn your gardening tools into handy measuring devices. It's easy to do. Use a file to mark your long-handled tools inch by inch from the top to the bottom. Then use stain or ink to fill in the file marks. Voilà! You've got an easy way to measure when you're tooling around the old garden.

Q. My lawn, flowerbeds, and vegetable garden are infested with grubs and several different kinds of moss. I treated the lawn with milky spore, and used some lime. Now what?

A. Milky spore takes about a year to get started, and then lasts four years. To destroy

PEST PATROL

What a Tangled Web They Weave

To get rid of spiders, put cedar chips into the toes of old panty hose, and hang the hose in areas where spiders spin their webs. To discourage spiders from starting webs, spray rubbing alcohol on windowsills, or leave perfumed soap chips scattered about.

moss, you need sunshine, good drainage, and moss killer. Before you apply the moss killer, spray the area with a mix of 1 tablespoon of baby shampoo per gallon of water.

Q. I transplanted sweet peas from along the roadside. They grew great for two years, but have very few blooms. What should I do?

A. You need to work an ample amount of chicken manure into the soil before you plant your peas this year.

Q. Can you give me some advice on starting a perennial flower garden with wildflowers?

A. Start with any of the many wildflower mixes that you can buy at garden centers or through gardening catalogs—they are all perennial mixes. The secret to keeping wildflowers producing is to mow them down to 3 inches in the fall, and then let the cut stems lay on the ground, where they will reseed themselves over the winter.

Q. Can I use shredded paper in my garden?

A. Absolutely! Either use it as mulch around your plants, or add it to your compost pile.

Q. In my area, gardeners use lots of superphosphate. I know that phosphorus is the second number in fertilizer and that it feeds roots, but is it important for clay soil?

A. It sure is, because roots

Jerry's Secrets

Use your finger to draw a ring in the soil around new plants. The water that collects in this mini-basin goes straight to the roots, where plants need it to grow their best.

Rub out Pests

Keep a bottle of rubbing alcohol on hand in your garden shed. It's a quick and easy way to get rid of all sorts of pests like mealybugs, spider mites, aphids, whiteflies, and gnats. Simply mix 1/2 cup of rubbing alcohol with a quart of water. Lightly mist-spray any infected plants.

have a harder time getting nutrients in clay soil. Anything you can work into the soil to improve its structure—shredded bark, compost, sawdust, green manure, and especially phosphate—will help.

Lay Off the Salt

The salt you use to melt your icy driveway and sidewalks can mean death to your lawn and nearby plants. So save your landscape and use these good ol' fashioned ice fighters instead: sawdust, sand, or ashes.

Q. I've heard about using tobacco juice to get rid of insect pests in my vegetable garden. This may sound silly, but will the vegetables absorb the nicotine and become a crop of tobacco?

A. No, the vegetables will not absorb the nicotine if you use it in the recommended amounts, and they won't become tobacco crops any more than they will become soap if you wash them with a good soapy-water solution. Tobacco was one of the first insecticides known to man, and it continues to be effective to this day.

Q. I have a problem with deer munching on my trees, shrubs, flowers—everything! What can I do?

A. Try "Deer Buster Egg Tonic," at right.

Q. A few months ago, I used beer in margarine tubs sunk into the ground to kill slugs. It worked wonderfully, but buying all that beer can get expensive! Is there a cheaper alternative that I can use?

A. Yes, there is—and it's grape juice. Believe it or not, it works just as well, and costs considerably less than beer.

CRITTER CONTROL

Deer Buster Egg Tonic

2 eggs
2 cloves of garlic
2 tbsp. of Tabasco sauce
2 tbsp. of cayenne pepper
2 cups of water

Put all of the ingredients in a blender, and purée. Allow the mixture to sit for two days, then pour or spray it all over and around the plants you need to protect.

MIXERS
&
ELIXIRS

Groundcover Grub

3 parts bonemeal
1 part Epsom salts
1 part gypsum

Mix all of the ingredients together, and add to the planting hole and soil surface when you plant any groundcover.

Q. I have a steep slope out back that I really don't want to plant with grass, because mowing would be too difficult. Any suggestions for an attractive groundcover besides the usual pachysandra?

A. For a twist, try thyme. It makes a good groundcover for banks, slopes, or terraces—anywhere it is difficult to grow and maintain grass.

. . . .

Q. How can I get rid of toads in my garden?

A. You shouldn't! Toads are gardeners' best friends, so never harm them. In three months, a single toad will devour 10,000 insects, including beetles, worms, snails, caterpillars, wasps, yellow jackets, and ants. They also lay more than 1,000 eggs per year. So please, cultivate a friendship with your local toads.

Keep 'Em Shallow

. . . .

When setting out young plants, try not to bury their roots under more than half an inch of soil beyond what they had in their flats. "Leggy" plants, like indoor-grown lettuce, can be safely set deeper into the ground.

. . . .

. . . .

Q. What do you recommend to bring down soil pH?

A. To correct high pH, mix 50 percent pelletized lime and 50 percent pelletized gypsum, and work it into the soil in both spring and fall.

. . . .

Q. I'm going to replace my deck, and I need to remove most of the flowers growing around it. When is the best time of year to remove and replant them?

A. From fall to winter, as long as the ground isn't frozen. This is one of the best times for planting, dividing, moving, or removing plants in your garden. To ensure a good restart, add a handful of dry oatmeal and human hair to the soil mix when replanting.

Q. Can I shred those glossy magazines and catalogs and use them as compost?

A. Not unless they're black-and-white and printed on recycled paper. The chemicals used in making glossy magazine paper and for printing color on the page are not healthy for your garden. So stick with black-and-white newspaper. To get it going, finely shred the newsprint first, mix it up with other compostable materials, and add some soil on top.

Q. I have a 40 × 50-foot garden, and the soil is all clay. I irrigate it with river water, and the furrows are really packed. How much gypsum should I apply to make the clay drain?

A. For really good drainage, you're going to need to apply upwards of 200 pounds of gypsum (10 pounds per 100 square feet). As you can guess, that will be rather expensive—but it will work! On the other hand, you'd be miles ahead if you build raised beds, and bring material in to fill them. A good mix would be ¼ sand, ¼ organic matter, ¼ clay loam, and ¼ topsoil. After you've got the beds up and running, work a good, dry, all-purpose plant food into the soil.

Q. How do I get rid of Queen-Anne's-lace? It's all over my yard!

A. Queen-Anne's-lace is an indicator of poor soil. It is difficult to get rid of, and it

Count on Compost

You know all the good things compost can do for the soil in your planting beds. What you may not realize is that you can also count on this "black gold" for:

☑ mulching around your established plants

☑ top-dressing your lawn

☑ improving potting soils or planting mixes

☑ side-dressing around your growing plants

So make the most of your compost, and put it to good use all around your yard!

Jerry's Secrets

Spread wood ashes around your vegetable garden, where they'll do double duty. First, they'll help lighten the soil, and second, they'll make a good slug roadblock. The slimy slitherers can't glide over the ashes without injuring their skin, so they don't dare cross the border.

multiplies very rapidly. The best solution for large infested areas is to plow it up and pick out all of the roots. Then get to work on improving your soil.

Q. Can I use maple leaves as a mulch around my rhododendrons?

A. Absolutely! They make a great mulch for rhododendrons because they are very alkaline, and tend to pack down to almost form a crust on the soil surface.

Q. Is it safe to add weeds to my compost pile, or am I just asking for trouble?

A. Sure, you can add weeds to your compost pile, as long as they're not in the seed-formation stage.

Q. There are ants all over my peonies. Are they harmful to the flowers?

A. Ants and peonies go together like hands and gloves. The ants aren't doing any harm—they're simply gathering the sticky substance from the buds.

Q. How do I treat soil that has been contaminated with automotive fluids?

A. The best treatment is to dig up the soil, and dispose of it properly. Absent that, mix 40 to 50 pounds of gypsum and lime with 2 pounds of sugar, and spread it heavily over the area. Repeat as necessary.

MIXERS
&
ELIXIRS

A Breath of Fresh Air

This tonic is like a breath of fresh air for your plants.

1 cup of 3% hydrogen peroxide
¼ cup of clear corn syrup
2 tbsp. of whiskey
2 tbsp. of baby shampoo
1½ cups of warm water

Mix all of the ingredients in your 20 gallon hose-end sprayer, and apply it liberally to your lawn and garden plants as new growth begins.

Turn Up the Heat

Spread a thin layer of compost on hot concrete, and stir or rake it several times. A 10-hour exposure to the sun reduces harmful microorganisms, making it safe to use with seeds.

CHAPTER 3

"To grow a successful garden, water and feed your plants regularly, and keep them clean and neat. Watch for trouble and act at once. In the garden, you must never put off for tomorrow what should be done today, or there won't be a garden tomorrow!"

Let's Water, Weed, and Feed

Water, Water, Everywhere

Of course, plants, like people, need water to survive. But there's a right way to water your plants and a wrong way—and watering wisely can mean the difference between a happy, healthy life and a slow, agonizing death for your plants. You can keep your plants alive and kicking by following my tried-and-true watering techniques.

THE BEST PART OF WAKING UP

The best time to water your plants is in the morning, to give them ample time to dry off before bedtime. If plants go to bed in wet pajamas, they are more likely to develop fungus troubles down the road.

Water enough to give the root area a good soaking, but don't water more than once or twice a week. And unless you're in the middle of a drought, you shouldn't have to water daily.

DON'T BE SHALLOW

The first rule of watering, whether you're an amateur or a seasoned professional, is to be sure to water deeply. Shallow watering does more harm than good because it causes your plants to develop shallow root systems, up near the soil's surface. This can mean trouble during prolonged dry spells.

So whenever you water your plants, slow and steady is the key, and be sure to really soak the soil well.

Jerry's Secrets

Annuals have shallower root systems than bulbs and perennials, so mulch and water them lightly, but do so more often than you do their hardier cousins.

Soak, Don't Sprinkle

A soaker hose is best for watering plants that grow from bulbs. If you have to use a sprinkler, just remember that you run the risk of burning foliage, especially if you water on a sunny day.

KEEP YOUR HANDS TO YOURSELF

The least effective method for watering your garden is with a handheld nozzle or watering can. Watering with a nozzle can tear up the soil surface, and using either of these methods more often than not results in water that is poorly distributed over the area. Besides which, both of these methods require a very patient person to do as thorough a job as a soaker hose or oscillating sprinkler would do, and as you know, I am the original Impatient Gardener, so I use the hose!

And anyway, do you really want to spend half a day watering your garden, or running back and forth from the spigot to the garden with a watering can? I'm sure we can all think of better things to do.

SELECTIVE SPRINKLING

If you water with a sprinkler, use what professional landscapers use—an oscillating type. These sprinklers cover a large area and produce rainlike drops of water. Don't use a rotating sprinkler—it tends to tear up the surface of the soil and covers only a small area.

Run your sprinkler for at least four hours in each area. This deep watering is best for your plants and will allow you to go longer intervals between waterings.

ALL SYSTEMS GO

Whether you water with a soaker hose or an oscillating sprinkler, be sure to thoroughly check out your watering system at the start of each season. It's easy for a bit of dirt or other debris to find its way into the hose (I've even found small, dead frogs in mine), clogging one or more of the holes. And sprinkler heads can become clogged by hard-water deposits. So give everything the once-over in the spring to get the most from your watering systems.

MIXERS & ELIXIRS

Just Desserts

This mix makes a great little dessert for all of your plants.

1 tbsp. of Epsom salts
1 tbsp. of baking powder
4 tbsp. of hydrogen peroxide
1 tbsp. of ammonia
1/2 tsp. of unflavored gelatin
1/2 tsp. of liquid dish soap
4 One-a-Day multivitamins with iron, dissolved in 1 cup of hot water
1 gal. of rain or filtered water

Combine all of the ingredients. To use, mix 1 cup of the dessert with a gallon of water, and water your plants liberally with the mixture.

WATER YOUR SOIL

When we talk about watering our plants, what we really should be talking about is watering the soil around the plants. This is where the water really counts, not on the foliage. A gentle, deep soaking of the soil will stimulate deep root growth and build stronger, healthier plants that can better withstand dry spells.

Watering, if done so that the soil is wet several inches deep, should last a week without rain. If there is no rain for seven days, then it's time to haul out the hose again.

Don't Neglect Bulbs After They Bloom

Bulbs need extra water when they're working hard to produce fantastic foliage and beautiful blooms in spring and summer. If Mother Nature isn't doing her part with plenty of nice spring showers, you need to step in. Remember, even after the bulbs have stopped blooming, they're still producing foliage, and if the foliage dries out and dies before maturing, your bulbs will be too pooped to participate next spring.

EVERGREEN S.O.S.

Evergreens like to drink a lot of water, but they can't stand in it. So water them deeply twice a week through the summer, but do not allow the water to puddle up, or your evergreens will actually drown.

GETTING TO THE ROOT OF THE MATTER

Here's a little secret that'll make watering a snap in your vegetable garden. Bury large coffee cans (with both ends removed) between your plants. Fill the cans with rocks, and water directly into the cans. The water will run through directly to the plants' roots.

COOL-WEATHER WATERING IS A MUST!

Most folks don't have a problem hauling out the soaker hose all summer long, but it's amazing how many of us quit watering our lawns and gardens once the cooler weather sets in. Well, how long can you go without a drink of water? I thought so! Think of your plants in the same way.

🐛 Without water, plant roots cannot absorb and distribute the nutrients and fertilizers you worked so hard to get into the soil.

🐛 Without water, plants can't produce and transport the sugars manufactured in their leaves to other parts of the plant

that need the sugars to grow.

🐛 In any event, plants don't use water very efficiently—they release much of what they receive right back into the atmosphere through their leaf pores. Talk about ungrateful!

So please remember how important water is to the health of your outdoor green scene no matter what time of year it is. A flourishing yard and garden is a healthy yard and garden, and it all adds up to more enjoyment for you!

WAGE WAR AGAINST WILTING

Don't let your plants wilt—it will seriously weaken them. If the weather is hot, sunny, or windy, water your outdoor plants at least once a day; twice a day is even better. Do this for a week or until the leaves do not wilt anymore. After that, water thoroughly to a depth of 6 to 8 inches every three or four days during the hot summer months, and cut back to once a week in cool weather.

Mulch is a great ally in winning the war against wilting. A mulch of peat moss, bark mulch, or cocoa mulch will conserve soil moisture and keep down weeds.

MIXERS & ELIXIRS

Evergreen Growth Tonic

To feed your evergreens in spring, lightly sprinkle a mix of 1 pound of gypsum and ¼ pound of Epsom salts on top of the soil out at the weep line, and then water with this tonic:

1 cup of liquid dish soap
1 cup of chewing tobacco juice*
4 tbsp. of Fish Fertilizer+
2 tbsp. of bourbon

Mix all of the ingredients in a 20 gallon hose-end sprayer.

*Take three fingers of chewing tobacco from the package, place it into the toe of a nylon stocking, and place the stocking in a gallon of hot water. Let it steep until the water is dark brown.

Jerry's Secrets

Swivel hooks are handy-dandy house-plant hanging helpers. Once you hang them up, you can turn the plant in any direction so all sides get sunlight. And gently spin your plants from time to time—they'll enjoy the ride!

DON'T LEAVE 'EM HIGH AND DRY

Surface-rooted plants like dogwoods, azaleas, blue-berries, and camellias need extra water in dry weather. Make sure the soil around these plants is moist at all times.

Be generous with the mulch, too. It will help to conserve moisture. My favorite mulch for these plants is 2 to 3 inches of shredded cypress. If you can't find that, pine needles will do just dandy, and they'll make the soil acidic, too!

QUENCH THEIR THIRST, DRIP BY DRIP

Here's a quick tip that'll get you growing like the pros: For a slow, continuous supply of water for your garden plants, punch small holes around the lower portion of a plastic soda bottle or milk jug. Fill the container with water, replace the cap, and place the container on the ground near your plants. Refill with water or tonic when needed.

Shake Your Blooms

The secret to watering flowers in bloom is to use a little extra care. Open flowers tend to rot if they catch and hold water. So after you water yours, give them a little shake to dislodge some of the drops from the petals.

KEEP FOLIAGE DRY

When you water your roses, make sure you don't get the foliage wet, because wet foliage helps to spread black spot disease. And once it has a toehold, believe you me, it's tough to get rid of. The best way to water roses is to use a soaker hose placed on the ground around the plant. Then the water can seep out to where it will do the most good—near the roots.

GIVE THESE BEAUTIES A DRINK

Roses get awfully thirsty. They need large amounts of water, and even where rainfall is plentiful, they benefit from an occasional watering. Roses thrive when they receive the equivalent of 1 inch of water every seven to ten days throughout the growing season.

Soak the soil around your roses thoroughly to a depth of 8 to 10 inches. Direct a small, very slow-moving stream of water from a garden hose around the bases of the plants. A heavy stream is wasteful—most of the water runs off and fails to penetrate the soil by more than a few inches.

SUPER-SOAK SOD

If you're laying sod in your yard, you must keep it moist. Immediately after rolling it out, give it a thorough watering. As a general rule, you should water every day to keep the sod moist until the roots have grown into the soil. Be sure to apply enough water so that the soil underneath the sod is getting wet, too.

Good rooting usually takes about two to three weeks. Once the sod is established, you can gradually reduce the watering to once a week or even less, depending upon when the grass begins to look thirsty—in other words, begins to dry out.

DROUGHT-PROOF YOUR LAWN

By alternately soaking your lawn to a depth of 10 inches or more and then allowing the top 2 inches or so to dry out, your grass roots will develop more deeply. And that's exactly what you want and need to develop a thick, healthy lawn. In return, this dense root growth will help save your lawn during a long drought.

Gum Up Gophers

If you see evidence of gophers (or moles) excavating in your lawn or garden, gum 'em up with this neat trick: Insert sticks of unwrapped Juicy Fruit gum (don't ask me why, but only this brand will do), slit lengthwise, into the gopher or mole runs.

The critters will eat the gum, but cannot digest it, and will die within a few weeks.

GRASS CAN'T SWIM!

That's right, and there's no easier
way to drown it than by overwatering.
You see, grass is just like us—depen-
dent on oxygen to survive. If it's watered
too heavily and the roots are kept submerged
under water for a period of time, or if the top of
the grass plant is submerged, then the plant smothers to death.

So if you see light yellow or soggy off-color spots in your lawn,
you know it's the result of too much water. The solution? Don't
water all day and all night in soil that doesn't drain well.

Clay soils, in particular, don't drain well. Grass will drown in
clay soil where there are pockets in the ground, or where the
ground is not level or has not been graded to let the water run off.

WHAT TYPE ARE YOU?

Water soaks into soil at different speeds, depending upon the
soil's composition. If you don't know your soil type, you can buy a
soil test kit at garden centers, through catalogs, or at your local
County Extension office. If you know your basic soil type, use the
table below as your handy-dandy guide to watering.

Jerry's Secrets

Let Mother Nature
lend you a helping
hand whenever she
can. Take your house-
plants out in the rain
for a good, quick
shower. And don't
overlook other "free"
water sources, such
as the water from
your defroster or
your dehumidifier.

	Soak It to Me	
SOIL TYPE	**SOAK RATE (INCHES PER HOUR)**	**SOAK TIME (PER INCH)**
Sand	2.0	$\frac{1}{2}$ hour
Sandy loam	1.0	1 hour
Loam	0.5	2 hours
Silt loam	0.4	$2\frac{1}{4}$ hours
Clay loam	0.3	$3\frac{1}{4}$ hours
Clay	0.2	5 hours

PUT HOUSEPLANTS ON A LOW-SALT DIET

If you're regularly watering your houseplants with household water that goes through a water softener, stop what you're doing immediately! Your plants will survive for a little while, but in the end, the salty water will do them in.

Here's my secret for making a low-cost water purifier. Start with a clean, one-gallon plastic milk jug. Use an ice pick, nail, or knitting needle to poke 12 holes in a 4-inch circle in the center of the bottom. Place a coffee-maker filter inside the jug, covering the bottom. Add charcoal from a pet store or garden shop to cover the filter completely. Top off the charcoal with a heavy layer of washed, crushed eggshells. Finish with two layers of marbles or well-boiled small stones.

Now place the jug over a pan or bowl and run water very slowly through the jug. Allow the water to pass through the filtering materials and out the holes in the bottom. Use this clean, filtered water to quench your plants' thirst!

Leave Fluoride at the Dentist's

Everyone knows that plants don't have teeth—so why are you watering your plants with your fluoridated tap water? Fluoride causes the tips of houseplants to turn yellow, while other chemicals in your drinking water make the potting soil crust over, slowing plant growth. So only use filtered water (see "Put Houseplants on a Low-Salt Diet," above) for all your plants.

RAIN, RAIN COME MY WAY

 My Grandma Putt sure knew what she was doing when she put sturdy oak barrels out to collect the rain. Of course, back then, rainwater was used for just about everything—from drinking and cooking to bathing and watering the garden.

Nowadays, there is no good reason why you can't collect rainwater for your garden and houseplants. And now it's even easier to do because you have a choice of any number of containers in all shapes, sizes, and colors that you can easily slip under a downspout. Just use the old noggin—don't use anything so large that it's impossible to move once it's full!

GIVE YOUR PLANTS A SHOWER

A great way to water several houseplants all at once is to put them in the shower. Just don't scald them—keep the temperature at a tepid 70°F or so. Once they've had a good soaking, dry off the foliage before putting them back in their sunny homes.

DOWN THE DRAIN

If you've been properly watering your houseplants and they still seem to be too moist, check to be sure that the drainage holes in your pots aren't clogged. Remove the plant and clean out the pot. Then put pieces of a broken clay pot, pebbles, or bits of broken brick in the bottom. Repot the plant and water. You should notice an improvement in the drainage.

PITCH A TENT

An easy way to increase the humidity for plants in a dry indoor environment is to pitch a tent for them. Place a plastic bag or plastic sheeting loosely over the plants at night. Be sure to remove the plastic in the morning before the bright sunlight causes excessive moisture to build up.

If you're going away, water your plants, then group them together. Put a plastic dry cleaning bag over a wire coat hanger to make a tent for the plants. This will help retain soil moisture for up to two weeks, so you won't have to worry about your little darlings while you're gone.

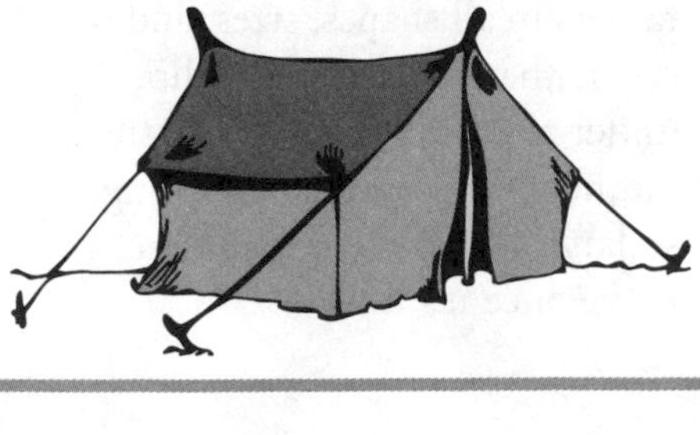

MIXERS & ELIXIRS

Container Plant Tonic

- 2 tbsp. of whiskey
- 1 tbsp. of all-purpose 15-30-15 fertilizer
- ½ tsp. of unflavored gelatin
- ½ tsp. of liquid dish soap
- ¼ tsp. of instant tea granules

Put all of the ingredients in a clean, 1-gallon milk jug, and fill it up with water. Mix, then mark the jug "Container Plant Tonic." Add ½ cup of this fortified mix to every gallon of water you use to water your outdoor container plants.

Humidity Helps

You can increase the humidity in your home by placing open containers of water around your houseplants. You can even place plants on pebble-filled trays and keep water in the trays, but just be sure to keep the plants above the water level, not sitting in it.

The Gender Gap

To make it easier to figure out what kind of plants you're dealing with, I like to think of and identify plants by their "gender." If a plant is known for its fruit, flowers, or berries, I think of it as a "girl" plant. If, on the other hand, the plant has thick, bushy, or trailing leaves, I consider it to be a "boy" plant.

3 STEPS TO HOUSEPLANT HAPPINESS

When the cold weather sets in, it's time to hustle in the houseplants that have spent their summer vacation lounging on the porch, patio, or deck. But a sudden change in temperature, light, or humidity can wreak havoc on your prized collection. To ease their transition back inside, give them a little TLC. Here's how:

Step 1: Take a look around the house for just the right spot to keep your plants comfortable this winter. Remember, a temperature range of 68° to 72°F is the perfect comfort zone for most houseplants (not to mention you and your pets, too).

Step 2: Steep a used tea bag in a quart of room-temperature water. Add 1 teaspoon of liquid dish soap or my Plant Shampoo and ½ teaspoon of ammonia, and pour the mix into a mist sprayer. Then give your plants a good once-over. Spray the whole plant—leaves and stalk—and the soil. Don't rinse.

The tannic acid in the tea helps plants manufacture more sugar and starch. The soap opens up leaf pores, which get clogged with dirt and dust, so the plants breathe better. The ammonia is a quick nitrogen boost.

Step 3: After you've given your plants their cleansing shower, put them on a balanced diet according to their "gender." (See "The Gender Gap," above.) Feed "girl" plants with low-nitrogen food and "boy" plants with high-nitrogen food. Be sure to follow the directions on the label when mixing the plant food.

MIXERS & ELIXIRS

Winter Wash

Give your winter-weary houseplants a misting with this formula twice a week to keep them looking moist and refreshed:

3 tsp. of baby shampoo
3 tsp. of ammonia
1 tsp. of antiseptic mouthwash
1 qt. of room-temperature water

Mix all of the ingredients together and apply to your plants with a hand-held mist sprayer.

THE HEAT IS ON

Houseplants are seriously affected by the humidity level in your home. So in the winter, when the heat is on, be sure to mist-spray leaf plants at least every other day in the early morning. Use weak tea water: Soak a used tea bag in a gallon of water plus 1 teaspoon of liquid dish soap until the mix is light brown. Follow this schedule in summer if your home dries out because of air conditioning.

I Smell Something Fishy

Here's a green-thumb tip: When you change the water in your fish bowl or aquarium, save the old water and feed it to your potted plants. The fish have already added the best natural fertilizer money can buy!

PEST PATROL

Mothball Magic

If your houseplants have been summering outdoors, there's a good chance they've picked up a few unwanted hangers-on. You don't want these pests taking up residence in your house, so give bugs the brush-off by placing a mothball on the soil of each houseplant one month before you bring them inside.

INSULATE YOUR PLANTS

If you have indoor plants that you keep on windowsills, you should move them on winter nights to protect them from the cold. If your plants are large or difficult to move, you can keep them in place—simply slip a section of newspaper between them and the window for extra protection from the cold.

NO-DRIP DRINKS

How many times have you given your thirsty hanging plants a drink only to have water rain down on your head (or carpet)? Well, say goodbye to drippy plants, with a secret the experts use—ice. You read right—ice, as in cubes. Simply place a few ice cubes on the soil of each hanging plant. The cubes will slowly melt right into the soil—no fuss, no muss!

PUT IT ON AUTO-PILOT

You can buy automatic watering pots that have a wick that hangs down into a reservoir of water. The wick brings the water to the soil, keeping it continually moist. This watering method is an excellent choice for many plants, especially African violets. It's also great for when you're starting seed in flats.

DON'T DROWN YOUR PLANTS WITH LOVE!

If you turn your flowerpots into miniature swamps, your houseplants will drown. When the cavities between the soil particles are filled with water instead of oxygen for long periods of time, the roots of your plants become oxygen starved and eventually decay. When this happens, you'll become painfully aware that your pampered plants are in serious trouble.

Here are a few hints to help you avoid houseplant tragedies:

🍂 Water your plants with "All-Purpose Houseplant Tonic" (at right).

🍂 Check your plants every day. Never allow them to wilt.

🍂 When watering is necessary, do so thoroughly, then allow all the excess water to drain away. The best time to water is in early morning.

🍂 If daily watering doesn't seem to be sufficient, you may need to repot the plant, leaving a depression in the top for water to collect in.

🍂 If the air in your house is very dry, try some of the secrets I recommend in "Pitch a Tent" on page 104.

🍂 Slow-growing plants, like mother-in-law's tongue and Christmas cactus, need far less water than rapid-growing plants, like ferns, fuchsias, begonias, and palms. Geraniums are happy with one good soaking a week.

🍂 One of the best investments you can make is inexpensive—a sprayer, which can be used for watering fragile plants or misting pest-control formulas. Most plants enjoy an occasional light spray, as well.

MIXERS & ELIXIRS

All-Purpose Houseplant Tonic

2 tbsp. of whiskey
1 tbsp. of hydrogen peroxide
1 tbsp. of Fish Fertilizer+
¼ tsp. of instant tea granules
½ tsp. of unflavored gelatin
½ tsp. of liquid dish soap
½ tsp. of ammonia
½ tsp. of corn syrup
1 gal. of warm water

Mix all of the ingredients together, and use this tonic instead of plain water when you water all of your houseplants.

CATCH THE RAIN

Always provide a catch basin around your newly transplanted trees, shrubs, and evergreens. Since the main requirement of any new transplant is sufficient water, it is important to build a saucer around the base of each plant to catch and retain water, especially rainwater.

Don't hill the soil around the base of a plant except in the fall, when you want the excess water to drain away.

DRENCH YOUR TREES

Newly planted trees need plenty of water so they can absorb the soil nutrients they need to get established and grow. A light sprinkling won't do the trick—you must drench the soil at least as deeply as the tree's lowest root tip. Once a week is none too often during a dry spell, and you should put on about twice as much water as you think is needed. Few trees have been hurt by overwatering through their first summer, but a whole lot have died because of underwatering!

SOCK IT TO 'EM

Here's a secret I learned long ago from my Grandma Putt, who never let anything go to waste. When your vegetable garden needs a drink, water it with the help of old socks. Put one sock inside the other, and use a short length of wire or a rubber band to attach the sock to the end of your garden hose. Now you've got a great soaker to lay over the mulch. Water for about an hour each day, three times a week.

Jerry's Secrets

The best way to water a tree is with a soaker hose laid on the ground in a circle out at the tree's weep line (at the tips of the farthest-reaching branches).

Flood Your Peppers

Take a tip from the pros—to get the hottest hot peppers in town, you need a flood. Flooding pepper plants with water shortly before harvest stresses the plants' roots, which then send out a signal to "turn up the heat." Your peppers will definitely be hotter, so be sure to save some water—for yourself!

SQUELCH SUMMER'S SIZZLE

When summer's heat is at its worst, every little drop of water counts. So be sure to water your garden in the early morning—between 5:00 A.M. and 9:00 A.M.—to minimize evaporation and give plants a chance to digest and dry off before nightfall. Use a soaker or an open-end hose with two layers of old socks tied onto the end, at least three times a week.

Water, M.D.

To get the most from your watering equipment, keep sprinkler heads clean so you get uniform water distribution. And check the washers in your hoses and outdoor faucets once a year, replacing them when necessary. Leaks make waste.

SUMMER SOOTHERS

When summer turns sweltering, we can run to the shelter of an air-conditioned house or spend the day at an air-conditioned mall. But what about our garden friends? They can't just get up and go! Any help you can give your trees, shrubs, and garden during the hot spells will be rewarded with abundant, healthy growth. One of the most important things you can do is keep them well watered. Here's how:

❦ Wrap tree trunks to prevent them from getting sun scorched. Mulch around trees with wood chips, straw, or grass to retain soil moisture.

❦ Mulch evergreens with shredded bark. Water them at midday with a sock tied over the end of the hose. (See "Sock It to 'Em," on the opposite page.)

❦ Recycle bath or dish water by using it on trees, shrubs, groundcovers, and flowers.

❦ Keep your flower garden soil mulched with grass clippings to retain moisture.

❦ Water your vegetable garden three times a week for a half hour each time with a soaker hose. If the weather is unbearably hot, rig up a lean-to with poles and cloth so you have a drop wall and roof to provide shade. Put this on the west end of your garden to block the intense sun.

PEST PATROL

Lethal Weapon

3 tbsp. of garlic-and-onion juice*
2 tbsp. of baby shampoo
2 tbsp. of skim milk
1 tsp. of Tabasco sauce
1 gal. of water

Mix all of the ingredients together in a 20 gallon hose-end sprayer, and spray on your vegetable garden every ten days to keep insects away.

* To make this juice, chop 2 cloves of garlic and 2 medium onions. Blend in a blender with 3 cups of warm water. Strain and use remaining liquid.

Chow Time

Could you live on a diet of water and nothing else? Of course not, so don't expect your plants to, either! Give them the nutrients they need to grow their best, and you won't be disappointed. You don't need a horticultural degree to help your plants thrive. Read on for my nutritional advice and feeding secrets that will keep your plants in the green of health.

THE HOWS AND WHYS OF MY TONICS

As you read through this book, you're going to come across dozens and dozens of my tonic recipes for everything from pest and critter controls to plant food to yard cleansers. You'll notice that many, if not most, of my tonics contain common household ingredients. I'm often asked just what makes these ingredients so effective. Here's a quick rundown for future reference:

Ammonia: a mild, immediately available source of nitrogen that helps to encourage leafy plant growth.

Beer: an enzyme activator that helps to release nutrients that are locked in the soil, plus it starts organic activity.

Molasses: a source of sugar that stimulates chlorophyll formation in plants.

Seaweed: contains a natural hormone that stimulates and increases plant growth.

Soap: softens soil and, when used on foliage, removes dust, dirt, and pollution so that osmosis and photosynthesis can more easily occur.

Tea: contains tannic acid, which helps plants digest their food faster.

DAILY DRINK— EVERYTHING BUT THE KITCHEN SINK

Give your garden this fortified daily drink and watch your plants grow to new heights. Take any combination of organic-based plant foods—like fish emulsion, table scraps (no meats or fats), potato peelings, and all other vegetable wastes—and put them in your blender. Fill with water and add a pinch of baking powder. Blend it all up, and feed it to your garden as often as you like.

DECIPHERING THE LABEL

Just what do those numbers on a fertilizer label mean? They're not the odds on your lawn living or dying! They simply indicate the percentages of nitrogen, phosphorus, and potash in the mix. For example, if the label says 5-10-5, that means the fertilizer has 5 parts nitrogen to 10 parts phosphorus to 5 parts potash. These nutrients are important for your plants because:

Nitrogen promotes vigorous plant growth, increases leaf yields, helps in chlorophyll formation, and is a building block for protein.

Phosphate hastens plant maturity, promotes cell division, stimulates healthy root formation, and plays an important part in other vital plant processes.

Potash is essential for photosynthesis, strengthens plant tissues, promotes fruit formation, and provides both disease resistance and winter hardiness.

NITROGEN ON THE SIDE

Most vegetables benefit from what we professionals call a side-dressing of nitrogen fertilizer, especially if they are not growing well or if they do not have a healthy, dark green color.

To side-dress a plant, simply scatter fertilizer on both sides of the row, several inches from the plants, and cultivate it in. Avoid getting fertilizer on plant leaves—it will burn them. Never side-dress when plants are wet, and don't apply soluble nitrogen in fall or winter, when rains will leach it out.

Apply side-dressing to leafy vegetables after the plants are up and well on their way. Apply to corn when it is 12 to 15 inches tall. Apply to tomatoes after the first fruits have set.

Annuals Eat Plenty

Lively annuals burn up a great deal of energy by constant flowering, so they need to eat heartily to keep it up. Try hand-spreading garden food once every three weeks, with a side order of my Fish Fertilizer+ in between to keep them in tiptop blooming condition.

MIXERS & ELIXIRS

Potted Plant Picnic

Here's a meal your potted plants will enjoy:

2 tbsp. of brewed black coffee
2 tbsp. of whiskey
½ tsp. of unflavored gelatin
½ tsp. of baby shampoo
½ tsp. of ammonia
1 tsp. of Fish Fertilizer+
1 gal. of water

Mix all of the ingredients together, and feed to all of your potted plants on a weekly basis.

LONG-LIFE LILIES

The secret to keeping your lilies strong and healthy is to feed them two or three times during the growing season. Scatter a handful of balanced fertilizer every few feet along with a pound of wood ashes every 20 square feet.

If your soil and water are alkaline, then scatter a pinch or two of agricultural sulphur over the soil, and water it in two or three times during the growing season.

Use peat moss as a mulch. It is slightly acidic, which is good for lilies, and it provides an ideal medium for the stem roots.

DIAGNOSING DEFICIENCIES

When plants are lacking in nutrients, their leaves usually tell the story. Here's a rundown of common foliage symptoms, the deficiencies that cause them, and what you can do to make things better:

Common Plant Problems

FOLIAGE SYMPTOMS	DEFICIENCY	REMEDIES
Paling to yellow of entire leaf surface; severe dwarfing or stunting soon follows.	Nitrogen (N)	**For houseplants:** 1 ounce of ammonium sulphate in 2 gallons of water. Use once a week for regular watering. Use my Fish Fertilizer+ for foliage plants. **In the garden:** Use primarily in spring when active growth begins on all woody caned plants. On vegetables and flowers, use before planting and as needed.
Margins of leaves turn yellow; tips and edges turn brown and dry; sometimes there is a purplish cast. Leaves fall.	Phosphorus (P)	**For houseplants:** 1 cup of bonemeal per bushel of potting soil, or 1 tablespoon of my SGH-15+ per quart of water around base of plant. **In the garden:** Apply my SGH-15+ in spring as a starter for bareroot plantings. Also use it to correct any deficiency noted during the previous summer.

FOLIAGE SYMPTOMS	DEFICIENCY	REMEDIES
Leaves spotted or mottled yellow; yellowing at edges; margins browning. Purplish along veins into entire leaf.	Potash (K)	**For houseplants:** 1 tablespoon of potassium sulphate scattered on soil around the plants, watered in. **In the garden:** Muriate of potash or potassium sulphate applied in spring. Apply wood ashes at the rate of 50 pounds per 30 × 50-foot area.
Leaf tissue from base outward darkens and dies due to the death of feeder roots.	Calcium (Ca)	**For houseplants:** 1/2 cup of dolomitic lime per quart of water per plant. **In the garden:** Dust soil with builder's lime; use dolomitic lime where magnesium is needed.
Leaves turn yellow between veins; veins remain green or faintly yellow.	Iron (Fe)	**For houseplants and in the garden:** 1 tablespoon of my Liquid Iron or chelated iron per quart of water per plant.
Yellowing or reddening of leaf centers. Dead spots appear between the veins.	Magnesium (Mg)	**For houseplants and in the garden:** 1 tablespoon of Epsom salts in enough water to dissolve per plant.
Top leaves yellow in centers, between the veins; no reddening.	Manganese (Mn)	**For houseplants and in the garden:** 1/2 tablespoon of manganese sulphate per quart of water per plant.
Leaves on top are thick and brittle; terminal buds die.	Boron (B)	**For houseplants and in the garden:** 1/4 tablespoon of borax or boracic acid per quart of water per plant.
Leaf veins lighter in color than the tissue in between.	Sulphur (S)	**For houseplants:** Sulphur dust as used for fungicide, worked into the soil. **In the garden:** Use agricultural sulphur per package directions.

PUT ROSES ON A LATE-SUMMER DIET

Never feed roses after August 15 in an area where temperatures drop below 20°F in winter. If you do, your roses will produce new growth, which won't have sufficient time to mature before winter sets in.

You should, however, apply a mixture of 1 cup of bonemeal and ½ cup of Epsom salts around the base of each bush before mulching and covering it for the winter. This is like packing your roses an organic breakfast to wake up to in spring.

MIXERS & ELIXIRS

Flower Feeder

1 cup of beer
2 tbsp. of Fish Fertilizer+
2 tbsp. of liquid dish soap
2 tbsp. of ammonia
2 tbsp. of hydrogen peroxide
2 tbsp. of whiskey
1 tbsp. of clear corn syrup
1 tbsp. of unflavored gelatin
4 tsp. of instant tea granules
2 gal. of warm water

Mix all of the ingredients together. Feed all of the flowers in your garden and yard with the mix every two weeks in the morning.

Banana Boost

Energize your tired old roses by feeding them rotten bananas. Just work the bananas, skin and all, into the soil around the base of the bushes. The potassium in the fruit and skin gives your roses a power-packed boost.

CAN IT!

Here's a timesaving tip: You can feed and water roses at the same time by using an empty 10-ounce frozen juice can. Cut the ends off of the can and push it all the way into the ground between two rose bushes. Then fill the can about halfway with pea-size pebbles. Once a month during the growing season, add a small amount of rose food to the can. Pour water directly into the can every time you water your rose bushes for no-fuss, deep penetration feeding.

SNACK ATTACK FOR BULBS

Do what professional growers swear by—give your bulbs a light snack in early spring. Once you see their noses sticking out of the soil, spread half a handful of garden food (4-12-4 or 5-10-5 formulation) over the soil.

KEEP 'EM PERENNIALLY FED

Perennials' extensive growing periods rob the soil of its natural fertility, so you must feed them regularly. Don't fertilize perennials heavily with inorganic fertilizers. Instead, feed them lightly to provide a continuous supply of nutrients, and you'll have plants that are easier to train or support on stakes. In addition, they won't have foliage so dense that it interferes with air circulation and moisture evaporation from the leaves.

If your soil has lots of organic nutrients like peat moss or compost in it, use a 5-10-5 fertilizer. Put little rings of fertilizer around each plant out at the tips of the farthest branches.

If your soil doesn't have a lot of organic matter, feed with my Fish Fertilizer+ or another natural organic fertilizer.

ANEMICS ANONYMOUS

Do your plants have iron-poor sap? Are they 98-pound weaklings? Yellowing leaves may indicate an iron deficiency. But don't panic. All you need to do is add an iron supplement, like a rusty nail, to the soil at the base of each plant once a year in early summer.

Trees, shrubs, and evergreens can suffer from anemia, too. Spray the foliage of azaleas, evergreens, and Southern foliage plants with "Iron Rx," at right.

Lawns can be sprayed or spread with liquid or dry iron and magnesium sulphate (Epsom salts), mixed in with your dry lawn food. No matter what form of iron is used, apply Epsom salts, too, to keep the greening action going.

Iron Rx

For those plants that look a little pale around the edges, try using this iron-rich tonic:

1 cup of hydrated lime
1 cup of Liquid Iron
1 cup of baby shampoo

Mix all of the ingredients together in a 20 gallon hose-end sprayer, and overspray your plants to the point of runoff.

DON'T LET PLANTS PIG OUT!

Plants can overeat, just like we can! So be sure to mix and apply my tonics at the recommended rate, and if you use commercial plant food, always apply it per the directions on the label.

HOOKED ON COFFEE

Azaleas, citrus plants, gardenias, and rhododendrons all need acidic plant food. While you can go out and buy it, there is a better way. Sprinkle three cups of used coffee grounds around the base of each plant, and that'll build up the acidity in the surrounding soil.

FERTILIZER FOR ALL

I'm often asked if there is any one fertilizer that's good for all flowers. The answer is yes—any garden food that's low in nitrogen and high in potash and phosphorus will do the trick. For bulbs and perennials, add some bonemeal to the soil. During the growing season you can add liquefied table scraps (but not meats or fats) to your flowerbeds, as well.

FEED PLANTS A BALANCED DIET

To avoid harming potted plants by overfeeding them, I only add 10 percent of the recommended amount of any plant food to the water each and every time I water. This way, my plants can eat a balanced diet at regular intervals, and I don't have to worry about overfeeding them.

To give your plants a boost, feed them the "Vitamin B_1 Booster Shot," at left.

MIXERS & ELIXIRS

Vitamin B_1 Booster Shot

1 Vitamin B_1 tablet
1 cup of hot water
2 tbsp. of hydrogen
2 tbsp. of whiskey
½ tbsp. of unflavored gelatin
1 gal. of water

Dissolve the B_1 tablet in the hot water. Then mix all the ingredients in the gallon of water, and feed your potted plants every time you water.

A Nice Warm Drink

Plants don't appreciate a cold drink, even in summer. So always mix your plant food with very warm water— plants will take it up faster.

HOT MEALS

Flowers and veggies don't need food just when they're young seedlings. After all, you wouldn't stop feeding your kids once they hit toddlerhood, would you? I didn't think so. Keep feeding your plants right through the summer months to keep 'em happy and healthy.

Flowers: Feed every two weeks with my Fish Fertilizer+ at half of the recommended rate, mixed with a cup of beer and a tablespoon of liquid dish soap per gallon of water.

Vegetables: Feed every three weeks with "Veggie Vitalizer," at right.

Know Your Nitrogen Needs

Flowering plants and plants with colorful foliage need plant foods that are low in nitrogen, while foliage plants need foods that are higher in nitrogen. So be sure to look at the nitrogen content (the first number in the sequence) in the plant foods you buy.

MIXERS & ELIXIRS

Veggie Vitalizer

½ can of beer
¼ cup of pepper/onion/ mint juice*
3 tbsp. of Fish Fertilizer+
2 tbsp. of liquid dish soap

Mix all of the ingredients in a 20 gallon hose-end sprayer, and apply liberally to your vegetable garden every three weeks.

* To make this juice, finely mince 1 onion, 1 green pepper, and 2 tablespoons of mint leaves. Add to 1 quart of hot water, and blend in a blender. Strain and use the remaining liquid.

KEEP FERNS FEISTY

A dose of castor oil does the trick. Just add 1 tablespoon of castor oil and 1 tablespoon of baby shampoo to a quart of warm water. Give each fern ¼ cup of the mix to keep them healthy.

GET YOUR POTTED PLANTS PLASTERED

Candy is dandy, but liquor is quicker, especially for your potted plants. Add a can of beer or a shot of bourbon, scotch, vodka, or gin to a gallon of room-temperature water. Add 1 ounce of liquid dish soap, and let it sit for half a day or so. Then add your favorite plant food, and water your potted plants with this boozy treat. The yeast in the alcohol seems to rejuvenate the old soil in the pot. Your plants will…hiccup…thank you!

FIDO CAN'T BE WRONG

Here's a little secret I discovered years ago—believe it or not, dried dog food contains many of the same nutrients found in organic fertilizers such as bloodmeal and bonemeal! So grab a handful and work it into the soil for an added energy boost when planting, or sprinkle it around growing plants.

A MATCH MADE IN HEAVEN

If you're like me, over the years you've collected dozens and dozens (maybe even hundreds and hundreds) of matchbooks from restaurants and hotels all across America. Well, now you can put them to good use with this gardening secret.

Take a pair of scissors and cut off all of the match heads. Sprinkle them on your garden soil before you spade or till it. Or you can drop three or four match heads in the bottom of each planting hole before planting your garden vegetables.

Why bother? The sulphur in the match heads is the key. It:

✎ releases elements that are locked in the soil;

✎ gives plants the sulphur they need in their diets;

✎ kills a multitude of insects;

✎ and gets those darned matchbooks out of your cupboard!

Jerry's Secrets

In my opinion, good old-fashioned manure is still the best all-around fertilizer. If you don't have the time to wait four to six months for it to break down in the soil, you can always buy ready-to-use dried manure at your local garden center.

A SPOT OF TEA, IF YOU PLEASE

Give your acid-loving plants, such as azaleas, rhododendrons, and blueberries, a midsummer pick-me-up by placing leftover tea bags on the soil underneath each plant. The tannic acid in the tea will make the soil slightly acidic, which these plants just love.

Dust Does 'Em In

Keep thugs away from your garden by sprinkling a light layer of diatomaceous earth around the bases of your plants and on their foliage. This sharp dust/powder scratches soft-bodied insects and slugs, causing them to dehydrate and die.

HUNGRY, HUNGRY HOUSEPLANTS

Because plants can ingest and digest only small amounts of food at one time, every time you water your plants, you should be feeding them, too.

To satisfy your houseplants' hunger, add 10 drops of any liquid dish soap per quart of water (or 2 tablespoons per gallon; 1 cup for each 10 gallons). Then water your plants before fertilizing them. The soap allows the fertilizer to better penetrate the soil and plant roots.

If the ends of the leaves suddenly turn brown, eliminate the fertilizer and only use the soapy water solution.

Timely Fruit Feeding

The best time to feed your fruit trees is in March and April if you have light soil. If you have heavy soil, feed them in November and December, when the soil is still frozen. Snow and rain will carry the food down through the cracks in the soil, and the food will be waiting there when the trees awaken in spring.

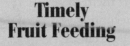

TOMATO NO-NOs

Don't use high-nitrogen fertilizer like chicken manure on your tomato plants. And don't use lawn fertilizer on them, either. High levels of nitrogen encourage foliage growth at the expense of flowers and fruit. So it'll be all show, and no tomato!

DON'T RISK YOUR GARDEN

I have seen many super-looking gardens die in a matter of days because one plant got sick and, instead of removing it, the gardener thought he or she could save it. Instead, it infected all the other plants, and they were soon "toast," as we say.

Unless you're an expert, don't take a chance if your ailing plant doesn't respond to food or water, and you can't see any bugs. Pull it out and burn it. Don't risk your whole garden for the sake of one plant.

MIXERS & ELIXIRS

Transplant Treat

When you transplant your houseplants into new pots, ease the transition by feeding them this terrific treat:

2 tbsp. of whiskey
1 tbsp. of unflavored gelatin
1 tbsp. of baby shampoo
2 tsp. of instant tea granules
½ tbsp. of ammonia
1 tsp. of Fish Fertilizer+
2 gal. of water

Mix all of the ingredients together, and use it to make your new transplants feel right at home.

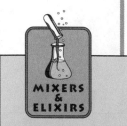

MIXERS & ELIXIRS

Shrub Grub

25 lbs. of garden food
1 lb. of granulated sugar
½ lb. of Epsom salts

Each spring, work this mix into the soil around your shrubs. Then mix the following ingredients in a 20 gallon hose-end sprayer, and overspray your newly fed shrubs:

1 can of beer
½ cup of liquid lawn food
½ cup of liquid dish soap
½ cup of ammonia
½ cup of regular cola (not diet)

PARCHED PALMS

Palms are some of my favorite plants (particularly now that I'm down in Florida), and they're also popular with plenty of gardeners across the country. Unfortunately, in summer, cabbage palms, windmill palms, and European fans tend to look a little washed-out and pale.

Here's the secret to bringing relief to parched palms. The first thing you should do is not allow them to get dry, especially if they are young plants. Second, give them a dose of magnesium by making a cocktail of two or three handfuls of Epsom salts mixed with enough water to make the salts dissolve. Then sprinkle it around the palms.

You can also mix the Epsom salts with an equal amount of manganese and dissolve this mixture in water. Both elements work well together by aiding in the plants' manufacture of chlorophyll. That's all there is to it!

EVERGREEN ROUTINE

Feed evergreens with a dry mix of natural organic garden food in early spring as growth begins, but no later than June 10. For best results, use an acid-type food specially formulated for evergreens.

The second year, add 4 inches of organic mulch to help keep the soil moisture adequate all year long.

EVERGREENS LOVE LAWN FOOD

Food that's good for your lawn is also good for your evergreens—except, of course, those lawn blends that contain weed killers like my Weed & Feed. To help you keep track of your feeding timetable, write this in your garden calendar in the first week of February, April, and June: "Feed evergreens."

Feed them with dry lawn food at the rate of ¼ cup per foot of tree height. Sprinkle the food on top of the mulch out at the weep line, which is at the tips of the farthest branches.

NEW ARRIVALS NEEDN'T EAT

Don't feed newly planted shrubs and evergreens right away. Let them get used to the soil in their new homes for a couple of weeks, and then give them a light snack of the "Evergreen Wake-Up" tonic, at right. Then feed them again a month later with a low-nitrogen, dry garden food (like 4-12-4 or 5-10-5) to stimulate root growth.

In the meantime, cover up the roots with a mulch of wood chips about 2 inches deep, all the way out to the ends of the bottom branches.

Last Call for Evergreens

• • • • • • • • • • • • • • • •

Never feed evergreens after August 15 if you live in snow country (they won't have time to digest it properly). If you live in the warmer regions, you can feed them in August and then again in October.

• • • • • • • • • • • • • • • •

CRISSCROSS FEEDING

Use my Grandma Putt's crisscross method to fertilize your lawn. Apply dry fertilizers at half the recommended rate, going back and forth from one side of your lawn to the other. Then apply the second half a week later by going back and forth from the top to the bottom of the lawn. That way, you'll avoid those embarrassing light green lines in the areas you miss the first time.

GIVE YOUR LAWN A FINAL FALL FAREWELL

 It's absolutely vital to give your lawn a good feeding before it goes dormant. A fall lawn uses the elements in the fertilizer to create and store food in its root system for the winter. So feeding a fall lawn means that your lawn will go to bed with a good supply of nutrients for best health and a great start for next year.

Your final feeding must be with a dry fertilizer, adding 4 pounds of Epsom salts to each 50-pound bag of fertilizer. Apply this mixture at half the recommended rate with your broadcast spreader set on the medium setting.

MIXERS & ELIXIRS

Evergreen Wake-Up

This elixir perks up shrubs and evergreens the same way a cup of coffee perks up you and me. Feed it to your greenery every three weeks, early in the morning, throughout the growing season.

1 can of beer
1 cup of baby shampoo
1 cup of liquid lawn food
½ cup of molasses
2 tbsp. of Fish Fertilizer+

Mix all of the ingredients together in a 20 gallon hose-end sprayer, and apply liberally to your shrubs and evergreens.

PEST PATROL

Garden Allies

Birds, toads, lady-bugs, garter snakes—they all can help you win the war on bugs. So do what you can to encourage them to visit your yard. These bug-hungry allies are worth their weight in gold when cutting down the local pest population.

FEED YOUR GRASS

The secret to effective lawn feeding is to water it the day before you apply any lawn fertilizer to it. Then apply the fertilizer before noon, and water lightly after application. This allows the grass to begin to digest the fertilizer soon after it has been applied.

Here are some of my other lawn-feeding tips:

Lawns need dry lawn food first thing in spring. A good formula is 4 pounds of Epsom salts with any 50-pound bag (or enough to cover 2,500 square feet) of your favorite lawn food. Apply at half the recommended rate with a broadcast spreader set on the medium setting. This should cover 5,000 square feet of lawn.

Use Lime Wisely

Contrary to popular belief, lime is not lawn food! It is a soil amendment (sweetener) that changes the acidity of the soil. It should be used only after a soil test indicates that your soil is sour.

In early spring, apply liquid lawn food every three weeks as a supplemental feeding, not as the primary food source.

Starting in May, you can use liquid lawn food as the primary food source. In addition to this food, overspray your lawn once a month with the following mixture: 1 can of beer, 1 cup of liquid dish soap, and 1/2 cup of molasses. Mix in a 20 gallon hose-end sprayer, filling the balance of the sprayer jar with ammonia.

STAY AWAY FROM A LIQUID DIET

Feeding your lawn with liquids at the same time you water is not a good idea. All too often, this causes overfeeding, and then the lawn burns. To avoid damaging your lawn, first water it, then apply liquid fertilizer with a hose-end sprayer. I consider this a light daily sprinkling, and it should be done *after* you've watered the lawn.

As for using automatic feeders, in a word, don't. They are definitely not for use by the average home gardener. Stick with hand feeding instead.

Take My Weeds, *Please!*

Whether you're growing flowers, fruits, or vegetables—or all three—you will, without a doubt, be dueling with weeds from the get-go. Your plants don't like to compete with weeds for the soil nutrients they need in order to produce strong foliage, healthy fruits, and fabulous flowers, so it's your job to see that they have no competition.

You can knock out weeds by hand with a hoe or other tool, or you can wage chemical warfare with pre-emergent weed killers. Whichever method you choose, the key to success in the battle against weeds is to get an early start.

BE THE GRIM REAPER

If you can't pull out all of the weeds in your vegetable patch, at least make an effort to do the next best thing—keep them from going to seed. Many weeds form seedheads that disperse over a wide area, and your problems will then multiply in successive years. So before weeds have the chance to develop their seedheads, use a grass whip or scythe to cut them down. You'll be glad you did!

Jerry's Secrets

Kill weeds between 11:00 A.M. and 2:30 P.M. because that's when they are the most vulnerable.

Cultivate Consistently

Begin cultivating your garden as soon as weeds appear. Don't wait until they threaten to take it over. Repeat as weeds appear, but don't over-cultivate, especially during hot, dry spells, or you will cause the soil to lose moisture more rapidly.

HOE, HOE, HOE

Here's a secret from master gardeners: There is no better way to cultivate while controlling weeds than to use a sharp hoe between rows of flowers and vegetables. A hoe is also great for deep spading of compost, leaves, animal manures, and green manures into the soil, ensuring years of abundant harvest.

MY BAKER'S DOZEN: RULES FOR SPRAYING SUCCESS

When you're ready to haul out your sprayer (or purchase one), whether for feeding or for insect and disease control, follow my 12 sensible rules for spraying success:

1. Select the right sprayer for the job. Buy the best quality you can afford. It will make spraying easier and, with the proper care, your sprayer will last for years. Be sure to get one that gives you full control of the spray mix and application.

2. Before you spray, be sure to read all the directions. Read the warranty, too. "Test drive" your new sprayer using water to see how it works and what it will do.

3. Mix your spray ingredients exactly according to the instructions. Use old measuring spoons and cups to measure everything—don't eyeball it.

4. Choose the right pressure. Use high pressure for a fine, penetrating mist (good for flowers). Use lower pressure if you want a heavier, wetting, nondrift spray (best for weeds).

5. Spot spray, don't broadcast. Spray only to the point of runoff. Avoid drenching, and you'll avoid waste.

6. Spray only where the trouble is. Since most plant problems start under the leaves, it is especially important that you spray there. Cover the entire stem system, too. Spraying on target avoids waste in time and materials.

7. Use an adjustable nozzle. This produces a fine, cone-shaped mist for close-up applications, and a coarser spray for long-range spraying or for spraying weeds.

THE TOOL'S THE THING

There are many different kinds of hoes and hand-weeding tools on the market, so choose your weapons wisely. My favorites are the Warren hoe and the hand cultivator.

The Warren hoe has a pointed, triangular blade, which makes it easy to work between plants without injuring them.

A hand cultivator is simply a three-pronged claw.

SOAP SMOOTHS THE WAY

I can't say this often enough—giving your plants a
good washing before applying liquid fertilizers, weed
killers, or pest controls can mean the difference between a garden that is just getting by and one that is healthy
and growing. Why? Soap removes dust, dirt, and pollution from
foliage pores, enabling plants to better take up the good stuff
that follows. So before you apply fertilizers or controls, give
your garden a bath with 1 cup of liquid dish soap applied with
your 20 gallon hose-end sprayer, or use my Plant Shampoo.

**8. Spray in the cool part of
the day.** For maximum effec-
tiveness (not to mention less
wear and tear on you), spray
either early in the morning or
after dinner.

**9. Never spray on windy
days**. This ensures that the
spray goes where it's needed
and doesn't drift to nontarget
areas of your yard.

10. Dress sensibly. Don't
wear shorts or a bathing suit.
It's a good idea to wear gloves, a
hat, and goggles if you're spraying above your head or at eye
level. Wear shoes. I recommend
that you wear
your golf
spikes when-
ever you're
working in the
yard. That way,
you improve your
traction on uneven

ground and aerate your
lawn at the same time.

**11. Thoroughly drain your
sprayer when you are finished.**
Then clean it with a solution of
mild soap and warm water.
Wipe it dry. A little extra care
will make your equipment last
for many, many seasons, making
it an even better investment.

**12. Store all sprays, dusts,
and plant chemicals out of
reach of children and pets.** A
locked cabinet is the safest
place to keep harmful chemicals
away from curious kids and
prying pets. Keep store-bought
sprays in their original containers, and be sure the labels are
kept on. Label all of your
homemade sprays, as well. And
do not burn empty spray containers! Wash them out, wrap
them up, and put them in the
trash for proper disposal.

Jerry's
Secrets

**If you prefer to dust
plants rather than
spray them, apply
the dust early in the
morning or later in
the evening, when
the air is still and the
dew on the plants
will help the dust
stick better.**

Year 'Round Refresher

Use this elixir every three weeks from spring through fall all around your yard and garden. In warm climates, you can use it year 'round.

1 cup of beer
1 cup of baby shampoo
1 cup of liquid lawn food
½ cup of molasses
2 tbsp. of Fish Fertilizer+
Ammonia

Mix the beer, shampoo, lawn food, molasses, and Fish Fertilizer+ in a 20 gallon hose-end sprayer. Fill the balance of the jar with ammonia.

CULTIVATE WITH CARE

Always cultivate shallowly to avoid damaging plant roots. Keep in mind that when weeds grow very near plants, their roots become intertwined. So take care to avoid pulling out both the plants you love and the weeds you hate at the same time!

When you're using a hoe, make short, shallow, scraping motions instead of chopping deeply into the soil. And use a rake to get at persistent weeds, such as purslane.

BETTER BARRIERS

Tomatoes, cucumbers, squash, and vine crops can't compete with weeds. So keep them happy by keeping them weed-free. If you aren't going to use chemicals in your vegetable garden, then use a physical barrier between the ground and the plants to cut down on weeds.

Weed barrier fabric is black fabric that you place down before planting. After securing the sides and corners with stones, you cut Xs through the fabric and plant your seedlings.

Newspapers are my choice because, at the end of the season, I can spade the disintegrating papers into the soil for next year. Simply place several sheets of newspaper around your seedlings, then cover with a few inches of soil to hold the layers in place. Add some mothballs and diatomaceous earth to keep away bugs and slugs, then cover with mulch.

KEEP WEEDS IN THE DARK

It's true—weeds can't grow without light. So the next time you're planting seedlings, cover the soil with a single layer of black-and-white (not colored) newspaper, and then add 3 to 4 inches of fresh grass clippings on top of the paper.

Weeds won't emerge from the darkness, and the grass and paper maintain soil temperature and retain soil moisture so your seedlings can grow up big and strong without any competition from weeds.

Use this weed-control method not just for seedlings, but also around flowers, trees, shrubs, evergreens, and veggies.

CONTROL LAWN WEEDS

Lawn weed control is better done in the fall than at any other time of year. The secret is to make sure that the weed killer does its job as quickly as possible, before it gets diluted by rain.

Always start your weed control program by first spraying the area with "Lawn Lather" (see below). This soapy solution will open up the pores in the weeds' leaves and soften the soil around their roots, allowing the weed killer to work twice as fast and twice as well. Then apply any good broadleaf weed killer according to the manufacturer's directions on the package.

NATURAL DEFENSES

A thick, healthy lawn actually keeps weeds out—there is simply no room for them to "muscle in." So to avoid using weed killers on your lawn, feed it regularly, dethatch often, and dig out what few weeds you do have. You can also spot-kill weeds with 2 tablespoons of vinegar mixed into $3\frac{1}{4}$ cups of water.

HAND-TO-HAND COMBAT

When I find a stubborn weed growing very close to a bulb, I like to engage in a bit of hand-to-hand combat rather than breaking out my weeding tool. That way I don't have to worry about cutting up the bulb or its delicate roots.

Hand weeding is also the best way to clear weeds out of a naturalized planting where you don't want a lot of bare soil showing.

LAWN LATHER

Lawns benefit from a good soapy wash as much as your garden plants do. Give your lawn this soapy lather every two or three weeks through spring and summer. It softens the soil for improved water penetration and removes pollution from grass blades so osmosis can take place. It also does a number on toadstools!

The recipe is simple: Mix 1 cup of liquid dish soap and one cup of ammonia in your 20 gallon hose-end sprayer. Then get out there, and liberally apply it to all of your lawn areas.

PEST PATROL

Fruit and Flower Defender

1 cup of liquid dish soap
1 cup of chewing tobacco juice*
1 cup of antiseptic mouthwash
¼ cup of Tabasco sauce
Warm water

Mix all of the ingredients together in a 20 gallon hose-end sprayer, filling the balance of the jar with warm water. Bathe all of your early bloomers with this super bug-buster in spring.

*Take three fingers of chewing tobacco from the package, place it into the toe of a nylon stocking, and place the stocking in a gallon of hot water. Steep until the water is dark brown.

MULCH AWAY WEEDS

I find that it is seldom necessary for me to use weed killers in my garden as long as I have an adequate amount of mulch down to protect the soil. Grass, leaves, shredded bark, peanut or cocoa shells, wood chips, and straw all fit the bill. Then all I need to do is pull or dig out the occasional weed.

This technique is known to gardening professionals as sheet composting—instead of piling up refuse in a compost heap, waiting for it to decompose, then hauling it back to the garden, I spread organic mulch over the garden, and allow it to decompose there.

If you want to give this technique a try, start by spreading a good, thick layer of mulch in your garden. As it decomposes into humus, replenish it with new materials to prevent weed seeds from sprouting in the rotted mulch.

Supplement straw, manure, and other basic mulching materials with kitchen vegetable refuse and anything else you would normally throw on a compost heap.

When you're ready to plant, just rake away the mulch from the row areas, make a furrow, and drop in seeds or set in seedlings. Firm the soil around newly planted seedlings, but don't rake the mulch back around them until the plants are well established.

Cover seeds with a light layer of soil, then strips of cardboard. Rake the mulch back up to the edges of the row. As soon as your seedlings sprout, remove the cardboard.

If you use this technique, you should be able to keep your garden practically weed-free year 'round.

Jerry's Secrets

Send weeds to a salty grave. Pour salt on weeds that are growing between stones, in driveways, and through cracks in patios and walkways. Just be sure to do this on a dry day, when there is no rain forecast, or the salt will wash away. In a day or two, the weeds will curl up and die from dehydration, and you can easily pull them out.

Spring into Weed Control

In early spring, when you're cleaning out your planting beds, make sure you remove all growing weeds. Then till up the soil, and put down a weed barrier fabric. When you're ready to plant your seedlings, simply cut holes in the fabric and plant them right through it.

MARIGOLDS TO THE RESCUE!

Studies have proven that the Mexican marigold (*Tagetes minuta*) actually fights weeds like ground elder, bindweed, and couchgrass. So if you're fighting these fellows, clear out the weeds as best you can, then sow marigold seeds in the area as a cover crop. They'll reach five feet or more in height—just be sure that you mow them down before they set seed.

Mexican marigolds also fight nematodes, parasitic worms that can do a number on your plants. Again, plant a cover crop and be sure to destroy it before it sets seed. In Georgia and Alabama, a cover crop of Mexican marigolds was found to reduce nematode populations in the soil.

Other marigold family members, such as African marigold (*T. erecta*) and French marigold (*T. patula*) have also been found to successfully fight nematodes in the soil. Simply plant these flowers among your crops or trees. You will see a substantial reduction in the nematode population.

CREATE A WEED-KILLER COCKTAIL

"How dry I am" is how the old song goes, and the weeds in your yard will be singing the blues when you hit 'em with this potent cocktail. Alcohol dehydrates almost any plant, so take advantage of its drying power and mix up a batch of this elixir, then watch those pesky weeds dry up right out of existence.

Simply put 2 tablespoons of rubbing alcohol into a handheld sprayer and thoroughly drench any unwanted plants with this mixture. A word of warning: This is a killer cocktail, so be sure not to get any of this mixture on surrounding plants or grass.

MIXERS & ELIXIRS

Wild Weed Wipeout

Zap those hard-to-kill weeds with this lethal weapon:

1 tbsp. of gin
1 tbsp. of apple cider vinegar
1 tsp. of liquid dish soap
1 qt. of very warm water

Mix all of the ingredients together in a bucket, then pour into a handheld sprayer to apply. Drench weeds to the point of runoff, taking care not to get any on the surrounding plants or grass.

DEALING WITH AQUATIC WEEDS

In the never-ending battle against aquatic weeds at lake- and shore-front properties, there are several battle plans available to you. Here's a quick rundown of your options:

Mechanical. Mechanical weed cutting is an immediate and effective short-term control. Long-term control, however, can only be achieved by cutting on a continual basis, which can be quite costly. Also, cut weeds must be removed as soon as possible to prevent fragments from re-establishing or spreading to other areas. You can tackle this job yourself by using small hand-operated equipment that is available from local rent-it centers.

Biological. Biological controls use plant-eating organisms and a variety of plant diseases to keep the weeds in check. The results with this method, however, are often slow and unpredictable.

Draw-down. Water draw-down, especially during winter months, can be effective on submersed weeds because the exposed plants die from drying out or freezing. This method does have its drawbacks, though, and care must be taken to prevent the destruction of fish and the wildlife habitat. Loss of recreational use may also occur. The other problem with this method is that marginal weeds may infest new areas and become a greater problem than the original infestation of submersed weeds.

Chemical. Chemical controls are currently the most commonly used, most effective, and most economical method of dealing with aquatic weeds. They last longer and are less costly than mechanical control. Chemicals can be applied to selected areas as opposed to the large areas that must be treated by other methods. Unfortunately, no single chemical is best for controlling all kinds of aquatic weeds. For best results, identify the weed first, and then consult a professional to assist you in selecting the proper product.

Jerry's Secrets

Control weeds with a 50-cent bag of peanuts. That's right! Just sprinkle a 4-inch layer of peanut shells as mulch around newly planted trees, shrubs, and evergreens, and you won't have to worry about weeds.

Jerry Tells All About...
Garden Care

Q. When do I fertilize strawberries, and what should I use?

A. After you're done picking for the year, wait until August, clean up the beds, and apply a 10-10-10 fertilizer at the rate of 2 cups per 100 square feet.

Out, Out Darned Spot!

Don't spray the "black spots" on delphiniums with a fungicide. These spots aren't a fungus—they're actually caused by mites, and are best controlled with Rotenone or nicotine spray, or by dusting them with fine sulphur.

Q. Is it OK to use horse manure in my flower garden?

A. Not unless it's a couple of years old. It's mean stuff if it's too young. Horse manure is full of weeds and humus foliage, and it can make plants too tall.

Q. I need help growing garlic. All I've gotten so far is small bulbs in the ground with tops like golf balls on the stems.

A. Dig a hole about a foot across and a foot deep, and fill it with ⅓ soil, ⅓ professional planting mix, and ⅓ builder's sand. Plant your garlic in it, and that should do the trick.

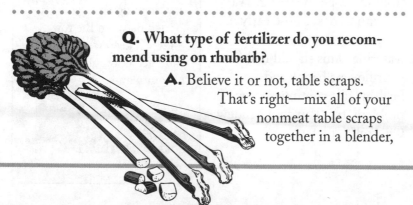

Q. What type of fertilizer do you recommend using on rhubarb?

A. Believe it or not, table scraps. That's right—mix all of your nonmeat table scraps together in a blender,

PEST PATROL

All-Purpose Bug/Thug Spray

To kill insects and diseases in one fell swoop, mix up a batch of my all-purpose spray.

3 tbsp. of baking soda
2 tbsp. of Murphy's Oil Soap
2 tbsp. of canola oil
2 tbsp. of vinegar
2 gal. of warm water

Mix all of the ingredients together, and mist spray your plants to the point of runoff. Apply in early spring, just as the bugs and thugs are waking up.

Powdery Mildew Control

4 tbsp. of baking soda
2 tbsp. of Murphy's
　Oil Soap
1 gal. of warm water

Mix all of the ingredients together, and apply with a handheld sprayer bottle when you see the telltale white spots on your plants.

add 2 tablespoons of Epsom salts, and purée. For fabulous results, pour this mixture on the plants every month or so.

Q. Please tell me how I can get rid of wild violets.

A. There's no secret to this one. Just mix 2 tablespoons of gin, 2 tablespoons of vinegar, and 2 tablespoons of baby shampoo in a quart of warm water, then zap 'em good!

Q. How often should I feed my flowers?

A. I feed mine a good, hearty meal in spring, and then during the season, I hand-sprinkle a light meal once a month.

Q. Is it necessary for me to add lime to my vegetable garden every year?

A. My general rule? It's not necessary unless the soil has become acidic. Don't ever use anything that isn't necessary.

Q. Why do my flowers look so dismal after I water them? Some even get a white powder on them.

A. The white stuff is powdery mildew, and it comes from improper watering. Water with a soaker hose early in the morning, and avoid top watering. This should make your flowers happy and healthy. If it continues to be a problem, try "Powdery Mildew Control" (at left).

Roll Out the Red Carpet!

Or any color carpet, for that matter! Cut your old carpeting and rugs into strips, and lay them down in your garden between the rows. They'll keep weeds down and act as a mulch around your plants.

Ward off Wilt

Don't let your plants wilt before you water them. If the soil is allowed to regularly dry out, the plant becomes dehydrated, resulting in leaf discoloration and stunted or lack of growth. Eventually, the plant will die. So check the soil daily, and provide adequate amounts of water.

Q. What causes tomatoes to turn gray or black on the top just before they ripen?

A. Blossom-end rot, which is the result of hot, humid weather—not enough water gets to the fruit. Well-mulched plants with a good irrigation program are seldom bothered. The best mulch is 6 inches of grass clippings. Put it down four weeks after you plant your tomatoes.

Q. How important is it to rotate crops in a small garden?

A. Because of the limited amount of soil—very important! I *always* recommend that crops be rotated regularly (with the exception of tomatoes, which can stay in one place for three years).

Q. My neighbor told me that I can use grass fertilizer to feed my cabbage plants. Is this true?

A. Yep, your neighbor is right. You can use lawn food for anything that grows above the ground, except for tomatoes.

Q. Is liquid cow manure good for tomatoes?

A. Only if the cows don't step on the tomatoes! Other good choices are fish fertilizer, liquid kelp, and any tomato food.

Coon Crunch

If raccoons are rummaging through your corn-fields, here's a simple way to keep them out: Take crumpled-up news-paper, and scatter it in and among your corn to keep the critters away. They can't stand to walk on it, so they'll beat a hasty retreat!

Q. How can I get a healthy, four-year-old trumpet vine to bloom? I've tried withholding water and beating the trunk with newspaper, but with no results. What can I do?

A. I want you to prune it back severely in fall, and then give it a pedicure—root prune all the way around the plant. Then sprinkle a mixture of 1/2 cup of Epsom salts and 1/2 cup of apple juice dissolved in 1 gallon of warm water into the cuts.

Q. I need your advice. I have four bigleaf hydrangea bushes. I had blooms the first year, but since then, I get big beautiful bushes, but no flowers. Please help.

A. It could be any of several problems—cold injury, improper pruning, or too much shade. Make sure that you mulch the plants well, prune them after they bloom, and/or prune the surrounding plants to let at least half a day's worth of sunlight in.

PEST PATROL

Super Spider Mite Mix

4 cups of wheat flour
1/2 cup of buttermilk
5 gal. of water

Mix all of the ingredients together, and apply to your plants with a hand-held mist sprayer. Spray to the point of runoff. This mix will suffocate the little buggers without harming your plants.

Can It!

If you don't have a large garden or yard to fertilize, there's no need to go to the expense of buying a spreader. Instead, punch holes in the bottom of a coffee can, fill with dry fertilizer, and shake, shake, shake your booty!

Q. I've heard that ladybugs are good for my garden. What do they do, and how can I attract them?

A. Ladybugs have voracious appetites; they can eat up to 40 aphids per hour! Other insects on their menu include mealybugs, spider mites, scale, thrips, and whiteflies. To attract ladybugs to your garden, plant marigolds, butterfly weed, yarrow, roses, or goldenrod. They're also kind of partial to cucumbers, peppers, and tomatoes.

Q. We have a lilac bush that is about a foot tall. It was doing great, but then I caught the neighbor's dog "doing his duty" on it. The bush turned brown, and lost its leaves. Can it be saved?

A. Possibly. First, apply pelletized gypsum all around the plant at the recommended rate. Then give it a good, thorough soaking with my Plant Shampoo. Two to three weeks later, apply a coat of Weather-Proof to the point of runoff. Finally, sprinkle some dog and cat repellent around the base of the plant to ward off any future sneak attacks by you-know-who.

Q. Which flowers are considered bug chasers?

A. The most common are marigolds, asters, nasturtiums, and mums.

Q. What exactly is bulb food, and is it necessary to use a special one?

A. Bulb food is usually ordinary garden food that has a liberal supply of bonemeal in it. And no, it's not necessary to use bulb food specifically, but you must feed your bulbs when they are blooming.

Q. What can I feed my peonies to keep them from flopping over and drooping?

A. It's not lack of food that makes peonies droop—their

Beat the Heat

Potted plants can take a beating when warm weather hits. But you can keep 'em comfy by placing each pot, plant and all, inside of a larger one. Then fill the space between the pots with peat moss. This will help keep the plants' roots moist and cool during hot weather.

Jerry's Secrets

Use grass clippings to mulch the soil around your sweet peas. This will keep the roots moist and prevent mildew from developing.

heads arc too heavy. You need to stake them up. The best way to do this is to tie them up with pieces of old panty hose.

Q. My roses were small and the leaves were yellow last season. What was wrong?

A. The plant was probably starving to death. You need to feed it every three weeks, up until August 15 in snow country.

Everything's Coming Up Roses

A mulch of peat, ground corncobs, spent hops, or well-rotted manure is great around your roses soon after growth starts. The mulch will maintain moisture and reduce weeds, giving your roses a bloomin' start.

Q. How often should I water my roses?

A. That depends on where you live and what the soil conditions are. In well-drained or sandy soil, water twice a week. In heavy soil, once a week should do it. In clay soil or extra-heavy soil, water very lightly once a week.

Q. I've got a problem—my lima beans get leggy and don't have many beans. What should I do?

A. Be sure you're planting them in a sunny, warm location with good drainage. Beans need very little food. And you must pick them just as quickly as they mature.

Q. How often should I feed my corn?

A. Never use garden food with newly planted seed, or it will rot. I use any lawn food to feed corn for the first time when it's a foot high, and then again when its beard, or silk, shows. There's no need to feed beyond that.

PEST PATROL

Act Fast!

Many plant pests—and diseases—spread very quickly. So be sure to spring into action at the first sign of trouble. This not only saves you time, effort, and material, but also results in better long-term control.

OLD-FASHIONED, FABULOUS FERTILIZERS

My Grandma Putt used everything she could find that had some nutritional value as fertilizer around her farm. Here's a sampling of a few of her old-time favorites:

Eggshells: Great for peppers and tomatoes; calcium is the main nutrient. Let crushed eggshells soak in water for 24 hours, then use it to water your plants.

Fish: Any and all fish parts, buried or composted. Native Americans used to "plant" fish right along with their crops to add nutrients to the soil.

Hair: Either animal or human, worked into the soil or the compost pile. It provides many nutrients including iron, manganese, and sulphur.

Mud: Pond mud or ditch scrapings were used as fertilizer because of the rich accumulation of nutrients. Some folks even used to drain their ponds every spring to grow crops in them!

Sawdust: This was generally composted with manure or vegetation. Today, it's still used as a good source of carbon, especially when it's mixed with fresh grass clippings.

Seaweed: A valuable fertilizer, but it also contains a large amount of salt, so dry it first by covering a pile of it with soil until the mixture gets a nice, soupy consistency.

Q. I want to grow my beets organically. What kind of plant food do you recommend?

A. Take your table scraps (not meat or bones), and put them in your blender. Add water to fill up the blender container, and liquefy the scraps. Pour this liquid onto your beets and the rest of your garden, and watch 'em grow!

Q. What does liquid seaweed do? Is there a substitute for it?

A. Liquid seaweed is a great natural fertilizer/soil conditioner that contains gibberellic acid and growth regulators, which make plants grow like crazy. One substitute is my Thatch Buster mixed with an equal amount of regular cola (not diet).

Q. Can you tell me what's the best feeding and watering routine for rhododendrons? I haven't had much luck with them in the past, but I want to try again.

A. Before the first of June each year, apply an acid-type fertilizer. A handful of cotton-seed meal is helpful, too. Work the fertilizer into the soil lightly with your fingertips. Never cultivate because the fine roots of these plants are right at the surface. Follow up immediately with a good drenching, then apply 2 to 3 inches of oak leaf or pine needle compost. All other times, water only when the foliage appears withery and fails to revive overnight. Use hard water sparingly; rainwater is best.

PEST PATROL

Cabbage Worm Wipe-Out

As your young cabbage plants develop heads, sprinkle a light coating of this mix on them:

1 cup of flour
2 tbsp. of cayenne
   pepper

Mix the ingredients together, and sprinkle them on your cabbage heads. The flour swells up inside the worms and bursts their insides, while the hot pepper keeps other critters away.

Don't Force the Issue

Most perennials grow slowly, and "forcing" them to grow bigger with high-nitrogen plant foods is not a good idea. Use a complete plant food that provides plenty of phosphorus and potash. Wood ashes and bonemeal are excellent sources.

Seeding Beats Weeding

Weeds are going to move in and overrun any bare ground they find, but you can beat them to it by filling the space with lots of cultivated plants. Then, when the weeds are up and growing, go back and thin your plants to the proper spacing. This is much more enjoyable and less tedious than hand weeding around a sparse stand of plants!

Q. Is liquid manure safe to use on mums?

A. Yes, it is. Apply it or fish fertilizer to mums just as the buds start to show color.

Q. Do you have any suggestions for feeding irises?

A. Yep. Mix 4 parts of bonemeal with 6 parts of hydrated lime, and sprinkle it around the plants. Work it into the ground when the soil is dry enough, and your irises will be off to a flying start!

Q. Should I water my garden plants every day?

A. Not unless you're growing in pure sand. Once or twice a week should be enough. The best time is in the morning, to give ample time for plants to dry before sundown. If plants are wet overnight, fungus troubles may develop.

Jerry's Secrets

Evergreens need water most in late fall, particularly after a dry summer. So be sure to thoroughly water them before the ground freezes.

Q. How much and how often should I spray my tomato plants to protect them from diseases and viruses?

A. If you mulch your tomato plants with a 6-inch layer of grass clippings and then wash them down every two weeks with my Plant Shampoo or "All-Season Clean-Up Tonic" (see "Green-Up and Clean-Up" on page 77), you should not have any problems with viruses.

Q. A former neighbor planted raspberry bushes too close to our lot line, and now the underground shoots are coming up on our side of the fence. How can we get rid of them?

A. Cut, chop, burn, and pray! Another option is to go with a chemical control—one of the systemic brush, weed, and grass killers like KleenUp. A third alternative is to drive a plastic or metal barrier 6 to 8 inches into the ground at the fence line, which will prevent anything from creeping into your yard.

Q. How can I keep whiteflies away from my plants?

A. First, cut 1-inch pine boards approximately 1 foot square, and paint them with a yellow-orange paint. After the paint dries, coat them with motor oil, mineral oil, or a commercial insect trapping compound. Suspend the boards by wires a few feet from your plants. When they're covered with pests, take them down, hose them off, and recoat them as necessary.

Q. Do you know of an inexpensive solution that I can make that will kill grass along my fence?

A. Really salty water has been a reliable weed killer for many, many years. In addition, there are several products on the market that are safe and effective to use. The best I know of is KleenUp, available at garden centers.

Doin' Double Duty

My Grandma Putt used dried bloodmeal to do double duty in her flower garden. First, by mixing it into the soil, it protected her bulbs from chipmunks and other varmints. Then she sprinkled it on the soil after planting, and its odor repelled the little critters. It also supplied a much-needed dose of nitrogen that made the bulbs very healthy the next year.

Q. My neighbor says I shouldn't spray my roses with the gardening hose to water them. Why not?

A. Wet foliage helps to spread black spot disease. A much better way to water roses is to use a soaker hose placed on the ground near the bushes. That way, the water can seep out near the roots—where it will do the most good.

Keep On Waterin'

Continue to water all of your woody caned plants right up until the first deep freeze of winter. Soil temperatures take longer to drop below freezing when there is ample moisture, so don't let up on your watering.

Q. I need help with dandelions and clover growing near a lake. Is there something I can use on my lawn around the water to kill the weeds without harming the lake water?

A. I don't encourage folks to use a weed killer on their entire lawn because it is generally a waste of time, money, and chemical control. This is especially true near water, where the control can run off and pollute the water. What you need to do is use what is called "selective weed control"—use any ready-to-use broadleaf weed control without fertilizer. Then only spray the weeds themselves.

Q. Please tell me how to get wild onions out of my lawn. Every time I look, there seems to be a few more of them!

A. Wild onions should be dug out of your lawn in the fall to get all of the little bulblets out. If there are simply too many, or if you want to attack them in spring, apply a good soapy-water solution followed by a good broadleaf weed killer.

CRITTER CONTROL

Snake Send-Off

To keep snakes out of your yard and garden, mix up a batch of this sandy send-off:

1 part builder's sand
1 part diatomaceous earth (DE)

Mix together and sprinkle a 3-inch-wide band around the area to be protected. Snakes won't dare cross this rough stuff. Now that's what I call drawing a line in the sand!

Q. What kind of commercial fertilizer should I use on rhubarb and strawberries?

A. You can use any dry garden food, as long as you mix in half a cup of sugar per 5 pounds of food. Broadcast this mixture over the area, and then water well.

Q. What can I safely use to keep weeds out of a fairly new asparagus patch? I planted the patch two years ago, and it is doing very well, but I am having a tough time keeping it clean and free of weeds.

A. If you know where the centers of the asparagus plants are, place a plastic container over them and then spray the area around them with a glyphosate control like KleenUp.

Q. I have a big row of peonies. There is grass and some weeds in between them, and I would like to know if there is anything I can apply to kill the grass and weeds, but not the peonies.

A. Since peonies are single-stem flowers, you can use a small sponge paintbrush to do the job. Dip the paintbrush into a systemic weed killer like KleenUp, and paint the grass and weeds dead without touching the peonies. It takes a steady hand, but it's worth the effort.

Get 'Em with Garlic

The strong smell of garlic apparently offends as many bugs as people. To make a pungent pest repellent, cut up 6 cloves of garlic, and mix with 1 tablespoon of baby shampoo and 1 quart of water. Spray it on your plants, and bugs will stay away.

Better Roses with Less Water

Roses are thirsty beauties, but you can save water by paying attention to where you plant your bushes. For starters, plant them where they will receive at least half a day of sunshine, but not all-day-long full sun. This will cut down on their water needs. And try to avoid planting rose bushes close to trees. The trees' roots can rob roses of essential nutrients and water.

Q. What's the best kind of fertilizer to use on my green peppers in the spring and summer?

A. Try using "All-Season Green-Up Tonic" (see "Green-Up and Clean-Up" on page 77) every three weeks throughout the growing season, and overspray once a month with a can of regular cola (not diet) in your 20 gallon hose-end sprayer. A pinch of Epsom salts will also help them grow an inch.

Sensible Strawberry Feeding

In small gardens, the soil fertility is usually high, so there's no need to use fertilizer when you first set out your strawberry plants. Wait until your plants get established (usually five to six weeks after planting) before using a fertilizer, and then give them only a light side-dressing of either an 8-8-8 or a 10-10-10 mix. And never apply the fertilizer when the plants are wet because any contact may burn the leaves.

Q. How do I fertilize overgrown shrubs that have been neglected for 12 years?

A. I would try using evergreen cartridges in a root feeder—check with your local garden center. You should also feed the shrubs every three weeks during the growing season with "All-Season Green-Up Tonic" (see "Green-Up and Clean-Up" on page 77). That'll get things growing!

Q. I've had two commercial applications of a weed and feed on my lawn this year. Are the clippings safe for composting or garden application next year?

A. My general rule is that it's not a good idea to use weed killer-tainted clippings for at least four weeks after application; six weeks is even better. After that, you should be OK.

Jerry's Secrets

The best time to feed your early-spring-flowering shrubs is the first two weeks of August. This late-summer meal encourages abundant spring growth.

PEST PATROL

Mighty Mosquito Mix

For natural control of mosquitoes, mix a batch of this tonic in your 20 gallon hose-end sprayer:

1 cup of lemon-scented ammonia
¼ cup of lemon-scented dish soap
Warm water

Put the ammonia and dish soap in your 20 gallon hose-end sprayer, filling the balance of the sprayer jar with warm water. Apply three times a week in early morning or late evening. Thoroughly soak any small puddles or low-lying areas where mosquitoes tend to gather.

Q. I fertilized my gooseberry and current bushes with liquid hog juice. They looked great, but bore no fruit. What can I do to counteract the hog juice?

A. Stop using it! It's too rich in nitrogen.

Q. What can I use to kill poison ivy?

A. You should first wash it down with soap and water (2 tablespoons of liquid dish soap per gallon of warm water), then spray with any of the commercial poison ivy killers available at garden centers.

Q. Can I use fresh-sheared sheep's wool for garden mulch? If not, can wool be composted?

A. Whether it's straight off the sheep's back or an old wool rug, wool makes a great mulch. Just remember, wool is slow to decompose. So if you're going to try to compost it, cut it into small pieces or clumps, then saturate it with a sugar source like regular cola (not diet) to speed up the process.

Handle with Care

To water plants properly, you should actually be watering the soil surrounding the plants, not sprinkling the leaves. One way to do this without straining your back is to attach a broom handle along the length of your hose, starting just behind the nozzle.

The handle helps direct the water to the roots, and you don't have to bend over to make sure it gets to where it needs to go.

Q. When is it too late to prune and fertilize a dogwood tree?

A. Prune these beauties when the blossoms fall, and don't feed after August 15.

Q. I have several clumps of Pampas grass in various full-sun locations in my yard. Last year, some did not bloom, and others weren't very full and looked like they needed a boost. Is there some fertilizer or growth food that I can give my Pampas grass to make it perk up?

A. Pamper your plants with "All–Season Green-Up Tonic" (see "Green-Up and Clean-Up" on page 77) every three weeks throughout the growing season, and make sure that the Pampas grass gets a good, healthy dose.

BLOOMIN' BASKET BASICS

MIXERS & ELIXIRS

Milky Fern Feed

To feed outdoor ferns, mix up a batch of this milky brew:

1 cup of milk
1 tbsp. of Epsom salts

Combine the ingredients in your 10 gallon hose-end sprayer, and over-spray the ferns until they are saturated.

I'm often asked about how to care for flowering plants in outdoor hanging baskets. Here's my advice for watering and feeding.

Under normal conditions, medium-size flowering plants in 10-inch-diameter baskets will need up to 1 quart of water at each watering. A thoroughly watered plant shouldn't require another watering for two to four days. But just to be on the safe side, check your baskets daily.

To feed, mix 1 to 2 teaspoons of a 20-20-20 or 15-30-15 water-soluble fertilizer per gallon of water, and apply every two weeks, depending upon the appearance of the plant (lack of blooms or yellow leaves are signs of insufficient feeding). Or you can sprinkle 1 or 2 tablespoons of slow-release, coated fertilizer on the soil surface in a 10-inch-diameter basket—one application may be all you need for the entire summer.

Q. I have a huge problem with my garden. Three years ago, I figured that if I fed the deer, I would have great fertilizer for spring planting. I sure did! But the alfalfa that I put out for the deer is now so heavy that I can't grow anything else. Help!

A. You've got to kill the alfalfa, roots and all, with any of the systemic weed killers like KleenUp in early spring. Wait a week to ten days, then till the dead vegetation under.

Q. How can I get rid of myrtle in my berry patch and flowerbeds? It spreads so fast and really crowds everything out.

A. Pull it up, mulch your berry patch and planting beds with straw, and then keep your fingers crossed. If you can put down a weed-block fabric before you mulch, you'll have a much better chance of eliminating this pesky weed.

Jerry's Secrets

Foliar feed young seedlings by mixing a little plant food and water in a handheld sprayer bottle, and giving them a blast or two in place of their regular feeding.

Q. I live along the New Jersey coast where it often gets flooded with salt water. What can I use on my lawn and garden to overcome all this salt water?

A. Apply pelletized gypsum and lime as soon as you can in spring. Then, on or before April 1, overspray everything with a mixture of 1 cup of my Plant Shampoo or 1 cup of liquid dish soap per 20 gallons of water. Follow this bath with the recipe

Window Box Watering

Beautifully planted window boxes are an attractive feature for your home in summer, but wilted, browning flowers aren't, so be sure you don't neglect their water needs. Water early in the morning, enough so that it runs out of the drainage holes. Then don't water again until the soil is dry to the touch. This may be necessary about twice a week, but check every day or so, and water as needed.

for "Vegetable Refreshers" on page 154 at three-week intervals, throughout the growing season.

for "Vegetable Refreshers" on page 154

Pin 'Em Down

Keep your soaker hoses in place on the ground by securing them with upside-down U-shape pieces of coat hanger. Simply cut an 8- to 12-inch-long piece from the coat hanger, bend it to fit over the hose, and press it firmly into the ground.

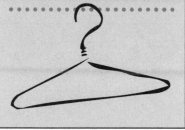

Q. I've heard about weed-blocking fabric, but I'm not sure how to use it. Do I mulch and then lay down the fabric, or do I lay down the fabric and then mulch?

A. Glad you asked! Weed-blocking fabric is a strong, synthetic fabric that lets in air and water while blocking out light and weeds. To use the fabric in a new planting bed, prepare the soil, install edging, then lay the fabric over the soil. Lay the fabric in strips, overlapping the edges about 6 inches or so. Then arrange your plants around the bed to get the effect you want. Cut slits through the fabric, and transplant your plants. Spread a layer of mulch about 3 inches deep over the fabric. You can water and feed as usual—it will soak down right through the fabric to the roots.

Q. How often should I water a fruit tree that is producing fruit?

A. These babies are thirsty, so you must get water deep down to the roots. This means plenty of water in spring, and twice a week in summer.

PEST PATROL

Super Snail and Slug Cure

I learned this super snail and slug cure after living and gardening in England for four years. When slugs appear, English gardeners fill shallow pans with beer or grape juice, and sink them into the ground as a lure. The next morning, they count the number of drowned pests to determine how big the problem is. Then they follow the slimy trail in the direction of the slugs' daytime resting spots.

That evening, dry aluminum sulphate is applied with a handheld spreader set on a medium setting, or 3 tablespoons are dissolved in a gallon of hot water, and sprayed on the surrounding area and plants. Try it, it really works!

Cut, Slash, and Burn

Cut off and burn all dead parts of diseased or insect-infested plants. These harbor insects that are always on the lookout for their next meal.

Q. How can I use weed-blocking fabric around my trees ?

A. Just follow these simple steps: First, use a hose to make a 4- to 5-foot-diameter circle around the trunk. Use a spade to remove a ring of sod just outside the circle. Pour a layer of builder's sand into the ring, and tamp it down. Lay a single row of bricks end to end in the sand. Tap the bricks down level with the sod to make an edging. Then lay strips of fabric across the circle, letting it overlap the bricks by about 6 inches. Use scissors to cut an opening for the tree trunk. Then lift the bricks one by one, and lay them on top of the fabric. Now add 3 to 5 inches of mulch on top of the fabric, and you're set to grow!

AFTER THE FLOODS COME

For those of you who suffer through heavy rains and flooding, don't despair. Here are a few of my tips and tricks you can use to revive your lawn after the floods and get it back into the green of health:

1. Direct any standing water away from low spots in your lawn, around trees, or in your gardens. Simple trenches will do.

2. Plug severely damaged turf areas.

3. Dethatch heavily flooded lawn areas either with a mower attachment or a mechanical dethatcher.

4. Apply gypsum at a rate of 50 pounds per 2,500 square feet to all low-lying areas.

5. Come fall, apply a good organic lawn food to power root growth and improve soil structure.

6. Last thing before winter, feed your lawn with a mix of 4 pounds of Epsom salts per 50 pounds of fertilizer.

Bulbs Aren't Picky Eaters

Bulbs don't need a lot of fancy food, and they don't demand or even particularly like hard-to-get gourmet items. When I plant my bulbs, I work a handful of compost and a teaspoonful of bonemeal into the soil in each hole before setting in the bulb. The only other feeding I give my bulbs is in early spring. When I notice they've begun to stick their noses out of the ground, I spread a handful of all-purpose garden food (4-12-4 or 5-10-5) over the soil. That's all there is to it!

Q. How can I increase the size and quality of our rhubarb?

A. Give them a good dose of chicken manure in the fall.

Q. Do you have a formula for making our papaya trees grow bigger?

A. Yes, and it's the same formula I use to make all trees grow from one end of the country to the other. Use the "All-Season Green-Up Tonic" (see "Green-Up and Clean-Up" on page 77) every three weeks, all season long.

Q. What should I be feeding my Oriental poppies?

A. Oriental poppies are heavy feeders that usually remain in one place for many years, so it's important to see that your soil is well supplied with nutrients. Old manure or compost is excellent—especially if it's supplemented with a handful of superphosphate or two handfuls of bonemeal per plant.

Q. How can I kill the morning glory that's growing in my shrubs without ruining the shrubs?

A. There are several sprays you can use, as long as your

Jerry's Secrets

To get rid of any particularly stubborn weeds, dig around the base of the plant, cut if off below ground level, and sprinkle a good healthy dose of salt on it. Just take care not to get any salt on the surrounding soil.

Chamomile Mildew Chaser

Chamomile is an excellent control for powdery mildew. So apply this elixir at the first sign of trouble (or in damp weather), and every week throughout the growing season to those plants that are especially susceptible to this devastating disease:

4 chamomile tea bags
2 tbsp. of Murphy's
  Oil Soap
1 qt. of boiling water

Make a good, strong batch of tea using the boiling water and tea bags, and let it steep for an hour or so. Let the tea cool, then mix with the Murphy's Oil Soap and apply with a 6 gallon hose-end sprayer.

groundcover isn't in the juniper family. I find that if I pull the morning glory stems in fall, apply a pre-emerge weed control, and repeat in early spring, I seldom have a problem.

Q. **How can I get rid of Japanese bamboo? I've pulled it out, cut the tops as soon as it flowers—even sprayed it with weed killer. Nothing works. Help!**

A. Thoroughly drench it with a good soapy-water solution, then apply a good broadleaf weed killer at the recommended rate. Follow up until it's gone.

Q. **How can I keep my pine grove free of underbrush growth? I would like only pine needles on the ground, but false lily-of-the-valley, ferns, and all kinds of scrub are growing there.**

A. Spray the brush with a good soapy-water solution followed by KleenUp. It will not hurt the trees or soil.

Q. **I put a nice, thick layer of grass clippings on my annual beds, but many of my flowers didn't bloom! What went wrong?**

A. You probably put them on too thickly. Grass clippings heat up as they decompose, which is bad news for your flowers! So, next time, be sure to put on a light layer, and distribute it evenly.

You Can Rain on Their Parade

Impatiens are some of the most rain-tolerant annuals around. Rain doesn't harm their blooms, which is one of the reasons why these flowers always look so fresh and vibrant.

CHAPTER 4

"You'd think that because I've been gardening for so long,
I'd take the results for granted. But I still get excited when
I pull my first radish from the ground, pick my first bush bean
from the vine, bite into the first tomato of the season,
or delight in the first blooms from my flower garden."

Show Off Your Green Thumb

Plentiful Produce

Vegetable gardening is a lot like playing baseball, except you're not one of the players—you're the coach! It's your job to make sure your vegetable team performs well. In earlier chapters, I told you how to select the lineup and make a game plan by choosing the right seeds and seedlings, laying out your garden, and improving the soil so your rookie plants could grow their best. Now your job is to rally your team on so you can end the season eating the fruits of victory!

PUT FAST STARTERS AND SLOW MOVERS TOGETHER

To get more out of your vegetable garden this year, try interplanting. Professional growers have used this secret for many years—all you've got to do is put rows of fast-growing vegetables between rows of slow growers. All of the crops are planted at one time, but they'll mature at different times. The speedy ones will be ready for harvest just about the time the slow ones start getting big and need more room to roam. So you can grow twice the crop in the same amount of space.

Jerry's Secrets

Stimulate your tomatoes into bloomin' action by mixing 2 tablespoons of Epsom salts in a gallon of warm water. Use this mix liberally to soak the soil around your plants just as they begin to flower, and you'll be rewarded with plants full of bountiful blooms.

QUENCH THEIR THIRST

Believe it or not, squirrels, chipmunks, and other varmints that take big chunks out of your tomatoes are often doing so to quench their thirst. So before you arm yourself to the teeth with all kinds of pest controls, install a birdbath or other water source in your yard. If you give the thirsty critters an easy drink, they just might leave your tomatoes alone!

KEEP UP THE GOOD WORK

Tomatoes and other vine crops should be kept up—up off the ground, that is. This makes caring for them easier and discourages disease and insect problems. Here are some of my favorite staking techniques:

Tomatoes: Use a single pole, tying the plant as it grows with small strips cut from panty hose. Or make a three-stick teepee over the plant, and wind the growing plant around it.

Bush beans: Place small twigs underneath the plants as they grow.

Pole beans: Train them to climb a wire or wooden fence. They grow better this way, and look attractive in the garden.

AN OUNCE OF PREVENTION

There's no way you can make absolutely sure that your plants will be insect and disease free, but you can come pretty close by following these timely tips:

🐛 Rotate your crops so that the same or a related vegetable isn't planted in the same area of your garden every year. This helps control soilborne diseases.

🐛 Keep an eye out for insects. Pick them off by hand, knock them off with a hard spray of water, or apply insecticides sparingly (at the recommended rates) before the little buggers multiply.

🐛 Water early in the day so the foliage can dry out by night. Leaf and fruit diseases thrive in damp conditions. During long periods of wet weather, keep plants covered with a protective layer of fungicide.

🐛 Dispose of plant remains as soon as you harvest each crop. Plow up the remains, leaving roots exposed for a few days to destroy nematodes (parasitic worms) in the soil. Then plow the plant tops and roots under the soil.

🐛 Keep weeds out of the garden. They take up vital space and nutrients, plus they provide a safe harbor for bugs, slugs, and other garden thugs.

🐛 Use enough fertilizer and lime to promote vigorous growth. A strong, healthy plant can oftentimes fight its own battles and is less likely to succumb to pests and diseases.

CRITTER CONTROL

A Little Dab'll Do Ya'!

Here's a neat trick that will drive raccoons, birds, and squirrels crazy, and save your ripening corn crop in the process. Place the toe of a nylon stocking over each ear of your corn after the pollen drops. Then just touch the top of the stocking with a dab of perfume. One whiff and the corn thieves will steer clear of your crop!

Vegetable Refreshers

Feed your vegetable garden every three weeks in the morning, alternating these elixirs every other time you feed. Mix each in a 20 gallon hose-end sprayer, and apply generously:

Refresher No. 1

1 can of beer
1 cup of Fish Fertilizer+
1 cup of ammonia
3 tbsp. of instant tea granules
1 tbsp. of liquid dish soap

Refresher No. 2

4 tbsp. of whiskey
2 tbsp. of instant tea granules
2 tsp. of liquid dish soap
Water to fill

GET A FEEL FOR YOUR GARDEN

Before I water or feed my vegetable garden, I always look at and feel the soil. That's right—I don't just go out, turn on the hose, and walk away. It's important to know what condition your garden is in before you jump the gun and give it water or food it doesn't need.

As a rule, plant foliage will droop down and roll over to indicate that it's thirsty. On the other hand, it will be limp if it's been over-watered. So before watering, force a dry stick deep into the ground, and let it sit for 15 minutes or so before removing it. Now feel the stick to see how deep the moisture is. This will save many a plant, and save you the time and effort of watering when it's not necessary.

SING AROUND THE CAMPFIRE

When the weather turns cold, it's time for your vegetable garden to camp out in a tent. No, you don't have to buy anything fancy—an old bedsheet will do. Simply drive a stake into the ground at each end of the garden, and stretch a rope or wire between the stakes. Then place an old sheet over the rope to make a tent. This will protect your plants from getting frostbite, and it will allow them to keep on growing.

A Pinch to Grow an Inch

If you want to grow whopper tomatoes (and who doesn't?), pinch off all of the suckers that develop in the crook between the branches and the main stem. This will make the plant stronger and the fruit much bigger.

DEM BONES, DEM BONES

Put last night's chicken dinner scraps to good use. Take the cleaned chicken bones, and dry them out in the microwave. Then place them in a heavy-duty plastic bag, and pound them to smithereens with a hammer. Sprinkle the bone shards in and on your garden soil for a nice nutrient boost.

POLLUTION SOLUTION

We can all do our part to keep our environment clean and green. I want you to set a good example for your neighbors by following these steps to taking care of good ol' Mother Earth:

🐦 If it can decompose, bury it or compost it.

🐦 Recycle anything that your community collects.

🐦 Properly dispose of toxic items and materials such as batteries, chemicals, and paint.

🐦 Avoid unnecessary use of possible pollutants if a milder, earth-friendly alternative is available. It may mean a bit more physical effort and time on your part, but that's just doing your bit toward a cleaner, greener planet.

🐦 Keep your yard and garden, trees, shrubs, and plants clean with a weekly bath of baby shampoo and water. Clean plants are happy, healthy plants that are safe from bugs and diseases, which means you don't have to resort to the more costly chemical pest controls.

🐦 When you must use chemicals, choose those that are derived from plants, like neem oil or pyrethrins.

🐦 When you have to use chemicals, start with the weakest dose first, then gradually work your way up.

🐦 Don't buy large containers of chemicals—buy only what you need so that you don't have to store the leftovers.

🐦 Don't mix and store any solutions, either garden or household, in food containers. Children, especially, could mistake them for something edible.

🐦 When using baits for mice, gophers, and moles, hide and protect them from children and pets.

🐦 Always be on pollution patrol in your own little corner of the world. If we all do our parts, we will all enjoy the rewards of living in a cleaner and greener environment.

Get a Leg Up

Abundant onions? Grab some hose—panty hose, that is—and tie them up. Put an onion in the toe, tie a knot above it, add another onion, tie a knot above it, and so on, until the leg is filled. Hang this leggin' in a cool, dry place. Then, when you need an onion, simply cut below the knot.

CRITTER CONTROL

Hair Scare

To keep rabbits and other small varmints out of your vegetable garden, wrap bunches of dog or cat hair in old nylon stockings, and hang them in various areas in and around your garden. The varmints will think that Fido or Fluffy is on duty, and they'll keep their distance.

GIVE ANTS A SIP OF SPEARMINT SPRAY

Antagonize ants in and around the house and garden with this minty mixture.

Put one cup of fresh or one-half cup of dried spearmint leaves in a blender. Fill the blender with water, and pulverize for 30 seconds. Strain out the liquid, and apply to ant-infested areas with a handheld sprayer. Apply twice a week until the ant problem is solved.

SEE YOU IN SEPTEMBER

Gardening professionals know that September is the *real* beginning of the growing year, not the end, like some folks think (you know, the ones who are marking the days on the calendar until they can padlock the tool shed!).

But what you do in your yard and garden between September and Thanksgiving will determine next spring's workload, so keep up the good work. Here's a quick list of what you should pay attention to in September, October, and November:

Vegetable garden: Plant any and all cool-weather vegetables. Harvest when ready, and don't let the crops die on the vines.

Flower garden: Pick all flowers, then dry or press them. Keep your roses cut, and plant new ones for next year.

Lawn: Continue to mow regularly at normal heights through the end of September; water and feed at the normal rate. Seed and sod after September 15 if you live north of the Mason-Dixon line, a month later if you live in the South.

CRITTER CONTROL

Garlic Gets 'Em

To rid your yard and garden of moles, open up their tunnels in different locations and drop in freshly cut-up garlic bulbs. Then cover up the holes you've made. The moles take one whiff, and run in the opposite direction!

Pumpkin Bonanza

Here's a little secret I learned years ago: To grow the biggest pumpkins, remove all but the biggest two fruits from each vine. And give your pumpkins plenty of water—they can grow as much as 8 inches per day!

SECOND-SEASON PLANTING

Many folks tend to call it quits in the vegetable garden around the middle of August. But you can continue to grow delicious vegetables far into fall and, in warmer areas, right through winter! There's no magic involved— just a few simple steps will keep you growing in the right direction.

Seed preparation: Properly prepared seeds are the secret to a super fall garden. Before planting, soak your seeds in "Seed-Soaker Solution" (at right). Then place them in the refrigerator for 48 hours. The shampoo softens the seeds' shells, the tea nudges them awake, and the refrigeration changes the seeds' life cycles. They think they've just woken up from a long winter's nap!

Soil preparation: For late-season planting, add 1 pound of Epsom salts per 10 square feet of garden area, and hoe in as deeply as possible. Then energize the soil with "Soil Energizer" (see page 158). When sprinkled over the soil, it should cover 20 to 25 rowfeet. The following day, start planting!

Planting: To decide when to plant, you need to know the average date of the first fall frost in your area, then back up from that date by the number of days it takes your plants to mature. Check seed packets or seedling labels for information on growing times. Be sure to add 14 days to the stated maturity time, since the plants will mature more slowly in the cool fall weather.

Mulching: For late-season vegetables, mulching is a must! As soon as your seedlings have two true leaves, or are tall and strong enough to stand upright, place a single sheet of newspaper on the soil beside them, and cover the newspaper with grass clippings. Add more clippings as your seedlings grow, until you have 4 to 6 inches of this mulch around the plants. This will keep the soil warmer longer. If and when it is necessary to cover the plants, the mulch will generate heat.

MIXERS & ELIXIRS

Seed-Soaker Solution

2 tbsp. of baby shampoo
1 tbsp. of Epsom salts
1 gal. of weak tea water*

Mix all of the ingredients together, and soak your seeds before planting.

*Soak a used tea bag in a gallon of warm water and 1 teaspoon of liquid dish soap until the mix is light brown.

AGELESS ASPARAGUS

Established asparagus beds can be productive for 35 to 40 years or more, if you keep the soil fertile and weeds under control. Here's how to keep your asparagus crop coming up strong:

Fertilize. Asparagus grows best with liberal annual applications of fertilizer. Apply well-rotted manure or compost at a rate of one bushel per 30 square feet. Once a year, spread a 10-10-10 or equivalent fertilizer at a rate of $1\frac{1}{2}$ to 2 cups over 10 feet of row. Apply it either in late fall, very early spring, or after the harvesting season has ended in late June.

Control weeds. Many old asparagus beds quickly become overrun with quackgrass or other wandering weeds. You can use a chemical weed control—just be sure to carefully follow the instructions on the label.

MIX UP A MUSTARD SHAKE

There's nothing more frustrating than putting a lot of time and energy into your vegetable garden, only to have it feasted upon by any and all bugs that walk, crawl, or fly by. Well, here's a surefire way to keep those pesky pests at the proper distance. Simply put 1 tablespoon of mustard (the hotter the better) in 1 quart of warm water, and shake it vigorously until it's well mixed. Lightly mist-spray your vegetable plants at the first sign of trouble.

Keep Their Tops On

Be sure to allow asparagus tops to stand over the winter to catch and hold snow. This may help prevent deep freezing and sudden changes in soil temperature. The added moisture provided by the melting snow is also important for the shoots produced the following spring. Once spring comes, you can lop off the dead tops.

LITTLE FLOWERS = LITTLE VEGETABLES

Peppers and eggplants often produce a lot of little flowers which, if you don't do anything about them, will result in a lot of small vegetables (makes sense, huh?). So remove some of the flowers, and your plants will spend their energy developing a few big vegetables rather than lots of little ones.

GIVE UNTO OTHERS

If your neighbors turn a violent shade of green when you show up at their door with yet another basket of your picture-perfect homegrown fruits and vegetables, and if you're tired of trying to figure out what to do with another 100 pounds of tomatoes and zucchini, don't relegate the fruits of your labors to the compost heap. Instead, donate your produce to your local shelter, soup kitchen, or other charity.

There are, unfortunately, plenty of needy families in this great country of ours, and they will be mighty glad to partake of some fresh food. And sharing your harvest will give you a great feeling while you're doing a good deed for others.

Foiled Again!

Aluminum foil reflects light, which some insects can't stand. So give 'em a good dose of sunlight by using foil as a mulch around your squash, cucumbers, and corn. This simple trick works wonders to keep the local insect population away from your produce!

DON'T GO FOR THE BURN

Professional growers know that you should never put chemical fertilizers into the soil just before setting out seedlings. Why? Because if the fertilizer comes into direct contact with small plant roots, it will burn them—causing serious injury, and even death. But that doesn't mean you can't feed your seedlings. Just remember to first dilute and then dissolve the fertilizer in water so that the plant roots can absorb it safely.

PEST PATROL

A Scratchy Solution

Don't throw away those used sandpaper discs—they make great slug busters. Cut a slit up to the center of the disk, and put the disk on the ground around the stem of your plant, like a collar. Slugs won't dare cross the scratchy surface!

Fabulous Fruits & Berries

Whether you're growing strawberries in a jar on the patio or you have a whole orchard of fruit trees growing out back, nothing beats the satisfaction you get from growing your own fruits and berries. And one taste of vine-ripened melon or the crunch of your first apple will convince you that it was all worth the effort. Follow these hints and tips, and I guarantee that your fruits and berries will be the pick of the crop!

THE FALL STRAWBERRY PATCH

What you do in the fall to make your berry patch safe and sound will determine how much work and worry you'll have next spring. What's the key? In a word—mulch! In the northern areas, mid- to late-October is the best time to mulch, while in the southern areas, where freezes are apt to surprise you and your strawberries, you can wait until December. Mulch after at least two killing frosts in the North.

Mulching materials include wheat, straw, cotton hulls or burrs, crushed corncobs, peat moss, wood shavings, sawdust, pine needles, and old hay.

Mulch helps prevent winter injury, keeps the fruit clean, conserves moisture, and prevents wind and water erosion. It also keeps the soil from becoming hardened, helps to prevent heaving (from alternate freezing and thawing of the soil), and adds plant food to the soil as it decomposes. A good fall mulching will also reduce weeds and grass growth the following spring. In spring, after the danger of hard frost has passed and new growth starts, you can encourage early fruiting by pulling part of the mulch back slightly from the row.

Jerry's Secrets

Oak leaves are best for mulching because their bitter taste deters those slimy slugs and grazing grubs. They also won't pack down like some of the softer wood leaves, such as maple.

Berry Basics

If you want a spring strawberry crop to really rave about, cover the soil area with a weed-blocking fabric in fall. Then place a layer of straw mulch on top of it. Follow up with a light dose of Epsom salts to power root growth and berry production.

PERFECT POLE PICKER

Make a handy apple picker with a pole, a nail, and an empty gallon-size plastic milk jug. Turn the jug upside down, and shove the neck onto the end of the pole (an old broomstick is a good choice). Then drive a small nail into the neck of the jug and through the pole to secure it in place.

Next, in the bottom of the jug, cut a hole that is big enough for the fruit to fit through, but not too much larger. Your fruit picker is ready to go. This handy helper can be used for picking peaches, pears, and other tree fruits as well.

TO GET THE BERRY BEST...

...don't fertilize strawberries with commercial fertilizer until your plants are well established (usually five to six weeks after planting). Then give them a light side-dressing of 8-8-8 or 10-10-10 fertilizer. Remember, never apply the fertilizer when the plants are wet from morning dew or after a rain because the fertilizer may burn the leaves. And burnt leaves are something you definitely don't want!

GREAT GRAPES

Grape pruning can be done any time after all of the leaves fall and before the end of winter; the point is to do it only when the vine is completely dormant, so you avoid "bleeding" (loss of sap). The amount of wood to cut away each year depends somewhat on the method of training that you're following. As a general rule of thumb, cut back all of the past season's growth, leaving not more than three buds (which will produce next year's bearing shoots) between the cut and the wood of the previous season.

PEST PATROL

The Ultimate Bug Spray

Many old-time gardeners swear by a spray made of ground-up bugs and water. Simply put as many dead insects as you can find in a jar, cover them with water, and allow them to "cook" for a few days. Then mix this buggy solution with 10 parts water, and apply it with an old hand sprayer or hose-end sprayer (you may not want to use it again).

No one is sure exactly why this works, but one theory I've heard is that the mixture passes along deadly bug viruses or other pathogens along to the target pests.

SECRETS FOR GERANIUM SUCCESS

Every year my mailbox is jammed with letters requesting information on saving geraniums. So, without further ado, here are my secrets for geranium-growing success.

First, keep in mind that your goal is twofold—to save the plant *and* to subject it to the least amount of trauma during transplanting. So plan on this process taking two to three weeks from start to finish.

1. Make the first cut. With a sharp trowel or long-bladed knife, cut a circle completely around the plant, about a third of the way into the soil, with the blade slanted toward the root. The circle should be a little smaller than the inside circumference of the pot you'll be transplanting the geranium into.

2. Prune well. Remove any buds or blossoms that are still on the plant, and cut it back quite severely, removing the oldest growth.

3. Lift the plant. Make a second cut around the plant, pushing the blade down further, then a third cut to completely sever the roots. Now you can remove the plant from the soil, provided the soil is moist enough. If the soil is dry, be sure to give it a thorough soaking several hours before you try lifting the plant out. Then cut off all of the long dangling roots. Cutting the roots in advance of repotting gives the plant a chance to recover from the shock, and also to form the new feeding roots that must be produced before it can establish itself in its new home.

4. Repot and feed. Repot the geranium, and give it a good feeding of 1 tablespoon of Epsom salts and a dose of "Transplant Tea" (at left) to stimulate new root growth. Keep the geranium in partial shade, such as under a tree, for a week or so before bringing it out into the full light for all the world to see.

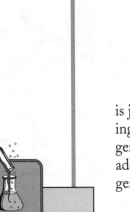

MIXERS & ELIXIRS

Transplant Tea

1 cup of beer
1 tsp. of baby shampoo
¼ tsp. of instant tea granules
1 gal. of warm water

Mix all of the ingredients together, and use to water your newly transplanted geraniums.

REACH FOR THE RASPBERRIES

Raspberries are definitely worth the wait! It's been my experience that these delicious fruits don't last too long after harvest because everyone gobbles them right up. You can be sure to get plenty of delicious raspberries by following these green-thumb tips from the pros:

🐛 Raspberries have shallow roots, so don't till or hoe around them to control weeds. Instead, mulch with a 2- to 3-inch layer of pine straw or a similar material. It's best to keep weeds out right from the start because weeding between thorny plants is no fun!

🐛 Raspberries need plenty of water to produce a good harvest. So be sure to water them well during dry spells—even in winter.

🐛 Prune red raspberries during the second winter after they are planted. Leave all but the five or six heaviest canes on each plant, and top them at 4 to 5 feet tall.

🐛 Prune black and purple raspberries during the first spring after you plant them, once they are 2 feet tall. Just nip the branch tips back 1 to 2 inches to force branching. From then on, prune in late winter, cutting each branch back to 8 to 10 inches. Then prune again in midsummer, removing just the top 2 to 4 inches from the tips of the canes.

🐛 Prune everbearers, such as 'Heritage' and 'Southland', as you do red raspberries, or cut them back to 2 to 3 inches above the ground in late winter. If you do this, the plants will bear only one large crop in the early part of the season.

Speedy Strawberries

Here's a tip that may come as a surprise to strawberry lovers: If you want to speed up production in your strawberry patch, remove the blooms that appear six to seven weeks after planting by snapping them off at the stem. This allows the plants to grow much faster and produce runner plants more readily. The result? A great picking bed the following spring.

PEST PATROL

Mother Nature's Barbed Wire

Keep garden-snacking varmints at bay by scattering cut-up thorny rose and berry stems into the mulch around your prized plants and shrubs.

Jerry's Secrets

Keep track of your garden tools by painting the handles bright yellow or orange. That way, you'll be sure to find them after you've set them down in the grass.

HEAD OFF FALL FRUIT TREE TROUBLES

More fruit tree troubles begin in fall than at any other time of year. But you can keep fruit trees healthy by following this advice:

Improve the soil. You must open up the soil beneath fruit trees. Use a hand spiker or wear golf shoes or my aerator sandals to aerate the soil in a circle around the tree. A 6-foot radius will do nicely.

Wash down the tree and trunks with a warm, soapy-water solution (use 1 cup of liquid dish soap and 1 cup of antiseptic mouthwash per 20 gallons of water). Apply the same solution to the soil beneath the tree. Wait a half hour, and apply Diazinon to the soil. I also suggest that you sprinkle some mothball crystals in a 3-foot circle under all fruit trees to keep insects at bay.

Prune in the fall. Fruit trees should be thinned out when they are dormant—in January and February. Use the proper tools. If a limb will not fit comfortably into a hand pruner, then use the big loppers. If you need more power, try a saw. When using a saw to prune, always make an undercut about 12 inches from the trunk, then cut the limb off 4 inches further from the trunk. Now go back and cut close to the trunk. This will prevent those unsightly and deadly bark rips.

Seal around the cut with pruning paint or latex paint, mixing 3 drops of liquid Sevin into every 8 ounces of paint.

Control insects. Many insects spend the winter safely tucked away as eggs in a crevice or crack of a tree. The problem comes when they hatch just before their food supply of young tender buds, leaves, or petals appears, with an appetite that would shame a bear coming out of hibernation.

Many newcomers to gardening, as well as some old-timers, are unaware of this, and are disappointed in the performance of their fruit trees after they have diligently followed feeding, watering, pruning, and in-season spray and maintenance programs. Little do they know that their insect and disease problems started long before the snow even started to fly. The solution is to dormant spray in late fall and early spring. (See "Spray to Save the Day" on the opposite page.)

SPRAY TO SAVE THE DAY

If you want to beat bugs to the punch and enjoy the bounty from your fruit trees, you must spray your trees with dormant spray in late fall and early spring. Dormant spray can be purchased as two separate chemicals that you mix, or they can be purchased premixed as a horticultural spray or ultra-fine oil. They are applied with any hose-end shrub and tree sprayer. If you mix the chemicals yourself, you will need lime sulphur solution and dormant oil (volk oil). I prefer to use the premixed version.

Begin applying the spray soon after the fruit tree has dropped all of its leaves. Be sure to spray your hedges, leafy shrubs, grapes, and berry bushes, too. Pick a comfortable fall day, between 11:00 A.M. and 2:00 P.M., when there is no threat of rain or freezing temperatures for at least 24 hours. Sometime before you begin, fill half of your hose-end sprayer jar with warm water, and add 1 cup of liquid dish soap and $1/2$ cup of antiseptic mouthwash. Add enough water to fill the jar, and you are ready to spray to the point of runoff. Once you're done, apply the dormant spray on top of the soap and mouthwash solution.

Then in early spring, before the buds swell up and open, repeat this process. The result will be the healthiest, happiest, and most abundant fruit trees you've ever seen!

KEEP YOUR GARDEN CLEAN

Fall garden cleaning is a close cousin of housecleaning—you get such a smug, virtuous feeling when the job is well done! But there is a second, more serious reason to keep your garden clean—to keep insects and diseases at bay. Here's a quick rundown for the backyard fruit grower:

🍂 Rake and burn all fallen fruits that are rotting on the ground. This will control brown rot of plums, cherries, and peaches, and black rot of grapes. It will also reduce the number of maggots in apples the following year.

🍂 Cut away and burn any apple and pear branches that were killed by bacterial fire blight. Make sure you cut several inches below the visibly infected portion.

🍂 Chop, pull, and burn any blackberries that were afflicted with orange rust.

🍂 Fight peach tree borers, either with a ring of mothball crystals about 1 inch away from the trunk and mounded over with soil, or by using any borer spray.

🍂 Remove any tent caterpillar egg clusters that may be encircling peach or apple twigs. If you don't want to cut off the infested branch, you can break the egg cluster, and slide it off into a paper bag for burning.

Garden Beauties

Wander down your garden path and see how those amazing annuals, perky perennials, beautiful bulbs, and robust roses are doing. I know you've been taking good care of them so far, but it's not quite time to start cutting and arranging them. Here's how to give your garden beauties the tender loving care they need to produce those bright, beautiful blooms.

ANNUAL REMINDER

1. Plant marigolds around your outdoor living areas (and your vegetable garden) to keep the mosquitoes away.

2. When planting annuals, sprinkle some seeds of the same type near existing annuals. That way, the new plants will bloom after the older ones have faded, and you'll have lots of blooms all season long.

3. Pick, pinch, or cut the flowers to stimulate more growth. Also, be sure to dead-head the plants (remove the spent blooms as soon as possible) for the same reason.

Midsummer Blooming

· · · · · · · · · · · ·

After a period of heavy bloom, cut snapdragons, verbenas, and stocks back, and give them a light dose of fertilizer. In return, they'll give you another show of healthy blooms.

· · · · · · · · · · · ·

Jerry's Secrets

With all the new germination fabrics available, you can cover newly planted seeds with a very light layer of soil, pat them down, and then tuck them in with strips of this material. Just remember to keep the seeds moist with "Soil Energizer" tonic (see page 158).

A FEAST FOR FLOWERING SHRUBS

Here's an old gardening secret my Grandma Putt passed along to me: For beautiful flowering shrubs, sprinkle ¼ cup of Epsom salts for every 3 feet of height on the ground at the tips of the farthest branches of the shrub. Do this in spring and late fall to deepen the color, thicken the petals, and increase root structure. You'll have the best-looking shrubs in the neighborhood, and everyone will be wondering what kind of "miracle food" you've been using!

GIVE TULIPS NEW BEDS

Take a tip from the pros: Don't plant tulips in the same bed for more than three years in a row. Repeated plantings in the same soil year after year are an open invitation to diseases such as fire blight. After three years, either change the location of your tulip bed, or replace the soil in the current bed.

An alternative to replacing the soil is to not use the bed for two years. Keep it well limed in the interim, and then in the third year, plant your bulbs again.

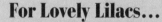

OFF WITH THEIR HEADS!

Cut off the tops of spent tulips and daffodils so they don't form seedheads. But don't cut the foliage down until it is brown and dry—green foliage stores nutrients that are needed for next year's growth.

DON'T LET THEM HANG AROUND

The spent flowers of phloxes, asters, and chrysanthemums often produce viable seeds that fall to the ground among the parent plants. There the seeds germinate and grow into vigorous specimens that usually end up choking out the choicer parent varieties. So be sure to pick spent flower heads before they have a chance to reproduce.

Jerry's Secrets

Not only does fresh manure stink to high heaven, annuals don't like it. It contains lots of nitrogen, causing them to produce too much green and not many flowers. So if you're going to use manure in your flowerbeds, be sure it has aged (dried) for at least two years. By that time, the potency of the nitrogen will have been reduced.

For Lovely Lilacs...

Keep suckers under control. The young suckers coming up from the base of the lilac plant drain it of nourishment. At least 80 percent of these suckers should be cut out as soon as they appear. Leave the remainder to replace old, diseased, or dying branches that may have to be cut out later.

KEEP 'EM FIT AND TRIM

Trim flowering shrubs in spring, while they are in full bloom. Lilacs, especially, should be cut frequently if you want the bush to bloom heavily for many years to come.

TEST YOUR FLOWER IQ

Here's a fun quiz to test your flower gardening knowledge:

1. **Tulip bulbs are best planted in:**
   ❑ Spring
   ❑ Summer
   ❑ Fall
   ❑ Winter
   ❑ Don't know

2. **When you purchase fertilizer, the first number on the chemical analysis (for example, 5-10-5) represents the percentage of:**
   ❑ Calcium
   ❑ Nitrogen
   ❑ Potassium
   ❑ Organics
   ❑ Don't know

3. **The official flower of the United States is:**
   ❑ Rose
   ❑ Trillium
   ❑ Marigold
   ❑ Geranium
   ❑ Don't know

4. **Which is the best mixture to pour into a vase before inserting fresh-cut flowers?**
   ❑ Cold water and aspirin
   ❑ Warm water and a few pennies
   ❑ Warm water and floral food (preservative)
   ❑ Don't know

5. **Petunias are classified as:**
   ❑ Annuals
   ❑ Perennials
   ❑ Biennials
   ❑ Don't know

6. **Which country is a major producer of carnations?**
   ❑ Greece
   ❑ Cuba
   ❑ India
   ❑ Colombia
   ❑ Don't know

7. **Which of the following fruits and vegetables can release ethylene gas into the air (which shortens the life of some cut flowers)?**
   ❑ Apples
   ❑ Oranges
   ❑ Onions
   ❑ Celery
   ❑ Don't know

8. **Which is the best schedule for watering an indoor flowering potted plant?**
   ❑ Water every day
   ❑ Water when the soil gets dry to the touch
   ❑ Water when the plant begins to wilt
   ❑ Always have a plant sitting in water
   ❑ Don't know

9. Which of the following plants was once thought to be poisonous?

❑ Potato
❑ Tomato
❑ Rutabaga
❑ Kale
❑ Don't know

10. Which plant develops flowers in response to the length of the day?

❑ Easter lilies
❑ Mums
❑ Roses
❑ Tulips
❑ Don't know

Answers: 1. Fall; 2. Nitrogen; 3. Rose; 4. Warm water and preservatives; 5. Annuals; 6. Colombia; 7. Apples; 8. Water when the soil gets dry to the touch; 9. Tomato; 10. Mums.

If you missed more than five questions, I suggest you join a gardening club. If you got them all right, you can join me and call yourself a master gardener!

DUST YOUR ROSES

You can prevent pests on your roses by following a regular program of dusting (or spraying). Once troubles set in, they may prove difficult to control, so don't wait until the damage is done!

🍂 My prepared Rose Dust is the best protection against insects and airborne diseases. Use a small hand-powered dusting machine if you have more than five bushes. It's simple to clean, and can be picked up and used in a matter of minutes.

🍂 Plan to first dust roses when the leaves are coming out in spring, and continue until growth stops in the fall. The best time of day for dusting is late evening when the air is still, and fresh dew on foliage catches and holds the powder. Hold the duster low, and shoot the dust up under the bushes without walking among them. Allow the protective cloud to settle gently over the whole bed.

🍂 The second best time to dust is predawn. When it rains, repeat the process immediately thereafter; in times of heavy dew, twice a week is about right. With light dew and the hotter, drier weather of summer, once a week is enough.

Jerry's Secrets

Here's a lesson I learned a long time ago—if you give your roses a bath once a week with a solution of 1 tablespoon of liquid dish soap mixed with 2 gallons of warm water, odds are, you won't need any chemical controls!

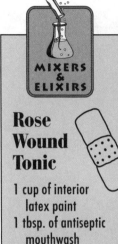

MIXERS & ELIXIRS

Rose Wound Tonic

1 cup of interior latex paint
1 tbsp. of antiseptic mouthwash
1 tbsp. of liquid Sevin

Mix all of the ingredients together, and pour them into a clear, empty white glue bottle. The pointed tip makes a handy applicator for small- to medium-size cuts. For larger cuts, use a foam paint pad to apply the mixture to your roses.

CONTROL POWDERY MILDEW

Powdery mildew is a fungus that can really do a number on your roses. While there are a number of commercial products on the market to control this disease, you can do it yourself with this organic formula: Mix ¼ cup of baking soda and 1 tablespoon of vegetable oil in 2 quarts of water. Spray on roses, zinnias, and lilacs early in the morning so the mildew-fighting effects last all day. Apply at the first sign of trouble, and every two weeks from then on to keep the disease under control.

THE KINDEST CUTS

Don't let roses die on the vine. The dead blooms are an invitation to pests and diseases. Always cut above a five-leaf cluster to encourage new growth, and then seal all cuts with "Rose Wound Tonic" (at left).

When cutting fresh roses to bring them indoors or to give away, make a slanted cut approximately ¼ inch above an outside leaf bud. This will encourage further growth in that direction. Cut only on healthy tissue, leaving two or more five-leaf clusters on the branch to encourage more flowers.

WINTER-READY ROSES

Getting your roses ready for winter weather is a simple task that doesn't take much time. Start by pruning them back in the fall, cutting them only enough to keep them from whipping in the winter wind. Climbing roses should be pruned only to keep them from rubbing the roof or walls. Seal the cuts with "Rose Wound Tonic" (at left).

Next, lightly tie your rose bushes with old nylon stockings. Use one stocking per bush, tying about ¾ of the way up the bush to keep it from breaking in a storm.

Remove all fallen leaves and petals from beneath the bushes. Spread mulch around each plant to a distance of at least 18 to 24 inches. Hang a piece of "No-Pest" strip from the branches, cover the plants with straw, and say "nitey-nite" for the winter.

COZY CONES FOR ROSES

Rose cones are good winter insulators for roses. They're made out of foam polystyrene with millions of tiny air chambers that keep the heat in and cold out. This promotes sturdier plants and ensures heartier growth in the spring.

Rose cones come in two sizes. The largest ones are for more mature bushes, and they eliminate the need for excessive pruning. The smaller ones are for younger rose bushes, and they can also be used for protecting tender perennials.

One word of caution: Don't paint rose cones a darker color. They will absorb the heat and damage your roses.

BOX 'EM IN

Another good way to protect roses in winter is with cardboard boxes. Here's how to use them for best results:

1. Prune your rose bushes after the first frost. Cut the canes back just far enough so that you can slip the boxes easily over the plants.

2. Cover each rose bush with a cardboard box, laying the flaps flat on the ground at the base of the bush. Use larger boxes for more mature bushes to eliminate the need for excessive pruning. Use smaller boxes for smaller plants. By the way, cardboard boxes also make great winter protection for tender perennials.

3. Weight down the box by putting rocks and soil on the flattened flaps. This serves two purposes: It helps insulate plant roots and also holds down the box during those blustery winter winds storms.

4. Remove the boxes after the last hard spring freeze. Or you can cut off the bottom of the box (which is now at the top) to allow air circulation on warm spring days; replace it if there's the threat of frost.

5. After you remove the box in spring, finish pruning your rose bush as you would otherwise, by cutting back the longer canes to 10 to 12 inches and removing the weaker canes. Start feeding your plants with "All-Season Green-Up" tonic on page 77 as soon as you can.

Better Borders

Border plantings need to be kept under control, especially if they're home to dominant perennials like phlox, Oriental poppies, or hemerocallis. These plants will soon take over the border if they are not kept in check. Keep your borders tidy by dividing these varieties every three years, discarding the extras if necessary.

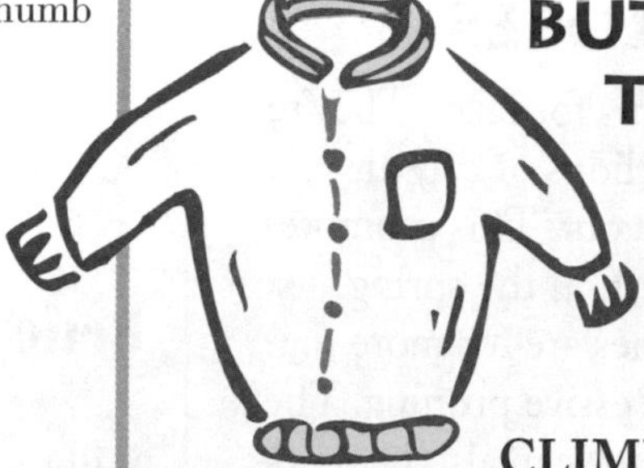

BUTTON UP THEIR OVERCOATS

If you live where the mercury falls to zero or below, you should protect climbers and other less-hardy varieties of roses from the harsh winter weather. Here's how:

CLIMBING ROSES

Protect the roots by covering the soil with a 3- to 6-inch layer of manure, partly decayed leaves, salt meadow hay, or straw.

If your roses are grown on an arch or pillar, and if the variety is fairly hardy, just tie the canes closely together and then cover them completely with corn stalks, sorghum canes, or something similar. Pieces of burlap, old carpet, and old bedspreads or quilts can also be used as covering. Tie the covering to keep it in place.

If your roses are growing on a trellis, take them down before bundling the canes together and covering them as described above. The tied-up bundle can then either be laid on the ground or fastened securely to the trellis.

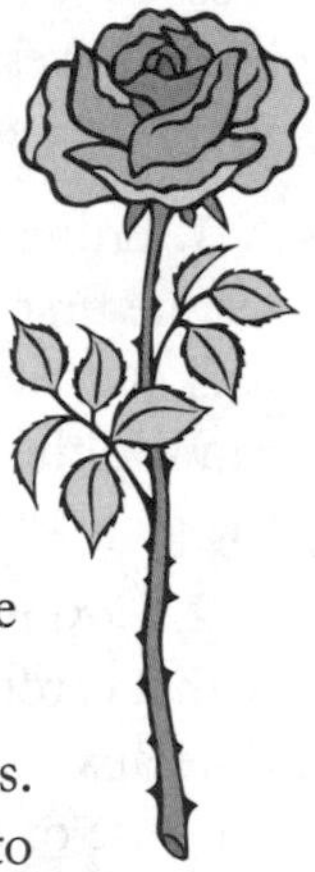

Don't be in too much of a hurry to cover up your roses because if you are, the field mice and other rodents may think you've put up an apartment for their benefit: They'll move in and feed on the bark during the long, cold winter.

Likewise, don't be in a hurry to uncover your roses. The covering will retard the bursting of buds, which is to your benefit if you have a late frost. However, the covering must be removed as soon as growth begins, so keep an eye on your bushes when the weather starts to warm up.

BUSH VARIETIES

Prune rose bushes after the first frost. Cut the canes back just far enough so you can slip a rose cone over the plant easily. (See "Cozy Cones for Roses" on page 171.)

Cover your rose bushes with the cones. Weight the base of

Onions on Call

Use onions to discourage aphids from dining on your roses. Chop up a medium-size onion, and place it in a blender with a quart of water. Pulverize, then strain off the liquid. Add 1 teaspoon of liquid dish soap to the onion juice, then liberally apply the mixture to your rose bushes with a hand-held mist sprayer.

the cones with rocks and soil so wintry winds don't tip them over. This helps to insulate the plant roots, too.

🥄 Remove the rose cone shelter after the last hard spring freeze. A removable top is available on some brands of the larger size cones to permit air circulation on warm spring days. You can put the cone top back in place if there's the threat of a freeze.

🥄 After removing the cone in spring, finish pruning your bushes as you would otherwise, by cutting back the longer canes to 10 to 12 inches, and removing the weaker canes. Give your bushes a dormant spray to prevent future insect problems, and start feeding them with a well-balanced rose food.

HELP YOUR ROSES SPRING INTO ACTION

Don't be too hasty to uncover your roses in spring. This gradual approach is best:

1. When new growth is ¼ inch above the winter covering of mounded soil, remove one quarter of the soil.

2. When new growth is between ½ and ¾ inch long, remove half of the remaining soil.

3. When new growth is 1 inch long, remove the balance of the mounded soil. Remember, it's better to leave the soil on too long to protect against a late freeze than to remove it too early and have frost damage.

4. Prune immediately after uncovering the plants. Seal all cuts with a mixture of 1 tablespoon of liquid Sevin and 1 tablespoon of antiseptic mouthwash added to ½ cup of interior latex paint.

5. Wash down all plants with a mild solution of 1 teaspoon of my Plant Shampoo and 1 teaspoon of my Rose & Flower Dust per gallon of warm water.

Jerry's Secrets

Prune large-flowered climbing roses the same way you do ramblers. The large-flowered climbers do not produce as many new canes as the ramblers do, so pruning them is simply a matter of removing the old flower clusters and cutting out enough old canes to make room for new ones to develop.

CRAZY FOR CHRYSANTHEMUMS

Most folks really go for hardy mums because they're easy to grow and care for. Just keep these tips in mind for the best chrysanthemums in town:

❧ Nip off the tips of the growing stems at least twice—once when the stems are 6 to 8 inches tall, and again about four weeks later. This keeps the mums from growing too tall and developing weak flowers.

❧ Divide and transplant your mums every two or three years, replanting the vigorous, outside sections of the clump. Discard the old center clump.

❧ Don't try to carry chrysanthemums over the winter in cold areas without giving them some protection. It's best to move them to a cold frame for the winter. If this isn't possible, protect them with a blanket of evergreen branches.

Jerry's Secrets

August is the time to pinch your annuals back severely. You may think it's going to hurt, but it's in their best interests. Then feed them with "Late-Summer Rejuvenating Mix" (see the opposite page). This little pick-me-up will stimulate your annuals into producing at least one more dazzling display of color.

Give Mums a Winter Break

If your mums die over the winter, don't blame the cold—the problem is usually too much moisture. So after the blooms fade, dig up the plants with as much soil as possible, and set them on top of the ground in a protected area. Then cover them lightly with mulch. Come spring, you can divide and replant them.

PETUNIAS: THE NATION'S PET!

Did you know that the petunia is the most popular garden annual in America? It certainly is one of the showiest, and one of the easiest to grow. And to add to their popularity, petunias have practically no pest or disease problems.

About the only thing you need to do to get these beauties up and growing is to fertilize them two or three times during the summer and water deeply at one- to two-week intervals, depending on the weather.

Some gardeners like to prune the plants back in midseason to encourage a heavier bloom. But even without this grooming, you won't be disappointed in these annual beauties!

IRIS IQ

If you're an iris lover like I am, you already know how important it is to separate these showy beauties every three to five years so that they have plenty of room to bloom. What you may not realize is that because irises are such heavy feeders, they will soon deplete the soil of nutrients, so it is important that you prepare their new beds well.

Using a spade to its fullest depth, thoroughly mix at least a 1-inch layer of peat, shredded dry leaves, and a mix of 25 percent Epsom salts and 75 percent bonemeal into the bedding soil.

After planting, drench irises with a mix of 1 gallon of warm water, Vitamin B_1 Plant Starter at 25 percent of the recommended rate, 2 tablespoons of liquid dish soap, and ½ cup of beer.

ZESTY ZINNIAS

Believe it or not, these blooming beauties are called Mal de Ojos, or eyesore, in their native Mexico! But most flower gardeners I know would not agree. Zinnias are easily grown in full sun in almost any soil, and they make a dramatic garden display in even the hottest weather. Here are my secrets to getting the most from your zinnias:

🌿 Although zinnias like moist soil, they are prone to mildew, so keep their leaves dry.

🌿 Use a fertilizer that is high in phosphorus, such as a 5-10-5 mixture. This will really strengthen the root structure.

🌿 These flowers are known as "cut and come again" because they really respond to cutting. So keep the scissors handy—you'll find that these plants are amazingly prolific bloomers!

Cut at Sunup

Flowers should be cut in the early morning, before the sun is in full force. Cutting is a form of pruning, so use a good, sharp pair of pruners to avoid hurting the plant. Sterilize the pruners before using them each time by rubbing them down with rubbing alcohol. Seal all pruning cuts with a mixture of clear nail polish and dirt.

MIXERS & ELIXIRS

Late-Summer Rejuvenating Mix

¼ cup of beer
1 tbsp. of corn syrup
1 tbsp. of baby shampoo
1 tbsp. of 15-30-15 fertilizer
1 gal. of water

Mix all of the ingredients together, and feed to all of your newly pinched-back annuals.

PICTURE PERFECT

Let your camera be your guide—use it to take pictures of your flowerbeds in spring when your bulbs are in all their glory. Why? For one thing, it will help you decide where you need more of the same or a different color next year. For another, you'll know right where everything is, which will help you avoid damaging existing bulbs when you plant new ones in the fall.

DOUBLE-DUTY DAHLIAS

Encourage your dahlias to do double duty by cutting the shoots when they are 6 inches tall. Cut them 1 inch above the base, and stick them in a mixture of half light sand, half compost. Water them and place them in a plastic bag in a dark location. In four to six weeks, they'll be ready to transplant into the garden.

FINAL FALL FLOWER PREP

If you're a cold-region gardener, the health of your future flowers depends upon fall preparation. As soon as frost has visited your garden, remove all summer annuals to the compost pile. Sprinkle 1 pound of bonemeal and 1 pound of Epsom salts per 100 square feet of flowerbed. Let it set for a week, and then till the soil under for the winter.

MIXERS & ELIXIRS

Bulb Soak

Prepare bulbs, tubers, and corms for planting by soaking them in this solution:

1 can of beer
2 tbsp. of liquid dish soap
¼ tsp. of instant tea granules
2 gal. of water

Mix all of the ingredients together in a large bucket, and carefully place the bulbs in the mix.

Call in the Reserves!

Even the best-kept flowerbeds have their share of disasters during the growing season. To combat this, be prepared. Keep extra plants on hand—in a cold frame or even in the vegetable garden—to use as replacements. Annuals fill the bill perfectly!

AZALEA ANTICS

Azaleas grow well without pruning, though you will want to prune them to remove dead or injured branches, to shape the plants, or to reduce their size.

If you want your plants to be bushier, cut growing twigs halfway back when they are 4 to 5 inches long.

Plants that have grown too tall can be pruned back severely to the size and shape you want. They won't have many flowers the next season, but in following years, the flowers will be more abundant than ever. If you ever need to thin crowded planting beds, snip the stems off close to the ground when plants are 4 to 6 inches tall.

Gorgeous Gardenias

Gardenia growers know that these flowers love slightly acidic soil. One way to keep them happy is to water them with a mix of 1 teaspoon of vinegar per quart of warm water. The vinegar adds acid to the soil—just what you need for gorgeous gardenias.

SOAK IT TO 'EM

Hostas love water, so plant them in wet areas. Or create one for them by directing your downspouts with a rain drain or gutter extension to bring the water right to your plants. They'll thank you for the soaking by growing bigger, better, and faster.

GO EASY ON HYDRANGEAS

Folks often complain to me about their French hydrangeas failing to bloom after a spring pruning. The problem isn't with the plant, it's with the overzealousness of the pruner! Most varieties of French hydrangeas produce the shoots that bear flowers only near the tips of the canes. Canes that have flowered can be cut back immediately after the blossoms fade, but don't cut back the whole plant to the ground. Limit your spring pruning to removing only those spindly canes and tips that have been injured over winter.

MIXERS & ELIXIRS

Out to Lunch

Give your fall-planted bulbs this organic lunch to snack on:

10 lbs. of dehydrated
    manure or compost
5 lbs. of bonemeal
1 lb. of Epsom salts

Mix and apply per 100 square feet of soil. For an extra treat, add up to 15 pounds of fireplace ashes to the soil.

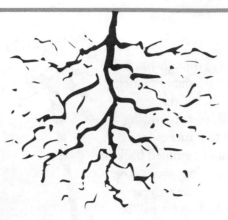

Flower Feast

1 can of beer
1 cup of ammonia
½ cup of liquid dish soap
½ cup of liquid lawn food
½ cup of molasses or corn syrup

Mix all of the ingredients together in a large bucket. Pour into a 20 gallon hose-end sprayer to apply. Feed this to your flowers once every three weeks in the morning throughout the growing season.

BE ROOTFUL AND MULTIPLY

Believe you me, perennials are habit forming! Once you start growing them, you'll want more and more. Unfortunately, your budget may put a crimp in your gardening style. But don't despair! Perennials are not only beautiful, they are very practical, too. That's because once you've established a good clump of your favorite perennial, you can easily propagate new plants from it, and they won't cost you a penny! One way to multiply your perennial plants is by root cuttings. Here's how:

Plants with slender roots (such as Japanese anemone, blanket flower, and butterfly weed): Lift a clump of perennials, and snip off 1- to 2-inch-long pieces of root. Then fill a shallow container with sand or garden soil. Lay the root pieces on their sides and cover them with an additional ½-inch layer of sand or soil. Firm the surface, and water carefully.

Place the container in a cold frame for the winter. When the cuttings sprout in spring, move the container outdoors until the new plants are large enough to be planted in their permanent homes.

Plants with thick roots (such as bleeding heart and Oriental poppy): Lift up a clump of perennials and cut off 3- to 4-inch-long root segments. In order to distinguish between the top and the bottom, make a straight cut across the top of the root segment and a diagonal cut across the bottom.

Then pot each segment individually, standing it upright in a 5- to 6-inch-diameter clay pot that has been filled with garden soil. Be sure you've planted the segment with the slanted end down into the soil. Set the segment in so that the top is about 1 inch below the soil surface. Water carefully.

Set the pots in a cold frame for the winter. In spring, when sprouts appear, move the cuttings outdoors to their permanent homes.

Frost-Free Flowers

If your flowering plants get hit by an unexpected heavy frost, water them lightly the next morning. This will thaw them out quickly, and they'll have a much better chance of survival.

PEONIES PLUS

If they're planted in a good location and get the proper care, peonies will continue to bloom for a good long time—20 years or more, if you're lucky. And to top that off, you can increase your peony yield by dividing your plants from time to time. When a peony root is divided, each piece of root that has a bud attached to it will grow and produce another plant just like the parent. What a deal!

Step 1: Start by digging up the entire plant, shaking the soil away from the roots. Cut the plant into divisions, each with three to five eyes.

Step 2: Thoroughly tamp down the soil in the planting hole. Set the plant in so that no eye is more than 2 inches below the surface. Cover with soil.

Step 3: Firm the soil to eliminate air pockets. Then cut off any aboveground stubs, and mulch well.

DON'T LET 'EM FADE AWAY

Remove faded flowers as soon as possible. This not only keeps your plants and landscape looking neat and well-groomed, but it also prevents seeds from forming. This way, you will prevent unwanted offspring and help conserve the plant's energy. Prompt removal of faded blooms also often encourages the plant to produce a second crop of flowers.

Even though some plants may not flower a second time, removing faded flowers allows the plant to conserve its energy and build a strong root system for the following year.

MIXERS & ELIXIRS

Flower Power

Feeding perennials is like satisfying a child's sweet tooth—make it sweet, and they'll eat themselves silly! Here's a mixture that'll give your perennials some real flower power!

Dry oatmeal
Crushed dry dog food
1 handful of human hair
½ cup of sugar

In a 5-gallon pail, mix equal parts of the oatmeal and pet food. Then add the hair and sugar. Work a handful of this mix into the soil just before planting your prize perennials.

JUST HANG IN THERE!

Clothes hangers are perfect for garden stakes. Fold the triangular base to one side, then squeeze tightly to form a "post." (You can tie the post with string or wire to keep it together.) Now bend the hook to one side so that it can curve around the stem of a sturdy plant. Shove the "post" into the ground next to the plant, and you're all set!

Fold over

Squeeze together

Bend hook

Hairy Mulch

Hair today, gone tomorrow! Keep moles and gophers out of your garden by adding human hair (from the barber shop or beauty salon) to compost, leaves, or other organic materials, and then working it into the garden soil. You'll need about two bushels of hair for every 100 square feet of garden area.

LOW-MAINTENANCE BLOOMERS

If your busy schedule doesn't leave you much time to keep up with deadheading your flowers (pinching off the faded blooms), choose from among the plants listed here. These low-maintenance bloomers have flowers that fall cleanly from the plant.

Ageratum	Begonia	Impatiens	Salvia
Alyssum	Coleus	Lobelia	Vinca

BATTLE THE BUGS

If you allow insect enemies to get a foothold in your perennial bed, they can do serious damage to and even destroy your plants. So keep your garden clean to prevent serious pest problems. Remove any and all weeds and dead plants that might harbor pests.

Then check your plants regularly for insects. If you see a few, simply pick them off by hand and drop them into a can of kerosene, or knock them off with a hard spray of water.

If you take care of the problem at an early stage, you won't have to resort to more serious warfare down the road.

Handsome Houseplants

Just about everyone I know has at least a few houseplants hanging around (literally!) or taking up windowsill space. Our potted friends purify the air, add color and interest to any room, and just make a house feel more like a home. I can't imagine living without them!

Whether you tend just a few or have every room filled with planters, pots, and vases, read on for my secrets to growing healthy, happy houseplants.

KEEP 'EM WARM AT NIGHT

A room with lots of windows is a great place for plants during the day. But if it gets cold at night, your plants won't be happy. You can solve this problem by removing the plants every night. Better yet, keep them in place, and bring in an electric space heater to warm up the room. Set the heater on a timer with multiple settings so it goes on for one hour at three-hour intervals.

To increase the warmth and save energy costs at the same time, put a fan up high on a bookshelf to blow the heated air back down into the room and around your plants.

LIGHT UP YOUR LIFE

If you use lights to keep your plants healthy, you must make sure the plants are close enough to the light source to actually benefit from it. As a rule, when using fluorescent tubes, plants should be between 6 and 8 inches away. When using incandescent bulbs, such as reflector floods and spots, plants can still benefit up to 6 feet away from the lights.

Do not use old light fixtures as makeshift plant lights. I cannot emphasize this enough—they can cause dangerous fires. Use only those lights specifically made for use as plant grow lights.

Fern Rx

A dose of castor oil is just what the doctor ordered to give ferns a new lease on life. Add 1 tablespoon of castor oil and 1 tablespoon of baby shampoo to a quart of warm water, and mix well. Give each plant $1/4$ cup of the mix.

IF THE SHOE FITS...

...make sure your plant is wearing it! Since every good gardener knows that plant roots are the feet, it only stands to reason that the pot is the plant's shoe. Always use clay, wood, or fiber "work shoes" for your plants. These materials breathe and let excess moisture escape. Glass, plastic, and metal should be considered "dress shoes," only used when company is coming.

Make sure your plants' shoes have holes in the bottoms, and when a plant's toes grow out of the bottom, move it up one shoe size larger (add an inch in diameter; for example, trade a 3-inch pot for a 4-inch pot).

Jerry's Secrets

Let 'em rock! Place your smaller houseplants on top of your radio, CD, or stereo system every once in a while, and treat them to a concert. Whether you're playing country, rock, pop, classical, or jazz, the vibrations will keep their circulation moving—and besides, they just love music!

PARE YOUR PLANTS

Take a tip from professional growers: Trim your houseplants to control their growth. Just think what you would look like if you never cut your fingernails! Plants are the same way—they need to be manicured. Here are three simple techniques:

Pinching is simply removing the tip of a growing shoot. You can do this by pressing it off with your thumbnail and finger. Pinching restrains overenthusiastic plants and promotes a compact, bushy growth habit. Pinching also checks strong shoots and stimulates the growth of buds that might otherwise remain dormant.

Disbudding is another form of pinching. In this case, you remove the buds so the plant is forced to conserve its energy until you want it to bloom.

Pruning is more severe than pinching and involves cutting back. It can also involve pruning roots as well as upper growth. Prune only with a sharp knife or pruning shears. Never hack at a plant with dull tools.

When pruning a branch, make your cuts just above a bud that is pointed in the direction you want the new shoot to grow in. If a branch needs to be completely removed, cut it close to the trunk or parent branch, and don't leave a stub.

If you need to prune because of disease, cut back to healthy tissue. Then be sure to disinfect your tools with denatured alcohol (rubbing alcohol) before using them again.

TREAT YOUR PLANTS TO ACUPUNCTURE

My Grandma Putt used to use acupuncture on her houseplants, and boy, did they ever love it! Why did she do it?

Well, watering reduces the pores (spaces) between the soil particles in the pots, which drives air out of the soil. Further waterings only increase the soil compaction and gradually choke the plant.

Soil in good condition should have about 50 percent pore space. If your plants are suffering from compacted soil conditions, try this: Take a long, large nail, and gently work it down into the soil. Go easy—you're aerating the soil, not trying to stab the plant to death! The number of holes you need to make depends upon the size of the pot. The larger the pot, the more holes you must poke.

After you've made the holes, water the plant. Remember, this treatment is not a cure, but it will give both you and your plants a breather until you have the time to repot them in new soil.

THE PLANT DOCTOR

I'm often asked to diagnose houseplant ailments. Over the years, I've seen just about every houseplant problem known to man. Here are some of the more common signs of an ailing plant, and what they mean:

Ends of leaves turn black: plant was in a cold location for too long.

Ends of leaves turn brown: plant was in a warm, dry draft or had too little humidity.

Leaves just wilt: plant is in a place where it is too hot, or plant needs water.

Mature leaves turn yellow and fall off: plant is starving.

Little tap leaves turn yellow: plant needs iron and more exposure to light.

Leaves fall off from the bottom: plant is being overwatered and isn't getting enough light.

Leaves fall off from the top: plant isn't getting enough water and humidity is too low.

Plant stops growing but looks pretty good: plant is getting too much light and is outgrowing its pot.

HOUSEPLANT 911

If you find a houseplant near death, it's time for you to take emergency action. Here's what to do:

1. Remove the plant from its present location, and put it into a room with a daytime temperature of 70°F, nighttime temperature of 60°F, and 50 percent humidity.

2. Remove the plant from its current pot, and repot it in a clean clay pot of the same size.

3. Drench the potting soil and spray the foliage with a solution of 1 tablespoon of liquid dish soap and 1 tablespoon of antiseptic mouthwash in one gallon of warm weak tea.*

4. Remove all disease-damaged foliage, and throw it away.

5. Be sure to wash your hands before touching any of your healthy houseplants.

* Soak a used tea bag in a gallon of warm water and 1 teaspoon of liquid dish soap until the mix is light brown.

THE TRUTH ABOUT AMARYLLIS

If your amaryllis isn't producing blooms, it could be that you're giving it too much to drink—or giving it the cold shoulder. Overwatering is one of the fatal mistakes amaryllis growers make, and the result is a plant that fails to bloom. The other big mistake is not keeping your amaryllis in a warm place.

Don't expose the bulb to below-freezing temperatures, or I can guarantee you that it will refuse to bloom.

Now, you may be discouraged by this picky plant, but once you give your amaryllis just the right water and temperature conditions, it will reward you with a bonus. Since the amaryllis is a true bulb, you can collect the bulblets that develop beside the main bulbs, and grow lots of new plants from them!

DEADLY POTS

Have you
taken a close
look at your
potted plants
lately? Do they
look a bit sickly?
If so, take a good
look at the pot itself. If it's
slimy, crusty, or otherwise icky,
you've got a deadly pot.

When inner and outer surfaces become coated with green slime, and the edges and upper sides build up with a white crust, you have several things to deal with. The green slime is an indication of overfeeding, overwatering, poor drainage, and overcrowded pots on your shelf or bench. The white crust tells you your plant has too much salt in its diet, usually caused by conditioned water (it's been through a water softener). Here's how to take action:

1. Transplant your plants into new pots (clay, wood, or fiber are best; see "If the Shoe Fits…" on page 182).

2. Wash the outsides and edges of the empty pots with a mixture of 2 tablespoons of liquid dish soap and a tablespoon of liquid bleach in a gallon of warm water. Use an old toothbrush or hand brush to really scrub the pots clean.

3. Rinse the pots well, then repot your plants.

4. Make sure that all plants are spaced at least 8 to 10 inches apart in a well-ventilated room, and put them all on a balanced diet.

5. If the plant is all foliage and no flowers, it needs a high-nitrogen plant food (12-6-6, 16-8-8, or the like). You can use liquid or dry food. Follow the package directions carefully.

6. Water your plants with filtered water. Make a simple water filter by washing out a quart milk carton and using a nail to poke several holes in the bottom. Fill the carton halfway with agricultural charcoal. Place the carton over a large bowl or a bucket and run your tap water through the carton. The charcoal will filter out harmful salts.

Jerry's Secrets

Never let dirty, moldy, salty pots lie around because that's just asking for trouble. I use a little soap and bleach in water and a scouring pad on clay pots, or one of those sponges that are soft on one side and rough on the other side for scrubbing my plaster, metal, glass, and ceramic containers.

WATER WISDOM

It's amazing how a simple thing like watering a plant can cause so many people so much grief! Seems like an awful lot of folks are either drowning their plants or neglecting them to the point of total dehydration. I am constantly asked how to water houseplants, but the truth of the matter is, there is no simple formula. The size of the plant, size of the pot, soil mix, time of year, light source, temperature, and humidity range all play a part in determining the watering needs of any particular plant.

Start by getting yourself a moisture meter (the ones that don't need batteries are best). They are available in garden centers and catalogs, and are reasonably priced. The meter will measure the amount of moisture in the soil. Then use the following chart as a guide to determining the soil moisture level that's best for your houseplants.

KEY

🪣 **Very moist:** keep wet at all times

🪣 **Moderately moist:** keep evenly moist

🪣 **Moderately dry:** let dry out from one watering to the next

Houseplant Water Needs

PLANT	PREFERRED SOIL CONDITIONS	PLANT	PREFERRED SOIL CONDITIONS
African violet	🪣 Moderately moist	Boston fern	🪣 Very moist
Aluminum plant	🪣 Moderately moist	Bromeliads	🪣 Moderately moist
Areca or butterfly palm	🪣 Very moist	Buddhist pine	🪣 Moderately moist
Artillery plant	🪣 Moderately moist	Burro's tail	🪣 Moderately dry
Asparagus fern	🪣 Moderately moist	Cactus	🪣 Moderately dry
Avocado	🪣 Moderately moist	Caladium	🪣 Moderately moist
Baby's tears	🪣 Moderately moist	Calathea	🪣 Moderately moist
Bella palm	🪣 Moderately moist	Cape primrose	🪣 Moderately moist
Bird's nest fern	🪣 Very moist	Century plant (American aloe)	🪣 Moderately dry

PLANT	PREFERRED SOIL CONDITIONS	PLANT	PREFERRED SOIL CONDITIONS
Chenille plant	Moderately moist	Dumb cane	Moderately dry
Chinese evergreen	Moderately moist	Elephant's foot tree (Ponytail)	Moderately moist
Chinese holly grape	Moderately moist	Euonymus	Moderately moist
Climbing fig	Moderately moist	False aralia	Moderately moist
Coffee plant	Moderately moist	Fan palm	Very moist
Coleus	Moderately moist	Fiddle-leaf fig	Moderately moist
Copperleaf plant	Moderately moist	Fishtail palm	Very moist
Coral berry	Moderately moist	Flame violet	Moderately moist
Corn plant	Moderately moist	Fluffy ruffle fern	Moderately moist
Croton	Moderately moist	Gardenia	Moderately moist
Crown of thorns	Moderately dry	Geranium	Moderately dry
Date palm	Very moist	Giant white inch plant	Moderately dry
Dracaena	Moderately moist	Gold dust tree	Moderately dry
		Golden trumpet	Moderately moist
		Gold vein bloodleaf	Moderately moist
		Hawaiian ti	Very moist
		Hibiscus	Moderately moist
		Holly fern	Moderately moist

Continued on the next page

Houseplant Water Needs (continued)

PLANT	PREFERRED SOIL CONDITIONS
Iron-cross begonia	Moderately moist
Ivy	Moderately moist
Jade plant	Moderately dry
Japanese aralia	Moderately moist
Japanese littleleaf boxwood	Moderately moist
Joseph's coat	Moderately moist
Jungle geranium	Moderately moist
Lantana	Moderately dry
Lipstick plant	Moderately moist
Maidenhair fern	Very moist
Medicine plant (True aloe)	Moderately dry
Ming aralia	Moderately moist
Moon Valley pilea	Moderately moist
Moses-in-the-bullrushes	Moderately moist

PLANT	PREFERRED SOIL CONDITIONS
Narrow-leaved pleomele	Moderately moist
Natal plum	Moderately moist
Norfolk Island pine	Moderately moist
Orange tree	Moderately dry
Orchids	Moderately moist
Peace lily	Very moist
Peperomia	Moderately dry
Philodendron	Moderately moist
Piggyback plant	Moderately moist
Pineapple	Moderately moist
Polka-dot plant	Moderately moist
Polynesia	Moderately moist
Polypody fern	Moderately moist
Pothos	Moderately moist
Prayer plant (Maranta)	Moderately moist
Purple heart	Moderately dry
Purple waffle plant	Moderately moist
Rex begonia	Moderately moist
Ribbon plant	Moderately moist

PLANT	PREFERRED SOIL CONDITIONS
Rosary vine	Moderately dry
Rose of Jericho	Moderately moist
Rubber plant	Moderately moist
Sansevieria	Moderately dry
Schefflera	Moderately dry
Screw pine	Moderately dry
Sensitive plant	Moderately moist
Shrimp plant	Moderately dry
Silver lace (table fern)	Moderately moist
Silver tree panamiga	Moderately moist
Spider plant	Moderately moist
Staghorn fern	Moderately moist
Strawberry begonia	Moderately dry
Striped inch plant	Moderately moist
Succulents	Moderately dry
Tahitian bridal veil	Moderately dry
Umbrella plant	Very moist
Variegated balfour aralia	Moderately moist

PLANT	PREFERRED SOIL CONDITIONS
Variegated mock orange	Moderately dry
Variegated wandering Jew	Moderately dry
Velvet leaf kalanchoe	Moderately dry
Velvet plant	Moderately moist
Wandering Jew	Moderately moist
Wax plant	Moderately dry
Weeping fig	Moderately moist
White-nerved fittonia	Moderately moist
White velvet tradescantia	Moderately dry
Yucca	Moderately dry
Zebra plant	Moderately moist

THE GIFT THAT KEEPS ON GIVING

I'm sure that most folks love receiving plants as gifts, yet the biggest complaint I hear is that the plants don't last long enough. That needn't be the case if you follow these precautions:

🖐 To begin with, the colorful foil wrapping, bows, and decorations that cover the pot are just for display. They are of no benefit to the plant, and can be harmful if left on for long, so remove them after several days.

🖐 Use your finger to poke a hole through the foil wrapping on the bottom of the pot. This will allow proper drainage. If your fail to do this, when you water the plant the excess water will have no place to go and your plant will drown.

🖐 Place the plant on a shallow saucer or pie tin filled with small pebbles. This helps to raise the humidity near your plant. After you have displayed the plant for a few days, select a temporary home for it in a south, east, or north window until it is time to move it outdoors.

🖐 When you move your plant to its windowsill home, remove the wrapping to let the clay pot breathe. Don't feed it for at least a month—it will have sufficient fertilizer from the greenhouse.

A LITTLE PAMPERING GOES A LONG WAY

Nearly all potted gift plants get along nicely at normal room temperatures of about 70°F during the day. To prolong flowering time, move plants to a cooler spot in the evening.

Watering is a snap—water well when the soil feels dry to the touch, then don't water again until the soil feels dry. Simple, right? The exceptions are mums, cinerarias, and hydrangeas. These flowers require a daily drink. Quench their thirst by filling a bucket about half full of tepid water and submerging the entire pot in the water. Let it sit for a few minutes, then remove and drain before returning the plant to its window seat.

Jerry's Secrets

This secret's all wet! You can make water "wetter" by adding 5 teaspoons of liquid dish soap to each quart of water (or 2 tablespoons of soap per gallon of water, or 1 cup of soap per 10 gallons of water). The soap acts as a wetting agent—it breaks through the static barrier caused by warm, dry, indoor air, so your plants can better absorb the water.

BRING PLANTS INDOORS WITH EASE

Folks who love their houseplants know that moving their loved ones outdoors when the weather warms up gives them a new lease on life. But how many of you take the time to ease their move back inside in fall?

If a plant is snatched up and brought inside to a too hot, too dry, and too dark or too bright location, is flooded with water, and force-fed tons of food, it's not going to survive.

You can, however, prevent this tragedy. Here's how:

1. Brew a batch of tea. Before you bring your plants back inside, give them a tea bath.

The tannic acid in the tea helps the plants manufacture more sugar and starch, and the soap opens up pores on the leaf surface, enabling the plant to absorb nutrients.

2. Get them back on a balanced diet. Take a quart of tepid water, and make a solution of 10 percent plant food. Then add 3 teaspoons of liquid dish soap. Use this every time you water.

3. After their first bath and feeding, leave your plants outside for the night. The next afternoon, around 3:00 P.M., lightly spray the foliage with the tea bath solution, bring the plants inside, and place them in their winter locations.

4. The following morning, about 9:00 A.M., take your plants back outside to their old spots and repeat the tea bath at 3:00 P.M. Then move your plants back inside for the night. Do this for three days.

5. On the fourth day, bring your plants outside at 10:00 A.M. and bring them back in at 2:00 P.M. After three days of this routine, take them out at 11:00 A.M., and bring them in at 1:00 P.M. By then, you'll have run out of time and patience. This process should take about nine days, but it is worth the effort. Your reward will be healthy, happy houseplants.

Tea Bath

Steep a tea bag in a quart of warm water, then add 3 teaspoons of liquid dish soap. Pour the solution into a mist sprayer and spray the top, bottom, and stem of each plant until the solution runs off. Don't rinse.

Jerry's Secrets

Don't cry over split leaves! You can repair torn plant leaves by applying clear nail polish to both sides of the leaf. It'll look good as new.

HOLIDAY HOLDOVERS

With a little care and patience, you can enjoy your holiday plants not just for days, weeks, or a month or two, but for years to come. Each type of plant has its own personality, its own likes and dislikes. If you pamper them from the beginning, they'll soon fend for themselves. Here's a little background info on my favorite holiday houseplants:

Easter lilies: Place in a window with a northern exposure. Pinch the yellow anthers inside the trumpets as soon as they arrive, and remove blossoms from the plant as they fade. Water when the soil is dry and be sure to let the water get all the way to the bottom of the pot. When the plant has died down, cut off the stems. When the weather warms, plant the base in a sunny spot in the garden.

Tulips and hyacinths: Place them in a window with an eastern exposure in a cool room. Water them daily with cool water, and don't let them dry out or become too warm. Plant the bulbs out-

doors when the weather permits, and enjoy them for years to come.

Poinsettias: Place near a warm, sunny window, but don't let the plant touch the glass. Check the soil every day and water when it's dry to the touch. Don't allow the soil to either dry out completely or remain soaking wet.

If you want to enjoy your poinsettia for another season, stop watering it and store it in a cool, dry place when the leaves fall off. In spring, water it again and cut the stems back to 6 inches tall. Keep the stems pinched back as the new leaves begin to form to make a short, compact plant. From early October until blooming starts, place the plant in a dark closet for 12 hours each night, say from 8:00 P.M. until 8:00 A.M. Keep the plant in a sunny window for the other 12 hours of the day.

Jerry's Secrets

Use extra care when transporting your holiday plants. Cover the plants with newspaper before taking them outside if the temperature is below 50°F. Warm up the car and park as close to the door as you can to keep them from being outdoors for too long. You don't want them to catch a cold!

TO BE CONTINUED...

Here are some popular plants that are often on the holiday gift list, along with my advice on how you can continue to enjoy these holiday plants—and keep them thriving—long after the holidays have passed.

Azaleas: Place in a fairly bright sunny window (eastern exposure is fine). Keep the soil evenly moist, and maintain a room temperature of 55° to 65°F. Spray the foliage three or four times a week to improve humidity. After the flowers have disappeared, sink pots and all into the ground in a semishaded area, and return them to the house in early fall.

Chrysanthemums: Place in a sunny window with a southern, eastern, or northern exposure. Keep the pot a little closer to the window because mums prefer cooler temperatures. Water daily. When the threat of frost has passed, cut the foliage all the way back and plant in the garden in a nice sunny spot.

Cyclamen: My favorite! Place it in a window with a southern, eastern, or northern exposure, and maintain a room temperature of 70°F during the day and 55°F at night. The leaves will turn over when the plant is thirsty. Water by submerging the plant, as described in "A Little Pampering Goes a Long Way" on page 190. When summer comes along, place your plant on the patio in a sunny spot, and return it to the house in fall.

Hydrangeas: Place in a window with a northern exposure after the plant has finished blooming. Water daily. Cut back the stems to the pot and when the weather warms, plant it in a good sunny spot, pot and all. In the fall, when you bring it back inside, cut it all the way back again and water daily. Feed hydrangeas once a week with my Fish Fertilizer+.

Padded Pots

Here's a neat trick: Place one potted plant, pot and all, inside of another, larger pot, and fill the space between the pots with peat moss. This will help keep the roots moist and cool during hot weather.

PEST PATROL

Give Bugs a Close Shave

Bugs won't call the soil of your houseplants home after this trick: Simply sprinkle pencil sharpening shavings onto the soil, or place a 3-inch slice of cedar pencil into the soil for every 3 inches of pot diameter (so a 6-inch-diameter pot would need two cedar slices, and so on).

AVOID A MOVING VIOLATION

Have you had bad luck when transplanting your houseplants—in other words, do they die shortly after they've made the move? If so, it's because they've gone into shock.

To transplant without trauma, first water your plant 24 hours beforehand. Then soak the new clay pot for an hour before transplanting into it, and fill the pot with damp soil.

Right after you set in your plant, feed it with plant food at 25 percent of the recommended rate. This should help your houseplant thrive in its new home.

Stand Up Straight!

Keep a leggy houseplant on the up-and-up by using a pencil as a stake. Insert the pencil into the soil next to the plant, and tie the plant to the pencil with a small strip cut from panty hose.

Jerry's Secrets

Don't get pricked when transplanting a cactus. Protect your fingers by using an old pair of kitchen tongs to lift and move your prickly plant.

WAIT FOR A SIGN

Every professional grower knows that there is no set schedule for feeding potted plants. Each variety of plant requires individual attention when it comes to food. Plants will tell you when they're hungry—you just need to know how to read their sign language.

If large, older leaves turn a tinge of yellow: Your plant is hungry. Feed it.

If new baby leaves are born yellow: Your parent plant needs iron. (Iron is available in catalogs or at garden centers.)

If the veins of older foliage are dark green, while foliage is yellowish: This is another indication of poor iron levels.

SHED SOME LIGHT ON YOUR CACTI

If your flowering cacti don't flower, they may not be getting enough light. Put them outside in the summer, starting gradually with exposure limited to several hours a day. This will activate buds that will blossom the next spring.

Jerry Tells All About...
Successful Growing

Q. Which vegetables grow the fastest?

A. If you want to have two or three different gardens a season, try these speedy selections: leaf lettuce, radishes, bush beans, onion sets, mustard and turnip greens, beets, and peas.

Q. Every time we put pepper or tomato plants in the ground, something breaks them off at the soil line. Any ideas what this could be?

A. That something is called a cutworm. Place 2-inch-high aluminum foil collars around the plant stems, making sure that 1 inch is below the soil. Then mulch with oak leaves. This should keep the little buggers out.

Q. I've heard that you can pinch tomatoes to make them climb, instead of spread out. Where do you pinch?

A. If you're going to train your tomatoes to grow up a stake, you should pinch out the side shoots that grow out of the crook of the main side stems.

Savory Neighbors

Plant herbs with strong odors in your vegetable gardens and flowerbeds to keep pests away. These odiferous neighbors can alternate with your food plants down rows, be planted together in alternate rows, or be planted here and there throughout the garden. The most common "pest-away" herbs are listed below:

Chives
Garlic
Mint
Rosemary
Sage
Thyme

MIXERS & ELIXIRS

Energizing Earthworm Elixir

To grow the sweetest, juiciest tomatoes and melons in town, mix up a batch of this soil-energizing mix before planting:

5 lbs. of earthworm castings
½ lb. of Epsom salts
¼ cup of instant tea granules

Mix all of the ingredients together, and put 1 cup in the bottom of each hole as you plant. Your tomatoes and melons will grow beyond your wildest dreams!

Q. When is it time to thin beans?

A. Never. I plant pole beans 2 feet apart and bush beans 9 inches apart. The seeds are large enough to plant separately.

Q. Is it true that you shouldn't cultivate around tomatoes?

A. It's a good idea not to disturb the roots, if at all possible. A 2-inch layer of mulch will eliminate weeds so you won't need to hoe, hoe, hoe.

Q. What's the earliest and the latest that I can plant beets?

A. The earliest is as soon as you can work the soil. The latest is around August 15 in the East and Midwest, and around July 15 in the North.

Q. Why don't my beets ever get any bigger than a ping-pong ball?

A. It sounds like the soil is too heavy; beets like light, loose soil. You can plant them in a trench 4 inches wide and 8 inches deep, filled with chopped or mowed leaves and sawdust.

COACH A WINNING TEAM

A good coach rotates his players in and out of the game to get the most from each one. You should do the same in your vegetable garden. To get the most from your plants, put your garden on a three-year rotation, like this one:

Year 1: Rotate the heavy feeders, like corn, squash, tomatoes, and melons.

Year 2: Rotate the heavy givers, like legumes (which return nitrogen to the soil), peas, beans, alfalfa, clover, and vetch.

Year 3: Rotate the light feeders, like beets, onions, carrots, turnips, kohlrabi, and parsnips.

Cucumbers by the Numbers

Here's a little secret that'll help you grow bigger, stronger cucumbers this year: Once the vines are off and running, only leave four fruits on the plant at any one time. Remove the tiny cukes as soon as they appear, and you'll be rewarded with a much better all-around harvest.

Q. Can I plant my broccoli, cabbage, and brussels sprouts together?

A. You sure can. All the vegetables you mention are in the same family, so you can give them all the same care and watch for the same insects. Just remember, they take up a lot of room, so keep that in mind when you plant your garden.

Q. Why do my carrots always grow all gnarled up, short and fat, or not at all?

A. They're probably in heavy soil. Carrots like rich, light soil that's 8 to 10 inches deep. If your soil is clay, just dig an 8- to 10-inch trench and fill it with sand, peat, leaves, and sawdust. Carrots don't do well in shade and prefer bright, sunny areas. Feed them with any garden food after foliage appears. I plant my seeds 3 inches apart, one at a time. I'd rather do the separating work sooner than have to thin them later.

MIXERS & ELIXIRS

Quick-Ripening Veggie Tonic

½ cup of apple juice
1 tbsp. of ammonia
1 tsp. of liquid dish soap
Water

Mix the apple juice, ammonia, and soap together in your 20 gallon hose-end sprayer, filling the sprayer jar with water to the 10-gallon mark. Use this tonic to hasten the ripening process of your vegetables at the end of the growing season.

Q. What makes my lettuce get mushy and slimy?

A. This usually happens when it is planted too late in the season. Lettuce doesn't like warm weather, but it can be grown in hot weather if it's grown in light shade. Lettuce is a very shallow rooted plant that needs plenty of food and must be kept damp at all times.

MIXERS & ELIXIRS

Tomato Blight Buster

To ward off early blight and other common tomato diseases, try using this mix on your newly transplanted tomato seedlings:

1 cup of compost
½ cup plus ¼ cup of powdered nonfat milk
½ cup of Epsom salts

Mix the compost, ½ cup of the powdered milk, and the Epsom salts together; sprinkle a handful of the mix into each planting hole. Then sprinkle the remaining ¼ cup of powdered milk on top of the soil after planting. Repeat every few weeks throughout the season.

Q. Do you have to take suckers off tomatoes?

A. No, you don't have to, and most folks don't want to go to the trouble. I do it because I plant fewer plants and want more fruit, so I remove the suckers that ride along for a free meal and don't produce.

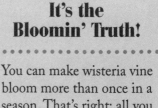
Q. I love turnip greens, but they don't do too well in the summer. How come?

A. It's because they don't like hot weather. Plant them early in May and again in August. You'll have some luck in the summer if you plant them in partial shade, but don't expect wonders.

Q. I can't get my parsnips to sprout. Can you tell me what the secret is?

A. Dig a trench 12 inches deep and 6 inches wide, and fill it with ⅓ sharp sand, ⅓ professional potting mix, and ⅓ local garden soil. Then plant your parsnips. You should see the results.

Q. My broccoli and cauliflower produce small heads that aren't very firm. What can I do to get bigger, firmer heads?

A. I want you to mix crushed eggshells into the soil around the plants to provide extra calcium, which these plants need to produce large, firm heads.

Q. I just don't have any luck with watermelons, and I've tried all kinds. I've planted them on a hill with good, rich, black soil. Why don't they like me?

A. It's not you—it's your garden location! If you planted on a sunny hillside, your watermelons would grow to the bottom of the hill before you could get there. Dry soil, in a sunny location, with really good drainage, is what they really love. And don't forget to remove any sick or dried blossoms.

Q. I had a problem with possums eating my strawberries, deer eating my roses and lettuce, and raccoons eating my tomatoes, plus the fish in my fish pond! Then I read about using mothballs to keep cats out of the garden, and I thought I'd give it a try to scare off the possums, coons, and deer. I scattered the mothballs all around my planting areas, and I didn't lose another thing all year! My question is, do the mothballs hurt the plants?

A. It depends on how heavily you apply them. Too much of a good thing can be trouble. To be safe, I'd rake 'em up at the end of each growing season, and properly dispose of them in the trash.

Q. How can I have good apples without bad worms?

A. You must dormant spray the trees in spring, and then

Give 'Em Room to Breathe!

Many folks get carried away when they're planting tomatoes. First, they plant far too many and then have to worry about harvesting a never-ending supply, and second, they tend to plant too close. You've got to give your tomatoes room to breathe. Plants that are crowded together don't get enough air circulation, and that invites garden pests, especially aphids. So plant fewer plants and give them plenty of elbow room. They'll thank you for it!

MIXERS & ELIXIRS

Tomato Shake

If your tomatoes have been bothered in the past by deadly diseases, try this milky shake:

1 part skim milk
9 parts water

Combine the ingredients and mist spray your plants and garden starting in early summer.

begin a regular spraying program with any all-purpose
liquid fruit tree spray every 14 days until harvest.
Be sure to dormant spray again in fall.

Q. My rhubarb turns yellow, then brown, about mid-season. Is this a blight?

A. Could be, so I want you to try feeding it with my Fish
Fertilizer+ and iron. And spray the plant at the beginning of
the season with 6 teaspoons of tomato vegetable dust in your
20 gallon hose-end sprayer.

Q. How do I keep my hydrangeas from turning all blue?

A. It's quick and easy—add one handful of aluminum sulfate
to the soil around each bush.

Q. Should clematis vine be trimmed each spring?

A. If they bloom on new foliage each year, you can cut them
back in fall or early spring. If they flower on old wood, don't you
dare touch them!

CRITTER CONTROL

Scat Cat Solution

Cats can be a real problem if they dig in your garden. Try this solution to keep them away from your prized plantings:

5 tbsp. of flour
4 tbsp. of powdered
   mustard
3 tbsp. of cayenne
   pepper
2 tbsp. of chili powder
2 qts. of warm water

Mix all of the ingredients together. Sprinkle the solution around the perimeter of the areas you want to protect.

KEEP THE BERRIES COMING

You can count on strawberries to produce for many
years if you handle them right. Buy good, healthy plants
and make sure your soil is rich, tilled, and light. Set the
plants 12 inches apart with rows at least 4 feet apart.
Don't set the plants any deeper than they were in
their containers. Feed and cover them loosely with
straw in fall, and uncover them in spring.

When the main plant grows runners, let them go,
but don't let them bunch up; spread them out all around
the mother plant. Then, at the end of three years, spade the
original plants under, and let the grown-up kids do their thing!

A Plastic Perch for Melons

I'm always reminding folks to save their plastic milk jugs because they sure do come in handy around the yard and garden. Here's another great use for them: Use milk jugs in the melon patch to prevent root rot. Simply cut a jug in half lengthwise, lay one half on the ground, and set the ripening melon inside. Not only will this plastic perch prevent root rot, but it will also discourage mites and their cousins from nibbling on your melons.

Q. For the last three years, I've had problems with sucking insects that take all the pulp out of my marigolds. The plants dry right up! I've tried everything. Help!

A. Try spraying your marigolds with "All-Season Clean-Up Tonic" (see "Green-Up and Clean-Up" on page 77) mixed with 1 tablespoon of any all-purpose liquid fruit tree spray containing malathion, methoxychlor, Captan, or Sevin every 14 days or so.

Q. Is there a weed control that I can use in my flowerbeds? I have weeded and weeded, and the root systems just keep coming back. I'm tired of weeding, so now what can I do?

A. Try using any of the systemic weed killers like KleenUp. Paint, roll, or spray it on anything you want to remove permanently. But don't touch the leaves of your good guys.

Q. Deer have overrun my gardens and yard. Are there plants that act as deer repellents? And are there plants that deer love, because I want to make sure I don't plant any of those!

A. Yes, and yes. Plants that deer detest are black locust, cucumber, geranium, peony, squash, verbena, and wisteria. Plants that deer devour include azalea, beans, English ivy, hosta, sweet

PEST PATROL

Quick Thrips Control

Thrips are tiny insects that bug your roses, hanging out in the flowers and discoloring the petals or stopping the roses from opening. Use this formula to attract beneficial green lacewings to your rose garden to feast on a diet of thrips:

1 part yeast
1 part sugar

Mix the ingredients with just enough water to make a thin paste, and dab a little bit of the mixture on each rose bud in early morning.

Double Exposure

Many pests spend time in the soil as eggs, larvae, or pupae. When you cultivate the soil, they become dislodged and exposed at the soil surface, where they may be eaten by larger predators or killed by the weather conditions. You can encourage this natural process by tilling your garden in the fall instead of waiting until spring. Till and leave the soil exposed until the first hard freeze, then cover with a winter mulch.

corn, tulip, winged euonymus. You can also try "Deer Buster Egg Tonic" (see page 91) to keep deer away.

Q. I need help growing garlic. All I've gotten so far is small bulbs in the ground with tops like golf balls on the stems. Can you help?

A. I want you to dig a hole 12 inches across and deep, and fill it with ⅓ soil, ⅓ professional mix, and ⅓ builder's sand. Then plant your garlic. You should have better results.

Q. My tomato plants started getting "early blight" in June. I tried to pick the leaves off, hoping to stop it from spreading, but this didn't work. The tomatoes were delicious, but the bushes eventually were destroyed. What can I do next year?

A. It sounds to me like your plants had wilt disease, which is incurable. It's caused by a soil-inhabiting fungus that infects only tomato plants. What you need to do is destroy all infected plants. Then next year, select only plants that aren't susceptible to wilt (look for the "F" when selecting varieties), and don't plant tomatoes where a wilt-infested plant grew this year.

Q. My spider plant has dried-out, discolored tips. What's wrong with it?

A. Drying leaf tips usually indicate a lack of humidity. To tidy up the plant, just snip the tips off. Then move it to a more humid location, like a steam-filled bathroom.

The Early Bird Catches the Maggot

If you've had trouble with maggots in your radishes, then an early planting is the cure. The key is to plant early enough to get a mature radish crop by June 1. Do this, and the roots will be practically free of maggots.

Q. I have a small garden that does real well, but for the last two years, I've had trouble with my cucumbers. They start out fine, but after a couple of pickings, the vines start drooping. What do I need to do to correct this problem?

A. Prespray the area with a fungicide containing Daconil in spring. Then add an all-purpose liquid fruit tree spray at 25 percent of the recommended rate to the "All-Season Clean-Up Tonic" (see "Green-Up and Clean-Up" on page 77), and use it throughout the season.

Q. My mom had a fern that was over 70 years old. When she was living, it stayed green and bushy. She passed away, and the leaves have turned brown. I have been struggling to keep it alive ever since. Can you give me any pointers?

A. A teaspoon of castor oil keeps the doctor away, so I want you to give the old fella a dose of it every now and then. Also, add a little ammonia to your watering solution every second feeding.

Equality for All

If your lilacs are tall and spindly rather than thick and bushy, it's probably the result of improper cutting. To cut lilacs the right way, you must remove branches from all portions of the plant equally. Tip-end cutting on most shrubs is OK, but long stems should only be taken when the shrub is heavily overgrown, and the stem should be cut back as far as possible to ensure graceful shaping.

Q. I have an African violet plant that's healthy, but has no flowers. Can I do something to make it bloom?

A. You sure can! The difference between a greenhouse and your living room is probably  the reason for not blooming. African violets flower best if they are kept standing on moist pebbles, which gives them a lot of humidity. Plenty of indirect fresh air is also important. Repotting may also be necessary. As soon as buds begin to appear, feed your plant with an African violet plant food according to the package directions. But don't feed during the short periods when the plant is resting and producing no new growth. And remember: Once your plant starts flowering, you must remove faded flowers promptly to prevent seed formation, which deters further bud development.

. . . .

Q. I have two hydrangeas in my garden. I've had them for 10 years, yet they've never bloomed. I feed them lime, but still, they have no buds or flowers. What could be the problem?

A. Sounds to me like they need to be root pruned. To do so, take a flat-backed spade and plunge it into the ground in a circle all the way around the bushes out at the weep lines. Then pour a mixture of 12 ounces of apple juice per gallon of warm water into the cuts in the soil around each bush.

. . . .

Q. Last summer, squirrels ate my tomatoes and roses before they opened. I've set out water in case they're thirsty, but to no avail. Please help!

A. If they're that bad, this year try using tomato cages surrounded by chicken wire or hardware cloth. And be sure to cover the tops of the cages to keep the little critters out.

Jerry's Secrets

If you want large peony blooms, pick off the side buds when they are very small, leaving just the main end bud on each stalk. This will focus the plant's energy on producing one gigantic flower.

Bird-Proof Your Hanging Baskets

Our fine feathered friends often mistake outdoor hanging flower baskets for ready-made condos! If you have birds making nests in your hanging baskets, don't despair. Take a section of chicken wire, cover the basket with it, and then pull the plants through it. That should stop the birds from feathering their nests!

Q. On my back fence, I have a beautiful clematis that didn't bloom this year. The plant covered the fence and was otherwise healthy. I didn't prune it last year, but I cut all of the dry vines off of the fence this spring. Do you think I did something to it that caused it not to bloom?

A. Probably not. The fact is, sometimes a clematis just skips a year. If yours blooms late, then cut it back in spring. If it blooms early, cut it back in the fall, root prune it, and sprinkle a handful of Epsom salts into the cuts.

Mother Nature's Moisture Meters

If you don't have the patience to go through your house every few days, sticking your finger into the soil of your houseplants to see if they need watering, I've got the answer for you—in a word, pinecones. Yep, these are Mother Nature's own moisture meters. Just stick a pinecone about two petals deep into the soil of each of your potted plants. The petals of the cone open when the plant is dry and close when it's wet, so there's no more poking around to determine when to water. It works great!

Q. Please tell me what to do with my two new wisterias that didn't bloom this year.

A. To make them bloom, you need to root prune them this fall, and sprinkle a handful of Epsom salts into the cuts. Then next spring, trim all of the suckers back. And be sure to keep all of the wild growth under control by pruning them frequently during the season.

Q. I need some information about black raspberry bushes. Should they be cut down? If so, at what time of year, and how?

A. You should cut down all of the dead canes after fruit bearing is done, when winter is just around the corner. Then mulch the plants heavily with straw and

Slug Screen

If slugs are bothering your young plants, screen 'em out. Take an old window screen, and cut 7-inch square sections from it. Make an opening in the center of each square and place the square down over your small plants, with the plants sticking up through the opening, and the screening flat on the ground. This will keep the slimy slugs away.

Ultra-Light Potting Soil

To keep your really big pots and planters from being back-breakers, fill them with this ultra-light potting soil mix:

4 parts perlite, moistened
4 parts compost
1 part potting soil
½ part cow manure

Mix all of the ingredients together, then use it to fill your planters to the top. Then keep an eye on the soil because this mix dries out very quickly, particularly in the hot summer sun.

wait for new foliage to appear in spring. Then cut the dead tops back to new growth, and seal the ends with a mix of latex paint and antiseptic mouthwash. To make them really produce, pinch off the tops of the new shoots when plants are about 2 feet tall.

Q. What is the best way to keep the shine on my houseplant leaves?

A. With a little shampoo and beer. Add ½ teaspoon of baby shampoo and ½ teaspoon of beer to a quart of warm water, then gently wash down the plant leaves.

Q. Is there any way to tell when a plant isn't getting enough light?

A. In most cases, you'll see pale, yellowish foliage, few flowers, and funny-shaped leaves. The leaves will begin to fall off from all over the plant, growth almost stops, and buds will only half open.

A Pot Full of Tea

To help your potted plants retain water and keep the roots moist in their pots, place three used tea bags in the bottom of the pot on top of the drainage pebbles before filling the pot with soil. The tea bags will not only help retain moisture, but they will also add much-needed nutrients to the soil as they decompose.

Q. When I put my houseplants outside for the summer, they get infested with mealybugs. What can I do to get rid of them?

A. Mist-spray them with a mixture of 1 teaspoon of baby shampoo and liquid Sevin at the recommended rate per quart of water until all signs of the bugs disappear.

Q. What temperature do houseplants like best?

A. As a rule, most houseplants like temperatures between 62°F during the night and 74°F during the day.

Q. If the foliage dries up on my houseplants, how do I get moisture back into it?

A. First, water the plant with warm water, and shower the foliage with soapy warm water. Then put a brick in the bottom of a bucket, set the plant on the brick, and pour boiling water into the bucket. Cover the bucket with a towel and leave your plant alone for a three- to four-minute steam bath.

Q. How can I tell when I've overfed my houseplants?

A. Generally the leaves will wilt, shrivel, and be soft. If you see these symptoms, water through the soil to flush it out—in other words, water heavily so the water drains out the bottom of the pot.

Q. Which plants are the best for me to use in my indoor hanging baskets?

A. Any plant that grows outside can grow indoors. Plants best suited for hanging baskets are fantana, Christmas cactus, wandering Jew, fuchsia, spider plant, strawberry begonia, hoya, ivies, and any of the melon or squash plants.

Don't Forget Your Plant Vitamins

Perk up your winter-weary houseplants by poking a children's vitamin or One-A-Day vitamin into each pot. This will supplement the nourishment they miss from the summer sunshine. Go ahead—the neighbors aren't watching!

Jerry's Secrets

I don't know why folks seem to think that all plants are night owls and want light 24 hours a day, but I will let you in on a little secret— plants only grow when they get proper sleep in the dark. If they stay up too long, they'll wilt just like you will, and their leaves will get burned spots.

Indoor Clean-Up Tonic

For those plants of yours that are indoors and exposed to all sorts of household pollutants, here's a tonic that'll keep 'em happy, healthy, clean, *and* mean:

1 tbsp. of liquid dish soap

1 tbsp. of antiseptic mouthwash

1 tsp. of ammonia

1 tsp. of instant tea granules

1 qt. of warm water

Mix all of the ingredients together, and put them in a handheld mist sprayer. Liberally spray on your houseplants, and wipe off any excess with a clean, dry cloth.

MOVE 'EM ON UP

After spending the summer outdoors, many container plants develop new shoots and new roots, too. This means the plants probably need more room—in other words, a larger pot. But don't rush out to buy huge containers. Plants that need to be repotted should be moved into pots that are just one size larger than their present ones. So a plant in a 2-inch pot should move up to a 3-inch pot, and no larger. The pot should just comfortably fit the roots without crowding them.

Once you've selected the right size pot, prepare it by placing pieces of broken clay pots or screening over the drainage hole in the bottom. Then add a layer of washed pea gravel, and a 1-inch layer of professional planter mix that has been mixed with one package of unflavored gelatin per 4-quart bag. This will get your plants settled comfortably in their new homes.

Q. Why do my houseplants grow crooked all the time?

A. You haven't been taking them for a spin! You need to turn the pots at least half a turn each day so the plants get the same light exposure all over. That should have them standing straight and tall.

Q. My gardenia blooms, but the blossoms fall off. What's up?

A. Gardenias need temperatures that don't drop below 60°F, with no surprise breezes. They like a lot of humidity, and a really rich composted mix of leaves, peat moss, sand, and manure. Gardenias are best planted in pots and set outside on the patio in summer, when the threat of frost is gone. Once there, they will fill the air with perfume! The younger the plant, the more flowers it will have. Two- to three-year-olds do best.

Q. The stems of the large lower leaves on my African violet turn brown and break or rot off. What could be the cause?

A. You would break or rot off, too, if your arms rubbed against a rough old pot edge for long enough! To fix this, take an old wax candle, and rub it like the dickens along the edge of your pot to give it a nice, smooth coat. You should also be diligent about removing older foliage, and using it to start new plants.

Q. When should I divide my African violet?

A. First, water it 24 hours before you divide it. To divide, use a sharp knife to remove any new crowns that look like they can take care of themselves. Keep as much soil as you can and some roots to ensure a good start. Repot them in 2¼-inch diameter clay pots that are clean and have been soaked in soapy water for at least an hour. Dampen the soil after transplanting, and keep your newly planted violets lightly shaded for a week.

HOUSEPLANT TOMATOES?

Yep—there's no law that says you can't grow tomatoes (or lettuce, peppers, even fruit trees) indoors, and I don't mean in a greenhouse! You can treat your tomatoes just like houseplants. Start by planting seeds of miniature varieties like 'Tiny Tim' or 'Patio', propagating from a cut branch of a bearing plant, or planting a seedling in a large pot. Keep your tomato plants away from gas stoves and out of drafts. They will do well if placed in a south or southeast window, blossoming and bearing fruit throughout the winter months. Even if you don't have a southern exposure, you don't have to miss out on the fun—tomato plants also do well under fluorescent light.

MIXERS & ELIXIRS

Perfect Potting Mix

If you've got a lot of potted plants, you need plenty of potting soil. So instead of constantly running out, mix up a batch of this blend, and keep it handy:

1 part topsoil
1 part peat moss
1 part vermiculite
1 part compost

Mix all of the ingredients together, and use for potting your plants, indoors and out.

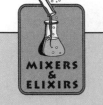

MIXERS & ELIXIRS

Flowering Houseplant Formula

Flowering houseplants need a little something extra to grow their very best. So to put on a big blooming show, supplement their regular diet with this special treat:

6 parts cottonseed meal
4 parts bonemeal
4 parts wood ashes
1 part Epsom salts

Mix all of the ingredients together, and apply at a rate of 1 teaspoon per 6-inch-diameter pot every eight weeks, working it well into the soil with an old fork.

Q. Why do the spikes of my aloe plant get all soft and spongy?

A. When the leaves are soft, it means the plant needs water. When the leaves are firm and hard, it has enough water. Aloe likes a lot of light (a western exposure is best), dry air, and temperatures above 55°F. Feed with any foliage food added to your water.

Give 'Em the Brush-Off

Dust off African violets, gloxinia, and other hairy-leafed plants with a soft baby's hairbrush. But go gently, and never, ever wash them off with water.

Q. I bring my azaleas in from the garden in the fall, but they never bloom again inside the house? Why not?

A. Azaleas bloom when the temperature is cool, and most of our homes are not. To keep the flowers longer, maintain the temperature between 50° and 65°F, and keep the soil damp, but not wet. Feed azaleas with any blooming plant food when you water them.

Q. If cactus is so easy to grow, why do I have so much trouble with mine?

A. Probably because you haven't gotten the point yet! Ouch! Cactus is best ignored, placed in a bright western window near heat. Water well, and then don't water again until the meat feels soft (I use a blunt stick to gently poke it). Keep the humidity down, and feed with foliage plant food. The soil mix should be sandy loam. By the way, succulents require the same conditions.

Q. My flowering cacti don't flower! What could be the problem?

A. They may not be getting enough light. Put them outside in the summer, starting gradually with exposure limited to several hours a day. This will activate buds that will blossom the next spring.

Q. I was overrun this past year by squash bugs that killed my vines and mites that snacked on my eggplants. What can I do to get rid of them?

A. At the first sign of trouble this year, I want you to mix 1 cup of my Plant Shampoo and 1 cup of my Total Insect Control in your 6 gallon hose-end sprayer, filling the balance of the sprayer jar with warm water. Then spray this mixture in the evening on all of your pestered plants at two-week intervals until the thugs are gone.

Q. I have purple Concord grape vines, and I need to know how and when to trim them. And what do you recommend for fertilizer?

A. Trim your vines in early March. Cut each limb back so there's only one bud per limb. Seal all cuts with "Tree Wound Paint Mixer" (see page 251). Feed them with any garden food in mid-April. Then spray them with an all-purpose liquid fruit tree spray at half the recommended rate after the grapes have set. Continue every two days for up to two weeks before the grapes are ripe.

BALE OUT

If you have limited growing space, terrible soil, or you just want to try something a little different next season, give bales a try. I kid you not—you can plant your garden seeds in bales of straw. Place the bale on a sheet of plastic or a cut-open trash can liner. Soak it regularly with water four to five weeks before planting to get the weed seeds in the straw to germinate. Then make small holes in the bale, fill them with rich topsoil or compost, and plant your seeds or seedlings in the topsoil. Keep the soil moist, and water every three weeks with my "All-Season Green-Up Tonic" (see "Green-Up and Clean-Up" on page 77).

Q. I have a striped spider plant and two that are solid green. They're doing well, but they have burning at the tips of their leaves. I put leftover coffee on them every day. Does this burn the tips?

A. No, but it sure builds up the acid in the soil! Don't add any more coffee, and only use "All-Purpose Houseplant Tonic" (see page 107) when you water.

• •

Q. I have a problem I'm hoping you can help me with. My canna, begonia, trumpet vine, and wisteria will not bloom. What can I do to get them to bloom?

A. It sounds to me like they're starving. I want you to feed them with a mixture of ½ cup of fish emulsion, ½ cup of regular cola (not diet), and ¼ cup of my All-Purpose Plant Food per 5 gallons of water.

• •

Jerry's Secrets

Use a large-toothed comb when repotting cacti to remove any particles of soil, peat, etc., that get caught in the cacti spines. It sure beats pickin' the stuff off by hand and suffering the prickly consequences!

Q. My rubber tree plant's lower leaves turn yellow and drop off. Other than that, the plant seems fine. Do you have any idea what's causing the lower leaves to drop?

A. The bottom leaves of rubber tree plants tend to turn yellow and drop with age— this is a natural process. If, on the other hand, your plant suddenly starts losing healthy, newer leaves, it's caused by overwatering. Water only when the soil is completely dry all through the pot. Use tepid water and apply very little in the winter months. When you do water, set the entire pot into a bucket so moisture can penetrate to the deepest roots.

Clean with Care

• • • • • • • • • • • • • • • • • • •

Cleanliness may be next to Godliness, but when it comes to houseplants, you do have to clean with care. Don't use any leaf-shining products on houseplant leaves. It clogs the plant's pores, and doesn't allow it to breathe. Instead, clean leaves every few weeks with a damp cloth that has been soaked in warm water and wrung out.

• • • • • • • • • • • • • • • • • • •

Step on It!

To grow the biggest onions around, use your feet! When your onions are about twice the size of your thumb, simply step on them, pressing them back down deeper into the soil. That's all there is to it!

Q. How long does it take before rhubarb matures? Our rhubarb is very good, but the rhubarb in the grocery store is much fatter. Does it make a difference if our stalks are fairly thin?

A. A two-year-old plant should be ready to please your taste buds. To fatten up your stalks, feed the plants in the winter by taking all of your nonmeat table scraps, pulverizing them in a blender, and adding a little regular cola (not diet) and beer to liquefy the mixture. Then pour it over the rhubarb mound.

Q. How can I sweeten the strawberries I grow? It seems that they have to be almost rotting before the sweetness occurs.

A. Sweetness has a lot to do with the soil the strawberries grow in. Feed them early in spring with a 4-12-4 or 5-10-5 dry fertilizer, adding 1 pound of sugar to the food. Then overspray with "All-Season Green-Up Tonic" (see "Green-Up and Clean-Up" on page 77) every three weeks through the growing season.

Q. How can I keep blight from killing all my tomato plants? I've used many different fungicides, and even moved the plants to different parts of my garden, but I still keep losing them. Do you have any ideas?

A. I want you to spray your garden soil late in the fall and early the next spring with a mixture of 2 tablespoons of bleach and 2 tablespoons of

Garlic Mist Formula

3 large cloves of garlic, minced
¼ cup of mineral oil
2 tsp. of liquid dish soap
1 pint of warm water

1. Soak the garlic in the mineral oil overnight.

2. The next day, strain the mixture. Take 2 teaspoons of the strained oil, and mix it with the dish soap in the pint of water. Now you have a formula for use indoors and out.

3. For houseplants, take 2 tablespoons of the garlic formula and add it to another pint of warm water. Mist-spray your plants with it every 7 to 10 days.

4. For outdoor use, put all of the garlic formula into your 20 gallon hose-end sprayer and fill the balance of the sprayer jar with warm water. Spray every two weeks in the early evening.

baby shampoo in a gallon of water. This will cover about 100 square feet of garden area. Then, during the growing season, spray the tomato plants every two weeks with an all-purpose liquid fruit tree spray.

Q. Last year, something ate the leaves off of my marigolds. Could it be slugs, and if so, what can I do to prevent a repeat?

A. Yes, it sounds like slugs to me. So this year, I want you to apply a mixture of 25 percent aluminum sulphate and 75 percent pelletized lime with your handheld spreader once every three weeks to the area you want to protect. Also, set out shallow pie tins filled with leftover beer for the tough guys—they'll fall in and drown themselves!

Q. I was given lovely pink impatiens last spring. They did well in the house and bloomed beautifully outdoors last summer. Now the leaves aren't looking so healthy. What can I do—should I cut them back? I don't want to lose them.

A. I would carefully cut back the plant so that there are three sets of leaves on each stem. Then add sugar to the plant food mixture you use, either in the form of regular cola (not diet) or sugar. Use the cola at the rate of 4 ounces per gallon of water, or use 2 teaspoons of sugar per gallon of water.

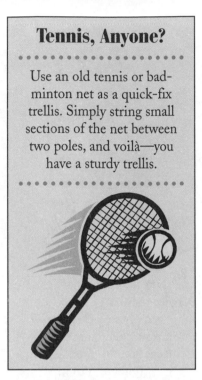

Tennis, Anyone?

Use an old tennis or badminton net as a quick-fix trellis. Simply string small sections of the net between two poles, and voilà—you have a sturdy trellis.

MIXERS & ELIXIRS

Berry Booster

1 can of beer
2 tbsp. of Fish Fertilizer+
2 tsp. of instant tea granules

Mix all of the ingredients together in your 6 gallon hose-end sprayer, and apply every three weeks during the growing season to keep those luscious berries coming.

CHAPTER 5

"No one ever tires of an attractive landscape, except perhaps
the homeowner who works too hard at keeping it that way.
Yes, it takes a little work, but it can be fun as well as
rewarding. After all, we all need exercise to stay healthy,
and there's nothing like a good workout or two each week
to make sure that both you and your yard stay in shape!"

Land Hoe!

The Grass Is Always Greener…In *My* Yard!

I want you to think of your lawn as if it were the hair on your head. People judge your hair—and your lawn—by its appearance. So make your lawn look like it just came back from the barbershop—clean, combed, and well cut. Here are my lawn grooming secrets. (And as for your hair, well, you're on your own!)

DINNER IS SERVED…WHEN?

Your lawn will let you know when it's hungry. As the soil warms up in the spring, plant roots stretch farther out through the soil, seeking food. When they can't find enough, their growth is stunted and the plants start to show signs of starvation. If your green lawn becomes spotty or lighter in color, pay attention—it's begging for food! Give it a hearty meal of "All-Purpose Yard Fertilizer" (at left), and watch it grow!

GIVE YOUR LAWN A NEW LEASE ON LIFE

Overseeding (broadcasting seed over your existing lawn) is the quickest and easiest way to improve an old lawn—it gives it better color and thicker growth, plus it builds resistance to drought and disease. This is especially important if your lawn is 8 to 10 years old because odds are the seed variety that was originally used was not as strong and disease-resistant as the new varieties that are available today. Through the miracle of modern science, today's varieties are resistant to traffic, insects, disease, drought, and shade.

Overseeding in the fall will give you a thicker stand of grass. But since most folks have had it with yard work by the time August rolls around, it's OK to overseed in spring, too.

GREEN-IT-UP

There isn't a single person I can think of who wouldn't like to have the greenest grass in the neighborhood. The trick here, my friends, is to have gorgeous green grass without giving up your golf, tennis, or other leisure pastimes, and without exerting any more effort than it would take to wash your car on a Saturday afternoon. Impossible, right? Wrong! Just follow these tips, and I'll show you how to *streeetch* your dollars and your time, so that you end up with "green" in your wallet *and* in your lawn:

🍂 Mow after 6:00 P.M. while wearing your golf shoes. Mowing late in the day allows the grass plants to recover from the shock before the hot sun and dry winds can take their toll the next day. The spikes in the shoes punch small holes through the "surface tension" barrier on the lawn, allowing food, water, and other controls to get down and dirty to the root area.

🍂 Feed your grass with my Liquid Lawn Food or "All-Season Green-Up Tonic" (see "Green-Up and Clean-Up" on page 77) every three weeks throughout the growing season. By applying milder and smaller amounts of fertilizer more often, your grass will stay greener and stronger—longer.

🍂 Clean grass is happy grass, and you want your grass to be delirious! So bathe your lawn every two weeks with "All-Season Clean-Up Tonic" in your 20 gallon hose-end sprayer (see "Green-Up and Clean-Up" on page 77) This tonic will destroy disease, discourage pests, and improve drainage. Plus, it'll make all of your other lawn applications more effective.

🍂 To ensure a healthy lawn, always water before 2:00 P.M. so the grass can "go to bed" dry. The best time is early in the morning—any time between 5:00 A.M. and 9:00 A.M.

🍂 For weed control, apply any good broadleaf weed control at the recommended rate when the weeds are growing.

Great Grass Seed Starter

If you're spot-seeding lawn areas in spring, soak your seeds in this starter mix first to speed up its sprouting time:

1 cup of liquid dish soap
1 gal. of weak tea water*

Soak the grass seed in this tonic, in the refrigerator, for at least 48 hours. Then take the seed outside and spread it out on your driveway to dry out. Once it's dry, it's ready to sow.

*Soak a used tea bag in a gallon of warm water and 1 teaspoon of liquid dish soap until the mix is light brown.

RULES FOR RENOVATION

You've heard of the Golden Rule? Well, here are my Golden Renovation Rules for redoing an old lawn. There are only three, and they are simple to follow:

Rule #1: Always remove excess thatch. (See "Attack Thatch" on page 231.) If you don't, the new grass seed you put down will not come into contact with the soil. It will simply set roots down in the thatch, and will quickly die when the hot, dry weather comes along.

Rule #2: Remember that all grass seed is not created equal, nor are all varieties the same. The seed you should use will vary, depending upon the climate in your area. The secret we professionals use is to mix as many different types of the same variety, using a major, middle, and minor type in a blend of 60-40-20. For example, if you live in the North, try using 60 percent bluegrass (as many different kinds as you can find), 40 percent perennial turf-type rye, and 20 percent fescue.

Rule #3: Keep overseeded lawns well watered, and feed with "All-Purpose Yard Fertilizer" (see page 216) as soon as you see sprouts sticking their heads through the soil.

SMART SEED SHOPPING

Over the years, I've seen many a homeowner buy grass seed simply because it was the lowest price. They soon discover that they've bought more trouble than they can handle. So don't fall into this trap—take my advice, and buy smart!

Your lawn can either add to or detract from your home's value. High-quality grass seed is the foundation of a good lawn, and it will prove to be one of the best long-term investments you'll ever make. That's right, it's an investment! How can you be sure that you're buying quality seed? First, choose a name brand because reputable companies do not put their names on inferior products. Second, read the seed label, paying close attention to the "seed mixture analysis." This tells you what's inside the box (see "Which Seed is Which?" on the opposite page).

WHICH SEED IS WHICH?

I tell you, shopping for grass seed can be a maddening experience, unless you know what you're looking for. There's an endless array of mixtures, quality, and packaging. But every bag of seed has a "seed mix analysis" that lists the components of the seed inside, so read the label. Here's a quick rundown on what it means:

Pure seed. You'll find the names of the grasses contained in the mix and their percentages by weight. Improved varieties of grasses will bear distinct names, like 'Victa' Kentucky bluegrass. Germination percentages tell you how much of that particular seed variety is capable of growing under ideal conditions.

Other ingredients. These are the undesirable contaminants in the mix. "Other Crop Seeds" can be grasses such as Timothy or orchard grass, which, once established, are extremely difficult to eliminate from your lawn. "Weed Seeds" refer to undesirables not normally grown as farm crops, and can include chickweed or dandelions. These can usually be controlled with herbicides. "Noxious Weed Seeds" are named and counted separately.

Inert matter. This is filler to make the bag look bigger so you think you're getting more for your money! Sand, which adds weight, and empty hulls and stems, which add bulk, are frequently used as fillers. Any seed you buy will have some inert matter, but watch out for those that have high percentages (8 to 10 percent), which means a large percentage of the bag is useless. And if a large percentage of the bag is useless, then the cost of that "bargain seed" just went through the roof!

Jerry's Secrets

I always try to plant, drill, or broadcast grass seed after 5:00 P.M. Plants grow in the dark, so I like to give them a head start!

Roll 'Em, Roll 'Em, Roll 'Em

That's right, keep those doggies rollin'! Once you've seeded your lawn, don't stop there! The next step is to roll your lawn to ensure good seed-to-soil contact. You can rent a lawn roller from your local garden center, or even get together with your neighbors and buy one for all to share.

		SEEDING	
GRASS	DAYS TO GERMINATE	(LBS) PER 1000 SQ. FT.	LIFE
Annual ryegrass	8	10	1 year
Baron	28	2	Permanent
Clover	10	6	Permanent
Delta	28	3	Permanent
Fescue	8	8	Permanent
Park	28	3	Permanent
Highland bent	28	3	Permanent
Kentucky blue	28	3	Permanent
Kentucky 31	10	10	Permanent
Manhattan rye	8	10	Permanent
Merion blue	28	3	Permanent
Newport	28	3	Permanent
Nugget	28	3	Permanent
Penncross bent	28	4	Permanent
Perennial rye	8	10	3 years
Red top	6	3	3 years

Turf Grasses at a Glance

TEXTURE	FOR SHADED AREA	FOR HEAVY WEAR	FOR QUICK COVER	FOR SLOPES & TERRACES
Coarse	No	Fair	Best	No
Fine	No	Good	No	Good
None	Fair	Best	Good	No
Fine	Poor	Good	No	Good
Fine	Fair	Fair	Best	No
Fine	Best	Fair	No	Fair
Fine	Poor	Good	No	Fair
Fine	Poor	Good	No	Good
Coarse	Fair	Best	Fair	Fair
Fine	Fair	Fair	Best	No
Fine	No	Best	No	Good
Fine	Poor	Good	No	Good
Fine	Poor	Good	No	Good
Very fine	Poor	Good	No	Good
Coarse	Fair	Fair	Best	No
Very fine	No	Fair	Good	No

THE BEST TIME TO SEED

The absolute best time to seed a new lawn for most parts of the country is between August 15 and September 15. Moisture and temperature conditions are great—and the gentle fall rains are best for establishing turf with minimal competition from weeds.

Grass that's seeded later in the fall may fail if the seedlings aren't able to grow enough to establish themselves before winter. However, a dormant seeding after early November is fine because low temperatures will prevent germination of the seeds until the following spring. So do it early or do it late; just don't do it in the middle!

STRAW SAVES THE DAY

Applying a good layer of straw mulch to your newly seeded lawn will provide consistent moisture and cool temperatures during the growing period, and it will reduce soil erosion and displacement of the seed. Hose the straw down with water after you spread it to help stabilize it on windy days. On those steep areas where erosion is a problem, cover the grass seed with burlap or twine netting instead of straw to reduce the amount of seed and soil that wash away.

When the grass is 1½ to 2 inches high, remove about half of the layer of straw. You do not need to remove burlap, cloth, or netting.

If you've seeded in spring, the remaining straw should decompose over the course of the season. If you've seeded in fall, remove the remaining straw before the first snowfall, unless, again, erosion is a problem in the area.

READY, SET, SEED!

Seeding a lawn takes a bit more effort than just going out there and throwing the grass seed to the wind! To seed like a pro, start by choosing the right day for the job. I know that it's not always possible, but you should seed your lawn when there is little wind. Otherwise, the light, chafflike grass seeds will blow away. Using a broadcast or drop-type spreader, apply half of the seed while walking from side to side across your lawn, and apply the other half while walking from top to bottom.

After seeding, lightly rake the soil to mix the seed into the top ⅛ to ¼ inch of soil. (An inverted metal or bamboo leaf rake dragged over the soil works great.) Now that's how to seed a lawn!

QUENCH YOUR NEW LAWN'S THIRST

Getting a new lawn started takes time, patience, and a whole lot of water. But over the years I've come up with these simple methods that'll save you water and money when establishing a new lawn:

🐛 If you can, reduce steep slopes while you're still in the design phase. Level surfaces allow water to penetrate into the ground, while steeper slopes encourage wasteful water runoff.

🐛 Install an irrigation system. A system delivers water much more efficiently and with less waste than hoses, sprinklers, and handheld hose-end sprayers.

🐛 Select drought-tolerant grass varieties that'll thrive in your area. Scientific grass breeding has developed many different varieties of improved turfgrasses, which you can find at your local garden center.

🐛 Sod, rather than seed. Turfgrass sod requires anywhere from 15 percent to as much as 60 percent less water to establish than seed does, depending on your geographic area and growing conditions. While sod is more expensive, it pays off in the long run if you live in an area with frequent dry spells.

🐛 Water in the early morning or early evening—never at midday when the hot, drying sun is beating down upon your lawn. There is less wind drift and lower evaporation rates early and late, also.

🐛 Mow higher than normal with a sharp, sharp blade. Larger grass blade surfaces hold more liquids, plus they shade the root zone. Dull mower blades damage the grass blades, which will increase moisture loss from the grass plants.

Hair Club for Lawns

If your lawn looks like it's going bald, fall is the time to overseed your old lawn as well as start a new one. To make grass seed sprout faster, place it in a refrigerator for 48 hours or soak it in chilled "Compost Tea" (at right) for 24 hours, then spread the seed out to dry. Sow it and then run for your life, because it's liable to grow right up your pant leg!

MIXERS & ELIXIRS

Compost Tea

This solution is great for seed starting and as an all-around plant pick-me-up. Simply put several shovelfuls of compost or manure into a large trash can. Fill the can to the top with water. Allow the mixture to sit for a day or two, stirring it several times each day. To use, dilute the tea with water until it is a light brown color. Give each plant about a cup of this tea every two weeks, and your feeding worries will be over.

Jerry's Secrets

You can get great results if you overseed (or dormant seed) your snow-covered yard in January. That's right—simply fill your handheld spreader with grass seed, and walk across your lawn, spreading the seed in front of you so that you step on it as you go. This will force it down into the snow (keeping it out of birds' beaks), where it will pick up moisture and swell up. Then, when the midwinter thaw comes, the soil will soften enough to swallow the seed. Once it freezes over again, the grass seed will be safe and sound until spring.

ZOYSIA: IS IT RIGHT FOR YOU?

There's no type of grass that I get more questions about than Zoysia. Although it sounds like a dream come true, if you live in an area where there is an early killing frost and a late spring, then "just say no." Here's why:

🌱 Zoysia loses its green color and turns tan at the first frost. It stays that way until the soil warms and night temperatures stay above 50°F. So in the North, your grass will be green maybe 4 months out of a year, at best.

🌱 It costs more to put in than most lawns.

🌱 It takes two years or more to completely fill in.

🌱 It can't handle even the slightest bit of shade.

🌱 It is not as fast or as full a grower as Bermuda grass.

Now, mind you, I'm not trying to be a stick in the mud; there are some advantages to Zoysia. If you live in the areas of the country it was designed for, like down South, and if you have the time to tend to it, Zoysia is hard to beat. Here's why:

🌱 It is a tough grass that resists wear, even when it's dormant.

🌱 It is slow growing, so you don't have to mow as often.

🌱 It is thick and attractive, but requires close mowing to keep its "carpet" look.

🌱 It is fairly disease-free, and insect pests give it two thumbs down—they don't seem to like it.

Watch Your Step

Keep off the grass! Grass will naturally go dormant during periods of drought, but will readily revive when water becomes available. Just be sure to keep people and pets off the lawn until it recovers. Otherwise, it's *hasta la vista*, baby!

DETER DROUGHT DAMAGE

At one time or another, most of us have lived through a summer drought. As a kid, it was great because you could play outside forever. As an adult—yikes, what happened to our lawn? Well, you certainly can't prevent a drought, but you sure can use that proverbial ounce of prevention to reduce the loss of your valuable lawn. Here's how the pros do it:

1. Water your lawn deeply, giving it at least 1 inch of water per week. Let the surface layer dry out to a depth of 2 inches or more. This will discourage shallow root growth, so the roots will grow down to where there is more moisture.

2. Alternately soak your lawn to a depth of 10 inches and then allow the top layer to dry out, as explained in Step 1. This ensures that your grass roots will develop in the lower level of soil.

3. When the drought hits, relax. By saturating the deep layer of soil while water was available, you stimulated deep, dense root growth that will now save your lawn during the dry spell.

SEND LAWN WEEDS A PACKIN'

If it seems like you had more weeds than grass last summer, fall is the time to solve your weedy woes and ensure that you won't see them hanging around your yard next spring.

Between August 15 and October 1, no matter what part of the country you live in, fill up your 20 gallon hose-end sprayer with water, and add a cup of liquid dish soap to it. Spray your entire lawn with this soapy water solution. Do it on a bright, sunny afternoon between 1:00 P.M. and 3:00 P.M. because those are the "killin' hours"—weeds die best between these hours.

Next, mix any good broadleaf weed killer as directed on the package, and respray your freshly shampooed lawn. The result will have you singing "bye-bye weeds."

MIXERS & ELIXIRS

Drought-Buster Tonic

1 can of beer
1 cup of Thatch Buster
1 cup of Liquid Lawn
  Food
1 cup of baby shampoo

Mix all of the ingredients together in a large bucket. Then pour into a 20 gallon hose-end sprayer, and apply to your lawn once a week in hot weather. Apply early in the morning to minimize evaporation and to give the grass plants ample time to digest it.

MIXERS & ELIXIRS

Lawn Pest Control Tonic

1 cup of Murphy's
  Oil Soap
1 cup of chew-
  ing tobacco
  juice*

Mix the
ingredients
together in
a 20 gallon hose-end
sprayer, and apply to
your lawn to chase insect
pests away.

*To make the juice, take
three fingers' worth of
chewing tobacco from the
package, place it in the toe
of a nylon stocking, and
place the stocking in a gallon of boiling water. Let the
tobacco steep until the water is dark brown.

LUSH LAWNS, LESS WATER

You don't have to drain the Hoover Dam every day to keep your lawn looking its best. You can have a healthy, lush lawn during times of drought if you just follow these water-saving tips:

🌿 **Mow as infrequently as possible.** Mowing puts the grass plants under additional stress, and when this happens, they scream for more water (so that's what that noise was!).

🌿 **Mow higher than normal.** Never remove more than 1/3 of the leaf blade in one mowing. Longer blades hold more water, shade the root zone, and result in deeper, more efficient roots.

🌿 **Water and mow early in the morning or early in the evening.** There is less wind and heat at these times, so water penetrates deeper and won't evaporate as quickly.

🌿 **Water for deep penetration.** Immediately stop watering when puddles form or when runoff occurs. Then allow the water to penetrate the soil before continuing.

🌿 **Aerate the turf.** Get out there with your golf shoes or aerating sandals on, and break some ground. By penetrating the surface tension barrier and breaking up the top layer of soil, you're helping water to penetrate more efficiently to the roots.

ALL WASHED UP

If you're using a broadleaf weed killer in liquid form, add 1 tablespoon of baby shampoo to each 5 gallons of spray. It will speed up the action of the weed killer by helping it stick to the weeds better.

If you're using a dry chemical control, wash the lawn first with a mix of 1 cup of baby shampoo per 20 gallons of water. But don't spray your whole lawn with weed killer if you've only got a small area infested with weeds. That would be like making your brother drink Castor oil when you were the sick kid. Wouldn't have done either of you much good, right? The same is true for your lawn—only apply weed killers to weeds, or you'll retard the development of your grass.

GETTING TO KNOW YOU

Or I should say, getting to know your weeds. The first step in any type of weed control is to know exactly what it is you're dealing with. Mother Nature has blessed us with two kinds of lawn weeds—monocots and dicots. Here's my quick Biology 101 lesson on what they are and how to deal with them:

Monocots: These are grassy weeds, like goose grass, crab grass, nut grass, foxtail, dallis grass, and witch grass.

Dicots: These are more commonly known as broadleaf weeds, and these are the bad guys you see most often. Purslane, chickweed, dandelion, henbit, oxalis, thistle, plantain, buckthorn, clover, ground ivy, and knotweed are all dicots.

How to kill 'em: Get at the monocots while they're asleep (dormant) with a "pre-emerge crabgrass control" that is available in either dry or liquid form. This kills the weed seed before it can germinate or sprout in spring. Keep in mind, however, that you have a relatively small window of opportunity—you must kill the seed before it germinates, or the pre-emerge control is worthless.

Tackle the dicots with 2,4-D, a growth-stimulator hormone that makes the plants literally grow themselves to death. This hormone is packaged with other herbicides in the mix, and is very effective any time the broadleaf weeds are thriving.

Jerry's Secrets

I'll keep on repeating this one until the cows come home: Whenever you apply any weed controls, do it on a calm, windless day. Even just a little bit of wind can scatter the chemicals, damaging nearby shrubs and flowers (not to mention the dog and the kids!) before you even realize what is happening. So be safe, rather than sorry!

KILL 'EM AS YOU SEE 'EM!

Serious (and smart) lawn lovers like me destroy our weeds one by one as we see them. You should, too. Simply fill a handheld sprayer with your favorite broadleaf weed killer and water, and take it with you when you go out to mow the lawn. Then, as you're mowing, stop, shoot the weed with the spray, and move on. If you do this, you'll never need to get involved in a full-blown weed battle; instead, you'll have knocked 'em dead one by one.

GO ON MOLE PATROL

There's nothing more devastating than having moles picnicking under your lawn. It may be hard for you to accept, but these harmless, ugly, furry, nearly blind critters are doing you a favor by digging in your lawn. Yep, that's because they're telling you that you probably have an overabundance of lawn-killing insects lurking beneath the sod. But before you can tackle the pest problem, you've got to control the moles. Here are my seven super secrets to scare 'em away and keep 'em away:

1. Add two tablespoons of Pine-Sol to a sprayer bottle filled with water, and squirt this mixture into spots along the runs.

2. Place ½-inch pieces of Juicy Fruit gum in the runs.

3. Mix human hair and mothball crystals, and place this mix along the runs.

4. Place pieces of rose stem or other thorny stems in the runs.

5. Place castor beans or castor oil in the runs.

6. Place Styrofoam or cotton balls the size of your little fingertip in and along the runs.

7. Place pieces of garlic and onion along the runs.

PEST PATROL

Worm Out

If your lawn is plagued by worms that leave small mounds all over the place, it's time to take action. Apply a light application of ammonium sulphate with your handheld spreader set on the lowest setting. Do this in early spring to send the worms a'wandering.

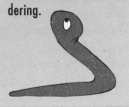

ARE YOU SURE IT'S GRASS?

Believe you me, not all lawns are grass! And some unsuspecting easterners have discovered this when they've moved west or south and met up with dichondra, a groundcover substitute for grass that's a member of the morning glory family. If you use a common weed killer on this type of lawn, you can kiss it all goodbye.

So a word to the wise—if you move to a new part of the country and cannot identify the "grass" variety that's growing in your lawn, play it safe. Take a sample of your turf to a local nursery and ask for help. Remember, always err on the side of caution.

DON'T NEGLECT YOUR SUMMER LAWN—OR ELSE!

By the time the hot, hazy
days of August roll around, the
mower blade is dull, and many
folks just want to find a shady
place to hang the hammock and
take a snooze. But your lawn
needs your support and encour-
agement in summer more than
any other time of year. It's an
unmistakable fact of life—summer is when diseases and insects rear their ugly heads. Start
your summer lawn program off
right by getting rid of lawn
pests. Use "Lawn Pest Control
Tonic" (see page 226) weekly to keep bugs in check.

Next, reseed any bare spots. Make sure the seed is refrigerated
for at least 48 hours before you sow it. Scuff up the soil, seed with
your spreader set at medium-light to medium, and cover the seed
with a 50/50 mixture of professional mix and garden soil. Pat it
down lightly, and keep it well watered.

Finally, toward the end of summer, I like to give my lawn a
hearty meal. This is the time of year when I mix just about every
leftover bag and box of dry lawn food, garden food, and flower
food together in a clean trash can, and apply it at half of the recommended rate over my entire yard, beds included. Then I wet it
down with a mix of 1 can of beer, 1 cup of liquid dish soap, and 1
cup of ammonia, ap-
plied with my 20 gal-
lon hose-end sprayer.
If you do the same,
your lawn will
thank you for this
summer bonanza!

MIXERS & ELIXIRS

Lawn Fungus Fighter Tonic

If your lawn develops
brown or yellow spots
that eventually die out,
fight back with this
fix-it-up formula:

1 tbsp. of baking soda
1 tbsp. of instant tea
    granules
1 tbsp. of horti-
    cultural/dormant oil
1 gal. of warm water

Mix all of the ingredi-
ents together in a large
bucket. Then apply with
a handheld sprayer by
lightly spraying the turf.
Do not drench or apply
to the point of runoff.
Repeat in two to three
weeks, if necessary.

Clipping Conditioner

If you don't pick up grass clippings after you mow, overspray your lawn once a month with this mix:

1 can of regular cola (not diet)
½ cup of liquid dish soap
¼ cup of ammonia

Mix all of the ingredients together in your 20 gallon hose-end sprayer, filling the balance of the jar with warm water.

MOWING MANIA

Everyone loves green grass, but most of us hate to mow it on a regular basis. Yet proper mowing is one of the simplest and least expensive preventive maintenance practices you can do for your lawn.

Each grass variety has a recommended cutting height that will make it grow vigorous and healthy. At its optimal height, grass will have greater root growth, less rapid regrowth, greater photosynthetic capacity, more density, and less stress (whew, what a mouthful!). And did I mention one other very important benefit? A tight, healthy turf also helps prevent weeds from getting started.

Check out the chart below for mowing heights and frequencies for some of the more popular grass varieties. These recommendations follow the general rule that no more than ⅓ of the leaf surface should be removed at each mowing. Under normal growing conditions, you should cut your lawn every six or seven days. Mow in the evening around 7:00 P.M., when it is more comfortable for both you and your lawn. And do it on a Thursday, so you've got the whole weekend to enjoy the great outdoors!

Mowing Heights		
GRASS VARIETY	**BEST CUT HEIGHT**	**MOW AT THIS HEIGHT**
Fine fescue	2"	3"
Kentucky bluegrass	2"	3"
Perennial ryegrass	2"	3"
Tall turf-type fescue	2"	3"
Zoysia	1" to 2"	1½" to 3"

ATTACK THATCH

What is thatch? It's what I call lawn dandruff. Every time you mow your lawn, the clippings you don't collect fall down near the base of the blades, leaving a thin layer of mulch. These clippings, along with other debris, build up into a matted, rotting layer of thatch.

While a thin layer of thatch helps to insulate grass roots from heat and cold, a thick layer blocks water, air, and fertilizer from getting to the roots below. So it's important for you to attack thatch before it gets the better of your lawn.

The best (and most expensive) way to remove thatch is with a motorized dethatcher or "power rake" attachment on your lawn mower. One warning here: The mower must have a powerful motor for good results.

My advice is to rent, not buy, a dethatcher to do the job because dethatching isn't something you'll have to do regularly.

Be sure to adjust the depth so the blades just reach the top level of soil. Once the thatch is brought to the lawn's surface, remove it either by raking, vacuuming, or picking it up with a grass catcher on your lawn mower. Then don't throw it out; add it to your compost pile.

Other ways to dethatch include using my Thatch Buster, "Thatch Control Tonic" (at right), or a dethatching rake, if you have a small lawn area.

MIXERS & ELIXIRS

Thatch Control Tonic

1 can of beer
1 cup of ammonia
1 cup of liquid dish soap
1 cup of regular cola
  (not diet)

Mix all of the ingredients together in a bucket, then apply to your lawn with a 20 gallon hose-end sprayer as soon as the temperature stays above 50°F in spring.

FALL INTO DETHATCHING

Dethatching is best done in fall. That's when vigorously growing grass plants will quickly repair any damage and fill in bare spots before weeds can invade the lawn. If you do it in midsummer, the grass plants are slow to recover because of the heat. On the other hand, if you wait too long in the fall, the plants may not have enough time to repair themselves before winter sets in.

A good rule of thumb is to remove thatch from your lawn when the layer is more than 3/4 inch thick. How can you determine its thickness? Take a sharp knife and cut a small section of the turf. Peel it back, and then measure the depth of the thatch.

COMPACTION IS FOR TRASH—NOT LAWNS!

If your lawn gets a lot of traffic, or if it's growing in clay soil, it's probably compacted. A compacted lawn feels hard, and the grass in it grows poorly and becomes thin. Even if you don't have clay soil, your lawn can become compacted if it's repeatedly walked on when it's wet. The solution is to aerate your lawn. Here's how to do it:

Start with an aerator. Both mechanical and manual aerators are available to remove plugs of soil from the lawn. Removing the soil plugs creates pathways for air, water, and fertilizer to make their way down to the grass roots. A manual aerator is only practical for small areas. If you've got a larger area, your best bet is to rent a mechanical aerator, not buy one.

Aerate your lawn in the fall, while you're in the mood for raking and fertilizing. The soil should be moist, but not wet, so the aerating tines can easily penetrate the soil.

Remove the soil plugs that are left on the grass, or break them up and spread them out with a rake or mower. If the compaction has developed over many years or your lawn has never been aerated, then you may have to go over it several times to remedy the problem.

Prevention is the key. If you get into the habit of wearing golf shoes or my aerating sandals every time you work in the yard, and you regularly apply "All Season Clean-Up Tonic" (see "Green-Up and Clean-Up" on page 77), you can all but kiss your lawn compaction problem goodbye.

OCTOBERFEAST

You should feed your lawn in October with a low-nitrogen fertilizer to establish a strong, healthy root system before the snow flies. Use a fertilizer with nitrogen-phosphorus-potassium proportions of 4-12-4, 5-10-5, or 6-10-4. In warmer climates, where the growing season stretches year 'round, fall is the time to use a fertilizer with a 1-1-1 ratio—that is, equal quantities of each nutrient, such as 10-10-10 or 12-12-12.

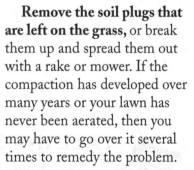

Luxurious Landscapes

There's more to an eye-pleasing landscape than just a lawn and garden—trees, shrubs, evergreens, and groundcovers count, too. I like to think of them as the framework for any great landscape. Anyone who's ever moved into a newly built home in the middle of a bare lot knows how empty the surroundings seem until the landscape gets growing. In this section, I'm gonna let you in on my secrets for selecting and caring for shrubs, groundcovers, and a variety of other landscape plants. To learn the whys and wherefores about trees, turn to page 244.

POLLUTION-PROOF PLANTS

Shrubs give you more bang for the landscape buck than nearly any other group of plants. As a rule, they are inexpensive, fast-growing, attractive, and demand little attention. If you live near a large city or industrial area where air pollution is a problem, you should select your landscape plants very carefully. My many years of experience have shown that some trees and shrubs are exceptionally tolerant of toxic fumes and dust. Here's a rundown of the best of the bunch:

Shrubs: Alpine currant, arrowwood, bayberry, drooping leucothoe, five-leaf aralia, honeysuckle, inkberry, Japanese barberry, showy border forsythia, shrubby cinquefoil, Siberian pea tree, Tatarian dogwood, and winged euonymus.

Trees: Amur cork tree, European linden, hedge maple, lavelle thorn, maidenhair tree, ornamental crabapple, thornless honey locust, and last but not least, Washington thorn.

I can't say this enough—it is absolutely necessary that you wash down your trees and shrubs on a regular basis if you live in a highly polluted area. Use a spot of baby shampoo at the rate of 1 tablespoon per gallon of water or 1 cup per 20 gallons of water, and hose down everything to the point of runoff.

Jerry's Secrets

Leave no leaf un-sprayed! To get rid of pests, you must spray plants thoroughly—especially under leaves, where most diseases start and many bugs hide from the light of day.

Fabulous Flowering Shrub Formula

For those acid-loving shrubs like azaleas, rhododendrons, and camellias, mix up a batch of this formula in a 5-gallon bucket:

1 bushelful of dried oak leaves
Coffee grounds, as much as you can find
Boiling water to cover the dry ingredients

Let it sit for a few days, strain, and use the liquid by sprinkling 1 cup of it on the ground around each bush. Soon, they'll be happy as clams!

SIMPLE STEPS TO A LOVELIER LANDSCAPE

Get out and take a good look around your yard. Are there any areas that have been planted for a lot of years that now look a bit overgrown and outdated? Has the way you use your outdoor space changed over the years? Are there places in your yard that could be turned into more attractive, inviting garden spots? If you answer yes to any one of these questions, then the time is right for you to plan a new landscape. It starts with these three simple steps:

Step 1—Assess your site. Get a notebook, and jot down the features in your yard that you want to redesign—note the amount and time of day they receive sunlight; what trees, shrubs, and other plantings are currently growing there; and so on. Then note the changes you want to make, how you plan to use the space, and what types of plants you want to include.

Step 2—Draw a simple sketch of the area. It's helpful if you draw this on grid paper, but an old paper bag will do just fine. Your drawing doesn't need to be exact, but it should include the permanent fixtures in the area you are renovating—house, driveway, patio, trees, garden, play area, and the like.

Step 3—Take lots of photographs of the yard. These will be helpful and allow you to share them with the experts at your local garden center or with a landscape professional.

Now you're ready to get growing on over to your garden center or landscape professional, where you can get help in planning a budget, sketching a new design, and choosing plants—everything you need to make your landscape dreams a picture-perfect reality.

Scrub Old Shrubs

Out with the old, and in with the new—don't expect shrubs to last forever. After 15 years or so, take a few minutes to evaluate your landscape plantings, and decide what needs to be replaced…now!

SHRUB SENSE

Most folks buy shrubs that soon outgrow their homes. To avoid this problem, first estimate how much height and spread you want in a certain area. Then, once you're armed with this information, talk with your local nurseryman about which shrubs have appropriate growth habits for your particular space. Of course, plants don't just stop growing at a certain height or width, but with a little forethought about proper selection, you'll find you'll need to use your pruning shears much less later on.

Make 'Em Wait

Don't feed shrubs immediately after planting. Wait at least four weeks. Since most shrubs aren't meant to grow more than 10 to 12 feet high, a well-balanced garden food (5-10-10) can be applied in early spring in most parts of the country, and in both fall and spring in the southern regions. You can also feed your shrubs by sprinkling ¼ pound of Epsom salts onto the soil beneath them and then watering with "Shrub Stimulator," at right.

ALL IN GOOD TIME

When's the best time to plant shrubs? In the colder climates, early spring is best. In the mild climate zones, plant in either spring or fall. In the southern regions, planting can be done whenever the plants are available. (You lucky dogs, you!) Follow these simple shrub-planting steps:

1. Dig the planting hole twice as large and 1 inch deeper than the one the plant was growing in at the nursery.

2. Add one handful of bonemeal, two handfuls of gypsum, and 2 handfuls of dry dog food to soil when planting.

3. Cover the soil with two or three layers of newspaper, and cover the newspaper with mulch.

4. Spray all newly planted shrubs with a mild all-purpose fruit tree spray to discourage insects from visiting.

MIXERS & ELIXIRS

Shrub Stimulator

4 tbsp. of instant tea granules
4 tbsp. of bourbon, or ½ can of beer
2 tbsp. of liquid dish soap
2 gal. of warm water

Mix all of the ingredients together, and sprinkle the mixture over your shrubs in spring.

The Super 6: Hard-Hitting, Natural Pest Controls

Everything old is new again, and that's especially true when it comes to old-time insect controls you can use to keep your landscape clean and green. Well, here are six super controls that still knock the stuffin' out of most bugs today:

COMMON NAME	WHAT IT DOES	HOW TO USE
Rotenone	Rotenone dust kills a wide variety of beetles and bugs. Made from derris roots, it eliminates pesky insects like Japanese beetles, flea beetles, loopers, pea weevils, fruit worms, and rose slugs on ornamentals, vegetables, and fruits.	Rotenone 1 percent is recommended for dusting. For spraying, Rotenone 5 percent gives better control. Dilute at the rate of 6 tablespoons per gallon of water, and apply at the rate of 10 to 20 pounds per acre.
Diatomaceous earth	The tiny mineral crystals in diatomaceous earth (DE) are sharp enough to cut through the skin of soft-bodied insects like aphids, thrips, slugs, and root maggots so they dehydrate and die. Insect eggs are also very susceptible to DE's dehydrating power.	Apply early in the morning with a Dustin Mizer, sprinkle on the soil surface, or mix with water and spray. The recommended rate is 8 to 10 pounds per acre. Dust frequently during bad infestations or while insect eggs are present.
Sabadilla	Sabadilla controls hard-to-kill harlequin bugs, green stink bugs, and striped cucumber beetles on squash, beans, cucumbers, and melons. It also effectively controls cabbageworms, loopers, green measuring worms, and diamond back moths on turnips, mustards, collards, and cabbage. Plus, it destroys leafhoppers on peanuts, beans, and potatoes, and eliminates citrus thrips.	Dust on the moist leaves of plants, and apply directly on insects. To use as a spray, dilute at the rate of 8 to 12 tablespoons per gallon of water, and apply at the rate of 5 pounds per acre.

COMMON NAME	WHAT IT DOES	HOW TO USE
Ryanodine or Ryania	Ryanodine is an effective control for codling moths. This plant resin is an internal stomach poison that kills leaf-eaters such as codling moths on apples and thrips on citrus. It is also effective against corn earworms and borers, gypsy moths, houseflies, fruit moths, and asparagus beetles. It affects pests adversely, but is gentle to beneficials, will not injure plant tissue, and is comparatively safe for mammals.	Dilute this powder at the rate of 5 tablespoons per gallon of water, and apply at the rate of 8 to 15 pounds per acre. Spray when the moths emerge at petal fall.
Bacillus thuringiensis	*Bacillus thuringiensis* (BT) is a caterpillar killer specific to the larval stages of the Lepidoptera moths (codling moth, tufted bud moth, leaf roller) that often infest fruit trees. It's also useful on tent caterpillars and bagworms. BT must be ingested by the caterpillar, so timing of the spray is very important because once the worms work their way into the fruit, they are unreachable.	Spray two weeks after moths first appear, just as the eggs are hatching. Apply at the rate recommended on the package.
Grasshopper disease spores	Grasshopper disease spores are an effective control for the Melanoplus group, the most destructive of all grasshoppers. The spores are applied to wheat bran. The grasshoppers eat the baited bran, get sick, and die. Migrating grasshoppers feed on the diseased carcasses of the previous herd, providing season-long control.	Introduce the disease in early summer, when grasshoppers are no more than 3/4 inch long. Apply at the rate of 1 pound per acre. It is most effective when large areas are treated.

PRUDENT PRUNING

My cardinal rule of pruning is that no cut should be made without a specific purpose. Here are my top five reasons to prudently prune your trees and shrubs:

1. Safety. You should remove dead, diseased, and structurally unsound plant parts before they fall and hit something or somebody. You should also be aware of this old nurseryman's trick—shift the weight of leaning trees by removing some branches on the leaning side, which will promote growth on the other side. I told you it isn't rocket science, right?

2. Health. Thin out weak or transplanted plants to balance the crown and root system, and to revitalize the remaining portion of the plant. This also allows sunlight to filter through to the ground, and it improves air circulation. Suckers literally sap the strength of the parent plant, so remove sucker growth and water sprouts as soon as they develop. Remove dead, dying, or diseased parts because they're more susceptible to attack by harmful insects, disease, or decay organisms.

3. Appearance. Prune trees, and especially shrubbery, to maintain their eye-pleasing characteristics or symmetrical shapes. They grow fast and tend to outgrow their allotted space unless they're reshaped periodically.

4. Structural integrity. Young plants, especially, should be trained through pruning to encourage them to grow the way you want them to—tall, wide, straight, or whatever. If at all possible, eliminate weak "V" crotches in young trees and shorten long, overhanging branches.

5. Damage correction. Most plant damage is caused by storms, vehicles, falling objects, or vandalism. If that happens to one of your prized possessions, then your objective is to save as much of the plant as possible. Remove any damaged parts and reshape what's left to as pleasing an appearance as possible.

Jerry's Secrets

When pruning with shears, keep the cutting blade toward the stump side of every cut. Cuts should be made horizontally across the branch that is to be severed. Avoid cutting down through crotches or up from underneath because you'll end up ripping or nipping the trunk.

TRIM WITH CARE

As you stand back and eyeball your flowering shrubs in anticipation of doing some pruning (something I highly recommend), keep in mind that you should cut back a branch only as far as the next strong-growing shoot because that shoot will provide next year's blooms. If you cut too much, there goes next year's color. Tip-end cutting of most shrubs is OK, but long stems should be taken off only when the shrub is heavily overgrown. If this is the kind of pruning that needs to be done, be sure to cut back the stems as far as possible to ensure graceful shaping. Then seal all wounds with "Tree Wound Paint Mixer" (see page 251).

MIXERS & ELIXIRS

Keep 'Em Neat

I don't like "hippies" in shrub beds, so I never wait until a shrub has become overgrown before I haul out my pruning shears. In particular, shrubs that are basal growers (they have many stems springing up out of the soil) need to be kept neat and clean by taking out stems, cutting them off at ground level. This type of pruning should be done every other year. The most popular basal growers are:

Autumn eleagnus
Drooping leucothoe
Flowering quince
Gray dogwood
Mock-orange
Oakleaf hydrangea

JUST A BIT OFF THE TOP, IF YOU PLEASE

You don't have to spend hours trimming hedges to get them all neatly lined up at the same height. Simply do what the pros do: Make a trimming guide by sticking two stakes or poles in the ground at either end of the shrubs. Then run a string tightly between the stakes, making sure that the string is perfectly level from one end to the other. Use this handy horizontal guide to trim your hedges to perfection every time.

If you're handy with a hammer and nails and you've got some spare 1 × 2s laying around, you can build yourself a more permanent guide to use year after year.

Disease Defense

Wet, rainy weather can mean an outbreak of fungus in your yard, especially in late winter and early spring. Keep your outdoor green scene happy and healthy with this elixir:

1 cup of chamomile tea
1 tsp. of liquid dish soap
½ tsp. of vegetable oil
½ tsp. of peppermint oil
1 gal. of warm water

Mix all of the ingredients together in a bucket. Mist-spray on your plants every week or so before the really hot weather (75°F or higher) sets in. This elixir is strong stuff, so test it on a few leaves before completely spraying any plant.

YOU'RE IN GOOD HANDS WITH...

...your insurance company, hopefully. If your landscape trees and shrubs are damaged or destroyed, you may be able to recoup some of your losses by turning to your homeowner's insurance. The plants may be covered under your policy. Many states have set a $500 maximum for reimbursement for a single tree, shrub, or plant. In addition, you may be able to deduct their value from your federal income tax. A deduction can be useful in case the insurance company doesn't cover all or part of your claim. Check with a qualified tax specialist for more information on this.

Finally, in the case of accidents or intentional damage due to the actions of others, you may be able to recover the plants' value through a civil court action. You gotta love those lawyers—attorneys report settling many of these cases out of court.

PEST PATROL

A Pair of Buggy Brews

If your plants are bugged by bugs, try these old-time repellent brews to send them heading for the border:

Dead Bug Brew

½ cup of dead insects (the more, the merrier!)
1 tbsp. of liquid dish soap
1 tbsp. of cayenne pepper
2 cups of water

Put all of the ingredients in an old blender (and I mean *really* old), and purée the heck of out them. Strain out the pulp using cheesecloth or panty hose. Dilute the remaining brew at a rate of ¼ cup of brew per 1 cup of water. Apply with a handheld mist sprayer to flowers, vegetables, and shrubs to the point of runoff.

Hot Bug Brew

3 hot green peppers (canned or fresh)
3 medium cloves of garlic
1 small onion
1 tbsp. of liquid dish soap
3 cups of water

Purée the peppers, garlic, and onion in a blender. Pour the purée into a jar, and add the dish soap and water. Let stand for 24 hours. Then strain out the pulp, and use a handheld sprayer to apply the remaining liquid to bug-infested plants, making sure to thoroughly coat the tops and undersides of leaves.

SMART SAVINGS FOR SPRING

Be a smart shopper. Buy liquid fertilizer in the fall or winter, when it's on sale. Then keep it tightly sealed and in a protected place where it won't freeze. Come spring, it will still be perfectly good to use, so you'll get more bang for your buck!

Hit the Ground

When pruning overgrown shrubs, the key is to keep (or restore) the plant's natural shape. If you simply cut off the ends of the branches, it will stimulate the remaining wood into sending out many side branches, making the shrub look dense and stubby, which just won't do. So aim for the ground—cut off the largest shoots at ground level, which won't alter the plant's natural shape.

WAIT FOR JACK FROST

If your flowering shrubs had major growth spurts during the spring and summer and they're looking a little shaggy come fall, you may be sorely tempted to get out the pruning shears. Don't do it! Pruning flowering shrubs in the fall before the plants go dormant will stimulate their summer-formed buds into growth that will be killed by the first frost. Yikes! Instead, wait until a hard frost has ended all growing activity for the season before you prune anything.

PLANT TO FIT

Pruning can help gently shape a shrub, but don't expect miracles. I've seen more folks buy the wrong plant to begin with, then get overzealous with their pruning shears, trying to turn the poor plant into something it's not. It's just like trying to squeeze a pair of size 12 dogs into size 8 shoes. It's not gonna happen!

It may sound obvious, but I will say it again and again: It is unrealistic to try to make a horizontal-growing shrub grow upright and fit into a limited space. And the opposite is also true: Upright-growing shrubs do not suddenly decide to grow horizontally, even if "aided" by a deftly wielded pair of pruning shears.

So please, avoid disappointment and wasted energy (yours *and* the poor plants'!) by buying plants that are appropriate for the spaces you want to put them in. You'll save hours of fruitless pruning time, and your plants will grow stronger, healthier, and happier.

MIXERS & ELIXIRS

Fabulous Foliar Formula

For the biggest, brightest, shiniest leaves in town, feed your nonfruiting and nonflowering plants this fantastic formula every three weeks:

1 can of beer
½ cup of Fish Fertilizer+
½ cup of ammonia
¼ cup of blackstrap molasses
¼ cup of instant tea granules

Mix all of the ingredients together in a 20 gallon hose-end sprayer, and apply thoroughly to the point of runoff.

TIMELY TRANSPLANTING

Here's an easy way to remember when to transplant trees, shrubs, and evergreens: Evergreens may be transplanted from the time the leaves of the lilac are the size of a mouse's ear until the leaves fall off in the fall. Deciduous trees are just the opposite—from the time the leaves fall in autumn until the leaves of the lilac are…well, you get the picture!

Of course, this doesn't mean that it's a good idea to transplant your rhododendrons at the end of July, or to try to hack out a young oak in frozen January, it's merely a general rule of thumb for remembering transplanting dates for woody plants.

GUARD AGAINST WINTER LOSSES

You can help your landscape perennials, evergreens, and deciduous shrubs make it through the harsh winter weather by taking a few simple precautions in fall:

1. Cut drains into any of your perennial flowerbeds to carry off standing water. Then rake away soggy leaves that are covering plant crowns, which will help prevent rot.

2. Cover the beds with 3 to 6 inches of noncompacting mulch like marsh hay, straw, or excelsior, which will keep the ground frozen until spring. This prevents the alternate freezing and thawing that causes heaving out of the soil.

3. Use peat or pecan, rice, or buckwheat hulls to mulch the soil around evergreens (like rhododendrons and azaleas) before it freezes. This keeps the plants from getting dehydrated, which, in turn, will keep them from being susceptible to wind- and sunburn. In addition, thoroughly spray both sides of the leaves with an antitranspirant agent like WeatherProof to prevent moisture loss.

4. Prevent azalea bark from splitting by mulching well and spraying with WeatherProof. To keep the sun off of the stems and tops of the plants, shield them with screens that are made of green burlap or evergreen branches.

GO FOR GROUNDCOVERS

Groundcovers can hide a multitude of mistakes, sore spots, and problem areas in your yard. Plant 'em thick, feed 'em after planting (see "Groundcover Starter Mix" on the opposite page), and keep 'em clean. They'll reward you with bountiful growth and beauty.

Over the Top

Groundcovers are often neglected because they never make a fuss—unless a winter disease sneaks in. But I've found that the top dressing at right, watered in with a can of beer and 4 teaspoons of instant tea granules in 2 gallons of water, makes groundcover thick enough to stop a rabbit!

BABY, IT'S COLD OUTSIDE

Just an ounce of prevention on your part will get shrubs through the winter with flying colors, and ensure that they'll add beauty to your outdoor scene for years to come.

🐌 Use your 20 gallon hose-end sprayer to wash down your shrubs with a solution of one cup of liquid dish soap and 1 cup of antiseptic mouthwash, filling the balance of the sprayer jar with water. Spray the soil underneath the shrubs as well. Then sprinkle a cup of moth-ball crystals on top of the soil directly under each shrub in a 3-foot circumference.

🐌 In snow country, gently tie your shrubs about halfway up with old nylon panty hose legs. This will prevent branches from breaking during snow and ice storms.

🐌 On a nice, warm, sunny, windless day, once they have lost all of their leaves, dormant spray your shrubs with a good horticultural/dormant oil. That'll catch and kill any bugs that are nappin' in the cracks and crevices.

🐌 As a final measure, apply a good, thorough coat of my WeatherProof. It's just like buying life insurance for your plants, only it's a whole lot cheaper!

That's it—a few simple steps will keep your shrubs happy and healthy through the winter months.

MIXERS & ELIXIRS

Terrific Top Dressing

20 parts Milorganite
10 parts earthworm
   castings
5 parts ground apple
½ bushel of peat moss

Mix all of the ingredients together, and use it as a dressing over top of your groundcovers.

To Tree or Not to Tree

Have you ever spent a sultry summer afternoon picnicking under the shade of a giant oak tree? Or maybe you've relieved stress and strain by taking a walk in a local tree-filled park. Now stop and think—a world without trees wouldn't be much to look at, would it? Absolutely not. So, it's worth the time and effort to learn about how to choose, plant, and care for those *tree*-mendous trees.

DIG WIDE AND DEEP

When planting trees, dig a hole deep and wide enough for the roots. In the center, dig another hole as deep as you can with a post-hole digger. Fill this second hole with "Tree-mendous Planting Mix" (at left). The roots of all trees, especially those with long tap roots, will benefit from this little bit of extra soil preparation.

IT'S A WRAP

Once your trees are in their new homes, you must provide them with protection from the elements until they become firmly established members of your landscape family. Young trees—especially dogwoods, beeches, and maples—have very delicate bark. So it's up to you to keep them from getting sunburned by giving them a wrap.

Simply wrap the trunks from the ground to the lowest branches with burlap, foil, cheesecloth, or tree wrap (made of waterproof paper). Take two firm turns around the base of the tree, then spiral the wrap up the trunk, overlapping the layers by about an inch to keep water out. Tie the top and bottom ends with cotton cords. The wrap should stay on the tree for about two years to give the bark time to toughen up.

MIXERS & ELIXIRS

Tree-mendous Planting Mix

5 lbs. of compost
2 lbs. of gypsum
1 lb. of dry dog food
1 lb. of oatmeal

Mix all of the ingredients together, and use it to improve the soil when planting trees.

8 STEPS TO TRANSPLANT SUCCESS

Mid- to late-August is generally an excellent time to move evergreens. Most have finished their growth for the year and have set their buds for the next year's growth. From that point on, most of the plants' efforts are concentrated on root growth.

Of course, you just can't dig them up willy-nilly. Here are my eight steps to transplanting success:

1. Soak the soil around the tree a day or two before you plan to move it. This keeps the soil from falling off the roots in all but the sandiest locations.

2. Dig the new hole one and a half times wider than and as deep as the rootball you intend to dig. Improve about one-fourth of the soil in the bottom of the hole (not less than 1 foot deep) with a half-and-half mixture of dried cow manure and moistened peat moss.

3. Cut down around the tree as deeply as you can with a spade or shovel, undercutting as you go, until you have completely severed the rootball from the earth.

4. Lift out the tree, but not by the trunk. Instead, pry and lift from the bottom with one or more shovels or spades. Depending on the size of the tree, you may need a helper.

5. If your tree is relatively small, you can slide it to its new location on the shovel. If not, lift it onto a piece of canvas or burlap bag and then, with a partner, drag the fabric "sling" to the new site.

6. When you get the tree into the new hole, fill halfway with improved soil, using manure and peat moss as explained in Step 2. Tamp the soil, and then flood it with water. When the water has drained away, finish filling the hole with soil, but do not tamp it down. Leave a basin in the soil around the tree to hold water.

7. To retain moisture, cover the soil around the tree and a foot or two beyond with 2 inches of mulch like ground corncobs, wood chips, shredded bark, or buckwheat hulls.

8. Spray the foliage thoroughly with my WeatherProof to prevent it from wilting and drying out before the roots are able to function properly in their new home.

MIXERS & ELIXIRS

Terrific Transplant Tonic

¼ cup of instant tea granules
¼ cup of whiskey
¼ cup of baby shampoo
⅓ cup of hydrogen peroxide
2 tbsp. of Fish Fertilizer+
1 gal. of warm water

Mix all of the ingredients together, and give each newly transplanted tree about a quart of the tonic.

START YOUR OWN FOREST

Here's something I learned years ago—if you want to make a large planting of evergreens, the Division of Forestry at your state's Department of Agriculture can help you. They have several different kinds of evergreens to offer, and they'll charge you considerably less than your local nursery.

The only drawback is that most states require a minimum order of 500 trees. If you don't want that many, share an order with some friends or donate the extras to a Scout troop, local school, library, nursing home, or what have you. The small seedlings are easy to transport and are easy to plant successfully.

Jerry's Secrets

I know this sounds ridiculously obvious, but don't plant trees too close to your house! You'd be amazed at how many folks don't give this a second thought when they choose a site for that cute little seedling, or transplant young trees from one part of the yard to another. You must consider a tree's mature height, and plan accordingly. A tree that will grow 100 feet tall should be planted at least 75 feet away from the house. A tree that will grow 20 feet tall should be planted at least 15 feet away. So use these figures as guidelines to determine where to locate your trees.

TREES ON THE CHEAP

In much of the country, you can buy surplus shade trees from your local, county, or state forestry or parks department in fall. The prices are usually excellent, the trees and shrubs are top quality, and they're usually good sized. How can you beat that?

Well, just be aware that these plants are bare root, not balled and burlapped. But don't let this deter you: I have planted hundreds of these trees and shrubs with 100 percent success. See "The Bare Facts about Tree Planting" on the opposite page for my surefire tips.

DRESS THEM IN ARMOR?

Sun and wind aren't the only problems that young trees face. Rabbits, mice, and even lawn mowers can gnaw away at tender bark. Tree wrap will protect your tree during its first year, but then what? Give your trees a suit of armor.

For each tree, cut a length of 2-foot-wide mesh hardware cloth large enough to form a cylinder that will stand about 2 inches away from the tree's trunk on all sides. Wrap the mesh cloth around the tree and wire the ends together. If there is mulch around the tree, push the mesh down into it. If the tree isn't mulched and you plan to hand-clip around it, leave the "armor" loose so you can easily raise it.

THE BARE FACTS ABOUT TREE PLANTING

If you're used to buying only balled-and-burlapped trees, planting a bareroot tree may seem a bit scary. Not to worry. Just follow my steps to bareroot planting success:

1. As soon as you get the trees, soak them in a solution of my WeatherProof and water. This will help prevent transplant shock.

2. While they're soaking, dig a very wide hole with ample room to spread out the tree's roots. Dig it deep enough to plant the tree 2 to 4 inches deeper than it was in the nursery.

3. Sprinkle this mix on the bottom and sides of the hole: 1 cup of Epsom salts, 3 cups of bonemeal, 1 handful of hair, and 1 teaspoon of medicated baby powder.

4. Place the tree roots into the hole, cover them with soil, and pack it down firmly to take out any air pockets. Continue to refill the hole, ending up with a 6- to 8-inch dike to hold and fill with water. Fill the dike with water, let it settle, and then refill.

5. Use tree supports to keep the tree straight during its first winter. On opposite sides of the rootball, drive two 6-foot-long stakes about 2 feet into the ground. Take heavy-gauge wire and thread it through a short piece of old garden hose. Loop the wire around the tree, placing the garden hose around the trunk to keep it from being cut by the wire. Then attach the wire ends firmly to the stakes.

6. Wrap the trunk with tree wrap and mulch with a thick layer of shredded bark.

Collar Cats

Keep cats and squirrels from climbing your trees by placing a 12-inch-wide piece of sheet metal or aluminum around the trunk, about 6 inches or so off of the ground.

PEST PATROL

Slug It Out

Slimy slugs will drink themselves to death if you offer them this out-of-this-world concoction:

1 can of beer
1 tbsp. of sugar
1 tsp. of baker's yeast

Mix all of the ingredients in a large bowl, and let it sit uncovered for a few days. Then pour the mixture into shallow, disposable aluminum pie pans. Set the pans below ground level in various areas of your lawn and garden, and it's *hasta la vista*, baby.

WATERING 1, 2, 3

If you have several large evergreens planted close together, you can water them more efficiently with my quick-and-easy watering system. Here's how:

1. Bury 10-inch-long PVC tubing that is 4 to 5 inches in diameter between your trees, standing upright, with the top of the tubing standing about 1 inch below ground level.

2. Fill the tubing with small rocks.

3. Let your hose run water directly into the tubing. This delivers the water deep into the soil, where tree roots need it most.

Stretch Your Limbs

Exercise your evergreens to keep them growing tall, full, and wide. Simply shake them gently from time to time. This gets rid of the dandruff (dead needles), too.

Say Bon Voyage to Borers

Protect trees that are bothered by borer insects by sprinkling a cup of mothball crystals onto the soil directly below and around the trunk in a 3-foot radius. This will send the beastly borers a packin'!

AIR CONDITIONING FOR YOUR TREES

To keep your trees cool, calm, and collected during the long, hot dog days of summer, wrap them with 4-inch-wide strips of burlap from the ground up to the first branch. Keep the wrappings on until fall.

MILK JUG JAMBOREE

Is watering your trees a real chore? You wander from tree to tree, then stand for what seems like forever as you slowly water, water, water your life away. You know you can't just skip it—your trees are depending on you, and if there was any way that they could water themselves, they would. But it does not have to be so time-consuming. Here's where those handy milk jugs come to good use.

Punch five or six tiny nail holes in the bottom of a plastic milk jug, place at the base of each tree, and fill with water. There is no standing around for long periods, waiting for the water to soak it. Just fill the jug and walk away. The water will soak in with no runoff, and you can run off to do other things!

GET POTTED

If space is a problem in your yard, you can still grow an assortment of trees—just pot them up! Use large wooden, plastic, or concrete tubs to cultivate dwarf trees. Just be aware that inexpensive tubs of lightweight wood, such as pine, don't last very long when filled with moist soil, so use tubs made from cypress, redwood, and other water-resistant woods. Look for tubs that are well made, with steel bands encircling them, or square sides bolted together with steel rods.

Regardless of the material, if the tub you choose doesn't have short legs, put some on before filling and planting. An easy way to do this is to stand the tub on bricks or other supports so that it is slightly raised off the ground or patio floor. If set directly on the ground or floor, drainage will be slowed, and the base will decay much more quickly. It's also a great idea to put casters on the tubs; that way, you can have ever-changing scenery as the mood strikes you.

EVER-GROWING EVERGREENS

In my opinion, fall-planted evergreens are always the best looking come spring. You can even get a head start by planting evergreens in mid- to late-August, unless drought holds you back. Good for planting in fall: broad-leaved evergreens like rhododendrons, Kalmia, and mountain laurel, as well as the conifers—pines, hemlocks, spruce, cedars, and so on.

As a general rule, keep any mass planting of evergreens well to the north or west of your house, especially if you're using them as a windbreak. If you plant them to the south, the shade they will provide after several years' worth of growth is sure to be too dense, creating a gloomy atmosphere.

Don't make the common mistake of planting your evergreens all in a row. An artistic grouping requires no more trees, and is just as effective as a windbreak as a stiff nursery-looking row is.

PEST PATROL

Spray Away Scale Today

Female scales can kill a whole tree by sucking the sap out of it with their long, needlelike feeding tubes. These insects vary in size from $1/8$ to $1/2$ inch long and are wingless. Once they insert their feeding tubes into a twig or branch, they stay there for life. To give scales the heave-ho, spray any infested trees with dormant oil in early spring; this will smother both the female scales and their eggs.

A STICKY SITUATION

To get rid of what's bugging your trees, create a sticky situation from which there is no escape. Here's my surefire method for sticking it to bugs:

1. Cut a piece of burlap about 10 inches wide and long enough to wrap around the tree trunk so that it overlaps by about 2 inches. Then spray one side of the burlap with Tangle Trap, axle grease, Vasoline, or some other sticky substance.

2. Wrap the burlap around the trunk, sticky side out. Secure it to the tree by tying a nylon stocking or rope around the center of the burlap. This will cause the top half of the burlap to fold over, which is exactly what you want.

3. As bugs climb up the trunk, they get trapped between the two sticky surfaces and die. Check the traps daily, and dispose of whenever needed.

News Beat

Don't spare the rod when it comes to your trees. Beat your tree trunks with a stick or rolled-up newspaper from the ground all the way up to the first branch to stimulate sap flow in early spring.

Mighty Mouse Control

Here I come to save the day! To keep mice and other small varmints from nibbling your young trees to nubs, drench the trunks with this highly effective varmint repellent:

2 tbsp. of Tabasco sauce
2 tbsp. of cayenne
    pepper
2 tbsp. of Murphy's
    Oil Soap
1 qt. of warm water

Mix all of the ingredients together in a container, then apply with a handheld sprayer starting in late fall.

GETTING TO THE ROOT OF THE PROBLEM

If your lawn has tree roots coming to the surface, you know how dangerous they can be, making walking and mowing difficult and giving the landscape a rough, uneven look. How did this happen? Well, shallow fertilizing and watering encourage surface rooting, but they're only part of the problem. Some trees, like poplars and silver maples, naturally have shallow root systems.

If the tree in question is one you want to keep, then it's best to call in a professional arborist to evaluate the situation before you go whacking away at the unwanted roots. Such a do-it-yourself treatment could cause serious injury to the tree, or even death. So be on the safe side, and seek professional advice.

DON'T WORRY, BE HAPPY!

I'm often asked about common tree conditions by anxious property owners who are convinced that their trees are dying. But there are a number of perfectly normal tree conditions that are nothing to worry about. Take a look at the list below. If your trees are experiencing any of these, relax—they aren't signs of impending doom:

Nails. Contrary to the surprisingly widespread belief, nails or spikes really can penetrate a tree without causing injury. Unlike us, a tree has no vital organs that can be punctured. Trunks and boughs can be studded with nails without damage, except to you when you try to cut it down and strike one. Ouch!

Frost cracks. These cracks, usually 1 to 2 feet long, appear vertically along the trunk, with no apparent cause. Frost cracks are caused by extremely rapid drops in temperature, usually at night after a warm, sunny day. A frost-cracked tree will not break apart.

When tree growth resumes in spring, the crack will gradually close and should eventually heal completely. If the healing process isn't quite complete, simply coat the exposed wood with "Tree Wound Paint Mixer" (at right).

Lichen and moss. If your tree has a patch of greenish-gray substance on the trunk, it's not a disease, it's a patch of either lichen or moss, the same vegetation that grows on rocks. A tree's bark is rough enough for lichen to cling to without needing to secrete an acid to cause crumbling, as it does on rocks. So no damage occurs. Moss is quite harmless to the tree. To remove moss, mix up a solution of ½ cup of bleach and ½ cup of liquid dish soap in 1 gallon of warm water. Apply it lightly several times until the moss dies.

Minor cuts. A simple gash on a tree will do little harm, but if the bark is stripped off the trunk more than halfway around, this could mean serious trouble. Minor wounds heal over quickly. Simply coat them with "Tree Wound Paint Mixer" (at right) so the exposed wood doesn't dry out.

MIXERS & ELIXIRS

Tree Wound Paint Mixer

1 cup of interior latex paint
1 cup of antiseptic mouthwash
1 tbsp. of Sevin

Mix the mouthwash and Sevin into the paint, and brush on all tree wounds. (Before using this tonic, clean the wounds with "Tree Wound Sterilizer Tonic" on page 259.)

LOOK MA, CAVITIES!

No need to call the dentist! I'm talking about large hollows in the trunk or in the larger branches of your trees. Believe it or not, a tree's trunk may be as hollow as a barrel, and yet the tree can still produce luxuriant foliage. Why? Because the life functions of the tree are carried out within the outer rim of the trunk, in the sapwood area. The inner portion, the heartwood, is normally composed of inactive cells. If the heartwood rots, the sapwood goes on living.

The only danger to a tree that has extensive hollow areas is that the tree could break in a strong wind. So it is best to fill large cavities. And keep in mind that if any hollow is positioned so that rainwater collects in it, the wood will gradually rot deeper. Such a cavity should be filled with Great Stuff Foam or covered with metal or a shingle cut to shape and painted black for a neat appearance.

IT (USUALLY) TAKES TWO

Just like the birds and the bees, all fruit trees require pollination to produce fruit. Without pollination, trees may blossom abundantly, but they won't bear fruit.

Some varieties won't bear fruit or won't bear consistently unless they're pollinated with a different variety. It's best to buy two or more varieties of apricot and sweet cherry to ensure pollination. All apples, peaches, pears, and plums are  self-fertile and will bear fruit without cross-pollination. But it's still a good idea to plant more than one variety of the same family of fruit, if possible.

CLIMATE COUNTS!

Don't set yourself up for disappointment by trying to grow hardy fruit trees in warm climates. Most of these trees need exposure to some cold winter weather in order to break dormancy and start spring growth. Without sufficient winter cold, spring growth is delayed, and when the growth does start, it is irregular and slow. So if you're trying to grow hardy fruits in a climate that is considerably warmer than their native one, the bottom line is, you won't be pleased with the results.

WASH AWAY TREE TROUBLES

Many folks just don't pay attention to their trees until there's a problem that hits them smack dab in the face!

I've got a simple tree-care program that I'd like to share with you. Now I know that some of you will complain that some of your trees are too big to reach the top of with a hose-end sprayer, or are too old to begin to feed. Well, although it's true that some trees will be too big, no tree is ever too old to feed. So let's get started:

Step 1: Once a month, while the temperature is above freezing, wash your trees as far up as you can. Use a mixture of 1 cup of baby shampoo or liquid dish soap and 1 cup of antiseptic mouthwash in your 20 gallon hose-end sprayer. Spray the wood to the point of runoff.

Step 2: Twice a year, in early spring and again in late fall, after your deciduous trees have dropped their leaves, spray them with a good horticultural/dormant oil to smother egg masses and destroy disease. This will cut down on 75 percent of potential tree problems.

Step 3: Sprinkle mothball crystals onto the soil beneath any tree that's bothered by borers. Apply from the trunk out to the weep line (the tips of the longest branches).

Step 4: Feed trees in early spring, no matter how big or old they are, by drilling holes 8 to 10 inches deep and 18 inches apart out at the weep line. Then mix 25 pounds of garden food with 1 pound of sugar and ½ pound of Epsom salts. Place 2 tablespoons of this mix in the holes, then fill the holes with topsoil. Sprinkle the remainder of the mix on the soil.

Step 5: Feed your trees every three weeks throughout the growing season with the "All-Season Green-Up Tonic" (see Green-Up and Clean-Up" on page 77).

Step 6: Root prune all of your flowering trees in midfall by forcing a spade down into the soil out at the tip of the farthest branches, in a full circle all the way around the tree. Then sprinkle 1 cup of Epsom salts into the cuts, and pour a mix of 1 cup of apple juice in a gallon of warm water on top of it. This will stimulate new root growth.

Calling All Calcium

To control insects around apple, peach, and plum trees, spread ground oyster shells, finely crushed eggshells, or gypsum around the roots of the trees. Lightly cover the ground from the trunk out past the tips of the longest branches.

GET YOUR BEARINGS

I'm often asked how long it takes for a fruit tree to bear fruit. The answer is, "that depends." A fruit tree normally begins to bear fruit after it becomes old enough to blossom freely, provided other conditions are favorable. Tree health and environment, bearing habits, and the cultural practices used can all directly influence a tree's ability to produce fruit. Adequate pollination is also essential to fruit production. If any of these conditions are not met, then yields may be reduced or the tree may not bear any fruit at all.

Most nursery-produced fruit trees have tops that are one to two years old. The length of time required for them to bear fruit after planting varies with the kind of fruit. The chart at left indicates the ages (from planting time) at which fruit trees can be expected to bear.

Fruit Tree Bearing Times	
TREE	BEARING AGE (IN YEARS)
Apple	4 to 7
Apricot	4 to 5
Citrus	3 to 5
Fig	2 to 3
Peach	3 to 4
Pear	4 to 6
Plum	4 to 6
Quince	5 to 6
Sour Cherry	4 to 5
Sweet Cherry	5 to 7

IT'S JUST A SCRATCH, DOC

If you have a fruit tree that isn't bearing fruit, be heartless—give it a few scratches to encourage it to begin fruiting. When a tree is slightly damaged, it will begin to concentrate its energy in order to heal its wounds. Sometimes, this burst of energy is just what is needed to stimulate the tree to bear fruit.

Use a utility or carpet knife to scar the tree on the trunk and some of the main branches. Don't overdo it, and be sure that you don't completely girdle the trunk or branches.

H₂ORCHARD SPRAY

Take this tip from professional apple
growers: dislodge insects with plain old water. Yep, just good 'ol
H₂O. Apple growers use a water spray in the spring for control of
codling moths. Spraying loose bark will dislodge harmful larvae.

The most effective way to use water is with a standard orchard
sprayer held 2 to 3 feet away from the tree and directed against the
trunk. Also spray large branches where bark is rough or loose, and
don't forget the crotch of the tree.

FALL FOR FRUIT TREES

What's the best time to plant fruit trees and other
fruit-bearing plants? The down and dirty answer is,
as early in the spring as the soil can be prepared. However, many
kinds of fruits can be planted in the fall with excellent results, especially from New York state southward. In fact, fall planting has
some advantages over spring planting, and commercial growers
often plant in the fall. Here are the pros and cons:

Pro: When you plant in the fall, you give the plants plenty of
time to get well established by spring, with new root hairs ready to
suck up water and plant food for an early start on the growing season. And in the fall, you will be able to find varieties that might be
sold out by spring.

Con: In central and northern regions, there may be some
danger of cold injury to fruit trees and berry bushes set in the fall,
especially if very cold weather hits before new roots have a chance
to form and take in adequate water. In heavier soils, fall-set plants
may heave out of the ground as the soil alternately freezes and
thaws. Winter rains can also compact the soil so that it may need
to be plowed again in the spring.

Even if you decide to wait and plant your fruit-bearing plants in
spring, you should still order them in the fall, when there is a good
supply of desirable varieties available. As a matter of fact, I would
prefer to have the trees delivered in the fall, and heel them in until
the following spring if they can't be planted immediately. (To learn
how to heel in trees, see "Winter Holdovers" on page 256.)

Jerry's Secrets

Don't use wood chips
around your fruit
trees because they
become a nesting
place for mice and a
breeding place for in-
sects and disease—
all of which spells
T-R-O-U-B-L-E
for your
trees.

WINTER HOLDOVERS

If you want to keep trees over the winter for planting in the spring, you need to carefully heel them in. What does this mean? Simply that you place them in trenches in a protected area. Here's how to do it:

1. Dig a trench about 15 inches deep in a sandy, well-drained area that is protected from high winds.

2. Open the bundled trees in the trench, and space them out enough so that the soil can be well worked around the roots. Do not leave any of the packing materials around the roots. The trees may stand upright or lean with their tops facing the south.

3. Fill the trench with soil and pack it down. Make sure the roots are fully covered.

4. Examine the trees frequently during the winter for signs of rabbit or mouse injury. If you have a rabbit problem, place chicken wire or hardware cloth around the trunks.

PLANTING POINTERS

Whether you plant your fruit trees in fall or spring, the planting steps are essentially the same. Dig a $10 hole for a $5 tree. Then set the plants at the same depth, or slightly deeper, than they were growing at in the nursery. Make holes of ample size. Work the soil thoroughly around the roots, and form it by tamping or stepping on it as the hole is filled. Don't put fertilizer or manure in direct contact with the roots. Instead, use this mix in the hole and on top of the soil after planting: 5 parts bonemeal, 2 parts gypsum, and 1 part Epsom salts.

All fruit plants should be pruned rather severely at planting time. This helps to compensate for the loss of roots that occurred when the plants were taken from the nursery. See "Pruning Principles" on the opposite page for pruning tips.

PRUNING PRINCIPLES

Most fruit trees are sold as two-year-old whips, and must be pruned when planted. To prune your fruit trees, cut the main stem back by about one-third to a fat bud, and prune side branches until you have removed about one-third of the total wood. Such severe pruning may seem harsh, but it will get your tree off to a faster, healthier start.

Sunlight must reach into the middle of the tree as it grows, otherwise fruits won't ripen. In order to ensure this, you may find yourself removing many more lateral branches and stems than you would like, and the result may not be the most pleasing-looking tree. But again, it's for your tree's own good because it aids proper fruit development and helps prevent disease by allowing good air circulation through the crown.

WINTER IS PRUNING TIME

Deciduous fruit and shade trees can be pruned anytime after their leaves have dropped in fall, but before they leaf out in early spring. But I think the best time for pruning is in January and early February, before the sap begins to flow again. Pruning is less difficult then because you can clearly see what you're doing. Also, not much else is going on in the garden, so it gives you a good excuse to get up off of the couch and get outdoors for a couple of hours.

WINTER WIND GUARDS

If some of your evergreens are tender or not well adapted to your area, it's a good idea to build a screen to protect them from winter wind and bright sun, both of which can cause harmful burning.

To make a screen, drive wooden stakes into the ground and staple a piece of burlap between them. If wind is the main threat, place the burlap screen between the evergreen and the direction of the prevailing wind.

If the evergreen is growing in full sun, erect screens on both the south and west sides.

Give 'Em a Trim

Take a tip from professional landscapers—when you're moving a tree, but cannot leave its rootball intact, cut off approximately one-third of the branches just before transplanting it. This compensates for the root sections that are lost. (Evergreens don't need to be pruned.) When pruning, do not leave stubs; remove the limb sections cleanly.

Fruit Tree Pruning

TREE	WHEN TO PRUNE	HOW TO PRUNE
Catalpa	While dormant	Repair as necessary
Flowering cherries, peaches, etc.	After blooming	Shape and thin occasionally
Flowering dogwood	After blooming	Repair as necessary
Fringe tree	After blooming	Repair as necessary
Golden rain tree	Early spring	Repair as necessary
Hawthorn	After blooming	Repair as necessary
Jacaranda	Whenever necessary	Repair as necessary
Japanese pagoda tree	Should not be pruned	—
Laburnums	After blooming	Repair as necessary
Linden	Should not be pruned	—
Redbud	After blooming	Shape when young
Royal poinciana	After heaviest blooming	Repair as necessary
Serviceberry	After blooming	Repair as necessary
Silverbell tree	After blooming	Repair as necessary
Smoke tree	Early spring	Cut out 2-year wood; thin 1-year wood
Sorrel tree	After blooming	Repair as necessary
Stewartia	While dormant	Repair as necessary
Tulip tree	Should not be pruned	—
Yellowwood	After blooming	Repair as necessary

GIVE 'EM SOME T.L.C.

Often neglected, seldom fed, and rarely thanked, our trees sure do put up with a lot of abuse! So this fall, make a commitment to treat your trees better. After all, they provide you with shade and beauty, so why not re-pay them with some tender loving care? How do you do it? Start by walking underneath them when you're wearing golf spikes or aerating lawn sandals. This opens up the root mass in the grass beneath your trees, and it lets water and nutrients down through to the tree roots.

Next, wash down the trunks and lower limbs with warm, soapy water (2 cups of liquid dish soap per 20 gallons of water). Also spray this mix on the soil you have just punctured. Then, wrap the trunks of trees up to 6 inches in diameter with tree-wrap. Spray with horticultural/dormant oil for insect control.

For larger diameter trees, tape a neatly cut strip of roofing paper the length of the trunk to the southwest side using nylon tape. By taking a few minutes to wrap your trees, you'll be guarding against winter bark split or winterkill.

PREVENT FREEZE-DRIED FRUIT TREES

If your fruit trees are exposed to extremely cold weather during their winter dormancy, it may kill their fruit buds. Then there's no fruit in the bowl next year. Peaches are the most sensitive to the cold, followed by sweet cherry trees. On the other hand, cold weath-er rarely threatens apples, pears, sour cherries, or plums.

You can prevent bud or blos-som injury by covering the trees when heavy frost is expected, provided the temperatures don't get too low or the cold weather doesn't last too long. Commercial orchardists heat their orchards during frosts, but this is not practical for most home gardeners. So about all you can do is cover up your fruit trees—use newspaper, brown paper bags, a floating row cover, or Harvest Guard—and hope for the best.

MIXERS & ELIXIRS

Tree Wound Sterilizer Tonic

¼ cup of ammonia
¼ cup of liquid dish soap
¼ cup of antiseptic mouthwash
1 gal. of warm water

Mix all of the ingredients together, and pour the mixture into a handheld sprayer bottle. Spray on tree wounds to the point of runoff. Then seal the cuts with "Tree Wound Paint Mixer" (see page 251).

KEEP 'EM COZY

If you live in an area where winters are often severe, you need to keep your evergreens comfortable during the cold weather. Here's how:

🌿 Start by spraying all evergreens with WeatherProof in late fall to prevent water loss, windburn, winterkill, and salt damage.

🌿 Give your evergreens a thorough watering in late fall just before the ground freezes. Evaporation through the foliage takes place in winter as well as in summer. And if the roots become dry, there will be little moisture in the tree, so the foliage may burn during periods of bright sunshine.

🌿 Spread an extra blanket of mulch around your evergreens in fall. It's best to use materials like straw, ground cornstalks, or buckwheat hulls, which don't pack down tightly. If the tree is in a windy location, place slats or boards down on the mulch to hold it in place over the winter.

🌿 Once winter weather sets in, try to keep snow from piling up on your evergreens. Branches and twigs are likely to break under the weight of a heavy mantle of snow.

🌿 Be careful when shoveling the driveway, sidewalks, or any area near evergreens that may have been treated with salt. You don't want any of that treated snow or ice on or under your evergreens.

A WORD ABOUT TREE TOPPING...

Don't! We've all seen topped trees along roadways; you know what I'm talking about—the utility companies send out a crew to chop off the tops of trees so they don't grow into overhead wires and cables. The result is not only ugly, but tree topping leaves large wounds and causes weak growth that can cause trees to break. Poor pruning like this also sends trees into shock and stress, which in turn causes a loss of vigor, insect infestation, dead wood, and—in many cases—death. Now I know you would never intentionally kill your trees, so stay away from tree topping, and don't let any landscaper talk you into letting him do it for you!

Jerry's Secrets

Some evergreens, like arborvitae and junipers, have multiple stems. To prevent snow from bending these down and breaking them apart, gather the tops gently together with long strips of cloth or nylon panty hose.

Landscaping

Q. I have grass seed left over from last year. Is it still good?

A. As a general rule, yes, but to find out for sure, fill a paper, plastic, or Styrofoam cup three-quarters full of water, and add a used tea bag for a minute or two. Then sprinkle a teaspoonful of seed on top of the water, and set it in a window that gets a lot of light. If it's good, in a couple of weeks you should see grass.

Q. What can I do to keep the birds off my new grass seed until it sprouts?

A. Adopt six or seven cats! Seriously, though, cover the seed with ¼ inch of topsoil, then pat it down or roll gently. You can also

slit an old tennis ball and force it over the end of a 6- to 7-foot piece of old garden hose. Draw two mean eyes and a nasty mouth on the ball, and place yellow strips of tape like Xs down the hose. Let this guest lie on the seeded area until the seed sprouts. Why? The birds think it's a snake. Eagles and hawks won't be fooled, but then, they don't eat grass seed.

Q. How often should I water new grass seed?

A. Enough to keep it damp (moist), and that depends on where you live and when you plant. Remember, I said damp, *not* soggy wet!

Start Seed off Right

To be sure your lawn gets off to a good start, buy the highest quality grass seed you can afford. Sow the seed when the days are warm and the evenings are cool. Be sure the soil is loosened to give the new roots plenty of room to roam. Then cover the seeds lightly with topsoil, and keep the area damp.

MIXERS & ELIXIRS

Seed Soak

1 cup of liquid dish soap
1 gal. of weak tea water*

Soak your grass seed in this solution and refrigerate for 48 hours. Then spread the seed out on a warm, dry surface to dry. Plant as recommended.

*To make weak tea water, steep a twice-used tea bag in a gallon of water with a teaspoon of liquid dish soap added until the water is slightly colored.

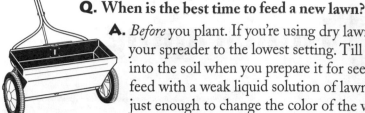

Q. When is the best time to feed a new lawn?

A. *Before* you plant. If you're using dry lawn food, set your spreader to the lowest setting. Till the food into the soil when you prepare it for seeding. I feed with a weak liquid solution of lawn food—just enough to change the color of the water in the container of my 20 gallon hose-end sprayer.

Q. Can I sow grass seed in winter?

A. Why not? And while you're at it, remember to topdress with a light layer of soil to keep the birds away from the seed.

Q. If grass seed freezes in the garage over the winter, can it still be used come spring?

A. Yes. If it goes to seed in the wild, do you think it builds a new house to keep warm in the winter? It just goes dormant (to sleep); it will wake up in time to give you a great new lawn.

Q. Do the numbers and dates on bags of seed mean anything, or do they just make them up?

A. They do mean something! The purity percentages indicate what percentage of the seed in the bag is the seed variety you're buying. Germination figures tell you the results of a sprout test the land grant college performed for

MIXERS & ELIXIRS

Fall Lawn Feed

Apply any brand of dry lawn food at half of the recommended rate, then water it in well with this elixir:

1 can of beer
1 cup of liquid
   dish soap
Ammonia

Mix the beer and soap in your 20 gallon hose-end sprayer, then fill the balance of the sprayer jar with ammonia.

Make the Most of Fertilizers

To make sure your lawn is getting the most out of the fertilizers you're putting down, keep this in mind: Always apply lawn fertilizer before noon. Be sure to water the lawn the day before you make the application, and then always water lightly again right after the application. This helps the grass plants to begin to digest the food right away, rather than just letting it sit there.

RAKE IT UP

Lawn raking is a job no one looks forward to—it's hard work! But it's necessary because excess leaves and grass clippings that lay on your lawn interfere with the turf's ability to breathe (manufacture chlorophyll), encourage thatch buildup, and rob the growing grass of nitrogen. So rake it all up. I recommend you use bamboo, flexible plastic, or flexible steel rakes. If your lawn is large, you may want to buy a lawn sweeper. Or you might look into sharing the expense with several of your neighbors.

Remember, the material you remove from your lawn is worth its weight in gold when it is converted into compost. So gather it up and put it in your compost pile—don't throw it out!

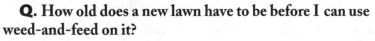

the state in which the seed was grown. The weed content tells you what percentage of weeds you can expect.

. . . .

Q. How can I fix the damage dogs do to my lawn?

A. To repair doggy damage to your lawn, overspray the turf with 1 cup of Plant Shampoo per 20 gallons of water, and then apply gypsum over the area at the recommended rate. One week later, overspray the turf with this lawn saver tonic: 1 can of beer, 1 cup of ammonia, and 1 can of regular cola (not diet) in your 20 gallon hose-end sprayer.

. . . .

Q. I had some grass seed that sprouted in the bag. My wife said it wouldn't grow, and threw it out. Was she right?

A. Sort of. In most cases, it would've had marginal growth, but it would have rooted. It's best to start with fresh seed.

Q. How old does a new lawn have to be before I can use weed-and-feed on it?

A. I like to have it undergo at least three mowings and one good, normal feeding before I use a weed-and-feed.

MIXERS & ELIXIRS

Summer Lawn Soother

To prevent extensive damage to your lawn in summer, overspray the turf once a week with this tonic:

1 can of beer
1 cup of Liquid Lawn Food
½ cup of Thatch Buster
½ cup of Plant Shampoo

Mix all of the ingredients in your 20 gallon hose-end sprayer, and apply the mix to your lawn early in the morning (before 8 A.M. is best).

TIDY TRIMMING

I've seen more hard-working, well-meaning homeowners make a mess out of an otherwise healthy lawn by not knowing how to trim or edge properly around beds, walkways, trees, and buildings. Here's what you need to know:

🐾 Buy a well-balanced, well-built trimmer, then learn how to properly use and maintain it.

🐾 If it's a gas-powered trimmer, be sure to use clean gasoline with the proper amount of oil added.

🐾 Clean your trimmer after every use. *Do not* use this tool for pushing, pounding, prying, digging, or pulling!

Q. How can I get rid of moss in my lawn?

A. Moss thrives in cool, dark, damp conditions, so it's usually found in lawns on the north side of trees and buildings where there is a lack of sunlight or there is poor drainage. Let the sun shine in, if possible, by thinning tree limbs. Then punch holes in the area to improve drainage, and apply gypsum at the rate of 50 pounds per 500 square feet. It may be necessary to correct the grade or tile the area if the water problem is too bad. Another alternative to use a commercial moss killer.

Q. How can I get rid of mushrooms in my yard? They're disgusting!

A. Use 2 cups of dry laundry detergent sprinkled over the area with your handheld spreader.

Q. When is the best time to destroy crabgrass?

A. For some reason, folks seem to think they should destroy the plant. To beat crabgrass, you need to kill the seed before it germinates. In most parts of the country, this should be done in

February or March. Wash down the area with soapy water, then apply a quality pre-emergent crabgrass killer.

· ·

Q. Is it really necessary to wrap the trunks of all new trees I plant?

A. I do, and after a year or two I change the wrap, and leave it on for a third year. Tree wrap keeps the moisture in and prevents bark split and sunscald.

· ·

Q. When is the very best time to plant a tree, any tree?

A. Nowadays, you can plant trees 12 months a year. Potted and balled-and-burlapped trees can even be planted when you have to break the frozen ground with a pick. But for the most part, late fall or early winter is best for balled stock. Late October and early November are also good times to plant bare-root trees.

· ·

Q. When is the best time to prune a birch tree?

A. In late June, because birch is a bleeder—the sap keeps running when you make a cut—and must be sterilized immediately with a solution of 2 tablespoons of ammonia per quart of water. Slosh this onto the wound. Then seal with "Tree Wound Paint Mixer" (see page 251).

Steady as She Goes

· ·

To keep a tree straight and steady when planting, tie the trunk to a long 2 × 4 that spans the planting hole. Remove the board after backfilling the hole.

· ·

CRITTER CONTROL

Worms Away!

My Grandma Putt knew the value of worms: They break down decomposable matter into fine humus, and help aerate the soil. But she also knew too much of a good thing when she saw it—an overabundance of these slimy creatures can render a fine lawn unsightly, as they cover the turf with their castings.

To take care of this problem, Grandma Putt would fill a coarse canvas bag with 2 pounds of mustard, and soak it in a tub of water. Then she'd drain off the mustard water, and sprinkle it over her lawn. This treatment soon brought the worms to the surface, where they could be gathered up and disposed of.

Q. I have a magnolia tree that has never bloomed, but the foliage is thick, green, and healthy. What's wrong?

A. Nothing. You have a seed tree, and I have known them to take 10 or more years to produce flowers. Be patient!

Q. Is it necessary to prune my trees every year?

A. A well-manicured tree will be healthier and prettier than one that is left to go its own way. But there may be seasons when they need no help, so you can relax.

Q. Can I mulch my trees with wood chips made from the limbs I've taken from the same tree?

A. You can if the limbs weren't removed because of insect or disease problems.

Q. Rabbits and mice eat the bark on my new trees. How can I stop them?

A. Wrap the bark with tree wrap right down to the soil. Then place medium-size stones around the base in a circle. If the problem is really bad, make a wire collar out of hardware cloth, and place it around the trunk from the ground up.

PEST PATROL

Grubs Be Gone

To kill grubs under a tree, poke holes in the soil and pour a mixture of 1 ounce of liquid dish soap per 10 gallons of water into the holes. Then apply diazinon at the recommended rate.

Fireproof Your Trees and Shrubs

If you live in an area that gets frequent or severe ice storms, you know the damage they can cause to your trees, shrubs, and evergreens by breaking limbs and branches. But did you also know that the ice creates a kind of fire glass for the sunlight? The concentrated rays of the sun can sometimes burn twigs and foliage as badly as a direct flame can. To "fireproof" your plants, put an old sheet or a piece of dry burlap over them after a storm while the sun is bright.

Q. What's the best way to get rid of a stump without digging it up?

A. Cut the stump at or below the level of the soil. Then drill a series of holes in it—the more the merrier. Make them as large and as deep as you can drill. Now fill them with a commercial stump remover that contains potassium nitrate, and plug up the holes. Let it set for one year. At the end of a year, remove the plugs, pour in kerosene, let it sit for an hour or so, then light it. The stump will smolder away to ashes.

Q. Can I use black enamel paint to seal tree cuts?

A. Absolutely not, because when the freezing weather comes, the paint will also freeze and crack, and then it won't act as a sealant any more. Use a commercial tree paint—it is flexible and will expand and contract as the weather  changes. Or use "Tree Wound Paint Mixer" on page 251.

Bye-Bye Fruit Flies

When you bring your harvest inside, do you soon find yourself swatting at fruit flies hovering over your baskets of fruits and vegetables? You can make a fruit fly trap out of an old fast-food carry-out  cup, a lid, and some regular cola. Simply fill the cup one-quarter full of cola, insert a straw so that it doesn't touch the cola, and leave about 1 inch of the straw extending out of the lid. Then set it on a counter near your fruit or vegetables. The flies fly down the straw into the cola, but they can't get out. Empty and refill the cup as often as needed.

Jerry's Secrets

It's a good idea to remove any mummified fruit and cankered branches from your fruit trees in February, before they spread disease spores to healthy branches. And while you're out there, tamp down any snow around the trunks (and around ornamental trees and shrubs) so that mice don't make runs to the trunks or feed on the bark.

Q. Should I keep my fruit and nut trees in a special area, or can I mix them up?

A. You can mix and match any group of trees. The idea is to make the trees and your landscape compatible—the size, height, shape, color, and commodity (fruit, nut, or berry). I don't put fruit trees too close to the patio or play areas, for the safety of both people and trees.

. . . .

Q. How can I keep dogs away from my evergreens?

A. Get a big, mean, cat. Seriously, though, you can dip pipe cleaners in tobacco juice and hang them on the plant, at dog sniffing height. Or spread moth crystals on the soil underneath the trees and shrubs. (This will also control some of the insects that try to move in.)

. . . .

Q. When's the best time to take cuttings from my cedar trees? And can I grow plants from them?

A. I take cuttings in the early spring and root them in sharp sand, then transfer to peat pots. Yes, you can grow your own plants, and they'll turn out to be the best kind because they're your babies.

. . . .

Q. Is it OK to use ground-covers instead of mulch under evergreens?

A. You bet! They are really great and, whenever possible, I use them. If you want to be the talk of the town, try strawberries as groundcover beneath evergreens. You can also use vinca, ajuga, or pachysandra, to name just a few of my favorites.

CRITTER CONTROL

Feed the Mice

If you've found mice munching on the mulch you put under your fruit trees in winter, try this trick that always worked for my Grandma Putt. Place small feeders on the ground near each tree, and fill them with mouse bait. That should take care of the problem.

When the Bough Breaks...

. . . .

You may be the one to fall! Ash, willow, horse chestnut, and redwood all have brittle wood, even when they're green. So climb these trees only for maintenance, and use a ladder instead of pulling yourself up branch by branch.

. . . .

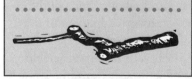

TREAT IT LIKE A ROSE

 Your mountain ash, that is. That's right—these close relatives of the rose and crabapple grow great if they're treated like a rose bush. Avoid high-nitrogen fertilizers, and instead use a rose fertilizer to keep them healthy and happy. Mountain ashes also respond well if they're given acid fertilizers.

Q. If you were going to use evergreens as a wind barrier, which would you use—pine, fir, or spruce?

A. I would go with the pine because they're much faster growing and generally less expensive. Spruce is a rather stodgy guy; handsome, yes, but he can be hard to get along with from time to time; and fir only likes it where it's cool and damp.

Q. I moved into an old house with an orchard of 12 trees. Some of the branches are dead, some have split bark, limbs are broken, and there are holes all up and down the trunks. Can I save any of them? There are 4 peach trees and 8 apple trees; I don't know the varieties.

A. I would sure give it a try. To begin with, cut down and remove all of the weeds in the orchard, then burn them. Next, remove all the dead and

MIXERS & ELIXIRS

Evergreen Elixir

If you want your evergreens to grow, you have to feed them in spring and early summer, but not after August 15 in areas where it freezes. Use a root feeder and alternate between the evergreen tablets and fruit tree tablets. On the upper soil, beneath the foliage and beyond, sprinkle ¼ pound of Epsom salts and 1 pound of gypsum under each plant. Then feed with this tonic:

1 cup of liquid dish soap
1 cup of chewing tobacco juice*
4 tbsp. of instant tea granules
2 tbsp. of bourbon
2 tbsp. of Fish Fertilizer+
2 gal. of warm water

Mix all of the ingredients together, and give each plant 1 quart of the elixir. Then water in well.

*To make the juice, take three fingers' worth of chewing tobacco from the package, place it in the toe of a nylon stocking, and place the stocking in a gallon of boiling water. Let the tobacco steep until the water is dark brown.

broken limbs. Then poke holes 3 feet apart and 8 inches deep in a circle out at the drip line, below the tips of the furthest branches of each tree. Use these holes to feed each tree with 15 pounds of low-nitrogen garden food. Then apply half a pound of moth crystals to the soil beneath each tree within 3 feet of the trunk. This will help to control borers.

Taters for Trees

Here's an old trick my Grandma Putt taught me: When planting a tree, line the planting hole with baking potatoes. They'll hold in moisture and provide nutrients to the tree as they decay.

Q. Is limestone a good groundcover to use under evergreens?

A. If it's washed, it's OK, but I don't like it as well as mixed stone or marble chips. Make sure you put down a weed-block fabric, covered with shredded bark, then the limestone.

Q. I am having a hard time growing grass under my shade trees. I've tried everything, including tilling the ground and reseeding. Please help.

A. Unfortunately, grass doesn't grow too well in the shade, so you must overseed every 16 to 20 days for the life of the shade tree, or plant a groundcover, such as myrtle.

Q. My town offers ground-up Christmas trees—needles and all—as a mulch. Is it safe to use in my yard?

A. It's a lifesaver, but remember: This mix will tend to make the soil acid. So if you use this material, add some lime in the spring.

CHAPTER 6

"The fondest memories I have of growing my first garden are of taking an old picnic basket, and going out to pick our evening meal. Crisp leafy lettuce, crunchy carrots, juicy red tomatoes, and tender string beans would find their way into the basket for a trip back to Grandma Putt's kitchen. Of course, there was plenty of sampling done on the spot—harvesttime is my favorite time of year!"

Gathering Up the Garden

Reap What You Sow

This is when all of your hard gardening work pays off! You'll realize that those months of weeding, feeding, watering, and worrying were worth the effort when you harvest fresh vegetables, fruits, and flowers at their absolute best. And you owe it all to yourself! So read on to reap the maximum returns from a winning growing season.

ASPARAGUS IS AN EARLY RISER

Asparagus is the earliest vegetable that you can harvest from your garden in the spring. The young, tender shoots usually reach cutting size by about mid-May. New shoots may be cut as often as every other day if temperatures and moisture conditions are favorable.

HOME COOKIN'

Asparagus Salad

This is a big, beautiful salad—perfect for a buffet.

1 lb. of asparagus
1 head of romaine lettuce, cleaned, separated, and dried
1 lb. of mushrooms
Juice of 2 whole lemons
½ cup of cream
¼ tsp. of paprika
Salt and pepper, to taste

1. Clean the asparagus, cut off the woody ends, and tie in a bundle. Boil in a sauce pan or steamer until the asparagus is tender-crisp. Cool quickly in ice water.

2. Arrange the lettuce on a large, round platter.

3. Clean and thickly slice large mushrooms; use small ones whole.

4. Make a dressing with the lemon juice, cream, paprika, salt, and pepper. Stir the mushrooms into the dressing, then use a slotted spoon to remove them.

5. Put the mushrooms in the middle of the lettuce. Surround them with asparagus spears, tips pointing out. Garnish with carrot curls, cherry tomatoes, and/or English walnut halves. Serve cold, with the dressing on the side.

SUPER CELERY

You can harvest celery all winter long, if you know what to do. Simply dig up the plants with a fair amount of roots attached to them before the freezing weather sets in, and then replant them in a deep cold frame. They will remain in great condition well into the winter, plus they'll be readily accessible even when the ground is covered in deep snow!

TOMATO TIME EXTENDER

You can greatly extend your tomato season by picking all green tomatoes before they're damaged by frost. Wipe off any dirt, and wrap each tomato individually in newspaper. Then pack the paper-wrapped tomatoes in a cardboard box, and store in a cool, dry place. They will continue to ripen, so check them often.

APPLES AT THEIR BEST

Timing is everything, especially when it comes to apples. Apples harvested at just the right time are always better in terms of flavor and keeping quality than those that are picked either before or after their peak of perfection. While it is darn near impossible to set down a hard and fast rule for determining the ripening times of the many different apple varieties, here are some of the general clues that I've picked up over the years:

🍂 Look for a change in the skin color, from leaf green to light greenish yellow or red. But, if you are planning on making applesauce from yellow apples that ripen in spring or

---

HOME COOKIN'

Quick-and-Easy Tomato Juice

Don't waste a lot of time and effort making tomato juice the old-fashioned way—by scalding, peeling, cooking, and mashing them through a colander. Instead, follow these simple steps. This method is not only faster, but it's also healthier for you because the skins are left on the tomatoes, providing you with more vitamins.

Fresh picked tomatoes
A blender

1. Wash and core tomatoes (work in batches of six or so, depending on their size), and cut away any bad spots.

2. Put the tomatoes in a blender, and blend on high speed or purée until smooth.

3. Can or freeze the juice.

---

early summer, it's best to pick them green.

🍂 If the fruit releases readily from the branch when you take it in hand and twist it up, it's ready to pick.

🍂 Early apples should be picked when they're still hard because they'll go soft if they're left on the tree for too long.

🍂 Hand-pick your apples; don't shake them off and allow them to drop to the ground. If you do, you'll end up with bruised fruit.

HARVESTTIME RECIPES

When you're drowning in zucchini, up to your elbows in tomatoes, and can't see the peppers for the peas, it's time to haul out the favorite harvesttime recipes, and put all of those good foods to good use! Here's a sampler of some of my all-time *Garden Line* favorites.

Zucchini Casserole

3 cups of peeled, grated zucchini
1 cup of Bisquick
1/2 cup of chopped onions
1/2 tsp. of oregano
1/2 cup of oil
4 eggs
1/2 cup of shredded
  cheese
2 tbsp. of parsley
1/2 tsp. of salt
Dash of pepper
Dash of garlic powder

Mix all of the ingredients together in a large bowl. Pour into a casserole dish, and bake at 350°F for 30 to 40 minutes.

Wilted Zucchini Salad

1 pound zucchini, thinly sliced
1/4 cup of chopped green onion
1/2 cup of finely chopped green peppers
1/2 cup of finely chopped red peppers
1/2 cup of cider vinegar
1/4 cup of sugar
1/2 tsp. of salt

Lightly mix all of the ingredients in a large bowl. Cover and chill before serving.

Cream of Zucchini Soup

5 to 6 medium zucchini
1 large onion, sliced
1 1/2 tsp. of curry powder
3 cups of chicken broth
1 cup of heavy cream
1/2 cup of milk
Salt and pepper, to taste
Garlic powder (optional)
Chopped chives

Cut the zucchini into small pieces, and place in a kettle with onion slices and curry powder. Stir to coat zucchini pieces. Add chicken broth and bring to a boil. Simmer for 45 minutes, then purée in a blender. Add cream, milk, salt and pepper, and garlic powder, if desired. Garnish with chopped chives on the side.

Baked Vegetables

2 sliced zucchini
2 sliced yellow
* squash*
1 red bell pepper
1 green bell pepper
1 small package of baby carrots
1 head of cabbage, sliced
2 cups of broccoli florets
1 large onion, sliced
Olive oil
Salt and pepper, to taste

Lay all of the vegetables in a long baking pan. Sprinkle them with olive oil, salt, and pepper. Bake in a 400° to 450°F oven, stirring frequently, until cooked to the desired tenderness.

Zucchini Cake

3 eggs
2 cups of sugar
3/4 cup of margarine, softened
2 cups of shredded zucchini
2 tsp. of vanilla
2 tbsp. of orange peel
1 cup of flour
1 tsp. of baking powder
1 tsp. of salt
1/2 tsp. of baking soda
1 cup of nuts (optional)
1/2 cup of milk

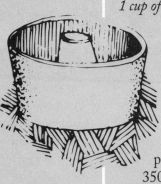

Beat the eggs into the sugar. Add the margarine, zucchini, vanilla, and orange peel. Add the remaining dry ingredients alternately with the milk. Pour into a Bundt pan or a 9 × 13-inch pan. Bake at 350°F for one hour in the Bundt pan or 35 to 45 minutes for the 9 × 13-inch pan. Cool. Top with frosting or glaze.

Zucchini Carrot Cake

4 eggs
2 cups of sugar
1 1/3 cups of oil
2 1/2 cups of flour
2 tsp. of baking soda
2 tsp. of baking powder
2 tsp. of ground cinnamon
1 tsp. of ground cloves
1 tsp. of allspice
1 tsp. of ginger
1/2 tsp. of nutmeg
1 tsp. of salt
2 cups of finely
* shredded carrots*
2 cups of finely shredded zucchini
1 cup of chopped pecans

In a large mixing bowl, beat the eggs and sugar until frothy. Gradually beat in the oil. Combine the dry ingredients and add to the batter. Beat 4 minutes. Stir in the carrots, zucchini, and nuts. Pour into three greased 9-inch round pans or a 9 × 11-inch pan. Bake at 350°F for 35 minutes or until the top springs back after being touched. Cool 5 minutes before frosting with your favorite cream cheese frosting.

Tomato Soup

1 qt. of tomatoes
1 qt. of milk
²/₃ tsp. of baking soda
Salt and pepper, to taste
Celery salt (optional)
Chopped chives (optional)

Heat the tomatoes in a
kettle or large saucepan
until they are very hot.
Remove from the heat and
add the milk and baking soda,
mixing well. Heat again, being careful not
to let it boil. Season with salt and pepper;
add celery salt and chives, if you wish.

Garden-Fresh Salsa

16 firm Roma tomatoes
2 red bell peppers
3 green bell peppers
4 mild onions
4 to 6 jalapeño
*   peppers (for mild,*
*   use only 2)*
2 yellow banana
*   peppers*
4 Anaheim green
*   chilies*
1 cup of fresh cilantro
2 fresh garlic cloves
1 cup of white vinegar
6 tsp. of garlic salt
2 tsp. of black pepper
2 cans of diced tomatoes with Mexican
*   seasonings, drained*

Using a food processor or a sharp knife,
coarsely chop and seed all of the cleaned
vegetables. Mix with the
vinegar and spices. Place
in a glass gallon jar, cover,
and refrigerate
before using.

Fried Green Tomatoes

1 egg, beaten
1 cup of buttermilk
1 cup of self-rising flour
¹/₃ cup of cornmeal
¹/₂ tsp. of salt
6 to 8 green tomatoes,
*   cut into ¹/₄" slices*

Mix the egg and buttermilk in a shallow
dish. Mix the flour, cornmeal, and salt in
another shallow dish. Working in batches,
dip the tomato slices into the egg mixture,
allowing excess to drip back into the dish.
Then coat with the flour mixture. Fry in
hot bacon drippings in a large, heavy skil-
let until browned, turning once with
tongs. Transfer to a colander to drain.

Pick When Berry, Berry Good

If you grow your own rasp-berries, blackberries, or other berries, congratulations! Having your own berry bushes nearby allows you to pick them when they are at the very peak of their deli-cious flavor. My rules of thumb? Pick red raspberries every day, and blackcaps and blackberries about every third day.

PEACHY PICKINGS

Peaches are so perishable that they are often picked by commercial growers when they are still too green. Because of this, many folks have never eaten a really ripe, sun-kissed peach, and so they have no idea how delicious they really are. So when folks plant their very first peach trees, they have no idea when they should harvest the fruit. Here are my tips that'll

guarantee the best-tasting, juiciest peaches around:

🍂 Remember that the quality of the fruit increases only while it's on the tree, where the leaves can manufacture sugars. So if you pick a peach too soon, it will not ripen properly.

🍂 Peaches grow rapidly, so the crop becomes greater as the fruit approaches tree-ripe con-ditions. One hundred bushels of peaches on August 15, if not picked until tree-ripe a few days later, will then become 124 bushels of much finer peaches.

🍂 Do not pick peaches until the color of the fruit changes from green to yellow (or to white, if you're growing the white-fleshed varieties).

🍂 Plan on two or three pickings over several days to make sure you get all of the peaches at their peak of flavor.

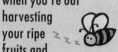

Bee Sting Relief

Chances are, sooner or later you're going to run into some bees when you're out harvesting your ripe fruits and berries because the bees know a good thing when they see it—and if you've taken my advice all along, that good thing is your delicious, juicy fruit! So if you get stung, whip up a paste made from baking soda and water or rubbing alcohol. Apply this directly to the bite to ease the pain.

THE MELON TEST

To determine whether or not your melons are ripe for the picking, check the blossom end (opposite the stem) by pressing on it. It should give way slightly and smell kind of sweet if it's ripe and ready for pickin'.

RE-MUM-BER THIS TIP

Want happier, healthier mums? Then lift chrysanthemum clumps after they bloom in the fall, divide and pot the plants, and set the new divisions in a cold frame. They will start growing much earlier the next spring. They'll also be less susceptible to any disease that was present in the parent plant than if you leave the whole clump undivided over the winter.

The Dirt on Berries

If your berries are dirty, don't wash them immediately after picking. Instead, put them in a plastic food-storage bag, and pop them into the refrigerator for a few hours. The cold air will firm them up in an hour or two, and then you can wash them without losing a lot of juice.

PEST PATROL

Good Reasons to Rake

By raking up and burning all fallen fruits rotting on the ground, you will be a step ahead in controlling brown rot of plums, cherries, and peaches, and black rot of grapes. And raking and burning fallen apples will reduce the number of maggots that come to feast on your fruit next spring.

KEEP IT SHORT

When cutting flowers to bring inside, here's a professional tip—cut the stems short for best results. With most perennials, the shorter the cut stems, the less damage there is to the remaining plant. And with most annuals, the shorter the stem, the more possibility there is that other flowers will be produced from the same plant.

SOCKS STOP SCRATCHES

Don't throw away those old, worn-out cotton socks—they come in "berry" handy for berry picking. Take a pair, and cut two holes in the foot of each sock; one hole for your thumb to slip through and the other one large enough for your other four fingers. Then pull one sock over each hand and arm to protect your skin from thorns—and go get those berries!

FLOWER ARRANGING 101

It's easy! Use a plastic mesh berry basket the next time you're arranging flowers. Turn the basket upside down, and place it in a bowl or large vase. Now insert the stems of your cut flowers into the openings. If your container is shallow, don't worry. You can drape moss over the top and sides of the berry basket to make it less noticeable.

For a Bountiful Flower Harvest...

...take a pail of tepid water into the garden when you go out to cut. Use a sharp knife to cut stems on a slant so that the largest possible surface is opened to absorb water. Immediately after cutting, stick the flower stems into the pail of water. Leave them up to their necks in water for at least a few hours; overnight is even better.

STRIP 'EM DOWN

When you're preparing cut flowers for arranging, keep in mind that the longer the stems, the less water will reach the blooms. The same can be said about leaves: The more leaves left on the stems, the less water will reach the blooms. So remove all but the top foliage.

If the plant has branching stems, cut off the branches and put them into the arrangement separately, so they don't tax the strength of the main stem.

Jerry's Secrets

The best times to cut flowers for arranging are either early in the morning or the evening, when the foliage contains a lot more moisture.

MIXERS & ELIXIRS

Repotting Booster Tonic

Once you've repotted your rooted cuttings, give them a dose of this tonic to help them adjust to their new homes:

½ tsp. of All-Purpose
    Plant Food
½ tsp. of Vitamin B$_1$
    Plant Starter
½ cup of weak tea
    water*
1 gal. of warm water

Mix all of the ingredients together, and gently pour the tonic through the soil of your repotted plant. Allow it to drain through for 15 minutes or so, then pour off any excess in the saucer.

*Soak a used tea bag in a gallon of warm water and 1 teaspoon of liquid dish soap until the mix is light brown.

COUNT ON CUTTINGS

You can enjoy your favorite garden plants indoors all winter long and have new plants for spring if you take cuttings in the fall. Coleus, lantana, geraniums, heliotrope, fuchsias, and begonias are only a few of the foliage and flowering plants that can be successfully carried through the winter in this way. Here's how to do it:

Build a box. Cuttings need high humidity and reduced air circulation. A tank-type terrarium or aquarium filled with wet sand makes a perfect propagation box. The sand should be moist or damp, but not wet or waterlogged. Use coarse, sharp sand that you have washed thoroughly (rinse until the water stays clean). Fill your container about 3 inches deep with sand; press down firmly with a piece of wood or a clean brick.

Although most professional propagators prefer sand, many home gardeners (like me) mix peat moss in with the sand to retain moisture. Perlite and

vermiculite are also good to use as rooting materials. Just be sure to water sparingly—these materials hold many times their weight in water, and you must avoid overwatering or the cuttings will rot.

Place your box so that it is out of the midday sun. A north- or west-facing window that has indirect light is best.

Take your cuttings. Take cuttings only from plants that are healthy and mature. Cut them on a cloudy day or early in the morning. Cuttings should be at least 4 to 6 inches long and should be mature stems. The tips should be soft and tender, while the bottoms should be hardy and strong, almost woody. If you take soft, immature cuttings, they are likely to decay. As you take your cuttings, loosely pack them in wet paper towels, and put them in a plastic bag. Keep the bag in the shade.

Turn Over a New Leaf

Some plants—such as African violets, gloxinias, rex begonias, and peperomia—root easily from leaf cuttings. Simply cut off the mature leaves with 2 or 3 inches of leafstalk, and insert them into the rooting medium until the leaf stands upright. For peperomia leaf cuttings, the blade of each leaf must touch the surface in order for the leaf to propagate. A bonus that comes with leaf cuttings—sometimes more than one plant grows from one leaf!

Once you're inside, use a sharp knife to cut each stem about ½ inch below a node or joint (the point where a leaf originates). Make a clean, smooth cut so it heals quickly. You can dip the bottom of each cutting into a rooting hormone before inserting it into the sand.

Insert each cutting into the sand gently to prevent the cut end from being injured. Be sure to insert it no deeper than is necessary to hold it upright. The plant needs oxygen both for healing and for forming roots, so it's best to have the cut end close to the soil surface.

Use the eraser end of a pencil or a small dibble to press the sand firmly around the cutting, but not against the stem. "Water in" the cuttings by gently flooding the box to make the sand adhere around the stems.

Trim the leaves. Trim the leaves of coleus, geraniums, and other plants that have large, soft leaves to about half their original size to reduce the evaporation area. Be sure to keep these succulent cuttings on the dry side—slight wilting is less harmful to these plants than excess dampness.

Be patient. Rooting should take place within three to five weeks; a few varieties may take a little longer. Increase their light exposure as soon as the cuttings become strong and sturdy. Don't remove cuttings from the sand until they are well rooted.

Once the cuttings are rooted, pot them up in small containers, like 2 × 2-inch pots. Use a light, porous soil mix. Once potbound, you can move the young plants into larger pots to await setting out in spring.

Jerry's Secrets

To start a few cuttings of your favorite garden plants in a flowerpot, put a glass jar over them to hold in humidity and prevent wilt. This should also help them root more quickly. Remove the cover once the plants are established.

KEEP YOUR COOL, MAN

When you walk into a florist's shop, you never see fresh-cut flower arrangements just sitting out in the open. No siree….they're all sitting pretty in refrigerated cases. And that's where your arrangements should spend their nights, if size permits. If they're too big, let them spend the night in a cool, dark place like the garage or basement. During the day, keep your fresh flower arrangements out of direct sunlight and away from heat sources like radiators or air vents. These simple steps will help prolong the life of any flower arrangement.

Vole Control

Voles, which are close kin to mice, run in mole runs and eat roots in winter, making a mess of your flowerbeds, lawn, young trees, and shrubs. Mix diatomaceous earth (DE) and Bon Ami cleansing powder with your fall lawn food to pep up the grass and discourage vole damage. Sprinkle the mix in your planting beds and around trees and shrubs. You can also sprinkle just plain ol' Bon Ami into bulb planting holes to keep these nasty little critters away.

SALAD SEASONINGS

For a colorful, tangy addition to any salad, try using calendula blooms or nasturtium flowers and leaves. The flowers not only add a fresh outdoor taste, but also can perk up the appearance of any salad. A word of caution, however: Use only those flowers and leaves that have not been chemically treated!

Get Your Lilies in Hot Water

To restore faded flowers to the height of their beauty, stick them in very hot water halfway up their stems, and allow them to remain there until the water cools. Then cut off the scalded portions of the stems and place the flowers in clear, cold water.

6 WAYS TO BOOM THE BLOOM!

There are many ways to extend the life of your beautiful cut flowers. Try any one of these techniques to see which works best for you:

1. Smash the stems of woody-stemmed plants with a hammer before placing them in water.

2. Mix 2 tablespoons of clear corn syrup per quart of very warm water before adding it to the vase.

3. Place 1 tablespoon of activated charcoal in the bottom of the vase before adding the flowers and water.

4. Place a copper penny in the vase, then add some sugar water (1 cube of sugar per pint of water) to it.

5. Use any one of the cut-flower extenders that you'll find sold in your local flower and garden shops.

6. Spray the flowers with hairspray or my WeatherProof.

FLOWERS LIKE THE FIZZ

You can enjoy the beauty of your cut flowers by keeping them in a mixture of 50 percent water and 50 percent lemon-lime soda. The sugar in the soda acts like an energy-supplying IV, and the citric acid slows down the growth of bacteria in the water.

HOME COOKIN'

Daylily Delight

I'll bet you didn't know this: You can eat daylilies. They taste like fried mushrooms (no, not chicken!). Rinse your homegrown, freshly picked flowers (don't use roadside ones, or any that may have been chemically treated), dry them on paper towels, and dip them into a thin pancake batter. Then panfry them until lightly browned, turning once. Put 'em on a plate, and serve as a different, but delectable, appetizer.

Putting the Garden to Bed

It's sad to see, but the last act of any gardening year is putting the garden to bed for winter. Some folks hardly give it any thought, but in many cases, it's just as important as all the TLC you gave your plants during the growing season. Actually, it may be more important than fertilizing, pruning, or any other thing you did this year. Read on for tips, tricks, and tonics to get it done the fast, fun, and easy Jerry Baker way.

Jerry's Secrets

To help your summer-flowering bulbs survive the winter, dust them with medicated baby powder before storing them in old onion sacks for the winter.

BATTEN DOWN THE BEDS

Proper fall preparation is vital to flowerbeds for those of you who live in the cold regions. As soon as Jack Frost has come nipping at your nose, remove all of your annuals and put them on your compost pile. Then cover the beds with finely mowed grass clippings and leaves, and overspray with a mixture of 1 can of regular cola (not diet), 1 cup of liquid dish soap, and ¼ cup of ammonia in your 20 gallon hose-end sprayer. Seven to ten days later, lightly spade in the clippings and leaves.

Sprinkle a mix of 5 pounds of all-purpose fertilizer, 2 pounds of gypsum, and 1 pound of Epsom salts per each 100 square feet of flowerbed, at least once in the winter. You can do this anytime; it's almost never too late.

GIVE ASPARAGUS BEDS A BREAK

Asparagus is like all other perennials—it should be allowed to keep its foliage until it dies down naturally in the fall. The reason, of course, is that root growth and preparation for next year's crop need this year's stalks and leaves to absorb nutrients.

So leave your asparagus stalks alone until they begin to turn yellow, and then cut them off cleanly at ground level. If they have berries on them, don't add them to the compost pile unless you're prepared to cope with unwanted seedlings scattered here and there later on.

6 STEPS TO SUPER GARDEN SUCCESS

When the gardening year finally comes to a close and the harvest has been gathered, unfortunately most folks are about ready to call it quits! But you're not quite done yet! I want you to rally your energy one more time and follow these six simple steps to ensure a ready, willing, and able garden next season:

1. Clean it up. Very few home gardeners ever clean up their garden as well as they should. I'm not just talking about neatness, although as my old kindergarten teacher beat into us, it does count! Here are three things that you will accomplish by doing a serious fall clean-up job:

🍂 limit the distribution of weed seeds;

🍂 help control both insects and diseases;

🍂 save yourself time next spring, when it's at a premium.

2. Plant a cover crop. It's fast and easy. Simply sow ordinary rye over the top of your rough garden, and then till it in. The cover crop returns nutrients to the soil.

3. Plant perennial vegetables. The more vegetables you plant that come up year after year (only if you like them, of course!), the less work you have to do. Makes sense, doesn't it?

4. Start a compost pile. If any of you who read, watch, or listen to me on a regular basis don't have some form of composting going on in your yard, then it's not because I haven't tried to persuade you! Now, please, get one going today.

5. Rough spade your gardens. I know it's hard work and I don't necessarily want you to do the whole job at one time, but I do want you to get it done before the ground freezes. (See "Last Call to Clean-It-Up" on page 288 for details.)

6. Drain any wet areas. If you have had a problem with too much water setting in your garden, now is the time to either begin to raise the garden bed, dig a runoff trench, or lay drain tile in the problem area. All will help eliminate those soggy spots.

MIXERS & ELIXIRS

Flowerbed Bonanza

After the fall cleanup, overspray your flowerbeds with this elixir:

1 can of beer
1 can of regular cola (not diet)
½ cup of liquid dish soap
½ cup of chewing tobacco juice*

Mix all of the ingredients together in a bucket, then apply with your 20 gallon hose-end sprayer.

*To make the juice, take three fingers' worth of chewing tobacco from the package, place it in the toe of a nylon stocking, and place the stocking in a gallon of boiling water. Let the tobacco steep until the water is dark brown.

Thwart Thrips

If your gladioli have been attacked by thrips, first clean them, then place the corms in paper bags along with 2 tablespoons of mothball crystals for every 100 corms. Twist the mouth of the bag closed, and keep them at a temperature of about 70°F for three or four weeks. Then remove the corms and store them as I described in "Dig 'Em Up and Bring 'Em In," at right.

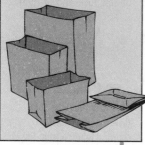

DIG 'EM UP AND BRING 'EM IN

Many of the plants that we think of as "summer-flowering bulbs" (including corms such as gladiolus, tubers, and fleshy rootstocks) cannot survive the winter outdoors in the northern states, so you have to dig them up to hibernate in safety. Here's how to protect some of my favorite flowering bulbs:

Begonia: Tuberous begonias growing in pots may be stored, pots and all, in temperatures between 50° and 60°F. Do not water them while they are in storage. If they are growing in the open ground, dig them up before the first frost, and pack them closely together in a shallow box with soil around their roots. When the tops have withered, remove the tubers, pack them in a shallow, topless box with leaf mold or peat moss around them, and keep them in a dry location for the winter.

Blue African lily: This plant doesn't go completely dormant during the winter. Leave it in its container, and store it in a cool, dry place where it will get plenty of light. Blue African lilies can withstand slight freezing, but the temperature should not fall lower than 25°F. You can keep these plants in an unheated sun porch, but keep a weather eye out because you'll have to bring it indoors when there is a chance that the temperature will fall too low. Water it only enough to keep the leaves from wilting.

Canna: When the foliage has been injured by frost, cut these plants down to within 6 inches of the ground. Then dig them up without making any special effort to shake the soil loose from the roots. Pack the plants close together with sand around them in shallow boxes in a cellar or room where the temperature stays between 40° and 50°F. Take a look at your cannas occasionally during the winter, and if there is any shriveling of the rootstock, moisten the sand ever so slightly.

Dahlia: When frost has blackened the foliage, cut the tops down to within a few inches of the ground. Then dig up the roots carefully (early in the morning), turn them upside down to drain any moisture from the hollow stems, and leave them exposed to sunshine

Ring around the Roses

Bush roses, especially teas and hybrid teas, should be covered with a mound of soil that's at least 6 inches deep to protect their lower stems through the winter. But don't make these mounds from the soil normally found around the plants, or you'll leave the roots exposed without enough covering. Instead, bring in additional soil for mounding, then cart it away in spring. And while you're at it, bury half a handful of mothballs in the new soil to keep thugs away.

until that afternoon. If you have an old-fashioned, dirt-floored, unheated cellar, stand the roots on the floor in some out-of-the-way area. Another storage method is to wrap each clump of roots in newspaper and pack them in a ventilated barrel or crate. A third method is to put the roots in a box that is 6 to 8 inches deep, and fill in and around them with granulated peat moss or sand. They should be stored in the coolest place available, provided that the temperature does not ever fall below freezing.

Gladiolus: This plant is capable of surviving winter temperatures as low as 0°F, provided it is planted at the normal depth and mulched in the fall with 3 to 6 inches of partially rotted leaves. But most folks dig up gladioli whenever the foliage begins to turn color, or when it has been killed by frost. Leave the tops attached until they become brittle; then they can easily be removed along with the loose scales and withered corms of the preceding year. Spread the plants out in shallow boxes or paper grocery bags, and keep them in a dry place between 40° and 50°F.

Summer hyacinth: Summer hyacinths are reasonably hardy, but they often fail to survive the winter. So just to be on the safe side, dig up the bulbs in fall and store them indoors at a temperature between 35° and 45°F.

Jerry's Secrets

Apply a temporary mulch to your rock garden plants as soon as the ground freezes hard. This will help the plants through the winter by stabilizing soil temperature, lessening heaving and thawing, and protecting the tops.

PRESCRIPTION FOR PEONIES

Cut off peony stalks, and remove them after they've died back in the fall. Be sure to cut them below ground level, or else you will give botrytis disease a chance to survive the winter. If it does, look out next spring!

LAST CALL TO CLEAN-IT-UP

If you have freezing temperatures in your area in the winter, make sure you remove all dead foliage and dropped vegetables from your vegetable garden after the first killing frost. Here's a neat little technique that I learned a long time ago: Dig a trench across one end of the garden, about 3 feet wide and a spade's head deep. Spread the soil over the garden and fill the trench with newly raked leaves, grass clippings, manure, table scraps, sawdust, ashes, and any other organic matter you can get your hands on.

Mix a batch of "Fall Garden Prep Tonic" (at left), and sprinkle it over the leaf mixture. Then dig the next 3-foot trench, throwing the soil on top of the finished trench to cover the organic material. Repeat this process until your garden is completely spaded. Let your neighbors know they can bring their leaves over to help out—they'll probably be glad to get rid of them!

When you have the whole garden spaded, sprinkle an all-purpose garden food on top at a rate of 5 pounds per 100 square feet. Then fill your 20 gallon hose-end sprayer with a can of beer, and drench the soil. Once that's done, you can sit back and let your garden rest and recuperate all winter long.

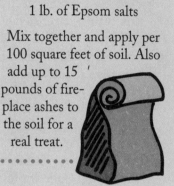

Pack 'Em a Lunch

Give your fall-planted bulbs an organic lunch by mixing:

10 lbs. of compost
5 lbs. of bonemeal
1 lb. of Epsom salts

Mix together and apply per 100 square feet of soil. Also add up to 15 pounds of fireplace ashes to the soil for a real treat.

MIXERS & ELIXIRS

Fall Garden Prep Tonic

2 cups of ammonia
1 cup of beer
½ cup of liquid dish soap
¼ cup of instant tea granules
2 gal. of warm water

Mix all of the ingredients together, and use it to give a boost to your composting materials.

STRIKE ONE FOR INSECTS

If soil insects have been "bugging" you this year, here's my little secret for effective control next year.

It's an organic control that's been around for ages: marigolds. This one takes a little bit of work because you need to collect all of the marigold plants and flowers in the neighborhood! Place them all in a row, and run your lawn mower over them with the catcher bag attached to it. Make sure you shred them finely. When you're done, sprinkle them over your freshly turned garden before you spray it with beer (see "Last Call to Clean-It-Up" on the opposite page).

A Frosty Reception

If Jack Frost snuck up on you and your vegetable plants before you had a chance to cover them, don't worry. You may be able to revive hardy crops like chard, collards, and mustard. Simply sprinkle them gently with water from your garden hose *before* the sun shines on them, and then wait to see what happens to them.

SOME LIKE IT COLD

I know that we bundle up at the drop of the thermometer, but to get the most from your winter plant coverings, you should only apply them *after* the ground freezes. Why wait so long? Because your real enemy is not temperatures; it's the wild fluctuations of heat and cold that you need to control. You actually want to protect your plants *to keep them cold* during those midwinter thaws that cause the ground to heave, which results in root damage. Unprotected plants that are heaved out of the soil can die from exposure, or they may just dry out. Likewise, unseasonable warm spells can cause dormant buds on unprotected plants to start growing, which will only be killed by the next freeze. But if you mulch soon after the ground freezes, you keep the ground colder, lessening the chance of heaving during a warmer spell.

MIXERS & ELIXIRS

Hibernation Snack

Give your vegetable garden and flowerbeds a hibernation snack by applying 25 pounds of garden gypsum, 5 pounds of bonemeal, and 10 pounds of garden food (4-2-4 or 5-10-5) for every 100 square feet. Then cover the entire area with a blanket of grass clippings and shredded leaves.

Fall Wash-Down Spray

Use this formula if you have a late-season infestation of bugs or just before you dormant-spray your trees and shrubs:

1 cup of tobacco juice*
½ cup of baby shampoo
6 tbsp. of fruit tree spray
4 tbsp. of antiseptic mouthwash
2 tbsp. of witch hazel

Mix all of the ingredients in your 20 gallon hose-end sprayer. Spray your plants to the point of runoff, making sure you get the spray inside your plants and onto the soil underneath them.

*To make the juice, take three fingers' worth of chewing tobacco from the package, place it in the toe of a nylon stocking, and place the stocking in a gallon of boiling water. Let the tobacco steep until the water is dark brown.

EVERGREENS UNDER WRAPS

Broad-leaved evergreens have large leaf surfaces that tend to lose a great deal of moisture during the sunny days of winter. If you live in the North and have bright, sunny winter days, protect your broad-leaved evergreens from scorching by setting up muslin covers over the plants. This reduces the effects of direct sun and drying winds. Likewise, planting evergreens on the north sides of buildings keeps them protected during both the summer and winter. My WeatherProof works wonders on these plants, too.

THE ROOTS OF THE MATTER

I'm always surprised at how many folks think that plants are entirely dormant during winter. The truth of the matter is that the roots of many evergreen and deciduous plants continue to function and absorb moisture from the soil throughout the winter months. In the cases of narrow-leaved (spruce, cedar, and so on) and broad-leaved (rhododendron, boxwood, and such) evergreens, a good deal of evaporation from the leaves takes place. The roots have to work harder to compensate for the moisture that is lost. Because of that, it is very important to thoroughly soak the soil around your evergreens in the fall, just before a heavy frost, and then mulch. And don't forget your trees' overcoats—a good thorough application of my WeatherProof in fall will lock moisture in while locking out the destructive elements like wind, sun, dirt, salt, and pollution.

HARDY PLANTS NEED PROTECTION, TOO

Normally, folks don't think that hardy shrubs and trees need any winter protection, but believe you me, they do! And you just can't beat mulch—it's quick, cheap, easy to apply, and it does a wonderful job. All of those lawn leaves that you rake up in fall make excellent mulches, and even if they mat down, they won't do any harm. Strawy manure also works well, if you can get it.

Broad-leaved evergreens may be mulched with leaves, peat, alfalfa hay, or coarse tobacco stems. Once spring rolls around, these materials can be left on or worked into the soil. If you live in northern areas where sunscald is a concern, see "Evergreens Under Wraps," on the opposite page, for tips on giving your plants extra protection.

SHADE TREE SECURITY

Landscaping professionals know this startling fact: 70 percent of your spring and summer shade tree bug problems return to the soil beneath those trees in fall to overwinter there, safe and sound. But you can surprise and destroy these insects by spraying the area from the trunk out to the weep line (at the tips of the longest branches) by applying Total Pest Control or Dursban at the recommended rates. This is especially critical if your trees are infested with borers.

All small trees should be sprayed with WeatherProof to prevent windburn, sunscald, and salt damage. This polymer material coats the tree, holding the moisture in while locking out the elements.

Last but not least, a good dormant spray in fall will destroy any insect egg masses that are deposited on branches or trunks, or in crevices and other handy spots. Dormant spray is a combination of lime sulphur and volk oil. You can purchase the ingredients separately or premixed. Apply it on a warm, sunny, windless day after all of the foliage has fallen. Make sure that you spray to the point of runoff in all of those troublesome areas.

CRITTER CONTROL

Wrap Out Rascally Rabbits

You know the importance of surrounding the trunks of young fruit trees with wire mesh to keep rabbits from eating the bark in winter. But did you know that azaleas and blueberry bushes are also favorites on rabbits' winter dinner menu? So protect them with wire mesh, too.

MAKE A CLEAN SWEEP

If you leave a large supply of loosely piled leaves under your trees, shrubs, and evergreens in fall, you're inviting trouble—mice, moles, rabbits, and rats love to nest around and feed on your defenseless plants. Plus, as the heat and moisture inside the pile build, disease-breeding bugs hibernate there. So the moral of the story is to sweep, rake, and remove any of last year's foliage and leaves to an area where you can mow them very finely, and add them to your garden soil. Then, just before the snow flies, shower everything and anything that grows with the "Fall Wash-Down Spray" (see page 290).

Jerry's Secrets

Don't prune back rose canes unless they're long enough to whip around in the wind and scratch each other. In my experience, any fall pruning beyond this seems to encourage pith borers and may result in more winter-killed plants.

BURN, BURY, OR COMPOST?

While we all know how important it is to clean up the yard and garden at the end of the growing season, how we should dispose of the plant remains is an ongoing debate. Do you burn it, bury it, or bequeath it to the compost pile? Some folks compost everything, and then treat the resulting product with chloropicrin before use. Others refuse to bother with compost and excuse their laziness by saying they are afraid of encouraging weeds and pests. I fall in somewhere between the two, burning material that is definitely diseased or insect-ridden (as well as woody stalks that are almost certain to harbor borers), and trying to compost everything that looks to be reasonably safe.

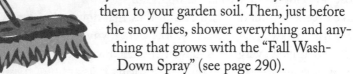

Most vegetable-disease organisms spend the winter in the vegetable rubbish that is left lying around the garden. Other destructive insect pests hibernate in old leaves or other garden debris, or at the bases of nearby weeds. It doesn't take a rocket scientist to figure out that if the cultivated area and the weeds 'round about it are cleaned up in fall, the battle against next spring's garden pests is half won. So hop to it now, and they won't be hopping around it later!

WINTER TOOL WRAP-UP

Yes, I've said this before, but it's worth repeating. When it's time to put your garden to bed for the winter, it's also time to put your tools to rest. If you just throw them in a box in the garage without taking a few minutes to clean and prepare them, come spring, you'll have a real mess on your hands. Here's how to wrap things up:

❧ Drain the oil and gas from all power equipment, and properly dispose of it.

❧ Wash off the dirt and grass buildup from under your mower deck. Use a product like Stay Clean to keep the deck in tiptop shape.

❧ Remove the mower blades, and clean and sharpen them now.

❧ Remove and clean or replace all spark plugs.

❧ Sand, prime, and paint rusted surfaces on any and all tools and power equipment.

❧ Oil springs, nuts, bolts, gears, and levers with WD-40.

❧ Wipe down your garden hose, electrical cords, and rubber/plastic parts with Armor All.

❧ Sharpen tool edges and paint metal parts with rust-resistant paint.

❧ Seal wood handles with a good water-sealing product.

❧ Burn or brand your name in the wood or etch it in the metal surfaces of all your tools.

❧ Clean, drain, and separate all your pressure sprayers and hose-end sprayers.

❧ Safely dispose of or store all garden chemicals out of reach of children and pets. A secure, locked cabinet works best.

Jerry's Secrets

Hole-y hoses! Don't throw away that old garden hose that leaks in a few places. Instead, add more cuts along its length, plug up one end, and you've got yourself a super soaker hose.

Lasting Mementos

When you've spent a fair amount of time lovingly tending to your flower gardens, it seems a real shame to only enjoy them for a few fleeting moments as they come into bloom and then quickly fade away. But there's no reason why you can't keep your garden beauties hanging around for months. All it takes is a little bit of know-how, and you can prolong the beauty of your garden flowers—even leaves and branches—to enjoy all year 'round.

KEEP THE BLOOM ON THE ROSE

…and on your other cut flowers, too. While we all know that cut flowers can't really be considered a "lasting memento" the way that dried ones can, you can still use some of these tips to keep them looking good for more than a few short days:

🌿 Split the stems and peel the bark from the ends of roses, honeysuckle, lilac, and other flowers with hard stems. Cut off a small portion of the stem every day, and change the water in the vase frequently.

🌿 Char the ends of chrysanthemum and azalea stems over a gas flame or a lit candle immediately after the flowers have been cut, and then put them in water.

🌿 Soak the stems of asters and delphiniums in a quart of water with a teaspoon of sugar for two hours before placing them in a vase.

🌿 Stand tulips in boiling water for 1 minute before placing them in a vase.

🌿 Put gardenias in a cardboard box and spray them thoroughly with water. Place the box in the refrigerator for about two hours before arranging the flowers in a vase.

🌿 Gather peonies just before the flowers open, and immediately put the stems into cold water.

Dapper, Deadly Daffodils?

Daffodils need a bit of extra attention when they're cut and brought inside. First, stand them in an inch of cold water and place them in the refrigerator for a few hours. Later, when you arrange them in a vase, do not put daffodils in with any other cut flowers—their stems excrete poisons that are harmful to anything standing with them in a vase of water.

5 STEPS TO SUCCESSFUL SILICA DRYING

My Grandma Putt dried late-summer and early-fall flowers in silica gel. While it can be somewhat expensive, Grandma Putt knew a bargain when she saw one—silica gel is reusable, and will last for many years. Don't be afraid to give it a try—silica gel comes with colored particles mixed in that indicate when the gel is saturated with moisture, which takes the guesswork out of the drying process. Here's how Grandma Putt got great results:

1. Gather flowers on warm, sunny days. They should be dry and at the peak of maturity. Cut off the flower heads, leaving about ¼- to ½-inch stems. Make new stems for the flowers (see "Give 'Em a Stem to Stand On" on page 296).

2. Add silica gel. Place 1½ to 2 inches of silica gel in the bottom of a container. Lay the flowers heads-up on the silica gel. Flowers with loosely spaced petals, like daisies, should be placed heads-down. Space flowers so that they are not touching each other. Bend the wire you added for stems in Step 1 at right angles to the heads of the flowers to support them. Sprinkle silica gel slowly and carefully around and inside the petals. Try to keep the petals in their normal positions. Bury the flowers completely.

3. Cover and seal. Cover the container with a tight lid, seal with tape, and place it in a warm, dry place where the contents won't be disturbed. Drying time varies, but it generally takes about two weeks.

4. Remove the flowers. When the petals are dry, carefully remove the flowers from the container. Gently shake, blow, or brush off all silica gel with a small paintbrush. Thick flowers like zinnias should be left on top of the silica gel after the petals have dried, to make certain that the undersides of the flower heads are thoroughly dry. Pour the silica gel into a container to save for another day.

5. Store the dried flowers. Keep them away from light, in a sealed, airtight container, to which you have added 2 to 3 tablespoons of silica gel to absorb moisture.

Jerry's Secrets

Before using your silica-dried flowers in arrangements, stretch and wind green florist's tape in a spiral around the wire stems. This makes them much more pleasing to the eye when they're arranged. And please remember to keep your dried flowers safely stored during humid weather. If you display them, they'll wilt!

GIVE 'EM A STEM TO STAND ON

Make new stems for flowers that you are drying by using green florist's wire. Use 18-gauge for large flowers, 20- to 22-gauge for smaller ones. Push the wire up through the short stem and through the center of the flower. Bend the top of the wire into a small fish hook, and pull it back into the center of the flower. For flowers with a hard calyx, such as roses, push the wire horizontally through the calyx only, allowing it to extend out of both sides.

USE IT AGAIN

When it was time to dry more flowers, Grandma Putt pulled out her container of used silica gel and poured the gel in a shallow baking pan. Then she heated it in the oven at 225° to 250°F for an hour or so, until the indicator crystals turned blue again. When you do this, remember to stir the gel from time to time.

Even this reactivated silica gel can be used again and again. Just keep it in sealed containers when it's not in use. You can keep on reusing it until the indicator crystals lose their color altogether.

A WORD ABOUT MICROWAVE DRYING

I've found that you can dry flowers and leaves in a microwave oven, but figuring out at what power setting and for how long can be a tricky and time-consuming process. However, there are several books available on how to dry flowers in a microwave, and some general flower craft books also have this information. The next time you're in your local library or bookstore, check 'em out.

It Just
Keeps on Going

Even though used glycerin
will darken, it's still good to
use. You may, however, have
to add more glycerin to the
old stuff before using it again
because the solution becomes
diluted with use by taking up
water from the air. When not
in use, store the glycerin in
capped bottles.

BRANCH OUT

When I was a boy, I mar-
veled at the branch and leaf
arrangements my Grandma
Putt and Aunt Ethyl concocted.
These natural arrangements
lasted a long time and never lost
their good looks. Grandma Putt
finally revealed her secret ingre-
dient to me—glycerin. If you
preserve branches and leaves in
glycerin, they will last for several years. Here's how Grandma
Putt and Aunt Ethyl did it:

**1. Choose branches that
have an attractive shape and
unblemished leaves.** Remove
any undesirable parts. Then
split or pound the ends of the
stems and remove some of the
lower bark to speed the absorption of the glycerin solution.

2. Mix one part glycerin to two parts warm (about 80°F) water.
You can use equal parts of glycerin and water for particularly stiff
foliage, such as mahonia, and for long branches.

3. Place the branches in tall, narrow containers. Use only
enough glycerin solution to keep the split ends covered. Be sure to
maintain the level of the solution as it is absorbed by the branch. If
the tips of the branches wilt before the glycerin reaches them,
warm the solution again to speed up the absorption. Absorption
takes anywhere from two to three days to three weeks or more, depending upon the size of the branch.

**4. When the glycerin has reached the tips, they will change
color and become pliable.** Hang the branches singly or in small
bunches upside down in a dark, dry place until you're ready for
them. Grandma Putt and Aunt Ethyl put the attic to good use as
their storage space.

Jerry's Secrets

Ivy and groundcovers
can also be preserved
with glycerin. Put
them completely in
the solution by
weighting them down
with small
stones.

HOT OFF THE PRESS

Pressing is a time-honored method of preserving flowers and leaves. My Grandma Putt was a real pro at pressing. She often made cards, bookmarks, and gift tags from recycled paper and decorated them by gluing on her dried flowers. But you don't have to be a pro to dry your own flowers—it's easy to do and doesn't require any special tools or materials.

All you need is a warm, dry area to work in, and a single layer of flowers on a piece of tissue paper. Cover them with another piece of tissue paper, and weight it all down with a heavy book, like a good, old-fashioned phone book or encyclopedia.

Grandma Putt always put her tissue-enclosed flowers on a hard surface—usually the dining room table, and sometimes on an uncarpeted floor—before weighting them down so the flowers would come out nice and flat. Just be sure to put them where they won't be bumped into or tripped over. Then leave them alone for a few weeks before peeking to see if they're dry. They're completely dry when the petals and leaves feel papery, and are no longer pliable.

If you plan on drying a large quantity of flowers, pressing under heavy books will take up a lot of time, not to mention floor space! Instead, consider buying a flower press. Then you can stack layers of flowers and get the job done more efficiently.

Jerry's Secrets

To retain the delicate beauty of roses in bloom and rosebuds, don't press them. Instead, bundle the stems with a rubber band and hang the roses upside-down in a dark, dry place.

Phone Book Bonanza

Another way to put the old phone book to good use is when drying individual flowers. Put each flower between sheets of tissue paper; slide them into the phone book, spaced out in various sections of the book; and place a weight on top. Leave the flowers inside for several weeks, or until they're dry.

Filling the Pantry

I remember thinking that fall was when the best smells came from my Grandma Putt's kitchen, but really, every day of the year smelled good, especially to a 10-year-old boy who had just run all the way home from school! Now I'm happy to share some of Grandma Putt's favorite recipes with you, along with a few others I've picked up from loyal readers over the years, plus tips on preserving and storing your produce. Believe you me, a gardener can never have enough recipes come harvesttime!

DRY IT, YOU'LL LIKE IT!

You don't have to give away everything you can't eat this season! Instead, give drying a try— it's a quick and easy way for you to preserve your bounty, and you don't need much storage space for the dried food.

The first thing you must know is kind of obvious—the bigger the piece of food, the longer it's going to take to dry. So you should slice foods thinly for best results. Another thing to keep in mind is that you want to choose only your best fruits and vegetables for drying. Blemished or bruised fruit will not keep. Fruit should be fully ripe, so that its sugar content is at its peak.

You have to prepare the food to be dried by blanching (pre-cooking) it in steam or boiling water for several minutes. Then you're ready to move and groove. Read on for a look at three tried-and-true ways to dry fruits and vegetables.

HOME COOKIN'

Do the Math

This isn't a recipe for something to eat, but it is a recipe to avoid disaster. When you dry foods, please, *please* keep in mind that a lot of produce goes a little, little way. What do I mean? Well, use this as a rule of thumb: 25 pounds of fresh vegetables dry down to between 3 and 8 pounds, depending on the size and moisture content of the vegetables. So do the math before you go promising everyone you know a box of dried home-grown goodies for Christmas!

HERE COMES THE SUN

Drying outdoors is the cheapest and easiest way to dry foods because you let the sun do all of the work. But you need to live in an area that gets plenty of hot, sunny days with low humidity and clean, unpolluted air. (Sound like your area?) But even then, when you dry foods outside, you must keep dust, dirt, insects, and animals away from the food. Sometimes that can be a mighty big chore.

Set the food out early in the morning, after the dew has dried, so it has a full day in the sun. Put the food skin-side-down on racks made from a wooden frame that has been covered with either nylon mesh or cheesecloth. You can use an old window screen, but first cover the screening with cotton fabric, freezer paper, or brown grocery bags opened inside out. This keeps the food from touching the metal wire, which can destroy the vitamins in the food or introduce a metallic taste.

Raise the tray up off of the ground by several inches to ensure good air circulation and to speed up the drying process. Turn the food often, and dry only on sunny days. If you're not going to bring the trays inside each night, then move them to a protected area and cover them tightly to keep insects, animals, and dew from spoiling your foods. Drying this way will take several days.

Jerry's Secrets

If you can dry food in a regular oven, why not speed up the process in a microwave? Seems like a good idea for time-pressed preservers, doesn't it? *Don't do it*—and here's why: You cannot control the temperature in a microwave, so your food will be cooked instead of dried.

PULL OUT ALL THE STOPS

If you're serious about drying large quantities of fruits and vegetables year after year, then consider buying a home food dryer. These give you shorter drying times, and they're dependable and convenient. The dryer comes with instructions on how to prepare foods for drying and how long to dry each type of food. When you buy a dryer, be sure it has a thermostat, a fan to improve ventilation, and sturdy, easy-to-clean shelves.

SOMETHIN'S IN THE OVEN

Oven drying is practical for folks who live in areas that aren't blessed with lots of warm, sunny days. When you dry foods in your oven, you can do so at any time of year, day or night, no matter what the weather.

Place the food skin-side-down directly on the oven racks, one piece deep. If the slats are too far apart, cover them first with finer wire cooking racks or cheesecloth, and then place the food on top. You can use regular baking sheets, but because they are solid, they don't expose the food to the dry air on all sides, so you must turn the food more frequently.

Set your oven no higher than 145°F. If your oven's lowest setting is 200°F, set it on "warm" and use an oven thermometer to check the temperature. Check the foods often, and turn them when the exposed sides are dried out and not sticky. Rotate the trays for more even heat distribution, and keep the oven door propped open a bit with a folded towel to get good air circulation. Drying will take anywhere from 4 to 12 hours, depending on the size and thickness of the food, and on how much you've put into the oven.

READY, OR NOT?

The toughest part about drying fruits and vegetables outdoors or in your kitchen oven is knowing when they're done drying. It may take a few batches before you get it right, and since everyone's backyard sunshine quotient and inside oven temperature is different, it's hard to give drying times. You'll just have to experiment, and keep notes on what works best.

I can give you some guidelines on what your food should look and feel like when it's done. Small pieces will dry faster (depending on size, thickness, and moisture content). Remove them from the trays, or they'll overheat and scorch before the rest of the tray is ready.

Fruit: should be dry and leathery on the outside and ever-so-slightly moist on the inside. It should still be pliable.

Beans, peas, corn: should be rock-hard.

Thinly sliced vegetables: should be leathery.

MIXERS
&
ELIXIRS

Broccoli Bath

Lots of bugs love to hide in and among broccoli florets. So here's a sure-fire way to make sure that your harvest is indeed bug free:

Fresh-picked broccoli
¼ cup of salt
1 tbsp. of vinegar
Cold water

Pour the salt and vinegar into a sinkful of cold water, and submerge the broccoli for 15 minutes or so. The bugs will float up to the surface, where they can be easily picked off. Rinse the broccoli under fresh water, and it's ready to eat.

KEEP 'EM DRY

After you've gone to all the trouble of blanching, slicing, and drying your harvest, don't throw it all away by improperly storing your dried foods. Once food is dry, pack it for storage right away because it immediately begins to absorb moisture from the air. Use jars with airtight lids, heavy-duty plastic bags, or metal cans with tight-fitting lids. If you're using metal cans, line them with brown paper to prevent food from coming in direct contact with the metal. If you don't have a dark storage area, you should also line glass jars and plastic bags

with brown paper to keep the light out. Check the food for mold from time to time. If you find any, throw away all of the food in that container, *not just the moldy pieces.*

Dried foods can be stored for anywhere from one month to two years, depending on how well they were dried and how well they were stored.

Stay Out of the Fridge!

. . . .

Don't store your dried produce in the refrigerator. Even though it's dark and a convenient storage place, it's dried food's worst enemy. The humidity and moisture in the cool, refrigerated air will rehydrate your food in no time, making it a worthless, ugly mess.

. . . .

INTO THE DEEP FREEZE

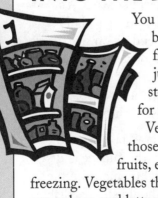

You can freeze your fresh fruits and vegetables, but only if you have a freezer that is separate from your refrigerator. A refrigerator freezer just doesn't get cold enough for long-term storage, and its small size makes it impractical for freezing large quantities of produce.

Vegetables that are best suited for freezing are those that you cook before eating, and almost all fruits, especially berries, are perfect candidates for freezing. Vegetables that are usually eaten raw, such as celery, cucumbers, and lettuce, do not freeze well.

As with drying, you must blanch the foods in either steam or boiling water before freezing. Then cool them by plunging them into ice water. Roll them in a towel to dry, then package them up for freezing. (See "Seal 'Em Tight" on the opposite page.)

SEAL 'EM TIGHT

The best freezer containers seal tight to keep
air out and prevent contamination and moisture
loss. Here are some of my favorite choices:

Plastic containers. Use only those containers with
lids that form and keep a good seal. Don't use yogurt or cottage
cheese containers, or other thin plastic containers—they crack in
cold temperatures, exposing your food to that yucky freezer burn.

Heavy-duty plastic freezer bags. Close the bags tightly with
a wire twist tie or rubber band set down close to the contents to
exclude as much air as possible. Don't use thin plastic bags like
grocery-store produce bags—they rip too easily.

Quart milk cartons. Save milk cartons and wash them out well.
Fill with food, fold down the top, and seal well with freezer tape.

MOTHER NATURE'S ICEBOX

If you live in a
cold climate where
the temperatures stay below
freezing for most of the winter,
you can store vegetables outside. They can be kept in shallow pits, in small barrels or nail
kegs, or in unused cold frames.
But if you live where winter
temperatures stay above freezing for several days at a time or
where winter rains are frequent,
outdoor storage is not for you.

If you use kegs or barrels, line
them with clean straw, then add
vegetables. Cover with straw or
leaves, then pile on enough soil

to prevent freezing.

If you dig storage pits,
locate them in soil that
drains well. Dig the pit
not more than 1 foot deep,
and line it with straw. Mound
the vegetables in a conical heap,
and cover them with 6 inches of
straw, then with 3 inches of soil,
allowing tufts of straw to stick
out to provide ventilation. As
the cold becomes severe, add
another 5- to 6-inch layer of
soil. When the surface freezes,
you can add 6 to 8 inches of wet
manure to generate heat.

Once you open a pit or barrel,
all the vegetables must be used,
so it's best to make plenty of
small storage areas or containers
instead of a few large ones.

GET A HANDLE ON HERBS

Herbs deserve careful preparation for storage. Since their flavors are fleeting, plan for only one year's supply at a time; don't save any beyond that.

The simplest way to preserve herbs is by quickly drying them after picking. Wash sprigs and leaves, gently pat them dry with paper towels, and spread them in a very thin layer to dry in an airy, shady place. Old window screens are ideal to use for herb drying trays and can be set up in an attic. While you're up there, you can hang small bunches of sprigs from the rafters. Herbs dry fairly quickly, so check on them often, and don't dry any of them beyond two weeks.

Store your dried herbs in glass jars with tight lids. Label the jars and keep them in a cool, dark place. Check them occasionally to make sure that no moisture is forming inside the jars.

Herb sprigs can also be frozen, but some cooks are not pleased with the results. The herbs tend to turn limp and begin to darken soon after thawing, so you must time their use carefully. To prepare herbs for freezing, wash and pat them dry with a paper towel, then wrap them in plastic food wrap and seal 'em up with freezer tape. Label each roll.

Aunt Ethyl's Ratatouille

Of all the vegetables, there always seems to be too much zucchini, which poses a storage problem for many gardeners. Here's an easy and delicious solution—a ratatouille-type mix that can be served over rice or used in soups and other dishes:

2 lbs. of unpeeled zucchini, sliced to make about 8 cups
2 lbs. of eggplant, peeled and cubed to make about 11 cups
3 medium tomatoes, peeled, cored, and cut up
1 large onion, chopped
1 medium green pepper, chopped
2 cloves of garlic, minced
2 tbsp. of fine herbs
1 tbsp. of salt
2 cups of water

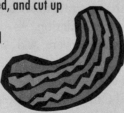

1. Combine all of the ingredients in a large pot and bring to a boil for 2 to 3 minutes, stirring once.

2. Cool by setting the pot in ice water.

3. Pack in freezer containers, seal, and freeze.

HERB CUBES, ANYONE?

If you use a lot of herbs in your cooking, you can have them on hand for quick use by freezing them in ice cubes. Then you can drop them into drinks (try mint cubes in ice tea), or herbs like rosemary, thyme, and basil can be cubed and used to season broths, soups, stews—just about any dish you want to flavor.

To make herb cubes, wash, pat dry, and chop up your favorite herbs. Pack them into ice cube trays, fill the trays with water, and freeze. When the cubes are frozen, wrap each cube separately in plastic food wrap, and store the lot in a large freezer bag. Come cooking time, just drop the cubes into the dish you're preparing. Isn't that easy?

PLEASE PASS THE SALT

Here's an old-fashioned secret—mints and parsley lose their flavor in drying, unless you use a salt solution as a fixative. Here's how to do it: Add 1 teaspoon of salt to each quart of water, and bring the mixture to a boil. Wash the herb leaves, place them in a strainer, and immerse them for 2 or 3 seconds in the boiling salted water. Then shake off the leaves, and place them on a screen to dry.

HOME COOKIN'

Pickled Watermelon Rind

7 lbs. of watermelon rind, diced
7 lbs. of sugar
1 qt. of vinegar
1 hot cayenne pepper, seeded
1 small piece of gingerroot
½ tsp. of oil of cloves
½ tsp. of oil of cinnamon
1 medium-size bottle of maraschino cherries
Salt
Water

1. Soak the watermelon rinds overnight in water to which salt has been added at the rate of 3 teaspoons per gallon.

2. The next morning, drain, rinse, and soak the rinds in ice water for 10 minutes. Then boil the rinds in the same water until they're tender.

3. Make a syrup with the sugar, vinegar, and 1 quart of water. Drain the rinds, and add them to the syrup. Boil for 10 minutes. Add the cayenne pepper, gingerroot, oil of cloves, and oil of cinnamon. Let stand overnight.

4. Drain the syrup from the maraschino cherries and save. Set aside the cherries.

5. Add the maraschino cherry syrup to the rinds, and boil for 15 minutes. Five minutes before the rinds are done, add the maraschino cherries and stir well.

6. Pack in sterilized jars, and seal.

Quick Dill Pickles

3 cups of white vinegar
3 cups of water
1/3 cup of pickling salt
4 lbs. of cucumbers,
    washed and cut into spears

6 heads of dill or 6 tbsp. of dill seed
3 peeled garlic cloves (optional)
9 peppercorns (optional)

Combine the vinegar, water, and salt, and heat to boiling. Pack the cucumbers into three hot, clean quart jars. Add 2 heads of dill or 2 tbsp. of dill seed, 1 clove of garlic, and 3 peppercorns to each jar. Fill the jars with the hot pickling syrup, leaving 1/2 inch of headroom. Adjust the lids. Process in a boiling water bath for 20 minutes. Remove the jars and complete the seals, if necessary.

Little Green Dilled Tomatoes

Grape leaves
Pickling spices
Fresh dill
Green cherry tomatoes

2 cups of salt
2 cups of vinegar
Stone crock
2 gal. of water

1. Line the stone crock with grape leaves and sprinkle them with the pickling spices.

2. Place a layer of fresh dill (stems, seeds, and flowers) on top of the spices, then pack the crock with the green cherry tomatoes, making alternate layers of tomatoes, dill, spices, tomatoes, dill, spices, and so on, until the crock is full.

3. Make a brine of the salt, vinegar, and 2 gallons of water. Pour it over the tomatoes.

4. Cover with a weighted plate, pressing the plate down into the crock, below the surface of the liquid.

5. Leave out at room temperature until it ferments (the warm days of August are best; it will take about two weeks).

6. Remove any scum that forms and pour off the brine into a large pot. Pack the tomatoes into sterile jars. Bring the brine to boiling, then pour over the tomatoes and seal the jars.

PICK A PECK OF CRISPER PICKLES

If your pickles are too pooped to participate (i.e., aren't crisp), then you've got a problem when you make dill pickles. Make sure you follow these simple steps next time:

1. Pick your cucumbers fresh from the vine early in the morning before they're heated by the sun. Pickle them immediately after picking. If you can't, then be sure to chill them right away until you can.

2. Remove all of the blossom ends from your cucumbers and wash them thoroughly.

3. If your recipe says to soak them in brine, keep them chillin' on ice.

4. Use full-strength (4 to 6 percent) vinegar and soft water, and make sure you completely cover the pickles.

5. Cap your jars immediately after packing, prior to processing, and then seal them airtight.

If you do all of the above, and your pickles are still not crisp and crunchy, add a little alum or a few grape leaves the next time you make them.

SAVE THOSE SEEDS

Anise, caraway, coriander, dill, sweet fennel, poppy, and mustard all have very flavorful seeds. If you'd like to collect these seeds, watch the plants carefully after they have bloomed because their seeds ripen quickly and fall off at the slightest touch. Cut the flower heads off and carefully put them in bags. When the seeds have fallen off, screen or sort out the debris, then wash and quickly dry the seeds the same way you do for herbs (see "Get a Handle on Herbs" on page 304). Store them in tightly sealed, labeled jars in a cool, dark place, and then use them to flavor your favorite dish.

EASY HERBED VINEGAR

I like to surprise my special friends with gifts from my garden—my own home-made herbed vinegars.

They're easy to make and wonderful to give. Simply place a few sprigs of thyme, chive, or tarragon into a sterilized jar or decorative bottle, and cover them with boiling vinegar. Leave the jar unsealed at room temperature until the vinegar has cooled. Then seal the jar and set it somewhere out of direct sunlight. The vinegar will be ready to sample in about two weeks.

HOME COOKIN'

Mighty-Fine Mustard Pickles

24 medium-size cucumbers, diced
1 qt. of small onions, finely chopped
2 cauliflower heads, divided into small florets
6 green peppers, seeded and chopped
2 qts. of small green tomatoes, diced*
Salt
Water

1. Soak the vegetables overnight in a brine solution made of 1 cup of salt to each gallon of water.

2. The next morning, heat the vegetables in the salt water until the water just comes to a boil. Drain them and set them aside.

Combine the following ingredients:

4 cups of sugar
¾ cup of flour
8 tbsp. of powdered mustard
1 tbsp. of turmeric
4 tsp. of celery salt

3. Mix well, then add:

3 qt. of vinegar

4. Stir in the vinegar slowly to make a smooth sauce.

5. Cook the sauce in a double boiler until thick, and then pour the sauce over the hot, drained vegetables.

6. Pack everything in sterilized jars, and seal.

* 1 cup of snap beans and/or 1 cup of carrots may be used in place of an equal quantity of green tomatoes.

FIGHT THE DARK SIDE

Many fruits will darken after they've been cut—unless you take action. One of my favorite old-fashioned cures is to mix 2 tablespoons of salt and 2 tablespoons of vinegar in a gallon of cold water. Then set the cut fruit in it for no more than 10 minutes. You can substitute 5 tablespoons of lemon juice for the salt and vinegar to get the same results.

Check out the chart below for a few more of my quick cures for fruit darkening.

To Prevent Fruit Darkening

CURE	FRUIT	HOW TO USE
Ascorbic acid crystals	Apples; other fruit	Mix 2½ tsp. per cup of cold water and sprinkle over cut apples. For other fruit, use 1 tsp. per cup of cold water.
Commercial antioxidant	All fruits	Follow label directions.
Saline solution (½ tbsp. of salt per qt. of cold water)	All fruits	Dip cut fruit into solution.

Jerry's Secrets

If you just can't wait to slice into a ripe, juicy melon, you can fast-forward their ripening time. Place your young melons on bricks while they're still attached to the vine, and the heat that the bricks absorb will speed up the ripening process.

FROM THE GARDEN LINE COOKBOOK

I can never get enough of that old-fashioned home cookin'. Throughout this book, I've shared many recipes with you, and I hope you like them as much as I do. Since I hate to end a book without giving you a little something extra-special, here are a handful (or should I say bellyful?) of my favorite *Garden Line* recipes that you folks have shared with me over the years. They're mmm, mmm…good, and they're a great way to share your garden with family and friends. Enjoy!

Baked Onions

1 medium white onion per person
1 beef bullion cube per onion
Salt and pepper, to taste
Pat of butter

Remove the outer skin from the onion. Cut a small core out of the top and place the onion on a square of foil. Place a bullion cube inside the cut-out, sprinkle on salt and pepper, and top with a pat of butter. Seal the onion in the foil and bake at 350°F for 1 hour.

Apple Cake Pudding

1 cup of sugar
1/2 cup of melted butter
1 well–beaten egg
5 apples, peeled and chopped

1 tsp. of baking soda
1 tsp. of cinnamon
1/2 tsp. of salt
1/2 tsp. of chopped nuts

Mix the sugar, butter, egg, and apples in a large bowl. Fold in the remaining ingredients. Pour into a 9 × 13-inch pan and bake at 360°F for 30 to 40 minutes.

Harvard Beets

2 cups of diced beets
1/2 cup of sugar
1 tbsp. of cornstarch
1/2 cup of vinegar
1/2 cup of water
Butter
Salt and pepper,
  to taste

Mix the sugar, cornstarch, vinegar, and water. Cook until thick. Add the beets and heat through. Add a small lump of butter, and salt and pepper to taste.

Pub Pickles

2 pickling cucumbers
1 tbsp. of salt
2 peeled garlic cloves

Cut off the ends of the cucumbers. Slice lengthwise into quarters and put into a plastic bag with the salt and garlic. Seal tightly and refrigerate for a few hours until marinated.

Broccoli Swirl Soup

2 tbsp. of butter
1/4 cup of chopped onions
1 can of cream of celery soup
1 cup of chopped broccoli
1/2 tsp. of dry dill weed
1/2 cup of milk
1/2 cup of light cream

In a saucepan, cook the onions in the butter, and stir until tender. Add the soup, broccoli, and dill weed. Pour the mixture into a blender or food processor and blend until smooth. Return the purée to the saucepan, and gradually add the cream and milk. Heat until warm, stirring constantly.

Sunshine Carrots

7 or 8 medium carrots, peeled
  and sliced
1 tbsp. of sugar
1 tsp. of cornstarch
1/2 tsp. of salt
1/2 tsp. of ginger
1/4 cup of orange juice
1/2 tbsp. of butter

Cook the carrots in salted water for 15 to 20 minutes, then drain and set aside. In a saucepan, mix the sugar, cornstarch, salt, and ginger, then add the orange juice. Cook, stirring constantly, until it thickens. Boil for 1 minute, then stir in the butter. Toss the sauce with the carrots and serve.

Superb Slaw

1 medium head of cabbage
1 medium onion, thinly sliced into rings
1/2 to 3/4 cup of sugar
1 cup of cider vinegar
3/4 cup of salad oil
2 tsp. of salt
1 tsp. of dry mustard
1 tsp. of celery seed

In a large bowl, alternate layers of shredded cabbage and onion rings. Top with sugar. Do not stir. Bring the remaining ingredients to a boil in a saucepan. Pour over the cabbage while still hot. Cover the bowl and refrigerate 4 to 6 hours. Then mix and serve.

Jerry Tells All About...
Harvesting

Q. How do you know when to pick kohlrabi?

A. That's a super question! Do you know that most folks who've grown it for years don't know the answer? Kohlrabi is part of the cabbage family, but you eat the base, not the foliage or the root. Pick it as soon as it's the size of a handball, or it will taste like you're eating a croquet ball—woody.

Q. How can I tell when my corn is ready for picking?

A. Pop 'em, then pick 'em! What do I mean? Start testing your corn about 15 days after the silk appears. Peel back the husk a couple of inches, and press on a kernel with your fingernail until it bursts open. If the juice is milky, the corn is perfect for picking. It it's watery, then give it a few more days. If it's pasty, then you're late, so you'd better get pickin'!

All in Due Time

The right time to harvest herbs depends on which part of the plant you want to use. Flowers should be picked when they blossom and are still only half open. Stems and leaves should be harvested before the plants flower because the essential oils are strongest at that time. Seeds should be picked when they are slightly hardened.

Jerry's Secrets

To remove silk from your corn quickly and with less mess, rub a damp paper towel along the ear. The silk will cling to the towel, not the corn.

Q. I like to harvest sunflower seeds to eat, but the birds usually beat me to most of them. What can I do to make sure I have some for myself?

A. Cover the head when the birds begin to feed on the seeds. Cut the head when the back of it is dry and brown, and leave about 2 feet of stem on it. Then hang it up to cure in a warm, dry place with good ventilation. When the back of the seedhead is entirely brown and papery, brush out the seeds. Store them in the refrigerator in an airtight container, but don't wash them. You can use the seeds raw in salads, or you can roast them.

Q. The cantaloupe I raised this year grew no larger than an orange. I put them in the same area each year—does this have any effect on them? Also, what type of fertilizer should I be using?

A. Next year, try growing your cantaloupe in bushel baskets with the bottoms removed, sunk into the ground. Place each basket 2 inches deep in the ground and fill with a mix of half professional planting mix and half garden soil (but someone else's, not yours). Then feed them every three weeks throughout the growing season with "All-Season Green-Up Tonic" (see "Green-Up and Clean-Up" on page 77).

Q. I usually pick my corn in the morning, before I go to work, and eat it that night for dinner. My neighbor says I should pick it just before I'm going to cook it. Does it really make a difference?

A. Yes! My Grandma Putt always picked her vegetables in the early evening, just before suppertime. In the case of sweet corn, she would have the water boiling before she went out to pick it. She said the less time spent between the stalk and your mouth, the better the corn will taste. And she was right! Research has shown that an ear of corn begins to lose its

Zap 'Em Dead Winterizing Tonic

1 cup of Total Pest Control
1 cup of baby shampoo
1 cup of tobacco juice*
1 cup of antiseptic mouthwash

Mix all of the ingredients together in your 20 gallon hose-end sprayer. Then give your yard and garden a heavy soaking in fall.

*To make the juice, take three fingers' worth of chewing tobacco from the package, place it in the toe of a nylon stocking, and place the stocking in a gallon of boiling water. Let the tobacco steep until the water is dark brown.

Herbal Switch Hitters

Dried and fresh herbs may be swapped in most recipes; depending upon the strength of the herb, use 3 to 5 times more fresh than dried. And to develop the flavor of dried herbs, soak them in the oil, vinegar, or lemon juice that is used in the recipe.

Pick 'Em Dry

Don't pick beans when the foliage is wet! Rust and other diseases are almost always present, and picking them when wet is the best way to spread the disease to the entire planting. To be safe, pick these delectable delights only when the foliage is dry.

sugar about 10 minutes after it's been picked. So listen to your neighbor!

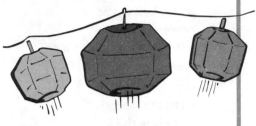

Q. How can I save my Chinese lantern blooms?

A. Cut them off on long stems, and then hang them upside down in a warm, dry place.

Q. How soon after planting can I cut asparagus?

A. Wait until the bed is well established. If it has started well, a few spears may be cut the second year, and it may be cut for several weeks the third year. But you shouldn't harvest a full crop until the fourth year.

Q. I have the loveliest tuberous begonias and gladioli in our garden. How can I make the blooms last longer?

A. Pinching off the withered flowers of your tuberous begonias will greatly extend the plants' flowering period. This is also true of gladioli in the ornamental garden. Pick the large bottom blooms off the glads first, which will help the blooms on top to open.

Q. Do you recommend burning dead floral foliage in the fall?

A. Not unless it's from sick, dying, or diseased plants. Otherwise, dead foliage belongs in the compost pile to make the grade for next year's garden food.

Q. The stems of my cut tulips seem to always end up curving. What can I do to make them stand up straight and tall?

A. To straighten up curvy stems, wrap the tulips in newspaper. Cover the flower heads, but not the lower third of the stems. Then recut the stems, and place the wrapped bunch upright in a container of cold water for an hour or two.

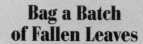

Q. No matter how careful I am when I cut my flower heads to harvest the seeds, I always lose a lot of seed on the ground. Am I waiting too long to harvest?

A. No—you're just using the wrong technique. Make it easy on yourself by placing a small plastic bag around the mature flowers, then shake the flowers. The seeds will fall right into the bag!

Bag a Batch of Fallen Leaves

Some gardeners bag leaves and put them on their beds of root vegetables to insulate them for the winter. Mark the spot with a brightly painted broom handle, and you'll be able to find your carrots, rutabaga, and parsnips when you want them!

Q. What's the best time to cut flowers to bring inside for display?

A. For the longest-lived cut flowers, gather glads when the first bud opens, peonies when outer petals unfold, dahlias when fully open, roses when buds are as soft as a finger, and poppies the night before they open. Once you bring them inside, avoid using vases with small openings; they don't provide adequate aeration of the water.

Q. **Do you have any tips for storing onions? Mine always end up mushy.**

A. You must provide them with plenty of air circulation. If you have a hammock, you can store your onions in it outside. To keep the dew off, throw a blanket over it at night, and if it rains, put a sheet of plastic over the hammock. When the onions are dry, bring the hammock inside, and hang it from the rafters in your attic or basement. The air will continue to circulate around the onions, which will keep them firm for use all winter long.

Q. **Is it OK to leave broccoli in the garden after the center head has been cut?**

A. Green sprouting broccoli varieties will produce smaller side-heads for a time after the center head has been cut. The plants can remain in the garden until hot weather makes them tough and poor tasting.

Jerry's Secrets

Work a handful or two of bonemeal around your old rose bushes before you cover them for winter, and I guarantee that you'll get spectacular blooms the next year.

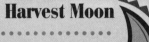

Harvest Moon

Plan to harvest your leafy vegetables by the light of the moon—or at least in the early evening—*not* during the day. That's because during the day, the sun burns up a lot of the vitamins and minerals stored in the plant leaves. But as soon as ol' sol starts to set, the plants begin to replenish and fortify themselves. So if you wait until evening, you'll be picking your vegetables when their vitamin content is at its peak.

Q. **I want to know how I can keep my impatiens growing and blooming in winter after I dig them up.**

A. Cut them back on September 15, and leave the pot outdoors in the shade for 10 days. Then bring them indoors, and place them in a southeast window.

Q. **How can I keep my cabbage heads from splitting?**

A. Heavy rains cause splitting after heads are well

developed, so it's important to harvest your cabbage promptly. If that's not possible, twist or pull the plant slightly to tear some of the roots, which will cut down on water absorption and the resulting splitting. Keep in mind that some varieties are more prone to splitting than others are.

Q. What do I have to do to my strawberry patch to get it ready for winter?

A. Not much, really. Just mow over the top of it, and cover the plants with a light blanket of straw or marsh hay. That's it!

Q. Why does my lettuce go to seed instead of producing a lush, leafy plant?

A. Hot weather causes lettuce to "bolt" and flower. To avoid this, you need to plant early with varieties that are indicated as heat-tolerant.

Q. Is there any way I can prevent my onions from going to seed?

A. I plant onion sets with bulbs that are no larger than ⅝ inch in diameter. Why? Because larger bulbs have a greater tendency to go to seed in the garden.

Q. When am I supposed to break the tops of my onions so they fall over?

A. Onion tops should fall over naturally. After about three quarters of them have fallen over, you can break

PEST PATROL

Moth-Chaser Sachets

Make a natural moth repellent for your home by mixing equal portions of:

Dried sage
Dried rosemary
Dried thyme

Place half a handful of the mix in a loosely woven cotton bag, and sew the bag shut. Hang the bags in closets or lay them in drawers among your clothes.

Carrot Capers

Carrots should be harvested when they're about 3 to 4 inches long. They can stay in the soil quite a while, but if you wait too long, they'll become tough and woody. Harvest all carrots before winter; if you don't, they'll be easy pickin's for slugs and wireworms.

Just a Spoonful of Sugar

When tomato fruits begin showing color, add a spoonful of sugar to their water. This will make the tomatoes sweeter and juicier.

down the others to help close their necks. However, onions that don't fall over naturally tend to be poor keepers, so you should keep them separate from the rest of the harvest, and use them first.

Q. I cannot get my parsnips to sprout; can you tell me what the secret is?

A. Dig a trench 12 inches deep and 6 inches wide, and fill it with ⅓ sharp sand, ⅓ professional mix, and ⅓ local garden soil. Then plant them.

Q. What vegetables can I harvest after frost?

A. In my book, there are two types—those that can withstand a light frost without suffering any injury, and those that can survive a fairly hard freeze. The former includes cauliflower, lettuce, chard, celery, and root crops like beets and carrots. The real tough ones are brussels sprouts, cabbage, kale, broccoli, turnips, and spinach. So plant your second-season garden accordingly.

Q. I had a problem with my carrots; they were stunted and deformed, and didn't grow very big. Do you have any idea what's going on?

A. It sounds to me like you've got a nematode problem (they're tiny microorganisms that live in the soil). To get rid of them, I want you to spread 5 pounds of sugar over every 50 square feet of garden area, and work it well into the soil. Then next spring, over-spray the area with a mix of 1 can of beer and 1 cup of molasses in your 20 gallon hose-end sprayer. That should do it.

MIXERS & ELIXIRS

Rapid Ripening Tonic

Once Jack Frost knocks at your door, it's the end of the growing season for most of your veggies. Here's a great tonic to speed up the ripening process so you can enjoy the fruits of your labor before frost sets in:

1 cup of apple juice
½ cup of ammonia
½ cup of baby shampoo

Mix all of the ingredients in your 20 gallon hose-end sprayer, filling the balance of the sprayer jar with warm water. This is a little trick on Mother Nature, but I'm sure she'll understand when Ol' Man Winter is waiting just around the corner.

Slug Buster

Get yourself an old handheld spray bottle, and fill it with ⅓ ammonia and ⅔ cool tap water. Set the spray nozzle on stream, and then any time slugs appear, give 'em a blast! You'll be delighted at the results!

Q. How can I attract ladybugs to my garden?

A. It's easy. All you have to do is plant marigolds, angelica, butterfly weed, yarrow, roses, and goldenrod in your flowerbeds, and cucumbers, peppers, eggplants, and tomatoes in your vegetable garden. Mother Nature will take care of the rest.

Q. I grew okra this past year in my garden, but it was tough and woody. What did I do wrong?

A. You probably waited too long to harvest it. Okra should be picked when the pods are barely finger length. I remember this by thinking that okra is finger lickin' good!

Q. I see lots of pearly white cabbage for sale in the store, but mine always turn yellow or purple. What am I doing wrong?

A. You're not protecting the cabbage heads from the sun. What you've got to do is pull the leaves together over the top of the head as soon as it begins to form, and tie them together at the tips to hold them in place. This will keep your cabbages perfectly white until they're ready to harvest.

Brush, Don't Wash

Sweet potatoes have thin skins and are susceptible to bruising, so handle them with care. After you dig them up, brush the soil off of them—don't wash it off. Cleaning them with water long before cooking only helps to spoil them.

Q. What causes tomato leaves to curl?

A. You've got to remember that plants that are soft and succulent, like tomatoes, require lots and lots of water. If it suddenly gets hot and dry (like in the summer), the leaves curl in an effort to reduce the loss of water. The solution? Soak 'em good at least once a week, and they'll stay straight as an arrow.

Can, Can? Not!

Not all vegetables are candidates for canning. Cukes, eggplants, and hot peppers are three that come to mind—they lose their flavor and crunchiness when they're under the pressure of the high temperatures of canning. So pickle a peck of them, instead.

Q. Is it true you can use cat litter to get rid of moles?

A. Yes, it is, with varying degrees of success. Sprinkle soiled litter in the runs every 3 feet or so. That should soon send 'em running!

Q. Should I burn the fallen leaves on my vegetable garden, or plow them under in the spring?

A. Plow or dig them under next spring instead of burning them. Anything that will decay should be turned into the soil so that it can add humus.

Q. After being thinned this year, my vegetable seedlings wilted badly. What happened?

A. Begin thinning your seedlings as soon as they are well up, and the soil is moist. If the plants start to wilt, water them and shade them with newspaper, leaving it on for a few days.

Q. Can I use bonemeal in place of eggshells to grow green peppers in my vegetable garden?

A. No—they are not substitutes for one another. Ground-up eggshells are a source of calcium, while bonemeal is a source of nitrogen. Use gypsum in place of eggshells.

Q. How can I battle whiteflies on my tomatoes?

A. Bathe your garden every two weeks with my Plant Shampoo. Then follow up with a little all-purpose liquid fruit tree spray at 25 percent of the recommended rate.

MIXERS & ELIXIRS

Magnesium Boost

Tomatoes, peppers, and eggplants will develop faster if you provide them with magnesium in a form they can use quickly. To do this, mix 2 tablespoons of Epsom salts in 1 gallon of water. Apply 1 pint of this mixture to each plant just as the blooms appear.

MIXERS & ELIXIRS

Java Jive

Next time you brew a pot of coffee, consider these five not-so-common ways to use it around your yard and garden:

1. Control red spider mites by spraying plants with brewed coffee diluted with water.

2. Combine coffee grounds with dead leaves or hay to create a mulch. (Don't use coffee grounds alone because they tend to cake together.)

3. Mix tiny seeds with dried grounds to keep the seeds from clumping, and to make them easier to handle.

4. Place coffee grounds in planting holes to boost the growth of various acid-loving plants like blueberries, gardenias, and evergreens.

5. Sprinkle grounds around your carrot patch to repel root maggots.

Q. How do I keep the neighborhood squirrels from eating my strawberries?

A. Cover your prized possessions with a chicken-wire tunnel. The other alternative is to sprinkle mothball crystals around the outside of the patch—squirrels can't stand the smell of them!

Egg-stra Calcium

Cabbage, broccoli, and cauliflower need extra calcium to grow their best. Provide some by mixing crushed eggshells into the soil around the plants. They'll thank you for it by producing bumper crops!

Q. My cherry trees had fruit on them, but the birds got there before I could harvest the cherries! What can I do to keep the birds away?

A. Try a mixture of 1 tablespoon of my Plant Shampoo and 1 tablespoon of ammonia per gallon of water. Spray it on the trees between rains.

Q. How can I get rid of the squash bugs and mites that plague my garden?

A. At the first sign of these bug troubles, mix 1 cup of my Plant Shampoo and ¼ cup of my Total Pest Control in your 6 gallon hose-end sprayer, filling the balance of the sprayer jar with warm water. Then spray this mixture in the evening at two-week intervals until the thugs are gone.

Q. How can I eliminate mushrooms that are growing in my mulched flowerbeds?

A. Rake up your mulch from time to time, and then overspray with a mixture of 1 cup of baby shampoo per 20 gallons of water. For small areas, sprinkle a handful of any dry laundry detergent over the area.

50 Fabulous Fixers, Mixers & Elixirs

Garden Cure-All Tonic

At the first sign of insects or disease, mix up a batch of my "Garden Cure-All Tonic" to set things right:

4 cloves of garlic
1 small onion
1 small jalapeño pepper
1 tsp. of Murphy's Oil Soap
1 tsp. of vegetable oil
Warm water

Pulverize the garlic, onion, and pepper in a blender, and let them steep in a quart of warm water for 2 hours. Strain the mixture, and further dilute the liquid with three parts of warm water. Add the Murphy's Oil Soap and vegetable oil. Mist-spray your plants with this elixir several times a week.

Fungus Fighter

Molasses is great for fighting fungus and disease in your garden. So at the first sign of trouble, mix up a batch of this brew:

1/2 cup of molasses
1/2 cup of powdered milk
1 tsp. of baking soda
1 gal. of warm water

Mix the molasses, powdered milk, and baking soda into a paste. Place the mixture into the toe of an old nylon stocking, and let it steep in a gallon of warm water for several hours. Then strain, and use the liquid as a fungus-fighting spray for your garden every two weeks throughout the growing season. I guarantee you'll have no more fungus troubles!

Caterpillar Killer Tonic

To keep caterpillars in check and away from your plants, mix up a batch of my "Caterpillar Killer Tonic":

1/2 lb. of wormwood leaves
2 tbsp. of Murphy's Oil Soap
Warm water

Simmer the wormwood leaves in 2 cups of water for 30 minutes or so. Strain,  then add the liquid and the Murphy's Oil Soap to 2 more cups of warm water. Apply with a 6 gallon hose-end sprayer to the point of runoff. Repeat as necessary until the caterpillars are gone.

Seedling Strengthener

To get your seedlings off to a healthy, disease-free start, mist-spray your plants every few days with this elixir:

2 cups of manure
½ cup of instant tea granules
Warm water

Put the manure and tea in an old nylon stocking, and let it steep in 5 gallons of water for several days. Dilute the "tea" with 4 parts of warm water before using.

Bulb Booster

Bulbs need a complete, balanced diet to grow their very best. So to boost your bulbs to new heights, sprinkle this mixture on top of the growing beds in early spring, just as the foliage starts to break out of the ground:

2 lbs. of bonemeal
2 lbs. of wood ashes
1 lb. of Epsom salts

Transplant Tonic

½ can of beer
1 tbsp. of ammonia
1 tbsp. of instant tea
1 tbsp. of baby shampoo
1 gallon of water

Mix all of the ingredients together. Use 1 cup of the tonic for each plant that you are transplanting.

Ant Control #1

4 to 5 tbsp. of cornmeal
3 tbsp. of bacon grease
3 tbsp. of baking powder
3 packages of yeast

Mix the cornmeal and bacon grease into a paste, then add the baking powder and yeast. Dab the gooey mix on the insides of jar lids, and set them near the ant hills.

Ant Control #2

1 cup of sugar
1 tbsp. of boric acid powder
3 cups of water

Add the sugar to 3 cups of water, and bring to a boil. Then add the boric acid. Place the mix in small jar lids, and set the lids in the middle of ant trails or near ant hills. Store any unused portion in a secure container, and keep everything out of reach of children and pets.

Super Slug Spray

For slugs that are too small to hand-pick or be lured into traps, try this super spray:

1½ cups of ammonia
1 tbsp. of Murphy's Oil Soap
1½ cups of water

Mix all of the ingredients in a handheld mist sprayer bottle, and over-spray any areas where you see signs of slug activity.

Compost Booster

To get your compost off to a roaring start, mix the following in a large bucket:

1 can of beer
1 can of regular cola (not diet)
1 cup of ammonia
1/2 cup of weak tea water*
1 oz. of baby shampoo

Pour this mixture into your 20 gallon hose-end sprayer, and saturate your compost pile every time you add a new foot of compost.

* Soak a used tea bag in a gallon of warm water and 1 teaspoon of liquid dish soap until the mix is light brown.

All-Season Green-Up Tonic

1 can of beer
1 cup of ammonia
1/2 cup of liquid dish soap
1/2 cup of liquid lawn food
1/2 cup of molasses or corn syrup

Mix all of the ingredients in a large bucket, then pour into a 20 gallon hose-end sprayer to spray your plants.

All-Season Clean-Up Tonic

1 cup of liquid dish soap
1 cup of chewing tobacco juice*
1 cup of antiseptic mouthwash

Mix all of the ingredients in a 20 gallon hose-end sprayer, filling the balance of the jar with warm water. Apply this mixture to your plants liberally to discourage insects and prevent disease during the growing season.

* Place three fingers of chewing tobacco in an old nylon stocking and soak in a gallon of hot water until the mixture is dark brown.

Squirrel Beater

To keep those pesky squirrels from chewing up everything in sight, douse your prized plantings with this spicy, surefire tonic:

2 tbsp. of cayenne pepper
2 tbsp. of Tabasco sauce
2 tbsp. of chili powder
1 tbsp. of Murphy's Oil Soap
1 qt. of warm water

Mix all of the ingredients together. Pour into a handheld sprayer, and liberally spray on all of your plants.

All-Purpose Houseplant Tonic

2 tbsp. of whiskey
1 tbsp. of hydrogen peroxide
1 tbsp. of Fish Fertilizer+
1/4 tsp. of instant tea granules
1/2 tsp. of unflavored gelatin
1/2 tsp. of liquid dish soap
1/2 tsp. of ammonia
1/2 tsp. of corn syrup
1 gal. of warm water

Mix all of the ingredients, and use this instead of plain water on your houseplants.

Seedling Starter Tonic

Give your transplants a break on moving day by serving them a sip of my starter tonic. This will help them recover more quickly from the transplanting shock:

1 tbsp. of Fish Fertilizer+
1 tbsp. of ammonia
1 tbsp. of Murphy's Oil Soap
1 tsp. of instant tea granules
1 qt. of warm water

Mix all of the ingredients in the warm water.
Pour into a handheld mist sprayer bottle, and mist the seedlings several times a day until they're back on their feet.

Chamomile Mildew Chaser

Chamomile is an excellent control for powdery mildew. So put it to good use in this elixir. Apply at the first sign of trouble (or in damp weather), every week throughout the growing season to those plants that are especially susceptible to this devastating disease:

4 chamomile tea bags
2 tbsp. of Murphy's Oil Soap
1 qt. of boiling water

Make a good, strong batch of tea using the boiling water and tea bags, letting it steep for an hour or so. Let the tea cool, then mix with the Murphy's Oil Soap, and apply with a 6 gallon hose-end sprayer.

Evergreen Growth Tonic

To feed your evergreens in spring, lightly sprinkle a mix of 1 pound of gypsum and 1/4 pound of Epsom salts on top of the soil out at the weep line, and then water it in with this tonic:

1 cup of liquid dish soap
1 cup of chewing tobacco juice*
4 tbsp. of Fish Fertilizer+
2 tbsp. of bourbon

Mix all of the ingredients in a 20 gallon hose-end sprayer, and saturate the soil.

* Take three fingers of chewing tobacco from the package, place it into the toe of a nylon stocking, and place the stocking in a gallon of hot water. Let it steep until the water is dark brown.

Shrub Grub

25 lbs. of garden food
1 lb. of granulated sugar
1/2 lb. of Epsom salts

Each spring, work this mix into the soil around your shrubs. Then mix the following ingredients in a 20 gallon hose-end sprayer, and overspray your newly fed shrubs:

1 can of beer
1/2 cup of liquid lawn food
1/2 cup of liquid dish soap
1/2 cup of ammonia
1/2 cup of regular cola (not diet)

Powdery Mildew Control

4 tbsp. of baking soda
2 tbsp. of Murphy's Oil Soap
1 gal. of warm water

Mix all of the ingredients together. Pour into a handheld mist sprayer, and apply liberally when you see the telltale white spots on your plants.

Super Spider Mite Mix

4 cups of wheat flour
1/2 cup of buttermilk
5 gal. of water

Mix all of the ingredients together, and apply to your plants with a handheld mist sprayer. Spray to the point of runoff. This mix will suffocate the little buggers without harming your plants.

Cabbage Worm Wipe-Out

As your young cabbage plants develop heads, prepare a batch of my " Cabbage Worm Wipe-Out" mixer:

1 cup of flour
2 tbsp. of cayenne pepper

Mix the ingredients together, and sprinkle the mix on your cabbage heads. The flour swells up inside the worms and bursts their insides, while the hot pepper keeps other critters away.

Aphid Antidote

To keep aphids and other pests off of your roses and prized perennials, mix up a batch of this amazing antidote:

1 small onion, chopped finely
2 medium cloves of garlic, chopped finely
1 tbsp. of liquid dish soap
2 cups of water

Put all of the ingredients in a blender, blend on high, and then strain out the pulp. Pour the liquid into a handheld mist sprayer, and apply liberally to your flowers at the first sign of aphid trouble.

Tomato Blight Buster

To ward off early blight and other common tomato diseases, mix up a batch of this "Blight Buster," and use it on your newly transplanted tomato seedlings:

1 cup of compost
1/2 cup plus 1/4 cup of powdered nonfat milk
1/2 cup of Epsom salts

Mix the compost, 1/2 cup of the powdered milk, and the Epsom salts together; sprinkle a handful of the mix into each planting hole. Then sprinkle the remaining 1/4 cup of powdered milk on top of the soil after planting. Repeat every few weeks throughout the growing season.

Perfect Potting Mix

If you've got a lot of potted plants, you need plenty of potting soil. So instead of constantly running out, mix up a batch of this blend, and keep it handy:

1 part topsoil
1 part peat moss
1 part vermiculite
1 part compost

Mix all of the ingredients together, and use for potting your plants, indoors and out.

Flower Feast

1 can of beer
1 cup of ammonia
¹/₂ cup of liquid dish soap
¹/₂ cup of liquid lawn food
¹/₂ cup of molasses or corn syrup

Mix all of the ingredients together in a large bucket. Pour into a 20 gallon hose-end sprayer to apply. Feed this to your flowers once every three weeks in the morning throughout the growing season.

Ultra-Light Potting Soil

To keep your really big pots and planters from being back-breakers, fill them with this ultra-light potting soil mix:

4 parts perlite, moistened
4 parts compost
1 part potting soil
¹/₂ part cow manure

Mix all of the ingredients together, then use it to fill your planters to the top. Be sure to keep an eye on the soil because this mix dries out very quickly, particularly in the hot summer sun.

Indoor Clean-Up Tonic

For those plants of yours that are indoors and exposed to all sorts of household pollutants, here's a tonic that'll keep 'em happy, healthy, clean, and mean:

1 tbsp. of liquid dish soap
1 tbsp. of antiseptic mouthwash
1 tsp. of ammonia
1 tsp. of instant tea granules
1 qt. of warm water

Mix all of the ingredients together, and put them in a handheld mist sprayer. Liberally spray on your houseplants, and wipe off any excess with a clean, dry cloth.

Energizing Earthworm Elixir

To grow the sweetest, juiciest tomatoes and melons in town, mix up a batch of this soil-energizing mix before planting:

5 lbs. of earthworm castings
¹/₂ lb. of Epsom salts
¹/₄ cup of instant tea granules

Mix all of the ingredients together, and put 1 cup in the bottom of each hole as you plant. Your tomatoes and melons will grow beyond your wildest dreams!

Flowering Houseplant Formula

Flowering houseplants need a little something extra to grow their very best. So to put on a big blooming show, supplement their regular diet with this special treat:

6 parts cottonseed meal
4 parts bonemeal
4 parts wood ashes
1 part Epsom salts

Mix all of the ingredients together, and apply at a rate of 1 teaspoon per 6-inch-diameter pot every eight weeks, working it well into the soil with an old fork.

Scat Cat Solution

Cats can be a real problem if they dig in your garden. Try this solution to keep them away from your prized plantings:

5 tbsp. of flour
4 tbsp. of powdered mustard
3 tbsp. of cayenne pepper
2 tbsp. of chili powder
2 qts. of warm water

Mix all of the ingredients together. Sprinkle the solution around the perimeter of the areas you want to protect.

Quick Thrips Control

Thrips are tiny insects that bug your roses, hanging out in the flowers and discoloring the petals or stopping the roses from opening. Use this formula to attract beneficial green lacewings to your rose garden to feast on a diet of thrips:

1 part yeast
1 part sugar

Mix the ingredients with just enough water to make a thin paste, and dab a little bit of the mixture onto each rose bud early in the morning.

Compost Tea

This solution is great for seed starting and as an all-around plant pick-me-up. Simply put several shovelfuls of compost or manure into a large trash can. Fill the can to the top with water. Allow the mixture to sit for a day or two, stirring it several times each day. To use, dilute the tea with water until it is a light brown color. Give each plant about a cup of this tea every two weeks, and your feeding worries will be over.

Fabulous Flowering Shrub Formula

For those acid-loving shrubs like azaleas, rhododendrons, and camellias, mix up a batch of this formula in a 5-gallon bucket:

1 bushelful of dried oak leaves
Coffee grounds, as much as you can find
Boiling water to cover the dry ingredients

Let this mixture sit for a few days, strain, and use the liquid by sprinkling 1 cup of it on the ground around each bush. Soon, they'll be happy as clams!

Lawn Fungus Fighter Tonic

If your lawn develops brown or yellow spots that eventually die out, fight back with this fix-it-up formula:

1 tbsp. of baking soda
1 tbsp. of instant tea granules
1 tbsp. of horticultural/dormant oil
1 gal. of warm water

Mix all of the ingredients together in a large bucket. Then apply with a handheld sprayer by lightly spraying the turf. Do not drench or apply to the point of runoff. Repeat in two to three weeks, if necessary.

All-Purpose Yard Fertilizer

Here's a new twist on an old favorite of mine that'll have your yard rolling in the green:

1 can of beer
1 can of regular cola (not diet)
1 cup of apple juice
1 cup of lemon-scented liquid dish soap
1 cup of ammonia
1 cup of my All-Purpose Plant Food

Mix all of the ingredients in a large bucket, then pour 1 quart into a 20 gallon hose-end sprayer. Apply to your yard to the point of runoff every three weeks during the growing season for fantastic growing results.

Disease Defense

Wet, rainy weather can mean an outbreak of fungus in your yard, especially in late winter and early spring. Keep your outdoor green scene happy and healthy with this elixir:

1 cup of chamomile tea
1 tsp. of liquid dish soap
1/2 tsp. of vegetable oil
1/2 tsp. of peppermint oil
1 gal. of warm water

Mix all of the ingredients together in a bucket. Mist-spray your plants every week or so before the really hot weather (75°F or higher) sets in. This elixir is strong stuff, so test it on a few leaves before completely spraying any plant.

Fabulous Foliar Formula

For the brightest, shiniest leaves in town, feed nonfruiting and nonflowering plants this fantastic formula every three weeks:

1 can of beer
1/2 cup of Fish Fertilizer+
1/2 cup of ammonia
1/4 cup of blackstrap molasses
1/4 cup of instant tea granules

Mix all of the ingredients together in a 20 gallon hose-end sprayer, and apply thoroughly to the point of runoff.

Dead Bug Brew

¹/₂ cup of dead insects (the more, the merrier!)
1 tbsp. of liquid dish soap
1 tbsp. of cayenne pepper
2 cups of water

Put all of the ingredients in an old blender (and I mean really old), and purée the heck of out them. Strain out the pulp using cheesecloth or panty hose. Dilute the remaining brew at a rate of ¹/₄ cup of brew per 1 cup of water. Apply with a handheld mist sprayer to flowers, vegetables, and shrubs to the point of runoff.

Hot Bug Brew

3 hot green peppers (canned or fresh)
3 medium cloves of garlic
1 small onion
1 tbsp. of liquid dish soap
3 cups of water

Purée the peppers, garlic, and onion in a blender. Pour the purée into a jar, and add the dish soap and water. Let stand for 24 hours.
Then strain out the pulp, and use a handheld sprayer to apply the remaining liquid to bug-infested plants, making sure to thoroughly coat the tops and undersides of all the leaves.

Dog-Gone-It!

Man's best friend can be your yard's worst enemy. To keep dogs out and away from their favorite digging areas, liberally apply this mix to the soil:

2 cloves of garlic
2 small onions
1 jalapeño pepper
1 tbsp. of cayenne pepper
1 tbsp. of Tabasco sauce
1 tbsp. of chili powder
1 qt. of warm water

Chop the garlic, onions, and pepper finely, then combine all of the ingredients. Let the mix sit for 24 hours, then sprinkle it on any areas where dogs are a problem.

Slug It Out

Slimy slugs will drink themselves to death if you serve them up a dose of this out-of-this-world concoction:

1 can of beer
1 tbsp. of sugar
1 tsp. of baker's yeast

Mix all of the ingredients in a large bowl, and let it sit uncovered for a few days. Then pour the mixture into shallow, disposable aluminum pie pans. Set the pans below ground level in various areas of your lawn and garden, and it's *hasta la vista*, baby, to slithering slugs.

Black Spot Remover

When black spot attacks your roses, fight back with a weapon you can gather from your garden:

15 tomato leaves
2 small onions
1/4 cup of rubbing alcohol

Chop the tomato leaves and onions into very, very fine pieces, and steep them in the alcohol overnight. Apply to your rose bushes with a small, sponge-type paintbrush, hitting the tops and bottoms of all the leaves.

Fall Wash-Down Spray

Use this formula if you have a late-season infestation of bugs, or just before you dormant-spray your trees and shrubs:

1 cup of tobacco juice*
1/2 cup of baby shampoo
6 tbsp. of fruit tree spray
4 tbsp. of antiseptic mouthwash
2 tbsp. of witch hazel

Mix all of the ingredients in your 20 gallon hose-end sprayer. Spray your plants to the point of runoff, making sure you get the spray inside your plants and onto the soil beneath them.

* To make the juice, take three fingers' worth of chewing tobacco from the package, place it in the toe of a nylon stocking, and place the stocking in a gallon of boiling water. Let the tobacco steep until the water is dark brown.

Mighty Mouse Control

Here I come to save the day! To keep mice and other small varmints from nibbling your young trees to nubs, give 'em a taste of this highly effective repellent:

2 tbsp. of Tabasco sauce
2 tbsp. of cayenne pepper
2 tbsp. of Murphy's Oil Soap
1 qt. of warm water

Mix all of the ingredients together in a container, then pour into a handheld mist sprayer. Drench young tree trunks with it starting in late fall.

Broccoli Bath

Lots of bugs love to hide in and among fresh broccoli florets. Here's a surefire way to make sure that your harvest is indeed bug free—give it a bath!

Fresh-picked
* broccoli*
1/4 cup of
* salt*
1 tbsp. of
* vinegar*
Cold water

Pour the salt and vinegar into a sinkful of cold water, and submerge the broccoli for 15 minutes or so. The bugs will float up to the surface, where they can be easily picked off. Rinse the broccoli under fresh water, and it's ready to eat.

Kick-in-the-Grass Tonic

After you've dethatched, mowed, fertilized, or seeded, apply this tonic to get your lawn off to a rip-roarin' start:

1 cup of Epsom salts
1 cup of antiseptic mouthwash
1 cup of liquid dish soap
1 cup of ammonia
1 can of beer

Mix all of the ingredients together in a large container. Then apply with your 20 gallon hose-end sprayer. But don't get carried away—nobody likes a lawn that's drunk on its grass!

Tea Time for Aphids

This garlic-and-parsley tea is a natural remedy to rid your roses of aphids:

1/2 cup of parsley flakes
2 tbsp. of minced garlic
3 cups of water

Mix all of the ingredients together, and boil down to 2 cups. Strain and cool. Put 2 cups of the tea in your 20 gallon hose-end sprayer, and apply to your rose bushes. And here's a shortcut—you don't even have to make the tea, just plant garlic and parsley between all of your rose bushes. That works, too!

Perennial Planting Potion

To get your perennials growing on the right foot, feed them this potion:

1/2 can of beer
1/4 cup of ammonia
2 tbsp. of hydrogen peroxide
1 tbsp. of liquid dish soap
2 gal. of warm water

Mix all of the ingredients together. Pour it into the planting holes, and sprinkle it over your blooming beauties throughout the summer.

Wild Weed Wipeout

For those hard-to-kill weeds, zap 'em with this wild tonic:

1 tbsp. of gin
1 tbsp. of apple cider vinegar
1 tbsp. of liquid dish soap
1 qt. of very warm water

Mix all of the ingredients together in a bucket, then pour into a handheld sprayer. Drench the weeds to the point of runoff, taking care not to get any on the surrounding plants.

Turf Builder

1 cup of baby shampoo
1 cup of ammonia
1 cup of regular cola (not diet)
4 tbsp. of instant tea granules

Mix all of the ingredients together in your 20 gallon hose-end sprayer. Use it to over-spray your turf after you apply a natural, organic fertilizer to it.

Index

Note: Page references in *italics* indicate tables.

A

African violets
    blooming problems with, 203-4
    broken stems on, 209
    dusting, 210
    when to divide, 209
Alcohol
    for bee sting relief, 277
    for black spot, 35, 330
    for pest control, 89, 90
    for weed control, 129
Alfalfa, killing, 146
All-Purpose Bug/Thug Spray, 131
All-Purpose Houseplant Tonic, 107, 323
All-Purpose Plant Food, 216, 280, 328
All-Purpose Yard Fertilizer, 216, 328
All-Season Clean-Up Tonic, 77, 323
All-Season Green-Up Tonic, 77, 323
Aloe plant, care of, 210
Aluminum sulphate, 147
Amaryllis, blooming problems with, 38, 184
American arborvitae, for wet areas, 35

Ammonia, 46, 54, 63, 67, 77, 82, 85, 97, 105, 107, 111, 119, 126, 127, 144, 154, 158, 178, 197, 208, 216, 230, 231, 241, 259, 262, 270, 288, 317, 318, 322, 323, 324, 326, 328, 331
Ammonium sulphate, 228
Annuals
    among perennials, 14
    care of, 166, 174
    cultivating, 85
    cutting back, 38
    for damp soil, 41
    feeding, 111
    manure for, 167
    most popular, 39
    problems growing, 89
    seedlings, 44
    soil pH for, 39
    suited to shade, 42
    uses for, *15*
    watering, 96
Ant Control #1, 39, 322
Ant Control #2, 39, 322
Ants
    controlling, 39, 156, 322
    on peonies, 94
    repelling, 156
Aphid Antidote, 137, 325
Aphids, repelling, 70, 137, 172, 325, 331
Apple Cake Pudding, 309
Apple juice, 197, 216, 317, 328
Apple picker, 161

Apples
    harvesting, 273
    recipe for
        Apple Cake Pudding, 309
    for top dressing, 243
Apple trees
    pest control for, 255
    spraying, 199-200
Arborvitae, American, for wet areas, 35
Ashes
    soil ruined by, 46
    uses for, 37, 49, 79, 85, 93, 210, 322, 327
Asparagus
    fertilizing, 158
    harvesting, 272, 313
    recipe for
        Asparagus Salad, 272
    weed control for, 142, 158
    when to harvest, 313
    winter preparation for, 158, 284
Asparagus Salad, 272
Asters
    for repelling insects, 135
    seeding of, 167
Audubon Society, 7
Aunt Ethyl's Ratatouille, 304
Autumn. *See* Fall
Azaleas
    blooming of, 210
    care of, 193

pruning, 177
repelling rabbits from, 291

B
Baby powder, 79
Bacillus thuringiensis, for pest control, *237*
Bacon grease, 39, 322
Baked Onions, 309
Baked Vegetables, 275
Baking powder, 39, 79, 97, 322
Baking soda, 41, 131, 132, 229, 277, 321, 325
Bales of straw, planting in, 211
Bargains, shopping for, 12
Barnyard tea, 28, 53
Basal growers, pruning, 239
Beans
lima, 136
location for, 19
planting distance for, 196
staking, 153
when to pick, 313
Beds. *See also* Flowerbeds
cleaning, 82
edging, 46
labeling, 28, 68
movable, 20
planning, 12, 13
raised, 50, 93
rebuilding, 39-40
Beer, 6, 51, 63, 67, 77, 114, 117, 121, 126, 147, 154, 158, 162, 175, 176, 178, 214, 216, 225, 231, 235, 241, 247, 262, 263, 285, 288, 322, 323, 326, 328, 329, 331
Bee Sting Relief, 277
Beets
organic, 138
recipe for
Harvard Beets, 309
soil for, 196

when to plant, 196
Begonias
blooming problems with, 212
extending blooms of, 313
winter protection for, 286
Bermuda grass, planting in, 39
Berries. *See also specific berries*
picking, 277, 279
washing, 278
Berry Booster, 214
Berry steams
for pest control, 163
Birch tree, when to prune, 265
Birds
attracting, 6, 7, 8, 9
information sources on, 7
locating feeders for, 8
necessities for, 7
for pest control, 122
repelling
from cherry trees, 320
from corn, 153
from grass seed, 261
from hanging baskets, 204
Blackberries, when to pick, 277
Black plastic sheeting, as mulch, 52
Black raspberry, cutting down, 205-6
Black spot, on roses, 35, 100, 141, 330
Black Spot Remover, 35, 330
Bloodmeal, 30, 140
Blue African lily, winter protection for, 286
Blueberries, repelling rabbits from, 291
Bon Ami cleansing powder, 282
Bonemeal, 30, 37, 79, 92, 177, 210, 242, 289, 322, 327
how to apply, 88

for rose bushes, 315
vs. eggshells, 319
Bones, chicken, for feeding soil, 154
Borders
controlling plants in, 171
for vegetable garden, 43
Borers
repelling, 248, 291
Boric acid powder, 39, 322
Bourbon, 82, 99, 235, 269
Branches, preserving, in glycerin, 297
Breath of Fresh Air, A, 94
Broccoli
eggshells for, 320
harvesting, 315
increasing size of, 198
for pest removal, 301, 330
planted with cabbage and Brussels sprouts, 197
recipes for
Baked Vegetables, 275
Broccoli Swirl Soup, 310
Broccoli Bath, 301, 330
Broccoli Swirl Soup, 310
Brussels sprouts, planted with broccoli and cabbage, 197
Bug-Be-Gone Spray, 9
Bugs. *See* Insects
Bulb Booster, 37, 322
Bulb Breakfast, 30
Bulb food, 135
Bulb planter, 32
Bulbs. *See also specific bulbs*
altering blooming of, 30, 31
choosing, 22
color blocks of, 40
drainage for, 37
feeding, 114, 135, 149, 288
forcing, 30
handling, 32
identifying top of, 74

Bulbs *(continued)*
  keeping foliage on, 74
  layering, 74
  location for, 31
  mulching, 38
  planning, 14
  planting depths for, *33*
  repelling bugs from, 31
  storing, 42, 284
  tools for planting, 32-33
  watering, 96, 98
  weeds near, 127
  when to plant, 45, 75
  winter protection for,
    286-87
Bulb Soak, 176
Bush beans
  planting distance for, 196
  staking, 153
Butterflies, attracting, 9
Buttermilk, 134, 325

C

Cabbage
  eggshells for, 320
  grass fertilizer for, 133
  planted with broccoli and
    Brussels sprouts, 197
  preventing discoloration of,
    318
  recipes for
    Baked Vegetables, 275
    Superb Slaw, 310
  repelling rabbits from, 45
  splitting of, 315-16
Cabbage worms, killing, 138,
  325
Cabbage Worm Wipe-Out,
  138, 325
Cacti
  care of, 210
  flowering problems with,
    194, 211

  repotting, 212
  transplanting, 194
Calcium, from eggshells, 69,
  319, 320
Calendula, in salads, 282
Canadian hemlock, for wet
  areas, 35
Canna
  blooming problems with,
    212
  winter protection for, 286
Canning, vegetables unsuitable
  for, 319
Canola oil, 131
Cantaloupes
  dwarf varieties of, 11
  increasing size of, 312
Carpet, for weed control, 132
Carrots
  care of, 197
  harvesting, 316
  increasing size of, 317
  recipes for
    Baked Vegetables, 275
    Sunshine Carrots, 310
    Zucchini Carrot Cake,
      275
Castor oil, 181
Caterpillar Killer Tonic, 36, 321
Caterpillars, controlling, 36,
  321
Cats, repelling, 29, 40, 200, 247,
  327
Cauliflower
  eggshells for, 320
  increasing size of, 198
Cayenne pepper, as repellent,
  49, 69, 91, 138, 200, 240, 250,
  264, 323, 325, 327, 329, 330
Cedar chips, uses for, 51, 89
Cedar pencil slice, for pest
  control, 193
Cedar trees, cuttings from, 268

Celery, harvesting, 272
Chamomile Mildew Chaser,
  150, 324
Cherry trees, repelling birds
  from, 320
Chicken bones, for feeding soil,
  154
Chili powder, 49, 200, 264, 323,
  327, 329
Chinese lanterns, saving blooms
  of, 313
Chipmunks, controlling, 152
Chores, calendar of, 6
Christmas trees, mulch from,
  270
Chrysanthemums
  care of, 174, 193, 278
  feeding, 139
  planning, 17
  seeding of, 167
Clay loam, 18
Clay pots, soaking, 24
Clay soil
  breaking up, 41
  drainage for, 86, 93
  phosphate for, 90-91
  planting in, 46
Clean-up
  after yard work, 59
  of beds, 82
  end-of-season, 285
  for fruit trees, 165
  for pest control, 292
  spring, 76
  of tools, 83
  before winter, 288, 292
  of yard, 3
Clematis
  blooming problems with,
    205
  trimming, 200
Clipping Conditioner, 230
Clover, killing, 141

Coffee, brewed, 111, 320

Coffee grounds, 18, 86, 116, 234, 320, 327

Cola, 6, 51, 63, 216, 230, 231, 285, 323, 328, 331

Cold frames, window wells as, 168

Companion plants, *65*

Compost, 5, 30, 177, 198, 206, 209, 223, 244, 325, 326, 327
  alternative containers for, 57
  cocktail, 63
  encouraging decomposition of, 60
  location for, 58
  maintaining health of, 59
  materials for
    dead foliage, 313
    green and brown materials, 60
    inappropriate, 57, 61, 63, 93, 143
    newspapers, 93
    nutrients in, *62*
    organic refuse, 61
    shredded leaves, 60
    shredded paper, 90
    weeds, 94
    wool, 144
  mushroom, 86
  preventing contamination of, 63, 94, 292
  recipe for, 61
  starting, 86, 285
  uses for, 62, 93
  ventilating, 60
  when to use, 88

Compost bin
  building, 58
  camouflaging, 58

Compost Booster, 63, 323

Compost Tea, 223, 327

Concord grapes, care of, 211

Container garden
  plastic containers for, 17
  repotting plants in, 208
  soil for, 18
  vegetables for, 18, 28

Container Plant Tonic, 104

Corn
  feeding, 136
  pole beans near, 19
  removing silk from, 311
  repelling animals from, 133, 153
  when to pick, 311, 312-13

Cornmeal, 39, 322

Corn syrup, 77, 94, 107, 114, 175, 178, 323, 326

Cosmos, seeding of, 27

Cottonseed meal, 210, 327

Cover crops, 285

Crabgrass, when to kill, 264-65

Cream of Zucchini Soup, 274

Crimson flag, location for, 21

Crocuses, planted in lawn, 71

Crop rotation, 133

Cucumbers
  care of, 203
  dwarf varieties of, 11
  increasing size of, 197
  pickling, 306
  recipes for
    Mighty-Fine Mustard Pickles, 307
    Pub Pickles, 310
    Quick Dill Pickles, 306

Cultivator, hand, 124

Curtain rod, for supporting plants, 76

Cushion, kneeling, 33, 34

Cutting garden, planning, 16

Cuttings
  care of, 280-81
  cedar tree, 268
  how to take, 79, 280-81

leaf, 281
  potting, 140
  root, for propagating perennials, 178

Cutworms, repelling, 195

Cyclamen, care of, 193

D

Daffodils
  cut, care of, 294
  cutting foliage of, 167
  when to plant, 45

Dahlias
  planting, 69
  preparing for transplanting, 176
  storing, 37
  winter protection for, 286-87

Dampness, annuals suited for, 41

Dandelions, killing, 141

Daylilies
  eating, 283
  locations for, 34
  planting, 34, 73

Dead Bug Brew, 240, 329

Deer
  plants attracting, 201-2
  repelling, 91, 201, 202

Deer Buster Egg Tonic, 91

Deficiencies, nutrient, remedies for, *112-13*

Delphiniums, black spots on, 131

Dethatching, 231

Diatomaceous earth, 141, *236*, 282

Diazinon, 266

Dichondra, as grass substitute, 228

Dirt, vs. soil, 85

Disease Defense, 239, 328

Diseases, preventing, 78, 153, 239, 328
  with burning, 119, 148
  in compost, 63
  with disease-resistant plants, 64
  with quick action, 136
  soil for, 64
Dish soap, liquid. *See* Soap, liquid dish
Dog food, 179, 244
Dog-Gone-It!, 264, 329
Dogs
  lawn damage from, 263
  repelling, 29, 268, 329
Dogwoods
  fertilizing, 145
  pruning, 145
  red twig, for wet soil, 37
Dormant spray
  for fruit trees, 165, 199-200
  for killing scales, 249
  for shade trees, 291
Double mock orange, 36
Drainage
  for bulbs, 37
  for clay soil, 86, 93
  end-of-season, 285
  test for, 56
  for trees, 19
Drought-Buster Tonic, 225
Droughts, protecting lawn from, 224, 225, 226
Dryness
  avoiding handling during, 76
  flowers suited to, 41

E

Earthworm castings, 195, 243, 326
Easter lilies, replanting, 192
Edging, materials for, 46

Eggplants
  increasing size of, 159
  recipe for
    Aunt Ethyl's Ratatouille, 304
Eggs, 91
Eggshells
  calcium from, 69, 319, 320
  as fertilizer, 137
  for pest control, 253
  in potting soil, 18
  vs. bonemeal, 319
Elephant's ear, location for, 21
Energizing Earthworm Elixir, 195, 326
Epsom salts, 18, 30, 37, 56, 78, 79, 92, 97, 120, 145, 157, 177, 195, 198, 210, 242, 319, 322, 324, 326, 327, 331
Evergreen Elixir, 269
Evergreen Growth Tonic, 99, 324
Evergreens
  balled-in-burlap, 36
  feeding, 120, 121
  groundcovers for, 268, 270
  location for, 20
  mulching, 291
  planting, 35, 249
  repelling dogs from, 268
  shaking, 248
  sources of, 246
  transplanting, 242, 245
  watering, 98, 108, 139, 248
  for wet areas, 35
  as wind barriers, 269
  winter protection for, 257, 260, 290, 291
Evergreen Wake-Up, 121

F

Fabulous Flowering Shrub Formula, 234, 327

Fabulous Foliar Formula, 241, 328
Fall
  bargains in, 12
  flower gardens in, 156
  lawn care in, 156
  preparing flowerbeds for, 176, 284
  strawberry care in, 160
  vegetable garden in, 156
  weather signs in, 5
  yard care in, 156
Fall Garden Prep Tonic, 288
Fall Lawn Feed, 262
Fall Wash-Down Spray, 290, 330
Feeders, bird, locations for, 8
Fence, for supporting plants, 76
Ferns, feeding, 117, 181, 203
Fertilizers. *See also feeding or fertilizing of specific plants;* Food, garden
  all-purpose, 116
  buying, 240
  dog food, 118
  15-30-15, 104, 175
  fish, 137
  hog juice, 144
  liquid seaweed, 55, 138
  manure, 118
  old-fashioned, 137
  side-dressing of, 111
  spreading, 134
  for successful garden, 42
  understanding labels on, 111
Fish, as fertilizer, 137
Fish Fertilizer+, 85, 99, 107, 111, 114, 117, 119, 121, 126, 154, 158, 214, 241, 245, 269, 323, 324, 328
Flea collars, for pest control, 184

Floods, lawn care after, 146-47, 148

Flour, 134, 138, 200, 325, 327

Flowerbed Bonanza, 285

Flowerbeds. *See also* Beds
    fall preparation of, 176, 284
    manure in, 167
    movable, 20
    pest control in, 195
    photographing, 176
    planning, 12
    repelling dogs and cats from, 29
    replacing plants in, 176
    weed control in, 201

Flower Feast, 178, 326

Flower Feeder, 114

Flower garden(ing). *See also* Flowerbeds; *specific flowers*
    fall care of, 156
    flower heights in, 43
    low-maintenance, 88
    manure in, 131
    quiz on, 168-69
    recommended size of, 42

Flowering Houseplant Formula, 210, 327

Flower Power, 79, 179

Flowers. *See also specific flowers*
    arranging, 279, 295
    cut
        care of, 294
        extending life of, 282, 283
    cutting, 16, 175, 278, 279, 314
    drying
        in microwave, 296
        in phone book, 298
        with silica gel, 295, 296
        stems for, 296
        when to pick flowers for, 296

faded, removing, 179
    feeding, 117, 132
    frost and, 179
    low-maintenance, 180
    for northern exposure, 36
    nursery-grown, choosing, 38
    planting
        according to height, 43
        in wagon, 20
    pressing, 298
    protecting trees, 73
    refrigerating, 282
    staking, 14, 75, 136, 180
    watering, 132
    wind protection for, 14

Flower Surge, 5

Foliage
    dead, for compost, 313
    and symptoms of plant problems, *112-13*

Food. *See also* Fertilizers
    garden, 5, 53, 120, 289, 324
    liquid lawn, 77, 121, 126, 178, 225, 263, 323, 326
    plant, 54, 216

Forsythia, blooming problems with, 43

Freezer
    for freezing fruits and vegetables, 302

Fried Green Tomatoes, 276

Frost
    flowers and, 172
    harvesting vegetables after, 317
    reviving vegetable garden after, 289

Frost cracks, on trees, 251

Fruit and Flower Defender, 127

Fruit flies, killing, 267

Fruits. *See also specific fruits*
    donating, 159

drying
    with home food dryer, 299
    microwave unsuitable for, 299
    outdoors, 299
    in oven, 301
    preparation for, 299
    signs of doneness for, 301
freezing
    containers for, 303
    freezer for, 302
    outdoors, 303
preventing darkening of, 308, *308*

Fruit trees. *See* Trees, fruit

Fruit tree spray, 290, 330

Fungus Fighter, 41, 321

G

Garden Cure-All Tonic, 42, 321

Garden food. *See* Food, garden

Garden-Fresh Salsa, 276

Gardenias
    acidifying soil for, 177
    care of, 208

Garden plans
    drawing, 2
    experiments with, 16
    for flowerbeds, 12
    using pictures in, 17

Garlic
    for deer control, 91
    for disease control, 42, 321
    as dog repellent, 264, 329
    as mole repellent, 156
    for pest control, 26, 34, 42, 81, 137, 142, 213, 240, 321, 325, 329, 331
    planting, 131, 202

Garlic-and-onion juice, 109

Garlic Mist Formula, 213

Gelatin, unflavored, 97, 104, 107, 111, 114, 116, 119, 323
Geraniums
    care of, 162
    for pest control, 26
Germination fabrics, 166
Gin, 129, 331
Gladioli
    extending blooms of, 313
    thrips on, 286
    winter protection for, 287
Gloxinia, dusting, 210
Glycerin, 81
    for preserving plants, 297
Gophers, controlling, 101, 180
Grape juice, 147
Grapes
    Concord, care of, 211
    pruning, 161, 211
Grass clippings
    for compost, 143
    proper use of, 150
Grass(es). *See also* Lawns
    clippings, as mulch, 52, 53
    mowing recommendations for, 230, *230*
    seed (*see* Seeds, grass)
    in shade, 270
    substitute for, 228
    types of, *220-21*
    Zoysia, 224
Grasshopper disease spores, for pest control, *237*
Great Grass Seed Starter, 218
Groundcover Grub, 92
Groundcovers
    care of, 243
    under evergreens, 268
    limestone as, 270
    preserving, in glycerin, 297
    thyme as, 92
Groundcover Starter Mix, 242
Grubs, killing, 266

Gum, Juicy Fruit, 101
Gypsum, 5, 53, 79, 92, 242, 244, 253, 289

H
Hair
    as animal repellent, 155, 180
    as fertilizer, 89, 137, 179
Hanging baskets
    best plants for, 207
    bird nests in, 204
    watering, 106, 145
Happy Herb Tonic, 82
Hardening off, 64
Harvard Beets, 309
Harvesting. *See harvesting of specific fruits and vegetables*
Heat, flowers suited to, 41
Hedgerows
    attracting birds, 6
    choosing plants for, 21
    trimming, 239
Hemlock, Canadian, for wet areas, 35
Herbs
    as borders, 43
    care of, 82
    collecting seeds from, 307
    dried vs. fresh, 312
    drying, 304, 305, 313
    in ice cubes, 305
    for pest control, 195
    planting, in ladder, 55
    in vinegar, 307
    when to harvest, 311
Hibernation Snack, 289
Hickory trees, difficulty planting near, 44
Hill, planting on, 44
Hoe
    uses for, 123
    Warren, 124

Hog juice, as fertilizer, 144
Hollows, tree, 252
Horticultural/dormant oil, 229
Hoses
    care of, 109
    soaker
        making, 293
        securing, 147
        watering with, 96, 97, 108, 132, 141
    storing, 83
Hostas, watering, 177
Hot Bug Brew, 240, 329
Houseplants. *See also* Potted plants; *specific potted plants*
    aerating soil of, 183
    best temperature for, 207
    choosing, 23
    cleaning leaves of, 212
    cold weather protection for, 181
    crooked, 208
    determining when to water, 205
    disbudding, 182
    dying, 184
    feeding, 119, 194, 207
    gift, care of, 190
    hangers for, 100
    hanging, watering, 106
    holiday, care of, 192, 193
    increasing humidity for, 104, 106, 202
    insulating, 106
    lights for, 181
    mealybugs on, 185, 206
    music for, 182
    outdoor care of, 196
    overfeeding, 207
    pest control for, 106, 183, 184, 185, 193
    pinching, 182
    pots for, 182

pruning, 182
returning moisture to, 207
shining leaves of, 206
signs of problems with, 183
staking, 194
tea bath for, 191
torn leaves on, 191
and transition to indoors,
105, 191
transplanting, 194
watering, 102, 103, 104,
106, 107, 186, *186-89*
Humidity, increasing, for
houseplants, 104, 106, 202
Hummingbirds, attracting, 9,
35
Hyacinths
replanting, 192
summer, winter protection
for, 287
when to plant, 45
wild, location for, 21
Hybrid plants, reproducing, 70
Hydrangeas
blooming problems with,
134, 204
care of, 193, 200
pruning, 177
Hydrogen peroxide, 72, 82, 94,
97, 107, 114, 116, 245, 323,
331

I

Ice, melting, 91
Impatiens
care of, 214
as rain-tolerant, 150
winter care of, 315
Indoor Clean-Up Tonic, 208,
326
Insects
controlling
tips for, 153

during yard work, 40
controlling, on
bulbs, 31
fruit trees, 164
marigolds, 201
perennials, 180
controlling, with
All-Purpose Bug/Thug
Spray, 131
aluminum foil, 159
birds, 122
Bug-Be-Gone Spray, 9
burning, 148
cayenne pepper, 69
cedar chips, 51
Dead Bug Brew, 240,
329
dead bug spray, 161
flowers, 135
Fruit and Flower De-
fender, 127
garlic, 142
garter snakes, 122
Hot Bug Brew, 240, 329
Knock 'Em Dead Tonic,
34
ladybugs, 122
Lethal Weapon, 109
marigolds, 135, 289
mothballs, 106
mustard, 158
Natural Bug Juice, 26
quick action, 136
Scare-'Em-All Tonic, 81
soil, 64
toads, 122
tobacco juice, 91
dead, for pest control, 161,
240, 329
Interplanting, in vegetable garden, 152
Irises
care of, 175

feeding, 139
location for, 44
Iron deficiency, 115, 194
Iron Rx, 115
Ivy, preserving, in glycerin, 297

J

Jalapeño peppers
for disease control, 42, 321
as dog repellent, 264, 329
for pest control, 42, 321
Japanese bamboo, killing, 150
Java Jive, 320
Juicy Fruit gum, 101
Just Desserts, 97

K

Kick-in-the-Grass Tonic, 331
KleenUp, 39, 140, 142, 146,
150, 201
Kneeling cushion, 33, 34
Knock 'Em Dead Tonic, 34
Kohlrabi, when to pick, 311

L

Ladybugs
attracting, 134, 318
for pest control, 122
Landscaping. *See also* Lawns;
Shrubs; *specific plants;* Trees
insurance coverage for, 240
planning, 234
winter protection for, 242,
243
Late-Summer Rejuvenating
Mix, 175
Lawn food, liquid. *See* Food,
liquid lawn
Lawn Fungus Fighter Tonic,
229, 328
Lawn mower, maintenance of,
84
Lawn Pest Control Tonic, 226

Lawns
  aerating, 232
  care of, 217
  compost for, 62
  crocuses in, 71
  dichondra, 228
  drought protection for, 224, 225, 226
  fall care of, 156
  fertilizing, 121, 122, 216, 232, 262, 263
  flooding of, 146-47, 148
  moss in, 264
  mowing recommendations for, 230, *230*
  overseeding, 216, 224
  raking, 263
  removing thatch from, 231
  renovating, 218
  repairing dog damage to, 263
  rolling, after seeding, 219
  seeding (*see also* Seeds, grass)
    best time for, 217, 222
    procedure for, 222
  straw mulch for, 222
  summer care of, 229
  trimming and edging, 264
  washing, 127
  watering, 101, 102, 223
  weed control for, 127, 225, 226, 227, 263
Leaves
  cleaning, on houseplants, 212
  for cuttings, 281
  as mulch, 51, 53, 160
  oak, 234, 327
  preserving, in glycerin, 297
  shining, on houseplants, 206
  shredding, for compost, 60

  tomato, for black spot, 35, 330
  torn, on houseplants, 191
  in vegetable garden, 319
Lethal Weapon, 109
Lettuce
  care of, 197
  planting, 28
  preventing seeding of, 316
Lichen, on trees, 251
Lilac bush, saving, 135
Lilacs
  cutting, 203
  trimming, 167
Lily(ies)
  bulbs, 31
  care of, 71
  Easter, replanting, 192
  fertilizing, 112
  location for, 13
Lily-of-the-valley
  location for, 21
  planted in moss, 87
Lima beans, 136
Lime, 79, 115, 122, 132
Limestone, as groundcover, 270
Liquid dish soap. *See* Soap, liquid dish
Liquid Iron, 115
Liquid lawn food. *See* Food, liquid lawn
Liquid seaweed, as fertilizer, 138
Little Green Dilled Tomatoes, 306

M

Maggots, on radishes, 202
Magnesium Boost, 319
Magnolia tree, blooming problems with, 266
Mail-order plants, care of, 23
Manure, 45, 53, 177, 206, 223,

  322, 326, 327
  as all-purpose fertilizer, 118
  in flowerbeds, 131, 167
  liquid, for chrysanthemums, 139
  for rhubarb, 149
  for tomatoes, 133
  types of, 56
Marigolds
  pest control for, 201, 214
  popularity of, 39
  for repelling
    insects, 26, 135, 289
    mosquitoes, 11, 40-41
    nematodes, 129
  for weed control, 129
Matches, for improving soil, 118
Mealybugs, on houseplants, 185, 206
Melons. *See also specific melons*
  preventing root rot in, 201
  ripening, 308
  when to pick, 278
Mexican marigolds
  for nematode control, 129
  for weed control, 129
Mice, repelling, 250, 266, 268, 330
Microwave, for drying flowers, 296
Mighty-Fine Mustard Pickles, 307
Mighty Mosquito Mix, 144
Mighty Mouse Control, 250, 330
Milk, 41, 109, 145, 198, 199, 321
Milky Fern Feed, 145
Milorganite, 243
Mineral oil, 213
Mint, drying, 305
Mites, controlling, 210, 320

Mixers & Elixirs
  All-Purpose Houseplant
    Tonic, 107, 323
  All-Purpose Yard Fertilizer,
    216, 328
  All-Season Clean-Up
    Tonic, 77, 323
  All-Season Green-Up
    Tonic, 77, 323
  Ant Control #1, 322
  Ant Control #2, 322
  Aphid Antidote, 325
  Berry Booster, 214
  Black Spot Remover, 35,
    330
  Breath of Fresh Air, A, 94
  Broccoli Bath, 301, 330
  Bulb Booster, 37, 322
  Bulb Breakfast, 30
  Bulb Soak, 176
  Cabbage Worm Wipe-Out,
    325
  Caterpillar Killer Tonic, 321
  Chamomile Mildew Chaser,
    150, 324
  Clipping Conditioner, 230
  Compost Booster, 63, 323
  Compost Tea, 223, 327
  Container Plant Tonic, 104
  Dead Bug Brew, 329
  Disease Defense, 239, 328
  Dog-Gone-It!, 264, 329
  Drought-Buster Tonic, 225
  Energizing Earthworm
    Elixir, 195, 326
  Evergreen Elixir, 269
  Evergreen Growth Tonic,
    99, 324
  Evergreen Wake-Up, 121
  Fabulous Flowering Shrub
    Formula, 234, 327
  Fabulous Foliar Formula,
    241, 328

Fall Garden Prep Tonic, 288
Fall Lawn Feed, 262
Fall Wash-Down Spray,
  290, 330
Flowerbed Bonanza, 285
Flower Feast, 178, 326
Flower Feeder, 114
Flowering Houseplant For-
  mula, 210, 327
Flower Power, 79, 179
Flower Surge, 5
function of ingredients in,
  110
Fungus Fighter, 41, 321
Garden Cure-All Tonic, 42,
  321
Great Grass Seed Starter,
  218
Groundcover Grub, 92
Groundcover Starter Mix,
  242
Happy Herb Tonic, 82
Hibernation Snack, 289
Hot Bug Brew, 329
Indoor Clean-Up Tonic,
  208, 326
Iron Rx, 115
Java Jive, 320
Just Desserts, 97
Kick-in-the-Grass Tonic,
  331
Late-Summer Rejuvenating
  Mix, 175
Lawn Fungus Fighter
  Tonic, 229, 328
Lawn Pest Control Tonic,
  226
Magnesium Boost, 319
Mighty Mouse Control, 330
Milky Fern Feed, 145
Out to Lunch, 177
Perennial Planting Potion,
  331

Perennial Punch, 6
Perfect Potting Mix, 209,
  326
Perfect Potting Soil, 18
Potted Plant Picnic, 111
Potted-Plant Potion, 54
Powdery Mildew Control,
  132, 325
Quick-Ripening Veggie
  Tonic, 197
Quick Thrips Control, 327
Rapid Ripening Tonic, 317
Refresher No. 1, 154
Refresher No. 2, 154
Repotting Booster Tonic,
  280
Rise-'n-Shine Clean-Up
  Tonic, 3
Root Revival Tonic, 78
Root-Rousing Tonic, 51
Rose Wound Tonic, 170
Scat Cat Solution, 327
Seedling Starter Tonic, 85,
  324
Seedling Strengthener, 45,
  322
Seed Soak, 261
Seed-Soaker Solution, 157
Shrub Grub, 120, 324
Shrub Stimulator, 235
Slug It Out, 329
Soil Energizer, 158
Squirrel Beater, 323
Start-Up Meal, 72
Summer Lawn Soother, 263
Super Seed Starter Solution,
  28
Super Slug Spray, 322
Super Spider Mite Mix, 325
Tea Time for Aphids, 331
Terrific Top Dressing, 243
Terrific Transplant Tonic,
  245

Mixers & Elixirs *(continued)*
  Thatch Control Tonic, 231
  Tomato Blight Buster, 198, 325
  Tomato Shake, 199
  Transplant Tea, 162
  Transplant Tonic, 67, 322
  Transplant Treat, 119
  Tree-mendous Planting Mix, 244
  Tree Wound Paint Mixer, 251
  Tree Wound Sterilizer Tonic, 259
  Turf Builder, 331
  Ultra-Light Potting Soil, 206, 326
  Veggie Tonic, 56
  Veggie Vitalizer, 117
  Vitamin B_1 Booster Shot, 116
  Weak Tea Water, 25
  Wild Weed Wipeout, 129, 331
  Winter Wash, 105
  Year-Round Refresher, 126
  Zap 'Em Dead Winterizing Tonic, 312
Molasses, 41, 77, 121, 126, 178, 241, 321, 323, 326, 328
Moles, repelling, 101, 156, 180, 228, 319
Morning glories
  killing, 149-50
  location for, 22
Mosquitoes, repelling, 11, 40-41, 144
Moss
  destroying, 89-90
  on lawn, 264
  planting in, 87
  on trees, 251

Mothballs, for pest control, 106, 199
Moth-Chaser Sachets, 316
Moth crystals, for pest control, 183, 248, 286
Moths, repelling, 316
Mound planting, 87
Mountain ash, care of, 269
Mouse bait, 268
Mouthwash, antiseptic, 3, 6, 9, 31, 51, 77, 105, 127, 170, 208, 251, 259, 290, 312, 323, 326, 330, 331
Mowing, recommendations for, 230, *230*
Mud, as fertilizer, 137
Mulch(ing)
  benefits of, 50
  bulbs, 38
  buying materials for, 50
  carpet as, 132
  from Christmas trees, 270
  compost as, 62
  evergreens, 291
  functions of, 86, 99
  grass clippings as, 52, 53
  for late-season vegetables, 157
  leaves as, 51, 53, 160
  newspapers as, 52
  plastic, 43, 52
  rhododendrons, 94
  rock garden plants, 287
  roses, 136
  shredded paper as, 90
  shrubs, 291
  strawberries, 160
  surface-rooted plants, 100
  sweet peas, 135
  tomatoes, 133
  trees, 266, 291
  types of, 53
  when to apply, 50, 289

  for winter protection, 289, 291
Mums. *See* Chrysanthemums
Murphy's Oil Soap, 3, 9, 42, 46, 49, 85, 131, 132, 150, 226, 250, 321, 322, 323, 324, 325, 330
Mushroom compost, 86
Mushrooms, killing, 264, 320
Mustard
  powdered, 200, 327
  for worm control, 265
Myrtle, eliminating, 146

N
Nasturtiums
  for repelling insects, 135
  in salads, 282
National Wildlife Federation, 7
Natural Bug Juice, 26
Nematodes
  on carrots, 317
  marigolds for controlling, 129
Newspapers
  as mulch, 52
  for repelling raccoons, 133
  as weed barrier, 126
Nitrogen, in plant foods, 111, 117
Nutrient deficiencies, remedies for, *112-13*

O
Oak leaves, 234, 327
  for mulching, 160
Oatmeal, 179, 244
Oil. *See specific oils*
Okra, when to pick, 318
One-a-Day multivitamins, 97
Onions
  as aphid repellent, 172
  for black spot, 35, 330

breaking tops of, 316-17
for disease control, 42, 321
as dog repellent, 264, 329
increasing size of, 213
for pest control, 34, 42, 81,
137, 240, 321, 325, 329
preventing seeding of, 316
recipes for
Aunt Ethyl's Ratatouille,
304
Baked Onions, 309
storing, 155, 315
wild, killing, 141
Organic matter, 18, 48
Oriental poppies, feeding, 149
Out to Lunch, 177
Overseeding, of lawns, 216, 224
Oyster shells, 253

P
Paint, interior latex, 170, 251
Palms, feeding, 120
Pampas grass, fertilizing, 145
Papaya trees, feeding, 149
Parsley
as aphid repellent, 331
drying, 305
for increasing rose fragrance,
203
Parsnips
planting, 198
sprouting of, 317
Peaches, harvesting, 277
Peanuts, for weed control, 130
Peas, sweet
feeding, 90
mulching, 135
Peat moss, 5, 53, 79, 87, 209,
243, 326
Pencil sharpening shavings, for
pest control, 193
Peonies
ants on, 94

dividing, 179
drooping, 135-36
increasing size of, 204
location for, 13
weed control for, 142
winter protection for, 288
Peppermint oil, 239, 328
Pepper/onion/mint juice, 117
Peppers
acidic soil for, 69
feeding, 143, 319
hot green, for pest control,
240, 329
increasing size of, 159
jalapeño (see Jalapeño peppers)
recipes for
Aunt Ethyl's Ratatouille,
304
Baked Vegetables, 275
Garden-Fresh Salsa,
276
repelling cutworms from,
195
watering, 108
Perennial Planting Potion, 331
Perennial Punch, 6
Perennials
annuals among, 14
choosing, 6, 22
dividing, 68, 69
edging, 4
feeding, 115, 138
marking, for winter, 314
pest control for, 180
planning, 3
planting, 26, 27, 67
planting depths for, 68
propagating, 79, 178
staking, 75
wildflower, 90
Perfect Potting Mix, 209, 326
Perfect Potting Soil, 18

Perfume, as animal repellent,
153
Perlite, 87, 206, 326
Pests. See also pest control for
specific plants
controlling
ants, 39, 94, 156, 322
aphids, 70, 137, 172,
325, 331
borers, 248, 291
cabbage worms, 138,
325
caterpillars, 36, 321
cultivation for, 202
cutworms, 195
fruit flies, 267
grubs, 266
with herbs, 195
insects, 9, 26, 31, 34, 40,
51, 64, 69, 81, 91, 106,
109, 122, 127, 131,
135, 136, 142, 148,
153, 158, 159, 161,
164, 180, 201, 213,
240, 329
marigolds for, 11, 40-41,
129, 135, 289
mealybugs, 185, 206
mites, 210, 320
mosquitoes, 11, 40-41,
144
mothballs for, 106, 199
moth crystals for, 183
moths, 316
with natural controls,
122, *236-37*
with rose and berry
stems, 163
scales, 249
slugs, 46, 91, 147, 159,
205, 214, 247, 318,
322, 329
spider mites, 134, 325

Pests *(continued)*
spiders, 89
spraying for, 233
squash bugs, 210, 320
thrips, 201, 286, 327
with tobacco juice, 91
wasps, 270
whiteflies, 140, 319
worms, 69, 228, 265
Petunias
care of, 174
popularity of, 39
pH, soil, 85, 92
Phloxes, seeding of, 167
Phosphate
for clay soil, 90-91
in fertilizer, 111
Pickled Watermelon Rind, 305
Pickles
recipes for
Mighty-Fine Mustard
Pickles, 307
Pub Pickles, 310
Quick Dill Pickles, 306
steps for making, 306
Pine trees, as wind barriers, 269
Planter bit, for planting bulbs, 32
Plant food. *See* Food, plant
Plant problems, diagnosing,
112-13
Plastic, as mulch, 43, 52
Poinsettias, care of, 192
Poison ivy, killing, 144
Pole beans
location for, 19
planting distance for, 196
staking, 153
Pollination, of fruit trees, 252
Pollution
landscape plants and, 233
preventing, 155
Pond, for water garden, 10
Pool, for water garden, 10

Potash
in fertilizer, 111
growing problems from,
39-40
Pots
clay, soaking, 24
cleaning, 185
for houseplants, 182
for repotting, 208
Potted Plant Picnic, 111
Potted-Plant Potion, 54
Potted plants. *See also* Houseplants; *specific plants*
feeding, 116, 117, 194
retaining moisture in, 206
warm weather care of, 135,
193
Potting soil, 18, 54, *55,* 62, 206,
326
Powder, baby, 79
Powdery mildew, controlling,
132, 150, 170, 324, 325
Powdery Mildew Control, 132,
325
Professional planter mix, 18
Pruning. *See also pruning of
specific plants*
best time for, 257
frequency of, 266
late-summer, 82
reasons for, 238
Pruning saws, protecting blade
of, 83
Pub Pickles, 310
Pumpkins
dwarf varieties of, 11
increasing size of, 156

Q
Queen-Anne's-lace, eliminating, 93-94
Quick-and-Easy Tomato Juice,
273

Quick Dill Pickles, 306
Quick-Ripening Veggie Tonic,
197
Quick Thrips Control, 201,
327

R
Rabbits, repelling, 45, 155, 266,
291
Raccoons, repelling, 133, 153
Radishes
maggots on, 202
planting, 28
Rainwater, for watering plants,
103
Rake, as tool holder, 84
Raking
fallen fruit, 278
lawns, 263
Rapid Ripening Tonic, 317
Raspberries
care of, 163
underground shoots from,
149
when to pick, 277
Ratatouille, recipe for, 304
Recipes
Apple Cake Pudding,
309
Asparagus Salad, 272
Aunt Ethyl's Ratatouille,
304
Baked Onions, 309
Baked Vegetables, 275
Broccoli Swirl Soup, 310
Cream of Zucchini Soup,
274
Fried Green Tomatoes,
276
Garden-Fresh Salsa, 276
Harvard Beets, 309
Little Green Dilled
Tomatoes, 306

Mighty-Fine Mustard Pickles, 307

Pickled Watermelon Rind, 305

Pub Pickles, 310

Quick-and-Easy Tomato Juice, 273

Quick Dill Pickles, 306

Sunshine Carrots, 310

Superb Slaw, 310

Tomato Soup, 276

Wilted Zucchini Salad, 274

Zucchini Cake, 275

Zucchini Carrot Cake, 275

Zucchini Casserole, 274

Red twig dogwood, for wet soil, 37

Refresher No. 1, 154

Refresher No. 2, 154

Replanting
best time for, 92
Easter lilies, 192
hyacinths, 192
tulips, 37, 192

Repotting
cacti, 212
procedure for, 208

Repotting Booster Tonic, 280

Rhizomes, planting, 67

Rhododendrons
feeding, 138
location for, 36, 46
mulching, 94
watering, 138

Rhubarb
discoloration of, 200
fertilizing, 131-32, 142, 149
indoor growing of, 70
mature, 213

Rinds, citrus, as plant starters, 28

Rise-'n-Shine Clean-Up Tonic, 3

Rock garden plants, mulching, 287

Root Revival Tonic, 78

Root rot, preventing, in melons, 201

Root-Rousing Tonic, 51

Rose cones, 171

Rosemary, in moth-chaser sachet, 316

Roses
black spot on, 35, 100, 141, 330
bonemeal for, 315
cleaning, 169
cutting, 170
feeding, 114, 136
increasing fragrance of, 203
moving, 70
mulching, 136
pest control for, 70, 169
planning, 12
planting, 72
from seed, 29
powdery mildew on, 170
preserving, 298
pruning, 173, 292
repelling aphids from, 172
uncovering, in spring, 173
watering, 100, 101, 114, 136, 141
where to plant, 142
winter protection for, 170, 171, 172-73, 287

Rose stems
for pest control, 163

Rose Wound Tonic, 170

Rotary tilling, 48, 88

Rotenone, for pest control, *236*

Rubber trees, leaves falling from, 212

Rust, removing, from tools, 83

Ryania, for pest control, *237*

Ryanodine, for pest control, *237*

S

Sabadilla, for pest control, *236*

Sage, in moth-chaser sachet, 316

Salads
asparagus, 272
flowers in, 282

Salsa, recipe for, 276

Salt, 301, 330
alternatives to, for melting ice, 91
for weed control, 128, 140, 149

Salt water, flooding lawn, 146-47

Salty air, flowers suited to, 42

Sand
builder's, 141
sharp, 18

Sandpaper discs, 159

Sawdust, as fertilizer, 137

Saws, pruning, protecting blade of, 83

Scales, on trees, 249

Scare-'Em-All Tonic, 81

Scat Cat Solution, 200, 327

Screen, for slug control, 205

Seaweed
as fertilizer, 137, 138
uses for, 55

Seedlings
annual, 44
feeding, 146, 159
perennial, choosing, 22
strengthening, 29
transplanting, 66
vegetable, wilting of, 319

Seedling Starter Tonic, 85, 324

Seedling Strengthener, 45, 322

Seed(s). *See also specific types*
for attracting birds, 8
flower, harvesting, 314
germinating, in dark, 44

Seed(s) *(continued)*
grass
buying, 218
frozen, 262
leftover, 261
repelling birds from,
261
seed mix analysis on,
219
sowing, 261, 262
sprouted in bag, 263
understanding labels on,
262-63
watering, 261
when to plant, 219
herb, collecting, 307
labeling, 28
for large vegetables, 27
leftover, 29, 66, 261
longevity of, *66*
old, 37
packets, 24
perennial
location for, 26
starting, 27
preparing, for late-season
vegetables, 157
protecting, from birds, 25,
261
sowing
in rows, 25
for small-seeded greens,
26
speeding sprouting of, 26
starting
in citrus rinds, 28
compost for, 62
indoors, 43
of slow sprouters, 27
for successful gardening,
41-42
sunflower, when to harvest,
311-12

tapes, 24
Seed-Soaker Solution, 157
Sevin, 170, 251
Shade
annuals suited to, 42
grass in, 270
plants suited to, 21
Shampoo
baby, 31, 54, 56, 63, 94, 105,
109, 111, 115, 119, 121,
126, 142, 157, 158, 162,
175, 181, 225, 245, 290,
312, 317, 323, 330, 331
plant, 263
Sheet composting, for weed
control, 128
Shrub Grub, 120, 324
Shrubs
choosing, 21, 235
evergreen *(see* Evergreens)
feeding, 121, 143, 235
flowering
care of, 166
trimming, 167
ice protection for, 266
mulching, 291
planting, 235
pollution-resistant, 233
pruning, 238-39, 241
replacing, 234
soil for, 16
sources of, 246
watering, 108
for wet soil, 37
when to transplant, 242
winter protection for, 243
Shrub Stimulator, 235
Side-dressing, for vegetables,
111
Silica gel, for drying flowers,
295, 296
Slug Buster, 318
Slug It Out, 247, 329

Slugs
killing, 147, 214
repelling, 46, 91, 159, 205,
247, 318, 322, 329
Smoking, ruining plants, 78
Snakes
garter, for pest control, 122
repelling, 141
Snake Send-Off, 141
Snapdragons, care of, 166
Soaker hoses
making, 293
securing, 147
for watering, 96, 97, 108,
132, 141
Soap, liquid dish, 6, 25, 34, 51,
72, 77, 78, 81, 82, 97, 99, 104,
107, 114, 117, 125, 127, 129,
137, 144, 154, 176, 178, 190,
197, 208, 213, 216, 218, 230,
231, 235, 239, 240, 259, 261,
262, 266, 269, 285, 288, 323,
325, 326, 328, 329, 331
Soap chips, 89
Sod, watering, 101
Soil. *See also soil for specific plants*
aerating, for houseplants,
183
ashes and, 46, 49
automotive fluids in, 94
barnyard tea for, 53
clay
breaking up, 41
drainage for, 86, 93
phosphate for, 90-91
planting in, 46
coffee grounds for, 86
compost for, 62
conditioners for, 87
moss in, 87
organic material for, 48
pH of, 85, 92
for planting shrubs, 16

potting, 18, 54, *55*, 62, 206, 326

preparing, 48, 88-89, 157

sandy, 87

second tilling of, 48

for successsful gardening, 42

testing drainage of, 56

types of, watering according to, *102*

vs. dirt, 85

when to spade, 88

when to work, 53

Soil Energizer, 158

Spade(ing)

  best time for, 48, 88

  end-of-season, 285

  for planting bulbs, 32-33

Spearmint, for ant control, 156

Speckled alder, for wet soil, 37

Sphagnum, 87

Spider mites, repelling, 134, 325

Spider plant, care of, 202, 212

Spiders, repelling, 89

Spreader, coffee can as, 134

Spring

  clean-up, 76

  holding trees for planting in, 256

  tilling in, 48

  uncovering roses in, 173

  weather signs in, 4

Sprinklers

  care of, 109

  types of, 97

Squash. *See specific types*

Squash bugs, controlling, 210, 320

Squirrel Beater Tonic, 49, 323

Squirrels, repelling

  from corn, 153

  from roses, 204, 247

  from strawberries, 320

from tomatoes, 152, 204

from trees, 247

Stakes

  for beans, 153

  hangers as, 180

  houseplant, 194

  for peonies, 136

  for perennials, 75

  prunings as, 75

  for tomatoes, 153

  umbrellas as, 14

  for vegetables, 153

Start-Up Meal, 72

Stocks, care of, 166

Straw, planting in, 211

Strawberries

  care of, 73, 200

  fall care of, 160

  fertilizing, 131, 142, 143, 161

  mulching, 160

  repelling squirrels from, 320

  speeding growth of, 163

  storing, 71

  sweetening, 213

  winter preparation for, 316

Stumps, killing, 267

Sugar, 39, 120, 179, 201, 247, 322, 324, 327, 329

Summer

  lawn care in, 229

  pruning in, 82

  watering in, 109

  weather signs in, 5

Summer hyacinths, winter protection for, 287

Summer Lawn Soother, 263

Sunflower seeds, when to harvest, 311-12

Sunlight

  lack of, signs of, 206

  overdose of, 207

  for producing blooms, 38

Sunshine Carrots, 310

Superb Slaw, 310

Super Seed Starter Solution, 28

Super Slug Spray, 46, 322

Super Snail and Slug Cure, 147

Super Spider Mite Mix, 134, 325

Supports. *See* Stakes

Surface-rooted plants, watering, 100

Sweet peas

  feeding, 90

  mulching, 135

Sweet potatoes, care of, 318

T

Tabasco sauce, 3, 49, 91, 109, 127, 250, 264, 323, 329, 330

Tea, 78, 82

  barnyard (*see* Barnyard tea)

  chamomile, 239, 328

  compost (*see* Compost tea)

  instant, 31, 67, 322

Tea bags, 25, 54, 118, 150, 206

Tea granules, 6, 45, 51, 85, 104, 107, 114, 119, 154, 158, 162, 176, 195, 208, 214, 229, 235, 241, 245, 269, 288, 322, 323, 324, 326, 328, 331

Tea Time for Aphids, 331

Tea water, 63, 72, 157, 218, 261, 280, 323

Terrific Top Dressing, 243

Terrific Transplant Tonic, 245

Thatch, removing, 231

Thatch Buster, 225, 263

Thatch Control Tonic, 231

Thinning plants, 78

Thrips, controlling, 201, 286, 327

Thyme

  as groundcover, 92

  in moth-chaser sachet, 316

Tilling
    in fall, 202
    in spring, 48
Toads
    benefits of, 92
    for pest control, 122
Tobacco juice
    for clean-up, 3, 77, 323
    for evergreens, 99, 269
    for flowerbeds, 285
    for pest control, 9, 91, 127,
        226, 290, 312, 330
Tobacco mosaic, preventing,
    78
Tomato Blight Buster, 198,
    325
Tomato(es)
    avoiding cultivation with,
        196
    blight on, 213-14
    curling leaves on, 318
    discolored tops on, 133
    dwarf varieties of, 11
    extending season of, 273
    fertilizing, 119, 133, 152
    increasing size of, 154
    indoor, 209
    leaves, for black spot, 35,
        330
    pest control for, 152
    pinching, 195
    preventing viruses in, 139
    recipes for
        Aunt Ethyl's Rata-
            touille, 304
        Fried Green Tomatoes,
            276
        Garden-Fresh Salsa, 276
        Little Green Dilled
            Tomatoes, 306
        Quick-and-Easy
            Tomato Juice, 273
        Tomato Soup, 276

removing suckers from, 198
repelling cutworms from,
    195
seeds, planting, 28
spacing, 199
staking, 153
sweetening, 317
whiteflies on, 319
wilt disease in, 202
Tomato Shake, 199
Tomato Soup, 276
Tonics. See Mixers & Elixirs
Tools
    choosing, 10
    cleaning, 83
    fork as, 84
    keeping track of, 164
    as measuring devices, 89
    for planting bulbs, 32-33
    removing rust from, 83
    safe use of, 84
    sterilizing, 256
    storing, 83, 84
    for weed control, 124
    winter preparation of, 293
Topsoil, 209, 326
Total Insect Control, 312
Transplants
    cactus, 194
    dahlias, 176
    evergreens, 242, 245
    houseplants, 194
    planting, 67
    protecting, 64
    seedlings, 66
    shrubs, 242
    timetable for, 242
    trees, 257
Transplant Tea, 162
Transplant Tonic, 67, 322
Transplant Treat, 119
Tree-mendous Planting Mix,
    244

Trees. See also specific trees
    attracting birds, 6, 7
    care of, 253, 259
    deciduous, winter protection
        for, 290
    drainage for, 19
    evergreen (see Evergreens)
    flowering, choosing, 22
    flowers protecting, 73
    frost cracks on, 251
    fruit
        bearing times for, 254,
            254
        clean-up for, 165
        encouraging fruiting of,
            254
        hardy, climate for, 252
        locating, 268
        pest control for, 253,
            255
        planting, 256
        pollination of, 252
        preventing problems
            with, 164
        pruning, 257, 258
        raking under, 278
        soil for, 164
        spraying, 165
        watering, 147
        when to feed, 119
        when to plant, 255
        winter care of, 259, 267
        wood chips and, 255
    holding, for spring planting,
        256
    hollows in, 252
    ice protection for, 266
    lichen and moss on, 251
    locating, 246
    minor cuts in, 251
    mulching, 266, 291
    nails in, 251
    nut, locating, 268

pest control for, 248, 249, 250

planting, 244, 247, 265, 270

pollution-resistant, 233

potted, 249

pruning, 238-39, 257, 266

repelling animals from, 266

safety issues and, 268

saving, 269-70

scales on, 249

sealing cuts in, 267

shade, pest control for, 291

soil for, 87

sources of, 246

surface rooting of, 250

topping, 260

transplanting, 257

watering, 108, 248

weed barrier fabric around, 148

when to transplant, 242

wrapping, 244, 246, 248, 265

Tree Wound Paint Mixer, 251

Tree Wound Sterilizer Tonic, 259

Trellis, tennis net for, 214

Trowel, for planting bulbs, 32

Trumpet vine, blooming problems with, 134, 212

Tulips

changing soil for, 167

cutting, 167

replanting, 37, 192

straightening stems of, 314

when to plant, 45

Turf Builder, 331

Turnip greens, when to plant, 198

U

Ultra-Light Potting Soil, 206, 326

Underbrush, killing, 150

V

Vegetable(s). *See also specific vegetables*

companion plants for, *65*

donating, 159

drying

with home food dryer, 299

microwave unsuitable for, 299

outdoors, 299

in oven, 301

preparation for, 299

signs of doneness for, 301

storage after, 302

fastest-growing, 195

feeding, 117

freezing

containers for, 303

freezer for, 302

outdoors, 303

harvesting, after frost, 317

large, planting seeds for, 27

leafy, harvesting, 315

perennial, end-of-season planting of, 285

seedlings, wilting of, 319

seeds, testing, 24

side-dressing, 111

when to plant, 77

Vegetable garden(ing)

borders for, 43

cold protection for, 154

container, 18

dwarf varieties for, 11

fall care of, 156

interplanting in, 152

late-season, 157

leaves in, 319

lime for, 132

location for, 11

marking, for winter, 314

pest control for, 158, 195

planning, 19

preventing weeds in, 126

in raised beds, 50

recommended size of, 42

reviving, after frost, 289

rotating, 196

watering, 98, 108

winter protection for, 285, 288

Vegetable oil, 42, 239, 321, 328

Veggie Tonic, 56

Veggie Vitalizer, 117

Verbenas, care of, 166

Vermiculite, 87, 209, 326

Vinegar, 129, 131, 301, 330, 331

herbed, 307

Vines, choosing, 22

Violets

African (*see* African violets)

wild, eliminating, 132

Vitamin B_1, 72, 116

Vitamin B_1 Booster Shot, 116

Vitamin B_1 Plant Starter, 158, 280

Voles, repelling, 282

W

Wall, for supporting plants, 76

Warren hoe, 124

Wasps, repelling, 270

Wasp Wipe-Out, 270

Water garden, planning, 10

Watering. *See also watering of specific plants*

according to soil type, *102*

automatic watering pots for, 107

best time for, 96, 109

cool-weather, 99, 141

Watering *(continued)*
    determining need for, 154
    equipment, 96, 97, 109
    frequency of, 139
    methods of, 96-98, 100, 144
    powdery mildew from, 132
    to prevent wilting, 99, 133
    with rainwater, 103
    for successful gardening, 42
    in summer, 109
    water temperature for, 116
Watermelons
    dwarf varieties of, 11
    location for, 199
    recipe for
        Pickled Watermelon
            Rind, 305
Weak Tea Water, 25
Weather, signs of, 4-5
WeatherProof, 64, 135, 242,
    243, 245, 247, 260, 283, 290,
    291
Weed barrier fabric, 126, 128,
    147, 148
Weeds. *See also specific weeds;*
    weed control for specific plants
    aquatic, 130
    for compost, 94
    controlling, with
        alcohol, 129
        broadleaf weed spray,
            141
        carpet, 132
        chemical-free spray, 45
        cultivated plants, 139
        cultivating, 123, 126
        dust, 125
        marigolds, 129
        newspapers, 126
        peanuts, 130
        salt, 128, 140, 149

seedhead removal, 123
sheet composting, 128
spraying, 124-25
weed barrier fabric, 126,
    128, 147, 148
Wild Weed Wipeout,
    129, 331
tools for removing, 123, 124
Wetlands, trees suited to, 45
Wetness
    evergreens suitable for, 35
    shrubs suitable for, 37
Whiskey, 54, 72, 94, 104, 107,
    111, 114, 116, 119, 154, 158,
    245, 323
Whiteflies
    killing, 140
    on tomatoes, 319
Wildflower(s)
    care of, 86, 90
    seeds, 35
Wild hyacinth, location for, 21
Wild onions, killing, 141
Wild violets, eliminating, 132
Wild Weed Wipeout, 129, 331
Wilt disease, tomatoes with,
    202
Wilted Zucchini Salad, 274
Wilting, preventing, 99, 133,
    319
Wind
    evergreens blocking, 269
    protecting plants from, 14
Window boxes, watering plants
    in, 146
Winter. *See also winter care of*
    specific plants
    clean-up before, 288, 292
    mulching for, 289, 291
    weather signs in, 4
    yard chores during, 80-81

Winter squash
    dwarf varieties of, 11
Winter Wash, 105
Wire mesh, for repelling
    rabbits, 291
Wisterias
    blooming problems with,
        45, 205, 212
    forcing blooming of, 198
Witch hazel, 290, 330
Wood chips, fruit trees and,
    255
Wool, composting, 144
Worms, repelling, 69, 228, 265

Y

Yard
    cleaning, 3
    drawing a plan of, 2
Year-Round Refresher, 126
Yeast, 39, 201, 247, 322, 327,
    329
Yellow squash, recipes for
    Baked Vegetables, 275

Z

Zap 'Em Dead Winterizing
    Tonic, 312
Zinnias, care of, 175
Zoysia, 224
Zucchini, recipes for
    Aunt Ethyl's Ratatouille,
        304
    Baked Vegetables, 275
    Cream of Zucchini Soup,
        274
    Wilted Zucchini Salad,
        274
    Zucchini Cake, 275
    Zucchini Carrot Cake, 275
    Zucchini Casserole, 274